English Literature in ᴸᵃᵘᶜᵉʳ

Longman Literature in English Series

General Editors:
David Carroll, formerly University of Lancaster
Chris Walsh, Chester College of Higher Education
Michael Wheeler, Chawton House Library and University of Southampton

For a complete list of titles see pages viii–ix.

English Literature in the Age of Chaucer

Dieter Mehl

An imprint of **Pearson** Education

Harlow, England · London · New York · Reading, Massachusetts · San Francisco · Toronto · Don Mills, Ontario · Sydney
Tokyo · Singapore · Hong Kong · Seoul · Taipei · Cape Town · Madrid · Mexico City · Amsterdam · Munich · Paris · Milan

Pearson Education Limited

Head Office:
Edinburgh Gate
Harlow CM20 2JE
Tel: +44 (0)1279 623623
Fax: +44 (0)1279 431059

London Office:
128 Long Acre
London WC2E 9AN
Tel: +44 (0)20 7447 2000
Fax: +44 (0)20 7240 5771
Website: www.business-minds.com

First published in Great Britain in 2001

ISBN 0 582 49299 8

British Library Cataloguing in Publication Data
A CIP catalogue record for this book can be obtained from the British Library

10 9 8 7 6 5 4 3 2 1

Set in 10/12pt Sabon
Typeset by 35
Produced by Pearson Education Asia Pte Ltd
Printed in Singapore

The Publishers' policy is to use paper manufactured from sustainable forests.

Contents

Editors' Preface	vii
Longman Literature in English Series	viii
Author's Preface	x
List of Abbreviations	xii

1 Introduction: The Age of Chaucer — 1

2 Geoffrey Chaucer — 8
- Reading and translating — 11
- *The Book of the Duchess* — 14
- *The Parliament of Fowls* — 16
- *The House of Fame* — 19
- *Troilus and Criseyde* — 22
- *The Legend of Good Women* — 32
- *The Canterbury Tales* — 36

3 John Gower — 60
- The Gower canon — 61
- *Confessio Amantis*: transmission and genesis — 62
- The frame and the tales — 64
- The lover's shrift and the closing of the frame — 72

4 William Langland — 80
- Text, texts and poem — 80
- *Piers Plowman* in its time — 82
- Structure and narrative discourse — 83
- Allegorical method, homiletic criticism and theological argument — 87

5 The *Gawain*-Poet — 108
- *Patience* — 110
- *Cleanness* — 113
- *Pearl* — 116
- *Sir Gawain and the Green Knight* — 119

6 John Lydgate and Thomas Hoccleve — 127
- Courtly love poems — 128
- Major translations and adaptations — 135
- A monastic hack-writer? — 144
- Thomas Hoccleve — 146

7 The Middle English Lyric — 157
- Love, fun and day-to-day trouble in the secular lyric — 158
- Carols and religious lyrics — 161
- Historical and political poems — 167

8 **Middle Scots Poetry**   173
   James I of Scotland: *The Kingis Quair*   173
   Richard Holland: *The Book of the Houlat*   175
   Robert Henryson   176
   William Dunbar   183
   Gavin Douglas   186

9 **Middle English Prose**   194
   Mandeville's Travels   195
   Prose writing of the English mystics   201
   The Book of Margery Kempe   207
   Prose narrative: Thomas Malory and *Morte Darthur*   211

Conclusion   224

Chronology   227

Bibliography   231

Index   246

Editors' Preface

The multi-volume Longman Literature in English Series provides students of literature with a critical introduction to the major genres in their historical and cultural context. Each volume gives a coherent account of a clearly defined area, and the series, when complete, will offer a practical and comprehensive guide to literature written in English from Anglo-Saxon times to the present. The aim of the series as a whole is to show that the most valuable and stimulating approach to the study of literature is that based upon awareness of the relations between literary forms and their historical contexts. Thus the areas covered by most of the separate volumes are defined by period and genre. Each volume offers new and informed ways of reading literary works, and provides guidance for further reading in an extensive reference section.

In recent years, the nature of English studies has been questioned in a number of increasingly radical ways. The very terms employed to define a series of this kind – period, genre, history, context, canon – have become the focus of extensive critical debate, which has necessarily influenced in varying degrees the successive volumes published since 1985. But however fierce the debate, it rages around the traditional terms and concepts.

As well as studies on all periods of English and American literature, the series includes books on criticism and literary theory and on the intellectual and cultural context. A comprehensive series of this kind must of course include other literatures written in English, and therefore a group of volumes deals with Irish and Scottish literature, and the literatures of India, Africa, the Caribbean, Australia and Canada. The forty-seven volumes of the series cover the following areas: Pre-Renaissance English Literature, English Poetry, English Drama, English Fiction, English Prose, Criticism and Literary Theory, Intellectual and Cultural Context, American Literature, Other Literatures in English.

David Carroll
Chris Walsh
Michael Wheeler

Longman Literature in English Series

General Editors:
David Carroll, formerly University of Lancaster
Chris Walsh, Chester College of Higher Education
Michael Wheeler, Chawton House Library and University of Southampton

Pre-Renaissance English Literature

* English Literature before Chaucer *Michael Swanton*
  English Literature in the Age of Chaucer *Dieter Mehl*
* English Medieval Romance *W. R. J. Barron*

English Poetry

* English Poetry of the Sixteenth Century *Gary Waller (Second Edition)*
* English Poetry of the Seventeenth Century *George Parfitt (Second Edition)*
  English Poetry of the Eighteenth Century, 1700–1789
* English Poetry of the Romantic Period, 1789–1830 *J. R. Watson (Second Edition)*
* English Poetry of the Victorian Period, 1830–1890 *Bernard Richards*
  English Poetry of the Early Modern Period, 1890–1940
* English Poetry since 1940 *Neil Corcoran*

English Drama

* English Drama before Shakespeare *Peter Happé*
* English Drama: Shakespeare to the Restoration, 1590–1660 *Alexander Leggatt*
* English Drama: Restoration and Eighteenth Century, 1660–1789 *Richard W. Bevis*
  English Drama: Romantic and Victorian, 1789–1890
* English Drama of the Early Modern Period, 1890–1940 *Jean Chothia*
  English Drama since 1940

English Fiction

* English Fiction of the Eighteenth Century, 1700–1789 *Clive T. Probyn*
* English Fiction of the Romantic Period, 1789–1830 *Gary Kelly*
* English Fiction of the Victorian Period, 1830–1890 *Michael Wheeler (Second Edition)*
* English Fiction of the Early Modern Period, 1890–1940 *Douglas Hewitt*
  English Fiction since 1940

English Prose

* English Prose of the Seventeenth Century, 1590–1700 *Roger Pooley*
English Prose of the Eighteenth Century
* English Prose of the Nineteenth Century *Hilary Fraser with Daniel Brown*

Criticism and Literary Theory

Criticism and Literary Theory from Sidney to Johnson
Criticism and Literary Theory from Wordsworth to Arnold
* Criticism and Literary Theory, 1890 to the Present *Chris Baldick*

The Intellectual and Cultural Context

The Sixteenth Century
* The Seventeenth Century, 1603–1700 *Graham Parry*
* The Eighteenth Century, 1700–1789 *James Sambrook (Second Edition)*
The Romantic Period, 1789–1830
* The Victorian Period, 1830–1890 *Robin Gilmour*
The Twentieth Century: 1890 to the Present

American Literature

American Literature before 1880
* American Poetry of the Twentieth Century *Richard Gray*
* American Drama of the Twentieth Century *Gerald M. Berkowitz*
* American Fiction, 1865–1940 *Brian Lee*
* American Fiction since 1940 *Tony Hilfer*
* Twentieth-Century America *Douglas Tallack*

Other Literatures

Irish Literature since 1800
* Scottish Literature since 1707 *Marshall Walker*
Australian Literature
* Indian Literature in English *William Walsh*
* African Literatures in English: East and West *Gareth Griffiths*
* Southern African Literatures *Michael Chapman*
* Caribbean Literature in English *Louis James*
* Canadian Literature in English *W. J. Keith*

* *Already published*

Author's Preface

One of the labels for the period covered by this volume is 'The Age of Chaucer', and one might well ask whether this is not a rather limiting description of what could more simply and correctly be called 'The Fourteenth and Fifteenth Centuries'. I have, however, decided to centre my account of the period's literature around Chaucer as the main focus, though this is admittedly a subjective view. It might wrongly suggest that Chaucer was in the main a typical exponent of the entire period's literary harvest, which is true only in a very restricted sense. Authors he may have known nothing about produced original work quite different from his, and the literature of his age includes works he could never have written or, perhaps, appreciated.

It seems to me, nevertheless, that to approach fourteenth- and fifteenth-century literature by way of Chaucer's poetry is, for the modern reader and student, justified not only by the familiarity of the texts, but also by their rich inclusiveness and their sensitive awareness of so many religious, social, intellectual and poetic issues of his day. They appear to put fewer obstacles in the way of the twentieth-century reader than many much later writings, and they alone, perhaps, give the impression of opening up immediately a whole period of history as few others can do. I take it that many critics, teachers and students have found this true in their own reading of Chaucer.

Beginning with a survey of Chaucer's poetry that attempts to assess his achievement as a uniquely responsive and at the same time original reader, translator, adaptor and recreator of nearly every poetic form and innovation that came his way, this volume tries to outline some of the major literary developments that, in a sense, culminated in his activity as a writer, went on side by side with it, or were substantially inspired and influenced by it. Much of fifteenth-century poetry, for instance, from Lydgate to Henryson, cannot adequately be appreciated without constant reference to Chaucer, although the traditional label 'Chaucerians' hardly does justice to their own, individual achievement.

In the space available to the present volume it seemed more profitable to concentrate on some of the major literary achievements of the fourteenth and fifteenth centuries and, while trying to present them in their cultural context, admit to the incompleteness of the picture. In an age where almost unlimited amounts of basic information and exhaustive bibliographies of texts, manuscripts, authors and library-holdings are available to the reader at a mouseclick, there is much less need for narrative accounts that aim at factual or bibliographical completeness of names and titles or for another basic work of reference. The goal of a more personal survey should rather be to awaken the reader's interest in the enduring quality and relevance of the *texts* and the intensity of their authors' concern with the cultural questions of their time as well as with the importance of a literary heritage freshly discovered by Chaucer and his contemporaries in the classical tradition and the vernacular literature of France and Italy. At the same time it must be insisted, though it cannot be demonstrated in every case, that the best-known works that have survived and are still capable of appealing to the modern reader, were not produced, read and transmitted in isolation, but are manifestations and eloquent witnesses of a rich culture in which literature played a significant but by no means exclusive part.

Every reader of Chaucer and his contemporaries is materially indebted to the great number of readers and critics, many a mute inglorious Walter Skeat or C. S. Lewis among them, that preceded us and helped us to understand and enjoy the texts. There is also the host of – often unsung – selflessly devoted editors, who preserved many of these texts from the ravages of Oblivion and made them accessible, and there are the many students, colleagues and friends with whom I have discussed them. The strictly scholarly debts and all those with local habitation and name, are, I hope, adequately acknowledged in the notes; but there remain many that defy pinning down to bibliographical references. I have received inspiration and encouragement from many academic teachers, colleagues and friends. My life-long appreciation of medieval literature would not have been the same without the late Wolfgang Clemen and Hugo Kuhn, two of my most impressive 'professors' in the best sense of the word, or without the long-standing generous friendship of Derek Brewer, Peter Dronke, Jill Mann, Derek Pearsall and many colleagues and friends all over Europe and America I have been fortunate to meet, to work together with and to learn from over the years. A particular 'thank you' is owed to the patience and trust of the general editors of the series, David Carroll, Chris Walsh and Michael Wheeler. Throughout the planning and execution of the project I have had the invaluable support of Christa Jansohn, who, first as my research assistant, then as a colleague and a friend, never failed me with competent advice, encouragement and practical help. Personal gratitude is also due to the unforgettable Patricia Shaw, whose warm sincerity and humane scholarship made her a model for all who were privileged to enjoy her friendship. It is to her memory I should like to dedicate this modest account.

Dieter Mehl
Bonn 2001

List of Abbreviations

The following abbreviations are used in the Notes and the Bibliography:

Archiv	*Archiv für das Studium der neuereu Sprachen und Literaturen*
EETS	*Early English Text Society*
EETS, ES	*Early English Text Society, Extra Series*
PMLA	*Publications of the Modern Language Association of America*

Chapter 1

Introduction: The Age of Chaucer

Geoffrey Chaucer's contemporaries, whether they knew him as his business associates, as his political patrons or as fellow-poets, would hardly have regarded themselves as citizens of the 'Age of Chaucer'. In terms of literary activities, they would have been exposed to a great variety of texts in a demanding variety of languages, dialects and poetic forms, and their reading must have been determined by accidents of transmission and accessibility to a far greater extent than ours. Even though many of Chaucer's first readers would surely have recognised his outstanding achievement as an English writer, they would scarcely have accorded him the status of a national poet or singled him out as the representative of his and their age. To the world outside the British Isles, he would remain a nonentity for some time to come, but this applies to practically all English literary production before the sixteenth century, the time of the Tudors.

One of the first observations to bear in mind about the status of Middle English literature is its insularity and indeed, apart from very few exceptional writers, its basic provinciality. All writing with any claim to international, that is, Western European significance, was in Latin or in French and, to a more limited extent, in Italian. Though many of the Middle English authors, especially those with some clerical education, were probably as good as bilingual as far as English and Latin were concerned, a majority do not seem to have been aware of important literary developments and innovations in France, and fewer still of the Italian authors.[1] On the other hand, the Continent also seems to have been largely unaware of what went on, in terms of original writing, beyond the English Channel.

The most important reason for this basic insularity has to do with the status of the English language during this period. In the centuries after the Norman conquest it had been pushed out of most areas concerned with public life, such as government, law-making, jurisdiction and the daily existence of the aristocracy, its reading, its sports and its feasting. It had been relegated to the uncultured and regionalised discourse of the 'common' people, to oral rather than written commerce. This is a sweeping generalisation, inaccurate in many details, but at least correct in its main outlines and in its consequences for the surviving literature. The overwhelming bulk of what was written in England between about 1100 and 1350 and beyond, was either in Latin, the common European medium for theological and philosophical discourse as well as for many other disciplines, or in French, mostly of the Anglo-Norman variety.[2] During the thirteenth and, more frequently, the fourteenth century, there was a steadily growing demand for writings in English, and French, once the

1

official language, was evidently fast losing in importance. This is one of the reasons why from this time an increasing number of works written in French were translated and adapted for those who preferred their reading in English, primarily works of unsophisticated devotion, instruction and entertainment. An anonymous romance-writer of the early fourteenth century puts the matter bluntly:

> Of Freynsch no Latin nil y tel more *or*
> Ac on I[n]glisch ichil tel þerfore: *I will*
> Riȝt is þat I[n]glische vnderstond
> Þat was born in Inglond.
> Freynsche vse þis gentil man
> Ac euerich Inglische Inglische can,
> Mani noble ich haue yseiȝe
> Þat no Freynsche couþe seye . . .[3]

The oldest surviving text of this romance is preserved in the famous Auchinleck manuscript, a comprehensive collection of romances, lyrics and religious literature, written probably in London around 1340. It is not quite clear which circles, which region and what period exactly the writer is speaking of, but his apology, if that is what it is, for the use of English is only one in a fair number of similar protestations.[4] The earlier instances generally agree in addressing themselves to the 'lewed', i. e. unlearned lay folk, without any Latin or French, but in the course of the fourteenth century this air of condescension disappears and there seems to be rather a feeling of pride in a new national and linguistic identity.

The use of the vernacular was an issue of particular concern for the authors of pastoral and homiletic texts. William Langland's *Piers Plowman* and the 'mystical' writers of the fourteenth century attempted, each in their own way, to bridge the gulf between Latin as the traditional medium of clerical discourse and the intellectually active laymen and to forge a vernacular capable of conveying complex abstract argument, rhetorical polish or inward vision so as to reach out to a new community of 'lewed' Christians. It is partly due to writers such as the hermit Richard Rolle, the author of *The Cloud of Unknowing* and Walter Hilton that English prose developed into an instrument of instruction, contemplation, theological reflexion and argumentative discourse not *per se* inferior and cruder than Latin. 'Written English, newly prestigious, easily translatable across dialect borders, and available to anyone who knew someone who could read, had by 1400 come to be perceived in ways only conceivable a century earlier.'[5] This is especially illuminating when authors are using Latin and English side by side or when their writings are translated in either direction, as in the case of Rolle or the *Cloud*-author.

When Chaucer addresses himself to 'every maner man / That Englissh understonde kan',[6] he is only using a familiar formula, without drawing particular attention to the language. Chaucer never apologises for writing in English and, unlike his contemporary and friend John Gower, he never seems to have attempted a major work in any other language although it is clear that

Latin, French and Italian texts were easily accessible and indeed familiar to him. His easy mastery of the first two is amply demonstrated by his perfectly competent translations of Boethius' *Consolatio Philosophiae* and the French *Roman de la Rose*. Almost immediately after his death (1400) he was praised by poets as the true father of English rhetoric and the first to show that the English language was capable of the same heroic eloquence and dignity as Latin and its vernacular successors, Italian and French.

The English of Chaucer and Gower, that is, the dialect of the London area and, presumably to a large extent, of courtly society, is the historical basis of modern standard English; but, at the time, this was by no means a foregone conclusion. England was divided into major dialect areas and major works were composed in varieties of English that must have seemed outlandish if not incomprehensible to the Londoner. While Langland's *Piers Plowman*, in alliterating long lines, might have appeared to Chaucer as a somewhat quaint discourse, but not a closed book, it is doubtful whether he would have found the works of the *Gawain*-poet, written in a West Midland variety of English, easy to appreciate, if at all comprehensible, and it seems to me difficult to believe that he would have taken very serious note of them. The language of Scotland must have been altogether foreign to the reader in the South of England, whereas some of the most acute criticism and appropriation of Chaucer is to be found in the work of some Middle Scots poets. Perhaps the greatest tribute paid to him is Robert Henryson's qualifying continuation of *Troilus and Criseyde* in his *Testament of Cresseid*, which starts from the pertinent question, 'Quha wait gif all that Chauceir wrait was trew?'[7] This, and the fact that early editions of Chaucer included Henryson's poem as if it were by the same author as *Troilus and Criseyde*, suggests that the dialect barriers were not quite as rigid for contemporary readers as we are at first sight inclined to assume, even though the literary traffic between London and the North may have been predominantly one-way. On the other hand, there was evidently a certain mobility of manuscripts and scribes across England and Scotland, certainly during the fifteenth century.[8]

When Chaucer's Parson, calling himself 'a Southren man', speaks dismissively of the alliterative poetry of the North – 'I kan nat geeste "rum, ram, ruf" by lettre' (X, 43) – he is clearly making fun of an outlandish poetic idiom, but we have no means of knowing, except by his own practice, whether Chaucer shared his contempt and what text he may have had in mind – the alliterative *Morte Arthure*, *Sir Gawain and the Green Knight* or The '*Gest Hystoriale*' of the Destruction of Troy? Chaucerians are still not wholly agreed about the extent of Chaucer's familiarity with English writings of the Midlands and beyond,[9] but there is no real evidence that he was aware of the full poetic range and sophistication of the texts produced in a dialect that must have sounded at best exotic to him. Like most of the urban or university-trained authors he looked to the other side of the channel for real inspiration and contact with the latest literary developments. On the other hand, the enthusiastic reception of Chaucer's and Gower's poetry beyond the Scottish border during the fifteenth century is proof that the linguistic barrier was not insuperable.

The presence of Henryson's *Testament of Criseyde* in sixteenth-century editions of Chaucer shows that literary traffic was not entirely confined to one direction, but this seems to be the exception rather than the rule. This is why the 'Age of Chaucer' includes the Middle Scots poets, who continually refer to their 'maisteris dere', Chaucer, Gower and, more often than not, Lydgate.

Though the Royal Court and, with it, the London area, had become something like the cultural centre of the realm, this does not necessarily apply to vernacular literature. Affairs at court were mainly dealt with in French, and literature written in English seems to have played a comparatively minor part.[10] John Gower, at the outset of his *Confessio Amantis*, claims that the work was written at the personal request of King Richard II,[11] but, even if this was more than an ingratiating fiction, it would have been the exception rather than the rule. Outside religious or ecclesiastical institutions, most vernacular literature was probably produced, or at least written down in the form we have it, in connection with major prosperous households, from wealthy landowning families and provincial gentry to the courts of powerful barons. Many of these were evidently highly educated and cultured men, with an active interest in learning and in books, or at least an idea that it was prestigious to give that impression and to bestow some patronage on grateful authors. One of the most active was the youngest son of King Henry IV, Humphrey Duke of Gloucester (1391–1447), a famous patron of the arts, though that was a generation or two after Chaucer.[12]

The authors of vernacular texts for the most part had some – more or less thorough – clerical training and the majority of them, at least well into the fifteenth century, would have been in some way connected with the clergy, unless they were directly attached to the court or, like Chaucer, held offices in the royal administration.[13] Some were chaplains in noble households; others may have been belonged to the important group of mendicant friars, and others, again, were attached to religious houses, not necessarily as monks confined to the cloister, but possibly as former pupils of one of the monastic schools. Lydgate is the best-known instance of an author in a basically monastic environment.[14]

These institutions also provided some of the oldest and most important facilities for copying texts and producing manuscripts. Other centres, however, became increasingly more important in the course of the fourteenth and fifteenth centuries, such as certain 'bookshops', where manuscripts were professionally copied and, probably, made to order,[15] or wealthy households, where single copies or anthologies could be produced according to the taste of the owner. Since all Middle English literature that has come down to us consists of copies and, more usually, copies of copies, often made at considerable remove from the author, readers of a later age are to a vital extent at the mercy of editors and textual critics. This is why, from the beginning of scholarly interest in medieval literature, the study of text-transmission and of individual manuscripts has always played a vital part.

The preservation, transmission and editing of texts provide the only access to what might be conjectured to be the 'original' or 'authorial' composition.

If, as in the case of the *Gawain*-poet, the texts, by a lucky accident, have survived in a single, anonymous manuscript, we can only make the most of what we have and speculate on the individuality of the author and the circumstances of the first creative process. If, on the other hand, there is a greater number of extant copies, as in the case of *The Canterbury Tales* or *Piers Plowman*, we are faced with the problem of different versions, questions of authorial revision, scribal interference and all the problems surrounding the genesis of a more ambitious work of literature.[16] And even in such instances, each manuscript and each copy presents a unique text and is the product of an individual act of more or less independent engagement with the author's original creation and as such a document of reception no less than of single authorship.[17] This is not only a matter of textual criticism and the importance of responsible editing; it bears on the whole concept of Medieval literature, the way it was produced, passed on and is to be understood by a later generation. As David Wallace has it in his introduction to the recent *Cambridge History of Medieval English Literature*: 'Medieval literature cannot be understood (does not survive) except as part of transmissive processes – moving through the hands of copyists, owners, readers and institutional authorities – that form part of other and greater histories (social, political, religious and economic).'[18]

Wallace's plea against the 'divorce of literature from history in literary history' (p. xx) is, of course, part of a general trend in literary criticism of the last generation, a determined departure from the more extreme views and practices of 'new criticism', where literary texts were often – though not as narrowly as is sometimes alleged – regarded as self-sufficient works of art, only distantly related to other histories. It is evident, however, that the great variety of literary productions in the 'Age of Chaucer', documented by the bewildering range of extant texts, is the reflection of a multi-layered, continually changing and regionally diversified society, heaving with violent religious controversy, social unrest and internecine political power-struggle.

Research and scholarship of the past thirty years has increasingly paid attention to the historical setting of all literary activity in the age of Chaucer and looked at texts within their religious, social and cultural contexts instead of merely concentrating on the best-known samples in isolation.[19] The first volume of the *New Cambridge History of English Literature*, published 1999, is a vigorous result of this development. This generous, deliberately innovative and revisionary collaborative survey boldly proclaims what this far more modest introduction cannot even attempt to achieve: 'to help ease the bottleneck that has formed in literary criticism and in curricular design around late fourteenth-century England' (p. xii). The reader in search of such wider spectrum can only be urged to turn to that stimulating and rich source of information, which claims to offer a comprehensive 'account of literature composed or transmitted in the British Isles between 1066 and 1547' (p. xi). Throughout the book, Middle English literature is viewed as part of mental, social and political processes and developments. The authors in this period were none of them freelance, independent poets, but figures in a complex system of economic ties, political loyalties and religious partisanship, and their texts cannot be properly read without some understanding of these forces.[20] On the other hand, literary texts often present true images of a generation's particular conflicts, anxieties and questions, even if they do not give, nor claim to give, faithful accounts of historical situations and events. To approach the fourteenth and fifteenth centuries by way of the poetry of Chaucer, Gower and Lydgate or the prose of Margery Kempe and Malory can lead to a teasing glimpse of some of the period's most burning issues: from the more than precarious equilibrium of power between the king's government and the rivalling ambition of his magnates, to the fundamental differences within the Christian church, its ecclesiastic hierarchy, monastic culture, and the challenge of the mendicant orders and Wicliffite ideas, as well as the changes in the feudal system and social upheavals.[21] All of this is reflected to a more or less explicit extent in the literature of late medieval Britain.

Notes

1. On English-Italian relations see *Chaucer and the Italian Trecento*, ed. Piero Boitani (Cambridge, 1983), especially Wendy Childs, 'Anglo-Italian Contacts in the Fourteenth Century', pp. 33–64.

2. For the large corpus of literature in Anglo-Norman see M. Dominica Legge, *Anglo-Norman Literature and its Background* (Oxford, 1963) and, more generally, the excellent survey by Susan Crane, 'Anglo-Norman Cultures in England, 1066–1460', in *The Cambridge History of Medieval English Literature*, ed. David Wallace (Cambridge, 1999), pp. 35–60.

3. *Of Arthour and of Merlin*, ed. O. D. Macrae-Gibson, *EETS*, 268, 279 (1973, 1979), Auchinleck manuscript, ll. 19–26 (Vol. i, pp. 3–5).

4. See my *The Middle English Romances of the Thirteenth and Fourteenth Centuries* (London, 1969), pp. 5–6, and Derek Pearsall, *Old English and Middle English Poetry*, The Routledge History of English Poetry, 1 (London, 1977), pp. 115–18, and pp. 145–6 on the Auchinleck MS.

5. Nicholas Watson, 'Middle English Mystics', in *The Cambridge History of Medieval English Literature*, p. 557.

6. *The House of Fame*, ll. 509–10. All Chaucer quotations are from *The Riverside Chaucer*, 3rd edn, ed. Larry D. Benson (Boston, 1987).

7. *The Testament of Cresseid*, l. 64, in *The Poems of Robert Henryson*, ed. Denton Fox (Oxford, 1981).

8. A notable example is the manuscript Arch. Selden.B.24 in the Bodleian Library, Oxford, which contains works by Chaucer and Scottish poems. See the facsimile, *The Works of Geoffrey Chaucer and* The Kingis Quair. *A Facsimile of Bodleian Library, Oxford, MS Arch. Selden.B.24*, with an introduction by Julia Boffey and A. S. G. Edwards and an appendix by B. C. Barker-Benfield (Cambridge, 1997).

9. See, for instance, Derek Pearsall, *The Life of Geoffrey Chaucer. A Critical Biography* (Oxford, 1992), pp. 73–7.

10. See V. J. Scattergood, 'Literary Culture at the Court of Richard II', in *English Court Culture in the Later Middle Ages*, ed. V. J. Scattergood and J. W. Sherborne (London, 1983), pp. 29–43. On the role of English at the English court see also Elizabeth Salter,

'Chaucer and Internationalism', in English and International: Studies in the Literature, Art and Patronage of Medieval England, ed. Derek Pearsall and Nicolette Zeeman (Cambridge, 1988), pp. 239–44.

11. See Confessio Amantis, ed. G. C. Macaulay, EETS, ES (1900), Prologue, 24–60*.

12. On Humphrey, Duke of Gloucester, see Derek Pearsall, John Lydgate, Medieval Authors (London, 1970), pp. 223–30; see also M. H. Keen, England in the Later Middle Ages. A Political History (London, 1973), pp. 411–17.

13. See below, chapter 2.

14. See the chapter 'The Monastic Background' in Pearsall, John Lydgate, pp. 22–48.

15. See the seminal article by Laura Hibbard Loomis, 'The Auchinleck Manuscript and a possible London Bookshop of 1330–1340', PLMA, 57 (1942), 595–627, and for useful description of about a hundred manuscripts, Gisela Guddat-Figge, Catalogue of Manuscripts Containing Middle English Romances, Texte und Untersuchungen zur Englischen Philologie, 4 (München, 1976).

16. See below, chapters 2 and 4.

17. For some pertinent studies see Crux and Controversy in Middle English Textual Criticism, ed. A. J. Minnis and Charlotte Brewer (Cambridge, 1992), Tim William Machan, Textual Criticism and Middle English Texts (Charlottesville, 1994) and, for a very helpful critical survey, Derek Pearsall, 'Theory and Practice in Middle English Editing', Text: Transactions of the Society for Textual Scholarship, 7 (1994), 107–26. For a critical and stimulating review of Machan's book by Hoyt N. Duggan see Text (1997), 377–88, with a rejoinder by Machan, 388–90. Another important area is the production of 'books' before the introduction of the printing press; see the valuable collection of studies Book Production and Publishing in Britain 1375–1475, ed. Jeremy Griffiths and Derek Pearsall, Cambridge Studies in Publishing and Printing History (Cambridge, 1989).

18. The Cambridge History of Medieval English Literature, p. xxi.

19. Earlier critics often attempted to take this into account by looking at the 'background' or 'context' of literature. A still valuable instance is Stephen Medcalf, The Later Middle Ages, The Context of English Literature (London, 1981), with chapters on religious, political, social and domestic conditions during the fourteenth and fifteenth centuries.

20. See the bibliography for some important references on the political, religious and cultural context.

21. Cf. M. H. Keen, England in the Later Middle Ages. A Political History, especially Section III, 'The changing world of the later Middle Ages', pp. 169–247.

Chapter 2

Geoffrey Chaucer

Geoffrey Chaucer is the most receptive as well as the most inventive English poet of the Middle Ages. It has been said of Shakespeare that he was 'a snapper-up of unconsidered trifles, hoarding like a magpie what others did not value, and transmuting it, at opportune moments, into dramatic gold'.[1] This could hardly have been Chaucer's way. The medieval poet prized learning more than originality and he was more likely to flaunt his reading than to disguise it. Chaucer habitually plays down his own, individual share in his writing, disguising rather than parading his inventiveness. And yet there is something Shakespearean in the way he defies being pinned down to definite sources. It is instructive in this respect to compare the existing collections of sources of the two poets, e.g. *The Sources and Analogues of Chaucer's Canterbury Tales*[2] and *Narrative and Dramatic Sources of Shakespeare*.[3] Both are admirable and very useful anthologies of otherwise not easily accessible texts, but they do not provide 'sources' in a strict sense of the word in as many instances as one might expect. Chaucer can be a very faithful translator when he chooses, as with Boethius' *Consolatio Philosophiae* or the *Roman de la Rose*, but whenever he embarks on works of his own he can hardly take over a single line from one of his sources without subtly changing and adapting it to his unorthodox design. He is anything but an uncritical reader, though he often likes to portray himself as one.

Chaucer's immediate successors and the first few generations of readers were chiefly impressed by his stylistic virtuosity and by the cosmopolitan quality he brought to English literature. John Lydgate, writing within twenty-five years of Chaucer's death, speaks of him as 'the first that euer elumined our language with flowers of rethorick eloquence',[4] and, less than eighty years later, William Caxton praised him in similar terms, as 'the worshipful fader & first foundeur & embelissher of ornate eloquence in our englissh'.[5] This is quite unlike the now conventional reputation of Chaucer as one of the earliest realists and humorists of English literature. What his first readers valued most of all was his achievement as a writer who introduced qualities traditionally associated with the classical authors into English literary discourse, making it thereby respectable and altogether less parochial. They admired not so much the rich originality of his imagination as his authority, in the double sense of being an 'author' (*auctour*) in his own right and having therefore the authority of a classical poet. The respect paid to him by generations of authors and his impact on their work can hardly be overestimated.

Chaucer's biography is not shrouded in mystery in the way Shakespeare's is (at least in the eyes of many amateurs and diehard partisans), but there is a basic uncertainty nevertheless which has evidently discouraged many a scholar from writing a straightforward 'Life'. The trouble is rather that we have plenty of documentary evidence for the life and career of one Geoffrey Chaucer, servant to the English Court, employed in a great variety of public offices and never really out of favour with any of the two ruling Kings between 1357 and 1400,[6] but there is not much substantial evidence, though overwhelming likelihood, that this is the same man as the author of a unique corpus of texts, who calls himself Geoffrey Chaucer. It is not really surprising that the documents relating to his public career do not contain any bibliographical references nor, given Chaucer's habitual evasiveness as regards his own person, should we expect a great deal of solid biographical information in his poems. One must be content with telling glimpses, such as the humorous sketch provided by the eagle in *The House of Fame*:

But of thy verray neyghebores,	*neighbours*
That duellen almost at thy dores,	
Thou herist neyther that ne this;	*You hear*
For when thy labour doon al ys,	
And hast mad alle thy rekenynges,	*accounts*
In stede of reste and newe thynges	
Thou goost hom to thy hous anoon,	
And, also domb as any stoon,	
Thou sittest at another book	
Tyl fully daswed ys thy look; (ll. 649–58)[7]	*dazed*

In fact, however, there is far more circumstantial evidence for the close relationship between Chaucer's biography and his literary activities than is often assumed and, as Derek Pearsall has recently demonstrated, to reconstruct a 'Life' of the poet is neither impossible nor futile,[8] as long as we do not assume a simple causal relationship between historical events that must have affected the poet profoundly and what he says or omits to say in his poetry. Chaucer the poet, like many of his French and Italian colleagues in the fourteenth century, deliberately appears to encourage an 'interest in himself, the poet, as an individual',[9] and, though we must beware of taking any information offered in this context at face-value, we are certainly justified in reading the texts with some curiosity as to the man behind them.

There are many areas of Chaucer's private life where speculation must always be idle and profitless, and biographies based on such kind of imaginative inference are at best entertaining, but not very useful as an approach to his poetry. Yet an idea of Chaucer's experience of life in fourteenth-century London, of his journeys abroad and of his various professional positions and activities is clearly desirable for an informed understanding of his poetry and is evidently taken for granted by the poet on the part of his audience. A passage like that quoted above obviously makes more sense to a reader who knows what exactly is meant by the 'labour' and the 'rekenynges' that occupy the poet's working day; what is much less certain is the accuracy of the portrait of him as an unsociable bookworm. It is just as likely that the comedy lies in the glaring contrast between this sketch and the personality familiar to his acquaintance, because it seems difficult to imagine a man who does not even know his neighbours and who goes to bed with a 'fully daswed' look being entrusted with a series of highly responsible public assignments and regular grants of royal favour. The puzzle serves again to highlight the complex and shifting relationship between authors and fictional characters, especially when the text suggests a very close proximity or even identity.

The documents referring to Geoffrey Chaucer suggest an unusually active and, in view of several political storms and upheavals, remarkably untroubled career. He had an unusually good start in life, coming from a settled and prosperous home in the city of London. His father's trade as a flourishing wine-merchant and his connections with the Court put him among the highest members of the merchant-class, those that 'could provide or buy for their offspring the privileges associated with gentility even though they themselves might not be "gentle"'.[10] His son (we do not know whether he had any other) is first mentioned in 1357 as a young page in the household of King Edward III's daughter-in-law, the Countess of Ulster.[11] This was as good a first step into 'gentle' society as any, and Geoffrey Chaucer evidently had the personal qualities needed to make the best use of the chances offered to him. He was several times on the Continent in the King's service, on diplomatic and trading missions to Spain, France and Italy, which evidently brought him into contact with French and Italian Renaissance poetry, in particular that of Dante Alighieri (1265–1321), Francesco Petrarca (Petrarch) (1304–74) and, above all, Giovanni Boccaccio (1313–75), the one great contemporary never mentioned by name in all his works, though perhaps the most influential.

Among the distinguished public offices Chaucer held, the longest and probably most important was that of controller of customs in the port of London, a post he occupied from 1374 to 1386, longer than most of his predecessors or successors in the fourteenth century. When he gave up this post, possibly to keep out of political harm's way, he became a member of Parliament for one stormy session and in 1389 he was appointed clerk of the King's Works, a strenuous job from which he was relieved two years later. Annual grants from King Richard II, continued by his successor Henry IV, who came to the throne in 1399, suggest strongly that Chaucer managed to keep in favour with both these political opponents, which by most scholars has been taken as evidence of a particularly kind and inoffensive character, by some others as a sign of a certain cautious opportunism or at least a gift for keeping out of harm's way in troubled times. This may well have included a reluctance to profess his commitment to any potentially contentious and therefore dangerous causes.[12] To what extent such speculations are relevant or helpful for our understanding of Chaucer's poetry, every reader must decide for himself.

We are on much more reliable ground when it comes to assessing Chaucer's reading and his literary preferences. His education almost certainly provided him with access to libraries and to individual bookowners, and his journeys abroad must have brought him into contact with the latest and the most influential literary productions in French and, later, in Italian. Though the older division of Chaucer's poetic career into a French, an Italian and an English period is somewhat too neat and misleadingly simplifies a rather more complex development, it is still true that the beginnings of Chaucer's literary activity were much more under the impact of French court poetry than his later production and that the preoccupation with French poetry seems to have given way to a new fascination with the Italian trecento poets, most of all Boccaccio and, to a lesser extent, Petrarch and Dante.[13] There is no exclusively 'English' period in Chaucer's poetic development, except for the fact that he became increasingly unconventional in the free use he made of his predecessors and contemporaries and drew on a wider range of literary material.

Reading and translating

There is no doubt that Chaucer was an insatiable and curious reader, and scholarship has succeeded in identifying many of the books that he found so absorbing. Two of them have to be singled out in particular, since Chaucer, by translating them, appropriated them in a singularly intimate way.

From a literary point of view, the *Roman de la Rose*, translated very early in his career, is perhaps the most important of all his literary models, though we also have to include the whole school of French court poets who were equally inspired by the *Roman*.[14] It is a kind of encyclopedia not only of courtly and uncourtly love, but also of favourite themes of medieval philosophy and, last not least, of narrative techniques. The first part (*c.* 1235), by Guillaume de Loris, is a genial fantasy about the dream of ideal love and the suffering of the lover who comes under its thrall, whereas the long continuation by Jean de Meun (*c.* 1275), making up more than three quarters of the whole work, is a huge collection of miscellaneous learning, an anthology of bits and pieces from a great variety of authors, presented with a mixture of pretentious authority and irreverent humour. For Chaucer, the *Roman* was evidently a text that served as a quarry for themes, characters and plots as well as a model for ironic narrative stances, but also one that raised fundamental poetological issues and provoked considerable controversy.

The *Querelle de la Rose*, a spirited and highly sophisticated literary and, indeed, theological debate about the alleged moral damage done by the *Roman* to its readers, fought out around the time of Chaucer's death, shows that the book, completed more than a century earlier, was still very much alive and able to excite and divide its audience. Its special importance for Chaucer, however, is manifested by the way it is introduced into the prologue of his *Legend of Good Women*, a much later work. There the God of Love accuses the unsuspecting poet of slander, and the first item in the case for the prosecution is the fact of his having translated the *Romaunce of the Rose*,

> That is an heresye ayeins my lawe,
> And makest wise folk fro me withdrawe; (F, 330–1)

11

The implication is clearly that, in the eyes of Chaucer's Cupid, the *Roman* has the effect of turning its readers against the kind of love this God represents instead of making them strive to be his servants. In the context of the *Legend*, this is evidently a misreading of the poet's (or at least the translator's) intentions; for later in the poem the *Roman* is explicitly linked with *Troilus and Criseyde* as a witness for the poet's good intentions; this is his famous apology for his poetry:

> For that I of Creseyde wroot or tolde,
> Or of the Rose; what so myn auctour mente,
> Algate, God woot, yt was myn entente   *All the time*
> To forthren trouthe in love and yt cheryce,
> And to ben war fro falsnesse and fro vice
> By swich ensample; this was my menynge. (F, 469–74)

Are we to take this at face-value? This is certainly one of the most tantalising questions raised by Chaucer's individual narrative stances. Like Pierre Col, the eloquent advocate of the *Roman de la Rose* in the *querelle*, Chaucer is arguing from a poet's point of view. He evidently insists that we cannot judge a literary text as if every sentence were an authorial pronouncement, but we must see the intention of the work as a whole. This is what Col aims at when he pleads for a dramatic reading of the individual speeches.[15] There are a number of instances, especially in the *Canterbury Tales*, to show that Chaucer was well aware of the absurd lengths to which this principle could be stretched, and yet his practice suggests that basically he agreed with it, at least to the extent that the true meaning and the authorial intention of every poetic statement has to be gathered from the whole of it, not from isolated quotations or possibly offensive utterances. The defence of the narrator in *The Legend of Good Women* seems to leave it open whether he really gives credit to the *Roman's* moral claims. But, as has been shown, the *Roman* offers a variety of precedents for Chaucer's narrative games that for a time were a favourite subject of Chaucer criticism[16] and this supports the impression of the sincerity of his dreamer's plea, even though he is not prepared to vouch for the purity of the author's intentions ('what so myn auctour mente'). Here, perhaps more than in any other text, Chaucer had a model of what seems to have been one of the most characteristic concerns of his literary activity: the mutual commenting, if not deconstructing, of 'ernest' and 'game', 'sentence' and 'solas', 'auctoritee' and 'experience'.

Why Chaucer translated the *Roman*, how much of it he actually did translate and for whom he did it, must remain a matter for speculation. The fact that only fragments have survived in a comparatively late manuscript suggests that it did not reach a wide audience.[17] Perhaps those who would be most interested in it were able to read it in the original, and Chaucer's own growing audience would not have found the work particularly congenial. It also soon went completely out of fashion during the following century.

Chaucer certainly would have known that Jean de Meun had also translated Boece's *Consolatio Philosophiae* and this might well dispose him to trust in the French author's moral seriousness. His own translation, mentioned in the 'Retraction' at the close of *The Canterbury Tales* as one of the books he has no reason to repent of, was heavily indebted to the French version. What must have appealed to Chaucer in the *Consolatio*, as it still does to us, is the depth and sincerity of the moral and philosophical debate, unmixed with any strictly theological and doctrinal argument, as well as the evident personal involvement of the author. Here, as in few other books, 'auctoritee' is the direct consequence of 'experience', and it is significant that Chaucer's Troilus quotes, or rather relives Boece's argument on predestination in his moment of profound despair (iv, 953–1078). This is no theoretical debate, produced in the study, but an argument immediately relevant to experience. For Chaucer it had the further interest of being not explicitly Christian, which is what evidently fascinated him about the Roman classics, not because he had any quarrel with Christian doctrine that we know of, but because the pre-Christian past allowed him to explore certain moral and philosophical issues without any bias or foregone conclusions.

The *Consolatio* raises fewer literary problems than the *Roman*, except that it would again be very helpful to know just what made him undertake the translation. One reason may have been that he wanted to make the book his own,[18] but I think it hard to believe that it was the only or even the principal one. He must have expected an audience for it, and the nine extant manuscripts show that such an audience was actually there. It is highly probable that among his own readers there were many who must have found it much easier to understand the famous treatise in English than in the original Latin.[19] It seems, therefore, not entirely far-fetched to assume that the audience Chaucer had in mind for his own writings was one that was also familiar with these two books, the *Roman* and the *Consolatio* and treasured them as valuable items of their literary inheritance. They are instances of the kind of medieval key texts that any modern reader of Chaucer should be acquainted with, whereas many of the other books Chaucer uses and quotes from in his writings may have been known only to a smaller group among his audience, or else, like Ovid and the Italian poets, have been first introduced by him into the literary discourse of his time.

Though we can never hope to follow up the entire cosmos of Chaucer's reading, his writings are an eloquent guide to what was available to a greedy reader of his time and place. Almost any of his poems could serve as an illustration: the brilliant absorption and transformation of classical, Italian, French and native English traditions in *Troilus and Criseyde* is not matched by any other writer of his time, but shows what could be achieved by an exceptional mind and talent. This in turn can serve as a point of reference to the reading and appreciation of other texts of the period, a kind of vantage point from which to try and survey the literary scene, to distinguish widely educated writers and avid readers from the more limited minds, with little access to, or interest in, the cultural debates of their generation.

Where Chaucer is, on the face of it, rather less (or more) than typical of his age, is in his evident refusal to be partisan, to take sides in fundamental questions of religion, politics, morals, or even characterisation. As a recent critic puts it: 'his analysis focused, finally, neither on moral standards nor on social conditions but on attitudes; that is to say, on socially determined and therefore historically contingent values and beliefs'.[20] This has not always been the predominant view, but it accounts for much of Chaucer's perennial appeal, though it also makes his texts, for some readers, more difficult to come to terms with.

The Book of the Duchess

Even Chaucer's first known longer poem, *The Book of the Duchess*, commemorating the death of Blanche, John of Gaunt's first wife (12 September 1368) shows this unconventionally evasive quality. It was clearly written as a tribute to the Duke of Lancaster, but it does not give the appearance of a specifically topical work. There are unmistakable references to the deceased, but they are vague enough for posterity to argue endlessly about the precise nature of the relationship between author and subject, between literary convention and personal involvement.

It is easy to overstate the topical quality of the poem, which has frequently been associated with the literature of consolation and even been claimed as a kind of liturgical extra for a funeral ceremony.[21] It certainly does not offer the kind of spiritual solace one would expect from a true fellow Christian. It is clearly a love poem, or to say the least, a poem on the subject of courtly love, making use of many of the conventions Chaucer found in the love poetry of his French contemporaries. Though the topical application to the death of Blanche is evidently there, the poem would be just as rich and meaningful without it. At the centre of it is the overwhelming experience of love, crowned by the lady's acceptance of her faithful wooer and cut off by sudden death. It is at the same time a lament for the loss of the most precious human being and a celebration of love and the beloved, cast in the conventional form of a dream vision, yet of unprecedented human immediacy and psychological insight.

The dreamer, like many similar figures in Chaucer's French models, becomes an eavesdropper listening to the outpourings of an apparently disconsolate knight; but, unlike most traditional dreamers, he attempts to establish some emotional contact with the bereaved, in an effort to offer consolation, not by traditional wisdom or edifying quotations, but merely by sympathetic attention. If there is any genuine consolation it consists in the uncomplicated practical solidarity, in sharing the other's grief. The dreamer throughout seems at a loss as to how one can respond to such intense human misery, but his 'strategy' (if one can call it that) of simply offering himself as a listener is perhaps the only effective reaction to the lover's complaint and, though the ending remains inconclusive, with the dreamer's plain words of sympathy and the sudden disappearance of the dream scenery, the reader is made to feel that the loss has somehow been softened. What remains is a powerful and moving impression of the enriching beauty of the love experience. There is, in this poem, very little of the self-conscious literary artifice of many of the French poems. What is perhaps most remarkable and original is the effortless contrast between the formal rhetoric of the lover's rhetorically ornate complaint and the very brief and spontaneous simplicity of the listener's reaction:

> 'Allas, sir, how? What may that be?'
> 'She ys ded!' 'Nay!' 'Yis, be my trouthe!'
> 'Is that youre los? Be God, hyt ys routhe!'   *a pity*
> And with that word ryght anoon
> They gan to strake forth; al was doon,
> For that tyme, the hert-huntyng. (ll. 1308–13)

The swift winding-up of the poem, when many readers would expect a more weighty and authoritative conclusion, is very characteristic of Chaucer's method, and the whole work already demonstrates a brilliantly independent handling of current poetic conventions.

The Black Knight's account of his love-service and of the exemplary perfection of its object makes up the greater part of the poem and forms its thematic centre, yet it is put into perspective by the frame and by the person of the dreamer. Right at the outset of his career Chaucer found his own characteristic way of introducing himself as first-person narrator of unmistakable individuality: the curious and sympathetic observer and listener, without any claim to superior experience or authority. Like any narration, this involves a more or less conscious act of role-playing, of speaking in an assumed voice; but this does not mean that the narrator is *per se* untrustworthy or that he is held up as an object of the reader's scorn. If the dreamer seems (to some readers and to the Knight himself) slow in understanding the situation, it is not from natural stupidity, but from pity and a feeling of helpless human commiseration. He is certainly not conceived as a comically inept figure; the dilemma of the impotent witness of another's grief is shown more truthfully in his attitude than it could possibly have been done by conventional authority and superior advice.

There has been much discussion of the dreamer's alleged obtuseness and of Chaucer's sophisticated handling of the narrative point of view. Much of it is of very limited relevance to Chaucer's art. As a theoretical concept, the fictional narrator is, of course, different from Geoffrey Chaucer the author, because he is part of the text and part of the fiction. Yet the audience of the poem's first 'performance', most probably by the author himself, would not, in fact, make this clear distinction. It would accept the 'I' of the text largely on its own terms, as would most readers through the centuries before the idea of a personal relationship between author and reader was obliterated by the mass production of books and the anonymity of their public. Chaucer does not deliberately put on a mask to hide behind a cloud of general irony. He does, however, delight in assuming different voices, thus involving the listener or reader in a personal dialogue with the text.

At the outset, the narrator complains of his own suffering from an unspecified ailment that has oppressed his spirits for eight years and he adds to the mystification by hinting at the only physician for his complaint who, for some reason, is no longer available. This may very well be an autobiographical detail no longer understood by non-contemporaries, but it is at the same time a personal gesture inviting the reader's emotional participation and setting the tone for what follows. The convention of the dream-vision is given a new slant by the introduction of the narrator's suffering from insomnia and by the device of inducing sleep by private reading. It is one of the earliest examples in English literature of a specific book, even a secular one, included as part of a fictional narrative. Like ourselves, the narrator finds enlightening information and emotional relief in fiction. The whole passage and the very personal retelling of a story from Ovid's *Metamorphoses*, not only testifies to Chaucer's early interest in the classics, but it also prepares us, by introducing the Greek God of Sleep and the theme of death and loss, for the situation of the Black Knight. Like the dreamer, Alcyone's husband, briefly brought back from the dead, can offer nothing but sympathy to the bereaved and there is no effective consolation; yet the incident still gives a hint on how to come to terms with the experience of death and loss:

> 'My swete wyf,
> Awake! Let be your sorwful lyf,
> For in your sorwe there lyth no red;   *lies no help*
> For, certes, swete, I am but ded.
> Ye shul me never on lyve yse.   *see alive*
> . . .
> And farewel, swete, my worldes blysse!
> I praye God youre sorwe lysse.   *lessen*
> To lytel while oure blysse lasteth!' (ll. 201–5, 209–11)

The intimate tone and the husband's loving concern for the widow's grief are Chaucer's additions to the story from Ovid's *Metamorphoses*, a book he was particularly indebted to for much of his classic story-material.

This highly original blending of courtly love conventions and poetic stereotypes with reading from the classics and, above all, deeply personal questioning of basic human issues makes *The Book of the Duchess*, for all its unpretentious conventionality, a minor masterpiece, not just the promising performance of an aspiring young court poet.

The Parliament of Fowls

The chronological order of Chaucer's early poems is uncertain, and a good case can be made for a dating of *The House of Fame* before *The Parliament of Fowls*, mainly, perhaps, because of the latter's superior metrical artistry and perfect structure. On the other hand, *The House of Fame* is much bolder in its claims and suggests a greater familiarity with Italian trecento poetry, especially the new concept of Fame and the wide-ranging literary concerns. It is altogether a much more ambitious work, which, however, does not necessarily put it later in the Chaucer canon.[22]

The Parliament of Fowls is closer to *The Book of the Duchess* in the concentration on the theme of love, though it evidently attempts to take a wider view and to put courtly love in the larger context of natural love and the social stratification of human society.[23] Again, Chaucer adopts the device of the dreamer in a love vision, and again he introduces this vision by the poet's looking for books to help him out of a personal dilemma. It is not sleeplessness that troubles him this time, but a general lack of orientation in a matter of great concern to him: the nature of love and its disturbing impact on the life of the individual. His obsession with Love's 'wonderful werkynge' (l. 5) of 'The dredful joye alwey that slit so yerne' (l. 3) shows that it is for him an existential problem, not just an idle interest and, furthermore, that what really unsettles him is the inexplicable contrast between the account of love's omnipotence found in books and his own complete lack of any personal experience of it. The desperate search for 'a certeyn thing' (l. 20), for some dependably reliable information, makes him dive into yet another book and this turns out to be an episode from the Roman author Cicero (the *Somnium Scipionis* [Scipio's Dream]), preserved together with a long commentary by Macrobius (*c.* AD 400), who claims that it contains the whole of philosophy. Thus, the fashionable theme of love is immediately placed into a cosmological context and, although the poet's reading only seems to increase his bewilderment, it produces a dream that continues the fundamental debate on the level of complex and suggestive allegory. In it (an instance of Chaucer's realistic dream-psychology), Scipio Africanus reappears and acts as a Dantesque guide to the poet whom he promises to show rewarding subjects to write about. Once more, the dreamer's own practical inexperience is confirmed and condoned. His guide compares him to a man who does not know a single trick of wrestling, yet likes to watch a good fight. The poet remains spectator for the rest of the poem, and all he can do after seeing the inconclusive end of the allegory is return to his books and hope for some more satisfactory message at a future date.

Combining the conventional love vision with the human search for some reliable view of our existence and with an all-embracing idea of love's binding and procreative purpose as well as its morally refining aspect, is Chaucer's most remarkable contribution to the genre. The poem's brevity contrasts with its astonishing inclusiveness: it juxtaposes essential elements from the *Roman de la Rose* and the graceful love-visions of Chaucer's French contemporaries with a surprising amount of classical mythology and Christian cosmology, without any pretension of learned exhibitionism or flat-footed didacticism.

The introduction of Greek and Roman Gods into the medieval allegory of the garden was evidently inspired by Boccaccio,[24] and Chaucer's adaptation puts the emphasis on the contradictory faces of human love. Venus clearly represents its most alluring and sensuous aspects, unmixed with any obvious moral bias, whereas Nature, a figure borrowed from the twelfth-century neoplatonist Alain de Lille, is described as 'the vicaire of the almyghty Lord' (l. 379),[25] i.e. God's deputy on earth. There is a deliberate contrast: Venus embodies the joys and perhaps also the dangers of love, though not necessarily its sinful aspects, whereas Nature offers a view of love acceptable even to strict moralists, that of fruitfulness in accordance with the will of God. Critics have sometimes overstressed the ominously seductive side of Chaucer's Venus and the atmosphere of shady sexuality; still, she represents only one side of the subject, one that turns out to be, for all its glittering attractiveness, severely limited.

The central part of the allegory, the birds' assembly and their choice of partners, is a particularly original and provocative variation on the theme of love. The basic idea behind it is that of a vast majority of cheerful creatures who have no problems with the alleged complications of refined love-sickness, but proceed straightaway with their mating in the service of all-creating Nature. Only the three aristocratic birds, competing for the favours of the perfect female find wooing a difficult labour and an occasion for sophisticated rhetoric. The narrative suggests that theirs is a very special kind of love, whose cult and ritualised manner of pleading may be fascinating to the connoisseur or the initiated, but remains 'cursede pletynge' (l. 495), holding up the essential business of love, to the rest of society.

The dream does not, however, take sides: though the unquestioning satisfaction and the cheerful carolling of the departing couples are to be envied, there is also much to be said for Nature's verdict of a year's delay, as an opportunity for the three wooers to prove the sincerity of their lofty protestations. This is clearly a higher form of love, even though it is only *one* way of fulfilling nature's universal purpose. There is no question of 'debunking' the refined rhetoric of courtly love and its sophisticated code of morals, although the sense of its artificiality is strongly brought out by the uncomprehending pragmatism of the lower birds. Their impatient clamouring for an end to the proceedings and their down-to-earth language provide a strong impression of natural reality, but there is no doubt that Nature herself is more particularly attached to her more finely touched creatures.

The answer to the poet's anxious questioning is not any hard-and-fast definition of love: all he is offered is the sight of nature's generous diversity, where everything, including the doctrine of *fin amour*, has its proper place. In many ways, this comes as near to putting the *Roman de la Rose* in a nutshell as any other work by Chaucer or his contemporaries, at least as far as the openly inclusive treatment of the love-theme is concerned. What Chaucer clearly learned from Guillaume de Loris and Jean de Meun, apart from the colourful allegory, was the close inter-relationship of courtly love and the concept of Nature, whose aim, above all, is procreation, whatever the refined rhetoric of the wooer may avow. The theme recurs, with profound psychological insight and dramatic directness, in *Troilus and Criseyde*.

Where *The Parliament* is totally different from the *Roman* is in its brevity and its allusive conciseness. There are no lengthy and circumstantial discussions, as in Jean de Meun's continuation, and there are certainly no encyclopedic claims. Instead, the reader is invited to share the dreamer's puzzling revelation and to make of it what he can. The poem does not stop to tell us what he learnt from his vision except that he will continue to search for new insight and new poetic material in books. The message, if the reader should expect one, lies in the whole panorama presented, not in any summarising conclusion. The fact that the poem has come down in fourteen manuscripts is proof that its consummate craftsmanship and undogmatic treatment of its subject was appreciated by Chaucer's first audience.

The House of Fame

Intellectually, *The House of Fame* is more innovative and more adventurous in its literary claims and in the search for new subjects than *The Parliament of Fowls*. It is also more thoroughly indebted to the Italian poets of the trecento and their exalted claims for the status of vernacular poetry and of its authors. Whether this argues for a later date must remain a matter of speculation. Stylistically, the poem (if it really came after *The Parliament*) would seem to be rather a backward step. The simple four-stress couplets, though handled with some virtuosity, are decidedly less flexible and expressive than the rhyme-royal stanza, which Chaucer seems to have mastered with astonishing ease from the very outset. Even so, *The House of Fame* has a remarkable range of voices, from the slightly pretentious scientific chatter of the eagle to the salesmanlike cry of the popular entertainer, from elaborate rhetorical description to easy, conversational narrative. The stylistic abundance reflects the ambitious theme. Though Chaucer has by no means abandoned his interest in the phenomenon of love, he now has come to see it as an aspect of a more universal concern: the origin of all our information and the role played by those who transmit it to posterity. 'Fame', for the poet, is not just a matter of personal reputation and glory, but is closely linked to the source of everything he receives from his predecessors and strives to pass on to posterity.[26]

In accordance with this loftier subject, Chaucer begins with a formal *Proem* and an Invocation. The *Proem* repeats much of the dream-lore discussed in the *Roman de la Rose* and elsewhere, and the Invocation picks up the motif of the God of Sleep, to whom it is addressed. Despite several classical allusions, this invocation is more in the manner of a popular romance, announcing to its listeners some famous story. The mixing of classical rhetoric and humorous address to the audience suggests that Chaucer does not really aspire to the heights of a Dantesque vision, but keeps a respectful distance through irony and modest self-effacement. He is evidently conversant with many poetic traditions newly discovered and revived by the Italian Renaissance poets, but he prefers to treat them with unassuming half-seriousness as if he were not certain how his readers would take all this novel subject-matter. Throughout the *House of Fame* there is this uneasy contrast between the bantering tone and the fundamental poetic issues that would seem to deserve a more serious treatment.

The initial dream image combines the subjects of love and fame. The temple of glass, the sanctuary of Venus, introduces the ever present love-theme, not, however, in the manner of the *Roman*, but by classical precedent and immediately linked to the question of literary transmission and the act of reading. Visual revelation gives way to writing on brass, and the first words the dreamer encounters are indeed the opening lines of Virgil's *Aeneid*, translated literally from the Latin. As the text proceeds and reaches its climax in the episode of

Aeneas and Dido, Chaucer seems to forget both its medium and its author: after reading the first lines, the dreamer introduces the rest of the narration with 'I saugh', repeated several times, as if the plot were actually acted before his vision or painted scene by scene in dramatic detail:

> Ther saugh I such tempeste aryse
> That every herte myght agryse   *shudder, tremble*
> To see hyt peynted on the wal.
>   Ther saugh I graven eke withal,
> Venus, how ye, my lady dere,
> Wepynge with ful woful chere,
> Prayen Jupiter on hye
> To save and kepe that navye
> Of the Troian Eneas,
> Syth that he hir sone was. (ll. 209–18)

It is not made clear whether the dreamer is reading or watching, but the question is less relevant than the recognition that through the text – Virgil's and Chaucer's – our imagination is stimulated to produce the illusion of observed reality. It is the words of the ancient poet that create this reality, and they are the only basis of our knowledge.

Just as important is the fact, perhaps not obvious to every contemporary reader, that Chaucer discredits Virgil's version of the story by largely adopting Dido's point of view, as he found it in Ovid's *Heroides*. It is not only an exercise in narrative perspective, but also a critical enquiry into the reliability of literary transmission. Chaucer exploits the existence of contradictory accounts to raise the issue of poetic and historical truth. Dido, as pathetic prototype of the forsaken woman, was to become a favourite subject of late medieval and Renaissance literature, but this reading had to be maintained against the conflicting view of the heroic Aeneas who had to follow a higher mission, sacrificing the lesser duty to the woman he loves.

When the dreamer comes to the question of guilt, he unexpectedly begins to talk of books and, by implication, returns to Virgil. Dido, 'as the book us tellis' (l. 426), wanted Aeneas to make her his wife, as he had sworn by everything he could swear by. And again, the dreamer adds, it is the book that, to excuse Aeneas, tells of Mercury's message, sending the hero off to Italy. All this is meant to undermine any simple trust in literary authority and to introduce an enquiry into the true source of all our information.

What the dreamer has been allowed to see so far has not answered any of his questions, but has left him even more disorientated because he does not even know the author of all these vivid images. When he decides to leave the temple and the whole allegorical scenery, by a little gate, he enters another symbolic landscape, a blank desert without any trace of life, of created nature or human activity. It is a complete contrast to the wealth of apparitions in the temple of glass and it makes him doubly conscious of their illusory character. Without any creature in sight to guide or to advise him, he prays to Christ to save him 'Fro fantome and illusion' (l. 493) and, raising his eyes to heaven, he sees a golden eagle descending; thus ends the first book.

The second opens with another *Proem*, again advertising the dream as something far more sensational than all the famous dreams in classical mythology or in the Old Testament. In the context of the whole poem, even this division into books has a slightly pretentious or mock-heroic air, but it supports, if in a rather light-hearted way, the poetological concerns and draws attention to the desperate effort of the poet to hold on to literary tradition as the only possibility of avoiding 'fantome and illusion'.

The eagle, traditionally a symbol of divine inspiration, and a playful compliment to Dante's *Divina Commedia*, where an eagle transports the poet into Paradise, offers himself as the next authority to enlighten his ignorance and, at Jupiter's request, to carry him to the House of Fame, as a reward for his patient and futile service to love. The whole second book from this point consists of a brilliantly comic dialogue between this learned and singularly communicative teacher and the frightened poet in his claws, whose curiosity about the structure of the physical cosmos is soon more than satisfied. In response to the eagle's word-happy rhetoric he becomes more and more monosyllabic, until at last he declines any further information on the nature of the stars, with the excuse that he is now too old (l. 995) and that he is quite prepared to believe them that have written about these matters, as if he had seen it all for himself. And why should he damage his eyesight looking at the stars? As they are approaching the House of Fame, however, the dreamer's interest is reawakening and he begins to hope for some more worthwhile information. The eagle seems to have provided mainly idle and pseudo-learned knowledge, not any helpful answers to what 'Geoffrey' (as the eagle calls him!) really wanted to know. What Jupiter, according to the eagle, has granted to show him are 'of Loves folk moo tydynges' (l. 675), and the third and last book ('lytel laste bok'; l. 1093), again introduced by an Invocation, promises at last to fulfil his expectations by taking him to the House of Fame.

The invocation addresses Apollo as the 'God of science and of lyght' (l. 1090) and it makes clear that the poetological concerns are more important than the love-theme or, at least, that the two are inseparably related:

> Nat that I wilne, for maistrye,
> Here art poetical be shewed,
> But for the rym ys lyght and lewed,   *without art or learning*
> Yit make hyt sumwhat agreable,
> Though som vers fayle in a sillable;
> And that I do no diligence
> To shewe craft, but o sentence. (ll. 1094–1100)

Not only the addressee, but also the insistence on 'sentence', the true aim of his poetry as opposed to mere formal craftsmanship or simple entertainment, underline the claim to poetic authority, and it is tempting, if rather fanciful, to regard the poem's abrupt conclusion on the word 'auctorite' as more than a mere accident of transmission.[27] Certainly, Chaucer's authorial mask, put on with some tongue-in-cheek solemnity and pretentiousness, gives additional point to the debate about the poets' activities of selecting and sifting their materials and presenting them in such a way as to convey their inner truth.

The whole of the third book, another firework display of fanciful and suggestive allegory, again does not do much to satisfy the dreamer's restless curiosity and uncertainty. It only demonstrates again, in a series of expressive images, the arbitrary and irrational quality of all the information handed down to posterity, in particular, the actions and reputations of men and women. Fame and defamation are not awarded according to merit, but according to the unpredictable whims of a goddess who cares nothing about the true deserving of her petitioners. For all the courtly masquerade and glamour, there seems to be no higher justice when it comes to reputation and fame, but only a chaotic mass of disorderly fragments of information, where any poet or newsmonger can take his pick. It is enough to turn the dreamer away from any ambition to be granted some fame of his own. All he asks for, when he is questioned about it, is that his name should not be bandied about after his death; as for the rest, 'I wot myself best how y stonde' (l. 1878). What he really desires is new material for his own poetic practice, and it soon appears that the House of Fame and its ruler are dependent on the whirling House of Rumour, where random items of 'tydynges' are released into the empty air to be received and judged by the capricious goddess of Fame.

At the height of the deafening and bewildering activity, the dreamer at last discovers someone who might help, the 'man of gret auctorite' – and here the text breaks off. We shall probably never know whether Chaucer wrote any more of this poem, whether accidents of transmission or Chaucer's own dissatisfaction or disinclination are responsible for the poem's unfinished state. Some readers and critics have felt that this is just the right inconclusive breaking off and have even praised Chaucer for it; but this is certainly mistaken. Most earlier readers took it for granted that Chaucer was unable to finish *The House of Fame* and some have even completed it for him, as Caxton did for the first printed edition in 1483. If we have to speculate, the most likely scenario is that the author left the poem before he composed the ending and somehow never managed to return to it. He may well have felt that he needed a little more time to reflect on the man of great authority and then was overtaken by other business before he could think of a satisfactory conclusion.

Judging by Chaucer's other works, it is more than improbable that this mysterious stranger would have come up with a solution that would have finally laid to rest all the dreamer's uncertainties. It would be most unlike his usual strategy to end with a crowning authoritative statement, and his investigation of the poetological issues is too searching and unconventional to admit of easy traditional answers. In spite of this tantalising rupture, however, the poem remains one of the most courageous and imaginative contributions to the ongoing debate.

Troilus and Criseyde

Troilus and Criseyde is Chaucer's first (and only) narrative on a major scale and in the tradition of the classical epic. After that, he returned again to smaller literary forms, but attempted to incorporate them in larger structures, such as

The Legend of Good Women and *The Canterbury Tales*. The poem was composed roughly between 1381 and 1386 when Chaucer evidently felt that he had reached a poetic status that at least made it not ridiculously presumptuous to address his own book in one breath with the monumental figures of Homer, Virgil and Statius (v, 1786–92).

He had read the story of the two lovers and their tragedy in the midst of the most famous campaign of classical mythology in several accounts, Latin and French, of the Trojan war; but what most impressed and challenged him to his own version was Boccaccio's youthful poem *Il Filostrato*. It is the first work to retell the episode on its own, set apart from the whole history of the siege of Troy, though the context of the war and the destined destruction of the city are ever present, creating a climate of doom and defeat.[28]

In fact, Chaucer's epic poem, or novel in verse, is basically a translation of the *Filostrato*, but only a comparatively small number of Boccaccio's lines have actually been turned into English; the rest is greatly expanded, rearranged and given a rather new interpretation. The story itself is hardly changed, but the proportions within it have been considerably altered: Boccaccio's heroine is from the first openly responsive to Pandaro's advances as go-between and she sees no great complications when confronted with the suggestion that she should take Troilus as her lover. The first night together, the climactic centre and almost exactly the middle of Chaucer's poem, comes somewhere in the first third of the *Filostrato*. For Boccaccio, the most important part of the story is Troilo's grief over the loss of Crisëida, which the poet, in his autobiographical introduction, compares to his own suffering as an unhappy lover, separated from his beloved. He offers his poem to the lady in question, to convince her of the depths of his sorrow and to move her to pity.

Chaucer from the start adopts quite a different role, that of the humble translator, who (once again) has no personal experience in love, but follows his 'auctour' as faithfully as he can, apologising whenever he has to relate something that might offend his audience or do injustice to one of the characters. For the reader who is able to check what the poet actually did to his sources, the mask becomes rather transparent and the assumed innocence reveals itself as a conscious and purposeful stratagem.

The narrator of *Troilus and Criseyde* has had almost too much critical attention.[29] He is, however, not a character in his own right; he remains the voice of the author and teller of the story; but his way of communicating with his audience or reader is so distinctively personal that one feels drawn into the process of narration and made to share not only the emotions of the characters, but, even more so, the translator's difficulties. This, in turn, strongly determines our response to the story and the impression formed in our minds of the actors. As in the *House of Fame*, the narrator suggests that he has to deal with an account of the story that may or may not be true to the historical facts, because these may have been misrepresented and distorted by previous authors. He is also very aware of the distance that time has built up between us and the past, of the changes in manners, forms of discourse and emotions. It is the subject of the Proem to the second book, where Chaucer, without any precedent in

Boccaccio's poem, warns his audience against judging the story according to their own conventions of speech and behaviour:

> Ye knowe ek that in forme of speche is chaunge
> Withinne a thousand yeer, and wordes tho
> That hadden pris, now wonder nyce and straunge   *curious*
> Us thinketh hem, and yet thei spake hem so,
> And spedde as wel in love as men now do;   *had success*
> Ek for to wynnen love in sondry ages,
> In sondry londes, sondry ben usages.
> . . .
> Ek scarsly ben ther in this place thre
> That have in love seid lik, and don, in al;
> For to thi purpos this may liken the,   *please you*
> And the right nought; yet al is seid or schal;   *And you not at all*
> Ek som men grave in tree, some in ston wal,   *cut, engrave*
> As it bitit. But syn I have bigonne,   *is fitting*
> Myn auctour shal I folwen, if I konne. (ii, 22–8, 43–9)

It is an explicit appeal to the historical imagination of the audience, in this case evidently addressed to a group of listeners present at the actual reading of the poem. Throughout *Troilus and Criseyde*, there are similar direct addresses, such as the companionable gesture (again not in Boccaccio) during the description of Troilus' love-sickness:

> For ay the ner the fir, the hotter is –   *nearer*
> This, trowe I, knoweth al this compaignye;
> But were he fer or ner, I dar sey this: (i, 449–51)

The narrator clearly tries to create an atmosphere of sociable complicity and a common ground of experience against the changes of time and the dubious trustworthiness of sources. This becomes even more insistent towards the end, when the story of Criseyde's betrayal has to be told, yet presented in such a way as to cast doubt upon the traditional cliché of the faithless woman. He is anxious to convince the reader that he is not prepared to endorse what people have said about the heroine, especially when it comes to her transferring her favours to Diomede. 'Men seyn – I not [*I do not know*] – that she yaf hym hire herte.' (v, 1050). This is followed by the narrator's famous apology:

> Ne me ne list this sely womman chyde   *I do not wish, poor woman*
> Forther than the storye wol devyse.
> Hire name, allas, is publysshed so wide
> That for hire gilt it oughte ynough suffise.
> And if I myghte excuse hire any wise,
> For she so sory was for hire untrouthe,
> Iwis, I wolde excuse hire yet for routhe. (v, 1093–9)   *compassion*

The appeal to compassion is a virtuoso move to provoke the reader to a dialogue with the text instead of just presenting him with a ready-made story. No other medieval version of Criseyde's fall succeeds equally in engaging our sympathy and discouraging us from easy judgement. It is Criseyde's sad fate and her tragic dilemma that the narrator feels should be worth our attention, not her treason and inconstancy that earlier historians have dwelt on, though, to be sure, this has not always been the effect the poem has had on its readers. A substantial minority at least has not been convinced by the poet's protestations in his heroine's defence and the clear message that he prefers to 'let other pens dwell on guilt and misery'.[30] And yet, from the very outset of his tale he has made clear that it is sympathy and pity, not moral judgement he asks from his audience in transmitting this distant story, and most of his own additions to the source as well as the countless modifications resulting in a complete transformation of tone clearly serve this object.

The most fundamental change concerns Chaucer's portrayal of love, and this, in turn, involves an entirely new view of the three central characters and their mutual relationship. Even a casual reader of the *Filostrato* will notice that what Boccaccio describes is really no more than an 'affair' like many others, arranged by Pandaro with the evident knowledge and complicity of the lovers themselves. Troilo has had similar experiences before, and Criseida at least knows from the start what to expect. For Chaucer's Troilus, the encounter with Criseyde is his very first real experience of love in all its intensity and a total claim on his person, and Criseyde, too, enters into the commitment with a full knowledge of what is involved. The difficulties, so brilliantly overcome by Pandarus, are not just the customary obstacles imposed by society or by the lovers' obligatory hesitancy, but they have their real roots in the complex nature of love and the seriousness of the choices involved. Troilus seems at first almost ludicrously inhibited by the conventions of 'courtly love', but he is, in fact, torn between his consuming desire and a genuine concern for Criseyde's safety from troubled apprehension and from public scandal. One of the first verbal expressions of his new state is the *Canticus Troili*, as it is labelled in several manuscripts, a fairly literal translation of Petrarch's sonnet CXXXII from the *Canzoniere*. It is a description of the paradoxical sensation of love, and there seems to be no reason to doubt that Chaucer was well aware of the basically spiritual dimension of Petrarch's infatuation, or rather his reverential devotion to his lady, purified of any selfish hope for a sensual reward. Troilus is soon persuaded by Pandarus that distant adoration is not what he really desires, but throughout all the subsequent scheming and manipulating he never loses sight of Criseyde's precarious situation nor does the reader ever feel that the eventual union is founded chiefly on physical attraction. Though Pandarus' view of love appears more 'realistic' than Petrarch's, it is manifestly much more limited, subordinating the most civilised and humane effects of love to its simple animal aspect. Troilus' earnest protestation, desperately vouching for the purity of his intentions, is answered by an amused and knowing laugh:

> For dredeles me were levere dye   *certainly, I would rather*
> Than she of me aught elles understode
> But that that myghte sownen into goode.'   *mean well*
>
> Tho lough this Pandare, and anon answerde,
> 'And I thi borugh? Fy! No wight doth but so. (i, 1034–8)
>   *Shall I vouch for you?*

25

What Pandarus seems to imply is that all the fine rhetoric of *fin amour* is no more than an ultimately meaningless game, good-humouredly attended to, but in practice ignored by the wiser friend. The equilibrium between these two extreme attitudes which the poem finally achieves is perhaps Chaucer's most remarkable triumph in this 'debate about love'.[31] Criseyde, too, though from different motives, wishes to believe that love can be limited to distant Petrarchan worship without practical obligations, but her intentions are dismissed with similar scorn:

> For pleynly hire entente, as seyde she,
> Was for to love hym unwist, if she myghte,   *without his knowledge*
> And guerdoun hym with nothing but with sighte.

> But Pandarus thought, 'It shal nought be so,
> Yif that I may; this nyce opynyoun   *silly attitude*
> Shal nought be holden fully yeres two.' (ii, 1293–8)

Her diffidence is not merely due to anxiety about her social reputation, though this is real and justified enough, but, as her long soliloquy in Book II reveals (ii, 701–808), she is well aware that personal freedom and independence are at stake and that accepting Troilus' love she will enter into a commitment no less total and binding than his.

The gravity of her decision is powerfully brought home to the reader by the elaborate stratagems Pandarus has to devise to bring the two together. The surface effect is chiefly that of a resourceful comedy of manners, and we may be forgiven if we sometimes feel that we have unawares been led into the world of the fabliau, where for the lovers to get into bed together is the sole aim of all ingenious scheming. This also appears to be the view taken by Pandarus when Troilus embraces Criseyde and he, satisfied that his inventive manoeuvering has been successful at last, lays him down to sleep, with a parting instruction to make the most of the present moment (iii, 1188–90).

But before this is achieved, an intricate game of deception and coercion has to be set in motion, which takes up the first half of the central book and is largely Chaucer's own invention. It is evidently enjoyed by Pandarus and joined in by Troilus and Criseyde without serious protest and, in the case of Criseyde, without the admission that she really knows what it is all about. There is a telling moment shortly before the family party arranged by Pandarus (without any precedent in *Il Filostrato*), when she suspects that something is afoot and asks whether Troilus will be there as well. Pandarus swears that he has left town, but adds that even if he were there she could absolutely rely on her uncle's secrecy (iii, 568–74). The narrator then adds,

> Nought list myn auctour fully to declare
> What that she thoughte whan he seyde so,
> That Troilus was out of towne yfare,
> As if he seyde therof soth or no; (iii, 575–8)

The obvious effect of this pretended ignorance is to raise doubts which we had no reason to entertain before and to suggest the possibility of Criseyde's silent complicity. Since she clearly loves Troilus and trusts in Pandarus' discretion her behaviour is blameless, as the narrator is at pains to assure us, whereas Troilus, more directly implicated in Pandarus' lies, at the critical point is so overcome with compunction that he falls into a swoon, which almost spoils Pandarus' finely-spun stratagem.[32] The comedy in no way subverts the reader's impression that both lovers are basically in unison with Pandarus, as they are with each other, and that the end more than justifies the means. Pandarus may have nothing more in mind than 'Th'olde daunce' (iii, 695),[33] but for the lovers this opens the door to an experience that includes much more than sensual fulfilment. In no other Middle English text is there such an effortlessly harmonious concord between a realistic assessment of sexual love and the stylised, idealistic concept of *fin amour*.

On a deeper level the comedy leading up to love's joyful consummation helps, by its very elaborateness, to convince us that the lovers' happiness is not lightly won and that it has a firmer basis than in *Il Filostrato*. The ravished bliss enjoyed by them is beyond what the sleeping Pandarus will ever comprehend, let alone experience for himself. The poem does not give us grounds for doubting the narrator's sincerity – or wisdom – when he bursts into an exclamation of envious enthusiasm as he recreates the scene:

> O blisful nyght, of hem so longe isought,
> How blithe unto hem bothe two thow weere!
> Why nad I swich oon with my soule ybought,
> Ye, or the leeste joie that was theere? (iii, 1317–20)

The last two lines have no equivalent in Boccaccio's poem and, in the context of the much harder won and much deeper felt mutual happiness, the narrator's sympathetic engagement also has an intensity absent in the source. In addition, Chaucer inserts two stanzas of authorial (or narratorial) comment on the difficulties of adequate translation and the shortcomings of his own version that make us sharply aware of the distance between ourselves and the characters, preventing a purely voyeuristic enjoyment, and at the same time intensify the impression of an exceptionally close union. Troilus repeats his assertion that, more than anything else, it is Criseyde's ease and comfort he has in mind, and she, on her side, welcomes him as 'my knyght, my pees, my suffisaunce' (iii, 1309). The poet leaves no doubt that the experience of love makes them both better human beings and brings them a happiness of a completely different order from 'the olde daunce'.

To betray such mutual affection and trust would seem to require more explaining and understanding than is needed in previous versions of the story, where Criseyde is simply the inconstant and untrustworthy woman tradition had made her by the time Chaucer came to reappraise the story. Critics have disagreed about the sincerity and the success of Chaucer's professed effort to 'excuse' his heroine. To the reader coming from *The House of Fame* it is not surprising that Chaucer would be particularly interested in the problem of the injustices done by capricious or biased transmission. The narrator's famous declaration, 'Iwis, I wolde excuse hire yet for routhe' (v, 1099), is not only a plea for sympathy with an unhappy woman, but also an appeal to our historical imagination and critical distrust of literary sources. All along the poet–translator has insisted on the hazards and deficiencies of previous accounts and has kept reminding us that all our knowledge of these people is indirect and derivative and that there is therefore no reason to take every detail and, in particular, every verdict, on trust. This justifies his attempt to rewrite the account of Criseyde's betrayal in a spirit of sympathy and, above all, of charity in the face of universal condemnation and of a consistently hostile tradition. The tragedy of the lovers is, then, at the same time, a subject for poets and books and a human story we are asked to read in the light of our own humanity. Chaucer again and again reminds the reader of his own difficulties in handing down a story he only knows at second or third hand, and he employs all the time-honoured formulas of epic poetry to foreground his humble role as faithful translator, as in the Proem to the third book, when, after a lively invocation to Venus as Goddess of Love, he calls on Calliope, the muse of epic poetry, for assistance:

> Caliope, thi vois be now present,
> For now is nede: sestow nought my destresse,
> How I mot telle anonright the gladnesse
> Of Troilus, to Venus heryinge? (iii, 45–8)   *praising*

The narrator's seeming diffidence reminds us of the text's artifice, but there is also something deceptive about it, because at this very point, as at many others, he is deliberately altering the order and the content of Boccaccio's text. In *Il Filostrato*, it is Troilo, happy in the success of his love, who chants the enthusiastic hymn in praise of Venus and of universal Love, actually based on Boece's *Consolatio Philosophiae*, whereas Chaucer puts his free translation of the passage into the mouth of the narrator at the outset of the book that is to tell the story of Troilus' rise to a state of short-lived bliss, thereby changing radically its tone and its authority. He also adds one or two details that give a more ambiguous quality to the concept of love, qualifying the enthusiastic praise by drawing attention to its wilful and at the same time very human nature.[34] Love is not only the divine principle, holding together the universe, from the harmony of the spheres down to the smallest creature; it is also the capricious force that made doting Jupiter pursue mortal women, sometimes successfully, sometimes in vain, as it pleased the whims of the Goddess. Whether Troilus' love belongs more to the first category or to the second is not stated in so many words; the text rather seems to suggest that his tragedy exemplifies the complexity and contrariness of the experience that makes any simple judgement impossible. Troilus' happiness in the fulfilment of his love is as real and genuine as his grief over the loss of it, and it seems to me misguided to read the whole poem in the light of its conclusion, as if Criseyde's pitiful betrayal invalidated the sincerity of her first love and, indeed, of all human love. The tragedy lies in the fact that even such genuine and, for a time, complete love is subject to the precarious inconstancy of human happiness.

Though Chaucer, in contrast to his source, devotes so much space and literary inventiveness to the wooing and winning of Criseyde, he puts hardly less weight on the portrayal of Troilus' misery, as the lovers are torn asunder by the cruel events of the war. The circular, or rather pyramidal structure imposed by the poet on the story impresses on the reader the height of the hero's fall from good fortune more intensely than in *Il Filostrato*, where more than two thirds of the text are concerned with Troilo's suffering, whose success in love had, in comparison, been rather lightly won.

Troilus, however, who has had to woo so patiently even for the slightest signs of favour from Criseyde, is facing a much more devastating sense of loss. Although the accounts of Criseyde's departure and eventual unfaithfulness run closely parallel in both poems, Chaucer, by a great number of small changes, omissions and additions, immeasurably heightens the pain of the separation and the experience of disillusionment. The time-scheme in *Troilus and Criseyde* is more subtly knitted than in *Il Filostrato*, giving an impression of day following day and of closely interrelated moments, while at the same time leaving the actual duration of events more vague. We are not told how long exactly the period of Troilus' wooing was, how long the happy union lasted and how long it took for Criseyde to transfer her affections from Troilus to Diomede.[35] Sometimes, indeed, there seem to be two time schemes, one suggesting breathless haste and continuous movement, the other suggesting the gradual and unhurried growth of emotions. Thus, we are told that Criseyde accepts Troilus as lover 'within the year in which the action starts',[36] but not before we have been explicitly urged by the narrator not to assume that this was an indecently hasty process.[37] The effect of this manipulation with time may vary from reader to reader. It certainly complicates our attitude to the characters, but it also adds to our sense of involvement in the action and its literary reconstruction.

Criseyde's change of heart, universally denounced by every author who wrote about her, is presented by Chaucer not as simply part of the story, but as a problem. The stark facts of the case are, if anything, made more shocking and indefensible in Chaucer's version; yet the narrator seems to try everything in his power to find excuses or at least mitigating circumstances for her and to grieve at what he has to report:

> For how Criseyde Troilus forsook –
> Or at the leeste, how that she was unkynde –
> Moot hennesforth ben matere of my book,
> As writen folk thorugh which it is in mynde.
> Allas, that they sholde evere cause fynde
> To speke hire harm! And if they on hire lye,
> Iwis, himself sholde han the vilanye. (iv, 15–21)   *they themselves*

The stanza, added by Chaucer to his source, firmly puts the responsibility on those who have handed down the story, refusing to judge the characters on the basis of mere reporting. Thus, even while aggravating Criseyde's guilt in one sense, the poet does not by any means put more blame on her, but leaves us to form our own opinion of what the texts tell us, not without adducing several considerations that should help us to understand her behaviour and

enter symphathetically into her anguished dilemma. If we still decide to con-
demn her, we should at least pause for a careful weighing of the evidence
before we do so.

There is, however, no uncertainty about the gravity and the pathos of Troilus'
ordeal. Since love had completely transformed his view of life and of virtuous
achievement, its loss leaves him more utterly at sea ('Al stereless withinne a
boot'; i, 416) than he was in his worst moments of love-longing, more funda-
mentally shaken even than the Black Knight in *The Book of the Duchess*. One
of Chaucer's major additions to his source, the substantial passage from Boece
on predestination (iv, 953–1085), shows that for the hero, his 'double sorwe'
raises more fundamental problems and agonising doubts than Boccaccio's
Troilo has to endure. Chaucer was evidently deeply fascinated with the question of God's foreknowledge and its consequences for human free will. Whether
he himself agreed with Boece's finely reasoned, orthodox solution we have no
means of knowing, but it is clear – and Chaucer, who himself had translated
the *Consolatio Philosophiae* into English, evidently intended the reader to be
aware of it – that his Troilus is denied any philosophical consolation. His
desperate questioning ends at the point where Boece's instructress expounds
her superior insight, and it is only at the very end of the poem and after the
hero's death that he, too, is granted a vision that converts despair and misery
into a serene contemplation of human helplessness.

Though Chaucer presents Troilus as a heroic figure, whose 'manhod' is
again and again stressed throughout the poem, many readers have felt that he
is at the same time a somehow weak or at least ambivalent character, especially when set against Pandarus' resourceful activities and Diomede's un-
scrupulous aggressiveness. His 'manliness' shows most clearly in the heroic
self-restraint he practises when he learns of Criseyde's impending exchange.
Though nearly dying with grief, he realises that any betrayal of strong concern
for Criseyde's fate on his side would endanger her reputation, which is more
dear to him than any selfish consideration:

> With mannes herte he gan his sorwes drye, (iv, 154)

The argument between Love and Reason in his mind is clearly decided in
favour of Reason: Troilus is firmly resolved not to proceed in any way without
consulting Criseyde and he is fully prepared to be ruled by her. In this he
combines, to an extraordinary degree, the traditional qualities of the exemplary knight and of the devoted lover who cares for his lady's peace of mind
more than for his own. The contrast comes out very strongly again in the
scenes of parting and in the lonely vigils of the deserted lover, torn between
bleak despair and hopeful expectation. In their last scene together Criseyde
almost seems more in command of the situation than he. Her protestations of
everlasting faith and her complaints against his seeming mistrust (iv, 1604–
10) may sound somewhat hollow when judged in the light of her subsequent
behaviour; but they are not presented as insincere, nor is the tragic irony of
her confidence directed against her own integrity. Her summing up of his
character – 'moral vertu, grounded upon trouthe' and 'gentil herte and manhod'

(iv, 1672, 1674) – rather suggests that she is not from the start unworthy of his love, that the two are, in fact, exceptionally well suited. It is the situation – fickle fate, unfathomable providence, and human frailty – certainly not the 'frailty-thy-name-is-woman'-sort! – that in the end shatters the lovers' happiness. Troilus' pitifully unrealistic suggestions are with some good reason rejected by Criseyde as impracticable; yet her trust in human constancy turns out in the end to be equally misplaced. One is sometimes tempted, not, I believe, without some gentle suggestion by the narrator, to find Criseyde's lamentable collapse no more directly blameworthy than Troilus' passive despair and his despondent, self-fulfilling premonitions. Again, the narrator warns against easy judgement and, more specifically, against taking the story's universally known conclusion as inevitable from the start:

> And treweliche, as writen wel I fynde
> That al this thyng was seyd of good entente,
> And that hire herte trewe was and kynde
> Towardes hym, and spak right as she mente,
> And that she starf for wo neigh whan she wente,   *died*
> And was in purpos evere to be trewe:
> Thus writen they that of hire werkes knewe. (iv, 1415–21)

The claim is slightly odd in view of Chaucer's usual scepticism regarding his sources, but he is clearly anxious to convince us that Criseyde's fall was not in any way a foregone conclusion and that in other circumstances she would have been as loyal as her lover for whom temptation evidently takes other forms.

While the fourth book, like the first three, opens with a formal proem and an invocation, this time to the three Furies, the fifth follows on immediately, without any new introduction apart from another brief glance at the three Fates. It may be that Chaucer originally believed he could relate 'the losse of lyf and love yfeere / Of Troilus' (iv, 27–8) all within the fourth book and only at a later stage found that he needed a fifth book, but there are no other signs of a deliberate change of design. The two last books are rather more closely linked together than the other books, thus stressing the inexorable pace of 'the fatal destyne' (v, 1) and the depth of Troilus' suffering. The fourth book portrays the lovers confronting their impending separation, while the final book relates the separate destinies, in particular Criseyde's lapse from truth and Troilus' agony and death.

After the deeply sympathetic, though in no way softening, relation of the stark facts the poem's conclusion comes as something of a surprise. The perspective changes repeatedly, as if the poet wanted to confess his own dilemma and admit his being at a loss how to wind up the story. He begins with a somewhat unconvincing apology to his readers for not relating all the details of the battle around Troy and a more particular apology to the ladies, asking them not to blame *him* for Criseyde's untruthfulness. His assurance that he would much rather write about Penelope's faithfulness and about the goodness of Alceste as well as his invective against faithless men seems to look forward to his next poem, *The Legend of Good Women*, and the farewell to his book appears to be a fit conclusion to the whole work. Yet he unexpectedly returns to Troilus and his death at the hands of Achilles. From Boccaccio's *Teseida* he then borrows the hero's ascent to a cosmic vantage-point that grants him full insight into the vanity of human desires and achievements and, in particular, the ridiculous insignificance of human grief. This finally leads the narrator to a sweeping condemnation of 'worldly vanyte' (v, 1837) and 'of payens corsed olde rites' (v, 1849) that seems to contradict the whole tenor of the poem so far and sounds like an all-out renunciation of it. The incongruousness of this conclusion can hardly be explained as a hasty retreat into safe orthodoxy or, even less so, as face-saving lip-service, but has to be seen as a kind of tentative succession of possible endings, expressing the poet's own inability (or refusal) to find a satisfactory single formula. Though he firmly asserts Christian commonplaces he is aware that, for all their undeniable truth, they do not provide easy answers to all the human uncertainties so movingly presented in Troilus' tragedy.[38] This is not to say that the poet does not believe in the truth of his final affirmation. It merely means that the poem cannot be reduced to a neat moral and the poet does not claim to provide simple answers to eternal questions. The haunting fascination the poem has had for many generations of readers since its first 'publication' can never be adequately or exhaustingly dissected. It combines classical symmetry and dazzling rhetorical artistry with realistic character analysis with an exploration of individual behaviour within a complex society that impresses us as at the same time mercilessly acute and humanely tolerant. It remains perhaps the most astonishing achievement in medieval English literature.

The Legend of Good Women

Chaucer's first attempt at a framed collection of tales has only of late come into its own again. Early readers and poets were evidently much impressed by some of Chaucer's retelling of classical stories, but many later generations all but ignored this intriguing poem, and it is only recently that it has been rediscovered and appreciated as one of Chaucer's most revealing discussions of his own art and his search for a new form of narrative.[39] It has often been suspected that the work's unfinished state suggests that the poet was bored with his venture and turned to the *Canterbury Tales* with some relief, but this is mere guesswork and might well give us a totally wrong idea of Chaucer's literary priorities. Nobody would deny, however, that the later collection is the more original and ambitious experiment and that it has always been infinitely more popular. *The Legend of Good Women*, though, has a formal and thematic unity that is lacking in the *Canterbury Tales*: it accounts for its intensity as well as for a certain monotony felt by most readers. Chaucer may well have found that tales that are too alike in subject and character can be wearying to the listener, an effect he dramatised by the string of 'tragedies' told by the Monk in the *Canterbury Tales* and the reaction of his audience.

More revealing than the tales themselves is their introduction as a work of enforced penance for poetic sins against the God of Love. The discussion between the poet and this God, with Alceste as mediator, almost certainly reflects some contemporary debate about the function of literature and, more specifically, about the portrayal of women in traditional male love discourse. It seems that Chaucer was blamed for translating the *Roman de la Rose* and, more surprisingly, for retelling the story of Criseyde's betrayal of Troilus. The poet's defence within the dream debate sounds sincere enough, and there is no obvious irony in his protestation that his intentions were of the best:

> For that I of Creseyde wroot or tolde,
> Or of the Rose; what so myn auctour mente,
> Algate, God woot, yt was myn entente   *All the time*
> To forthren trouthe in love and yt cheryce,
> And to ben war fro falsnesse and fro vice   *beware of*
> By swich ensample; this was my menynge. (F, 469–74)

There is no precedent in Middle English for this public profession of poetic intentions. Chaucer's decision to raise such issues within his own poetry and to speak in this undisguised way about his own work is evidence of a new kind of literary awareness and sophistication. It is clear that his God of Love is a parody of narrow-minded and wrong-headed critics who would like to lay down the law and give orders to poets if they could. The circumstances and the terms of the verdict make the sentence appear in a somewhat dubious light:

> Thow shalt, whil that thow livest, yer by yere,
> The moste partye of thy tyme spende
> In makynge of a gloryous legende
> Of goode women, maydenes and wyves,
> That were trewe in lovynge al here lyves; (G, 471–5)

It is a rather demanding commission and the reader may well wonder whether the outcome is likely to be serious poetry of the highest order. It is therefore hardly surprising that some critics have cast doubt on the sincerity of the whole venture and have assumed a generally subversive purpose, mainly at the expense of the poet's judges who get what they ask for with a vengeance. This reading, however, taken to its limit, would turn the whole work into a joke and would make the *Legend of Good Women* more antifeminist even than anything the God of Love had blamed the poet for.[40] But Chaucer's irony is generally more local and certainly does not undermine the seriousness of the whole poem. The divine verdict playfully introduces a subject that Chaucer was deeply interested in throughout his career; at the same time he experiments with a narrative strategy that avoids humourless dogmatism as well as corrosive satire. As a poet he evidently recognises the problem that women have traditionally been defamed by male authors, and, though being male himself and unmistakably speaking as a man, he sets himself up as women's champion. It is an elaborate piece of role playing that may well puzzle or frustrate literary criticism, especially when confronted with issues of twentieth-century academic feminism and with a totally different cultural environment.

Chaucer's strategy was successful at least to the extent that the Scots poet Gavin Douglas more than a century later described him as 'all womanis frend',[41] which may not have been meant as an unqualified personal compliment, but at least shows an understanding of what Chaucer was trying to do. In rewriting some of the most heterogeneous stories of famous women, turning them all into Love's martyrs, he was again clearly inspired by Ovid's *Heroides* and by Boccaccio's *De Mulieribus Claris*, though Boccaccio's collection of exemplary female biographies is by no means confined to virtuous women, but includes heroines exemplary only by their destructive viciousness, like the sorceress Medea, or at least of very ambiguous fame, like Cleopatra. Chaucer's narrator, admittedly writing under compulsion, unashamedly manipulates his source material in order to translate even the most notorious *femme fatale* into a model of suffering innocence and their men, even some of the most renowned classical heroes, into faithless profligates. It would be a mistake, however, to overestimate the amount of subversive irony and to conclude that Chaucer was just the opposite of 'womanis frend'. His chief object rather seems a problem of poetics and consists in a search for reliable truth in books. In a way, the *Legend* continues and extends the debate begun so insistently in the *House of Fame*.

At the outset of the Prologue the poet claims that there are many things we have to believe, even though we can never know them by experience and the testimony of our own senses. No living person has ever visited Heaven or Hell (*pace* the poet Dante[42]), yet we have to give credence to books that authoritatively tell us about the existence of such truths. The same applies, as Chaucer has explained in the *House of Fame*, to the stories of men's and women's past deeds. But instead of taking everything the books say on trust, we may well enquire into the basis of their authority. Poets can make or mar reputations, and thus the poet, ordered to write stories of virtuous women, can create these models at will out of the most unpropitious material.

Cleopatra, the heroine of the first legend, is not by any stretch of poetic imagination the natural choice for a saint, though Chaucer has brilliantly succeeded in presenting her as a pathetic victim and an exemplar of wifely loyalty unto death.[43] She seems a typical instance of what poets can do with traditional reputations and with differing historical reports. Her 'Legend', as far as is known, is the first version of her history in English, and Chaucer can hardly have been unaware of the differences between his own account and the most widely known portraits of her.

The second legend, relating the tragedy of Pyramus and Thisbe, seems a less controversial case. Chaucer, following Ovid's version in the *Metamorphoses* pretty closely, hardly alters the plot, yet the moral he draws from it is not necessarily the only possible one. Both the star-crossed lovers remain true to their ideal of love, even to death, but this does not make Thisbe a martyr let alone a victim of male agression and faithlessness. The poet admits as much and his conclusion reads like a concession – behind the God of Love's back – to his male readers, almost an apology for his feminist stance:

And thus are Tisbe and Piramus ygo.
Of trewe men I fynde but fewe mo
In alle my bokes, save this Piramus,
And therfore have I spoken of hym thus.
For it is deynte to us men to fynde   *delightful*
A man that can in love been trewe and kynde.
Here may ye se, what lovere so he be,
A woman dar and can as wel as he. (F, 916–23)

The poet is, after all, one of 'us men' and he clearly hints that there are other conclusions one may draw from the story than the official one.

In the case of Dido, whose tragedy Chaucer had already related in the *House of Fame*, the poet was quite aware of the existence of two conflicting traditions and again he clearly takes sides with the heroine against Virgil's account. The divine command to Aeneas to leave Carthage in obedience to his mission is dismissed as a cheap excuse invented by eager poets, if not by the false lover himself, though the tensions within Chaucer's version, some implied sneaking sympathy with Aeneas' position, may well raise some doubts on the reader's part as to other areas of meaning.

Any pretense at impartiality is, however, thrown to the winds in the twin legend of Hypsipile and Medea, where Jason is vigorously denounced as the 'sly devourere and confusioun / Of gentil wemen', who uses all the traditional paraphernalia of courtly love, 'feyned trouthe ... obesaunce and humble cheere ... contrefeted peyne and wo' as sinister strategies of seduction and who betrayed two where others betrayed one (F, 1369–77). He is the obverse side of Troilus, in seemingly perfect fulfilment of the Love-God's command. But the legend seems more eager to warn against false men than to glorify women's *trouthe*, which can hardly be what the God meant:

Yif that I live, thy name shal be shove   *made known*
In English that thy sekte shal be knowe! (F, 1381–2)

The victims, or martyrs, are, however, treated in a rather perfunctory way, and the narrator explicitly refers the reader to Ovid's epistles for a more lengthy treatment of their pathetic fate, too long for him to repeat.

The story of Lucrece, in contrast, needed no reinterpretation to fit into the thematic scheme of the collection. It was widely known through Ovid and the Roman historian Livy and it was also the subject of an influential theological discussion by the Church father Augustine. Chaucer refers explicitly to all three accounts, but he ignores the criticism of Augustine, choosing to commemorate the 'verray wif, the verray trewe Lucresse' who 'for hyre wifhod and hire stedefastnesse' (F, 1686–7) was praised not only by those pagans, but also pitied by the Christian Saint. Chaucer's Lucrece is first of all a faithful wife and in that respect she differs, if only in emphasis, from most previous versions. She kills herself not so much because of any dishonour she feels herself, but because she does not want her husband's good name to suffer.[44] This, as Chaucer thinks it necessary to explain, has to be seen as a result of the

35

Romans' particularly high regard for honour and good name. There is no idea that she could have resisted her rape more determinedly, as Augustine had suggested. Chaucer firmly rules out this possibility by insisting that Lucrece was practically unconscious with fright and did not really know what was happening to her.

It is interesting to note, as in this case, that all the martyred saints in this collection are married and thus belong, in the traditional classification of women quoted in the Prologue ('maydenes, widewes, wyves' (G, 282–3, 294–5) to the least perfect of the three states. All the husbands turn out to be seducers and betrayers who promise marriage, even when there is no mention of matrimony in the sources. Thus the stories of these unhappy women are made much more alike in Chaucer's telling than in previous versions.

It is difficult to know what precisely induced the poet to this deliberate act of reinterpretation, but his evident interest in the poetological problems involved makes it seem likely that he was attracted by the idea of collecting classical stories within a frame that gave unity and some kind of common point of view to the whole work, though modern readers find it all but impossible to agree on a definition of such a viewpoint. Like Ovid's unconventional rewriting of well-known biographies, Chaucer's 'legends' defy unambiguous classification as either 'pathetic' or 'ironic'; they evidently mean very different things to different readers. More than any other work by Chaucer, they can serve as examples of the 'Instability of Meaning'.[45]

The Canterbury Tales

Chaucer's best-known narrative work is, at first sight, the most accessible and least 'medieval'. It does not employ, so it seems, dated conventions, such as the dream-opening, and it offers an unorthodox and pluralistic variety of styles and subjects that strikes twentieth-century readers as distinctly modern, at least until they come to 'The Tale of Melibee' or 'The Parson's Tale', both of which few even of the most ardent admirers of Chaucer's story-telling will have read from start to finish. Yet they are as much part of the whole design as are the 'The Miller's Tale' or 'The Nun's Priest's Tale'.

Perhaps the most crucial fact about *The Canterbury Tales* is the poem's unfinished state. The framed tales make up one of the most fascinating fragments in world literature, and, like Dickens's *Mystery of Edwin Drood*, they leave many questions for ever unanswered and unanswerable. It is, for one thing, by no means clear that Chaucer even had a definite and precise plan as to the final form the complete work was to take. It seems at least likely that the poet changed his mind more than once in the course of composition, and it may well be that he was more interested in the possibility of a convenient folder for an indefinite number of heterogeneous tales than in any grand design.[46] It seems, therefore, more sensible to enjoy the invigorating plenty of tales and tellers than to insist on discovering a general theme that holds them together. The fascination with limitless possibilities of storytelling by an equally limitless variety of individuals is probably the only motive most readers would readily agree on and it is this openness, more than anything else, that distinguishes the *Canterbury Tales* from other medieval story-collections.[47] Most of these have either one single narrator or a fairly homogeneous group of narrators and, within the frame, only one particular type of narrative.

In Boccaccio's *Decameron*, for instance, which comes nearest to being Chaucer's model, the impressive symmetry of the design and the uniformity of tales and tellers are clearly intentional and stand in sharp contrast to the unpredictable capriciousness of the *Canterbury Tales*, where Chaucer exploited to the full the fact that different individuals tell different tales and tell them in different ways. In poetic practice, this goes clearly against the principle of decorum and the ruling conventions of stylistic unity. It also appears to cater for a rather mixed audience, an audience, moreover, that is free to choose and take its pick from the rich menu offered, according to taste, education and religious views. This idea is explicitly put forward by the narrator, when he apologises for the low and possibly offensive tone of the Miller's tale:

> And therfore every gentil wight I preye,
> For Goddes love, demeth nat that I seye
> Of yvel entente, but for I moot reherce   *evil intention, relate*
> Hir tales alle, be they bettre or werse,
> Or elles falsen som of my mateere.
> And therfore, whoso list it nat yheere,
> Turne over the leef and chese another tale;
> For he shal fynde ynowe, grete and smale,
> Of storial thyng that toucheth gentillesse,
> And eek moralitee and hoolynesse.
> Blameth nat me if that ye chese amys. (I (A), 3171–81)   *choose wrongly*

The situation envisaged by the text seems to hover between an oral and a written narrative, between a listening audience and solitary readers; for who decides when to turn over a leaf and skip a possibly unacceptable story? Within the frame, it is mostly the host who sets the tone and pronounces judgement. In the 'Miller's Prologue', however, it is clearly the author himself addressing the reader of the *Canterbury Tales*, thus creating a complicated fictional dialogue between implied audience and fictional audience, between narrators within the fictional narrative and their listeners and between us and the creator of the whole work.

The elaborate introduction or opening part of the frame, usually referred to as the 'General Prologue', is a masterpiece of ambiguity. It begins with a teasing description of pilgrimages suggesting at the same time naive piety, devotional business and worldly sociableness. The detailed portrayal of the individual members of the group gathered at the Tabard Inn also leaves us in some doubt as to their real motives; only a small fraction of them appear to be genuinely moved by religious fervour. Most of the others are so obsessively engrossed in their professional skills, in money-grabbing, cheating and manipulating others, that it seems something of a miracle they can spare the time for this pilgrimage. The poet in his own person, or rather his *persona*, presents himself as a close observer, who refuses to judge others, though he is acutely aware of their deficiencies. Unlike William Langland, he is not angered or moved to satirical rage by the imperfections around him, but relates what he sees and politely agrees with everyone. When his turn comes to tell a story, he contributes two extreme specimens of narrative: first, the outrageous parody of 'The Tale of Sir Thopas' and, when this is stopped by the Host, the undramatic and highly serious prose tract of 'The Tale of Melibee', the most undiluted piece of didacticism in the whole collection, if we except the homily of the Parson, which hardly qualifies as a 'tale' at all.

The famous portrait gallery of the prologue does not, however, describe a random assortment of individualised characters, but presents something like a comprehensive panorama of medieval 'estates', or at least a series of representatives of different ranks and professions, leaving out the very highest and the very lowest. It has usefully been connected with similar galleries in medieval versions of the Dance of Death or, more relevantly, medieval estate satire.[48] Chaucer could not, for obvious reasons, present a complete anatomy of Middle English society; yet he gives a strong sense of rank and profession that reflects some basic divisions and degrees of status, education, wealth and authority. The Knight would, in fact, rank below a whole hierarchy of aristocratic dignitaries, from the King downwards, but he would, in his own estimation and the conventions of his society, be distinctly above the mixed group of lower clergy, whose superiors, deans, abbots and bishops would hardly be found on this kind of pilgrimage. The citizens, again, would fall into groups not normally meeting under such relaxed conditions, but pursuing different occupations and following their own professional rules of social intercourse. Below them, a large majority of anonymous labourers, entertainers and beggars populated the countryside, but would certainly not have the means to join the group at the Tabard Inn.

Though Chaucer's series of pilgrim portraits is a virtuoso piece of brilliant characterisation and social analysis in its own right, its chief purpose is to prepare for the unprecedented diversity of the tales that are to follow. For all the liveliness of the individual figures and their biographies, Chaucer is careful not to arouse too much interest in their own histories, so as not to detract from their contributions to the story contest. Accounts of the *Canterbury Tales* claiming that the tales are really subservient to the 'roadside drama', as dramatic monologues serving to characterise the speakers, give a mistaken idea of the work's balance and of Chaucer's narrative priorities. Nowhere in the whole work does the frame assume the kind of independence found in some other story collections, and it seems unlikely that Chaucer would have provided this could he have finished the poem. There are a great number of recurring themes and motifs linking individual tales and even groups of tales, and there are also many close correspondences between tellers and tales; but the overall design, both in respect of formal structure or of thematic coherence, is anything but rigid, and its most important feature is an openness that allows for the inclusion of the most heterogeneous material. In this, the *Canterbury Tales* is the very opposite to the preceding collection of the *Legend of Good Women*, where the frame imposed a severe limitation on the subject and the interpretation of the individual stories. When the poet abandoned that self-imposed 'penaunce', he seems to have determined not to suffer any more strangling restrictions, but to exercise complete freedom as a narrative poet, untroubled by laws of form, genre or stylistic decorum. Thus the *Canterbury Tales* grew into an almost complete inventory of medieval types of narrative, from the unashamedly popular to the obtrusively learned, from the openly secular to the piously spiritual, from the seemingly most artless to the highly sophisticated.

In their attempt to introduce some order into their discussion of the *Canterbury Tales*, many critics divide them into groups according to subject or genre, the most usual being 'romances', 'religious tales' and 'fabliaux' or 'comic tales'.[49] This can be useful as a preliminary approach, but it may give a misleading idea of the tales' general conformity to any one particular genre pattern. In fact, only a small minority of them can be easily fitted into one of the traditional classifications, although most of them begin innocently enough as legend, romance, fable, or exemplum. A certain unity is imposed by the metrical form: the whole of Fragment I(A) and the greater part of the rest is written in decasyllabic or pentameter lines rhyming in couplets and used with consummate suppleness and inventive variety of tone, pace and syntactic complexity. There are, however, two long tracts in prose, several of the religious or exemplary tales use the seven-line rhyme-royal stanza, and the hilarious mock-romance of Sir Thopas makes deliberate fun of the popular tail-rhyme stanza. Nor is there any premeditated pattern in the order of the tales. The idea of a social hierarchy is first introduced in the Prologue, when Chaucer begins the series of portraits with the Knight, the Squire and their servant, but we soon lose the sense of a systematic breakdown of estates or ranks, and near the end of his account, the narrator feels it necessary to apologise for his failure to 'set folk in hir degree / Heere in this tale, as that they sholde stonde' (I, 744–5).

The apology is more apt than Chaucer's easy manner suggests, because the reality of rank and of gradation is a crucial fact of medieval society, governing and restricting social relations and generally preventing the kind of easy intercourse between different estates dramatised in the *General Prologue*. Only by a very bold stroke of poetic imagination could this utopian community of pilgrims and the shuffling of different levels be presented in fiction. This unprecedented breaking down of social barriers in some ways anticipates the many-layered world of Elizabethan comedy.

Similarly, when it comes to the telling of stories, the idea of rank and precedence seems simultaneously acknowledged and brushed aside by the drawing of lots and by the 'accident' of the Knight being chosen to tell the first story. Whatever scheme the Host has in mind when he calls on the Monk to succeed the Knight is frustrated by the drunken Miller who insists on pushing in with his own contribution. From then onwards the order seems all but arbitrary, except that some pilgrims are provoked into immediate retort by tales that explicitly attack or ridicule their own profession. This, again, is very different from other framed collections, most conspicuously the *Decameron*, where there is an almost ritual symmetry of tales and tellers, underlined by the number of

stories (ten times ten) and days (ten). Chaucer deliberately casts aside any suggestion of a constricting plan in order to leave himself completely free in the
choice and sequence of tales, though the surviving 'fragments' have a kind of
formal and thematic unity of their own.[50] It also seems clear that he intended,
at least at one stage, to conclude with the Parson's penitential sermon. This,
however, would have left other threads dangling in mid-air, such as the idea of
a contest and the final supper, quite apart from the unsolved problem of the
home journey with the return to Southwark and the eventual number of stories.[51]

These are questions that have received an almost excessive amount of attention from critics, since they are so closely related to the poem's unfinished state
and to the uncertainties of its transmission. It is impossible to be sure about
exactly what Chaucer left on his desk at the time of his death and how far he
had finally made up his mind as to the finished form the collection should take.
From the surviving manuscripts it appears that there was a number of more or
less completed fragments, including more than one tale, as well as a number of
'floating' tales of varying ascription, and probably various attempts by early
scribes to make some sense of the unconnected portions and genuine or spurious
links between them.[52] The evidence strongly supports Pearsall's view that
'Chaucer left the work as a partly assembled kit with no directions' and that
an ideal edition should present it 'partly as a bound book (with first and last
fragments fixed) and partly as a set of fragments in folders, with the incomplete
information as to their nature and placement fully displayed'.[53] Such an edition
would prevent the impression produced by seemingly 'definite' texts, such as
the *Riverside Chaucer*, and would give a clearer idea of what we in fact have
left to go on: a teasing series of fragments, yet part of a whole, with a wealth of
suggestions as to their guiding principle and poetic coherence and, most importantly, some two dozen of the richest narrative performances written in English.

Though it is instructive to examine these stories by genre and thus to discover
how freely Chaucer handled traditional epic material and literary conventions,
the reader will most appropriately approach the collection through the Prologue
and Fragment I(A) and thus share the experience of the first audiences for
whom the tales were part of a larger, but indeterminate design and of an open-
ended performance. The individual tales together clearly make up the bulk
and the centre of the whole work, but they are not isolated pieces of poetry,
but have to be read in their context, as narratives within a narrative, as part of
a social occasion. This is made very clear from the outset in the Prologue and
by the brief exchanges between the pilgrims that link many of the tales. As in
the *Decameron*, the listeners comment on the performances of their fellows,
but often in such a way that the very personal character of their reactions is
made clear. Though often very brief, these comments are as unpredictable as
the tales themselves and thus alert the reader to the complexities of literary
production and to the readers' responsibility.

Chaucer deliberately starts with the greatest possible contrast: the highly
rhetorical and philosophical story of the Knight, almost a minor epic poem in
its own right, is followed by the bawdy fabliau forced upon the company by
the drunken Miller and capped immediately by the Reeve's revenge.

'The Knight's Tale' is a very free and brilliantly condensed translation of Boccaccio's *Teseida*, reduced to about a quarter of its size and transformed into one of Chaucer's most finished courtly narratives. It combines highly wrought stylistic artifice with lavish descriptive virtuosity and colourful action. Above all, it is a study of human relationships and individual impotence in the face of omnipotent fate or 'necessity'. The poem was a favourite with later poets; John Dryden (1631–1700) made a free translation[54] and Shakespeare, together with John Fletcher, based the tragicomedy of *The Two Noble Kinsmen* (*c.* 1613) on it and we know of two earlier dramatic versions. The prologue (probably written by Fletcher) is remarkable for its eloquent praise of Chaucer:

> It [the play] has a noble breeder and a pure,
> A learned, and a poet never went
> More famous yet 'twixt Po and silver Trent.
> Chaucer, of all admired, the story gives;
> There, constant to eternity, it lives. (ll. 10–14)[55]

Chaucer evidently wrote the poem as a work to stand on its own, before the *Canterbury Tales* were conceived.[56] Nevertheless, it is perfectly suited as an introductory chord to the storytelling contest and as the particular contribution of the 'verray, parfit gentil knyght' (I (A), 72). To begin a collection of stories with a work of such large scale and poetic ambition suggests that Chaucer had a truly major work in mind, but the immediate sequel, with the Miller's rude interruption and his own 'cherles tale' as his contribution to the entertainment, followed by two even more vulgar and obscene stories, also proves that something of unprecedented novelty and variety was envisaged. The third of the comic items, 'The Cook's Tale', breaks off after 58 lines, to which the earliest copyist added, 'Of this Cokes tale maked Chaucer na moore'.[57] It is not unlikely that he had more reliable information than we and this would confirm the impression that, after this vigorous start, Chaucer, instead of continuing with the poem according to a predetermined plan, composed only free-floating individual tales or little groups of tales, to be allocated and strung together after the eventual working out of the whole design. This was not to happen in his lifetime, so that no more is left to do than to enjoy a work in progress.

In tale after tale we can observe the poet pick up a traditional type of narrative or subject and turn it into something unexpected and original. Not one of the tales is exactly like any other, but nearly all of them share a sense of communal experience and an awareness of the audience. Some of the tellers preface their contribution with a more personal statement or address to the company, and two of them introduce themselves at some length with an elaborate plea for sympathy or, indeed, complicity, before they actually enter into the narrative contest. This gives additional substance to the frame and helps to create the fiction of a social group of characters, each with his or her individual biography. This applies in particular to the Wife of Bath, whose apology for women's enjoyment of sex and their desire for marital dominance has made her one of the best-known characters in English fiction, quite apart from her own tale. Her eloquent defence of marriage, with a spirited attack on clerkly misogyny, and the dramatic account of her putting a stop to her husband's antifeminist reading show the poet exploring new ways of dramatising character through speech. No less original is the Pardoner's boastful demonstration of his seductive salesmanship (VI (C), 329–462), introducing his own contribution to the story-contest and, to cap it, an outrageous attempt to turn the entertainment into business by offering his pardons and his false relics to the fellow-pilgrims. The Host's taunting and offensive rebuff creates another moment of open discord among the company and keeps the reader aware of latent tensions and animosities among the audience.

Finally, 'The Canon's Yeoman's Prologue and Tale' provide an unprecedented addition to the framed collection of tales. His surprising appearance among the pilgrims gives another twist to the fiction of the pilgrimage and provides one more element of action and conflict that affects both the tales and the listeners.[58] The episode is perhaps the nearest approach to what critics have called 'roadside drama' and creates a particularly close interrelationship between the lives of the narrators and the tales. The newcomer's 'tale' is an immediate sequel to the 'prologue', an extended anecdote, taken from the Canon's Yeoman's own experience, with a claim to real truth. Whatever final connection between frame and stories Chaucer had in mind, the present fragment suggests that he kept experimenting with changing narrative stances and sophisticated variations of distance and audience involvement. Thus, the *Canterbury Tales* becomes not only a miscellaneous anthology of stories, but at the same time an exploration of methods and problems of storytelling.

Though many critics feel that Chaucer was, in the end, chiefly interested in finding a suitable vessel for a great variety of his stories, he was evidently unable to repress his narrative drive when it prompted him into some exuberant digression that possibly had not been part of his original design. In the minds of many readers, some of the earliest among them, the Canterbury pilgrims live as a company of individuals, not just as narrative voices or tellers of tales.[59] This is mainly due to the spontaneous comments on some individual performances or performers, quarrels between some of the pilgrims, and, not least, vociferous protest from listeners against a number of contributions, bringing some stories to a sudden, premature halt. Such is the case of the Monk's dreary series of tragedies and Chaucer's own first attempt, the romance of 'Sir Thopas'. All this is evidence of the author's particular interest in the narrative situation and the close rapport between narrator and audience. For all its incompleteness and the central importance of the tales themselves, the collection derives much of its vitality and of its literary impact from such metafictional suggestions.

Most of the plots used by Chaucer have their source in classical literature, in medieval romance, religious legend or folklore, but hardly any of the stories run strictly true to type and few could serve as typical specimens of traditional genres. Nearly all of them are embellished by rhetorical flourishes, by surprising touches of realism or unexpected twists of individual irregularity and, more often than not, by teasing authorial comment and humorous understatement. Any of the tales could be selected as examples of Chaucer's personal method and inimitable tone of voice, even in those cases where he seems to follow his model very closely, almost to the point of translating it.

The tale offered by the Clerk is an eloquent instance. Chaucer chose to render the famous story of patient Griselda, the concluding tale in Boccaccio's *Decameron*, translated into Latin by his friend Petrarch and also available in a French version.[60] The narrator introduces his contribution to the storytelling contest as a tale he 'Lerned at Padowe of a worthy clerk' (IV (E), 27), with a brief tribute to the late poet, whose fame he evidently knows how to appreciate:

> Fraunceys Petrak, the lauriat poete,
> Highte this clerk, whos rethorike sweete   *Was called*
> Enlumyned al Ytaille of poetrie, (ll. 31–3)

It is clear that the Clerk is familiar with the literary landscape of Europe and the latest poetic developments. He gives a brief outline of Petrarch's introduction, which he dismisses as irrelevant to his purpose, and then proceeds with a more or less faithful rendering of Petrarch's text. The most radical departure from the source is the change from prose to rhyme royal, which alters the tone and produces more pointed effects. Apart from that, the Clerk seems unable to suppress a certain discomfort with some aspects of the story and impatience with the lordly husband. He cannot accept Petrarch's text uncritically as just a parable, like Petrarch himself, without being touched by its human appeal. This is why he emphasises the pathos of Griselda's situation and his own disapproval of Walter's cruelty. He follows Petrarch's warning against a literal reading: Griselda is not held up as a model to be imitated by all wives, but as an image of Christian patience. Yet he will not leave it at that, but adds an outrageous 'Envoy', turning the whole performance into a joke, appealing even to the Wife of Bath and 'al hire secte' (l. 1171). The potentially offensive message of the Griselda-story is thus defused, and this is compounded by the reaction of the Host who can only take the story on a rather vulgar level as a lesson for unruly wives. He applies it, rather in the spirit of a comic *fabliau*, to his own domestic situation.

Here, as throughout his anthology, Chaucer refuses to offer narratives that ask for a single, definite interpretation, but presents alternative, indeed contradictory readings that challenge the audience and invite discussion rather than unanimous assent. The challenge sometimes consists in the juxtaposition of mutually exclusive points of view, at other times in provocative narrowness and extreme limitation of perspective. Some of the speakers seem quite unaware of the confrontational effect of their contribution, while others deliberately provoke a heated response. The Reeve is angered by the Miller's tale of a duped carpenter and procedes to 'quyt' him by his own story of a cheated Miller. This, in turn, amuses the Cook who promises a tale of a Host. Similarly, the Friar and the Summoner vent their professional enmity in their stories. The Friar who, during the Wife of Bath's performance has been casting angry looks at the Summoner, offers to tell a joke about a summoner and the fellow-pilgrim defiantly accepts the challenge. The anecdote of the sincerely meant curse, probably of folk origin, and extant in many medieval versions, is considerably expanded by Chaucer; the dialogue between the devil and the friar is a master-piece of irony and concise theology. The corrupt summoner immediately recognises a kindred spirit and enters into a compact with the fellow-cheater, thus choosing his own descent into the fiend's abode. There is no need for any false pretences on the devil's part because the summoner's grasping eagerness makes him immune against all danger signals, such as the devil's promise that his companion's curiosity in matters of the strategy of hell should soon be fully satisfied. Chaucer brilliantly combines satiric comedy and literary allusion in this dramatic exchange:

> Thou wolt algates wite how we been shape;   *for ever*
> Thou shalt herafterward, my brother deere,
> Come there thee nedeth nat of me to leere,   *learn*
> For thou shalt, by thyn owene experience,
> Konne in a chayer rede of this sentence   *Be able, teach*
> Bet than Virgile, while he was on lyve,
> Or Dant also. (III, 1514–20)

This is what happens, and the friar concludes his tale with a cynically insincere prayer for the repentance of summoners.

The summoner-pilgrim is so angered by this tale that he shakes in his stirrups and immediately embarks on his retort, a much coarser joke on a greedy friar, again of evidently popular origin, enriched with vivid domestic detail and outrageous scholastic farce. The practices of the mendicant orders, often satirised and particularly resented by the local clergy, are held up for ridicule and contempt and, as in the 'Miller's Tale' and the 'Reeve's Tale', aggressive obscenity is used as the hallmark of 'cherles' and their stories. The sequence breaks off at this point, and the end of the quarrel is not related, but the heated hostile exchange is a particularly successful instance of Chaucer's method of adapting his story material, dramatising the act of narration and shaping the tales to suit the speaker and the situation.

Geoffrey Chaucer's own part in the competition presents a more sophisticated, literary challenge to the audience's judgement. 'Sir Thopas' is an unashamedly mocking parody of trite popular romances which the Host angrily rejects for the wrong reasons, evidently blind to its real poetic purpose and accurate humour. When the offended narrator recites the massive prose tract of Melibeus instead, it is tempting to suspect another parody or least some kind of pointed retaliation. There is little doubt, however, that this long didactic dialogue on patience is quite seriously meant and is more than a long-drawn-out joke. On the other hand, there is surely a strong element of comedy in the fact that Chaucer, the author of the whole collection, offers first the most trivial and oral popular romance and then – leaving aside the Parson's penitential treatise – the most learned undramatic and unpoetic of all the items, a close translation from the French *Livre de Melibée et de Dame Prudence* by Renaud de Louens. The two 'tales' contributed by the author himself mark the two extreme poles of this most ambitious literary project, pure 'solas' and undiluted 'sentence'. The contrast between these two texts could hardly be more conspicuous, and the fact that, at least in the present fragmentary form of the *Canterbury Tales*, Chaucer himself is the only pilgrim who is allowed two tales also points in the direction of some self-conscious humour. His justification of the 'litel thyng in prose' (VII, 937) again highlights the range of the whole work, as laid down by the Host: 'som murthe or som doctryne' (VII, 935) and introduces a serious note of literary theory.[61] The poet evidently wants to draw the reader's attention to himself and his versatile art.

At one other point of the work he refers to himself by name, though we are never told that the Chaucer quoted as a familiar figure and author of many love stories by the Man of Law (II, 45–89) is the same individual as the 'I' of the frame and the narrator of 'Sir Thopas'. The bibliography given by this lawyer is one of the most remarkable literary self-portraits in Middle English literature and a unique document of the poet's confidence in the value of his art. 'The Man of Law's Tale' is a polished version of the very popular story of Constance which Chaucer found in an Anglo-Norman chronicle and, most probably, in his friend John Gower's *Confessio Amantis*. On the face of it, it seems one of the less original of Chaucer's retellings of familiar material, but comparison with analogues soon shows that he was particularly interested in the story's sensational and emotional appeal, its combination of pathos, adventure, piety and moral instruction. Like the 'Clerk's Tale', it is not a saint's legend nor a straightforward romance, but one of countless medieval exempla of trial, suffering and faith, borne with patience and resilience and finally rewarded.[62] What Chaucer adds to his own version is mainly a heightened sense of extraordinary fortitude in the face of injustice and affliction and the narrator's engaging sympathy. He is moved to pity by his heroine's unprotected plight and he appeals to an audience that extends far beyond the road to Canterbury:

> O queenes, lyvynge in prosperitee,
> Duchesses, and ye ladyes everichone,
> Haveth som routhe on hire adversitee!
> An Emperoures doghter stant allone;
> She hath no wight to whom to make hir mone.
> O blood roial, that stondest in this drede,
> Fer been thy freendes at thy grete nede! (II, 652–8)

The narrator's pity is an important aspect of the tale's rhetoric, another is the surprising shifts in tone, from high seriousness to sudden lapses into an almost flippant, humorous perspective as his comment on the wedding-night:

> They goon to bedde, as it was skile and right;   *proper*
> For thogh that wyves be ful hooly thynges,
> They moste take in pacience at nyght
> Swiche manere necessaries as been plesynges
> To folk that han ywedded hem with rynges,
> And leye a lite hir hoolynesse aside,
> As for the tyme – it may no bet bitide. (II, 708–14)   *better*

In a romance, this remark would be entirely unnecessary; in a saint's legend all but offensive, but in the present context it appears like a bold attempt to have it both ways: as so often in Chaucer, the reader is at a loss quite how seriously to take the characters or, indeed, the author, but it would be misreading the story to let the occasional humorous tone detract from the pathos and the pity. Chaucer is not making fun of pious legends and romantic miracles; he assumes an urbane attitude to all forms of entertainment and enjoys experimenting with narrative tones of voice. Perhaps the Man of Law, Chaucer's own creation, for all his disclaimer, is trying to do better than his creator in the way of stylistic refinement, and Chaucer the poet is thus entering into competition with himself. The little incident again demonstrates his exuberant delight in literary role-playing and self-referential masquerade.

Moreover, many of the stories document again, in their various ways, Chaucer's deep interest in problems of love, in classical mythology, philosophical debate and in controversial issues. One of these, as his earlier poetry has shown, is the nature and the truth of dreams; another is the controversy surrounding divine predestination and freedom of will. Both of these subjects return in stories where one would not normally expect them, e.g. in the animal fable of the Cock and the Fox, told by the Nun's Priest and the story of the rash promise, told as a Breton lay by the Franklin.

The 'Nun's Priest's Tale' is a justly celebrated virtuoso demonstration of what can be done with a simple episode. It derives from a brief fable and, again, Chaucer has enriched it with a display of rhetorical fireworks that almost buries the actual plot. The dramatis personae are developed into very human characters within a very clearly drawn social environment and the domestic dispute between the cock and his spouse turns into a moving little treatise about the significance of dreams, quoting authorities from Macrobius to the Bible and Greek myth. The narrator adds to this teasing mixture of comedy and seriousness a dazzling array of learning and traditional lore, by introducing the subject of predestination, one of Chaucer's favourite topics, not without mentioning Boece. The mock-heroic lament of the hens when the fox is carrying away the cock almost anticipates Alexander Pope's *Rape of the Lock* (1714) in its comic use of classical references:

> Certes, swich cry ne lamentacion
> Was nevere of ladyes maad whan Ylion
> Was wonne, and Pirrus with his streite swerd,
> Whan he hadde hent kyng Priam by the berd,　　　　　　*seized*
> And slayn hym, as seith us *Eneydos*,　　　　　　　　*the* Aeneid
> As maden alle the hennes in the clos,
> Whan they had seyn of Chauntecleer the sighte. (VII, 3355–60)

The Nun's Priest evidently enjoys such display of wide and miscellaneous reading to support his theory of writing, defined by a rather free application of St Paul's statement that everything that is written is written for our instruction.[63] It is obvious, of course, that St Paul is referring to the canonical scriptures, not to just any entertaining stories. In the context of the *Canterbury Tales*, however, the Nun's Priest's claim competes with other literary claims and is thus part of an ongoing debate about the moral use or abuse of 'auctoritee'.

In the broadest sense it agrees with Chaucer's own statements in the prologue to the 'Miller's Tale' (I, 3171–81) and in his own 'Retraction' at the end of the work (X, 1083), where the quotation from St Paul is repeated, to the effect that it is the reader who is responsible for any good or bad effects of literature in general. The rich plenty of the *Canterbury Tales* provides the reader with many opportunities to test this maxim and apply it to himself.

'The Franklin's Tale' is another example of Chaucer's adaptation of traditional material for his particular dramatic purposes and for a rhetorical exercise in creating moral dilemmas. It is difficult to be certain about the narrator's character and person because the state of the manuscript transmission suggests that Chaucer had not arrived at a final ascription. In the Ellesmere manuscript and several others, the Franklin interrupts the Squire's glittering romance by praising his promising youth, adding with some regret that he wished his own son were like it. In the earliest and to some scholars most authoritative manuscript (Hengwrt) the words are given to the Merchant, a notably different character. There is much to be said for the traditional view, however, that this sincere and somewhat envying admiration for 'gentillesse' belongs to the Franklin and fits in excellently with his tale: a competition in gentle or 'free', i.e. truly generous behaviour.

The Franklin begins with an enthusiastic and perhaps a little utopian picture of a perfect marriage in which there is no 'maistrye', but equality in all things. It stands evidently in complete contrast to all the much less harmonious marriages featuring in many other tales and it has a suspicious resemblance to the besotted old merchant's dream of blissful wedlock. But the Franklin evidently believes in the reality of this ideal equilibrium, and his tale shapes the events in such a way that each of the four characters involved emerges in the end as a model of 'gentil' behaviour. In the series of trials it is first the wife who is tested. Her grief over her husband's absence leads her into desperate questioning of God's providence and this, in turn, provokes her rash promise to the lovelorn squire. The condition playfully laid down by her moves him to extreme measures and expense well beyond his means. The real test comes when he tells her that the condition has been met and that she is bound by the law of 'trouthe' to grant him her love. According to the moral premises of the story, Dorigen is trapped in a true conflict of loyalties. Her long complaint provides another opportunity for the poet for an emotional debate and for quoting a series of precedents from antiquity, most of them with tragic outcome, such as the most famous classical representative of ravished innocence, Lucrece:

> Hath nat Lucresse yslayn hirself, allas,
> At Rome, whan that she oppressed was
> Of Tarquyn, for hire thoughte it was a shame
> To lyven whan she hadde lost hir name? (V, 1405–8)

We are not told in so many words why Dorigen does not choose this course: Chaucer was evidently interested in another side of the dilemma and in a more surprising solution. The husband's reaction to his wife's tearful confession reveals his moral quality: for him, 'trouthe' is the highest value in the system of 'gentil' behaviour. His sudden fit of weeping shows the emotional cost of this decision. It is not an easy solution, but a firm moral choice, and the narrator is anxious to answer possible objections on the part of the listeners. Evidently, he cannot be sure of their unquestioning approval:

> Paraventure an heep of yow, ywis,
> Wol holden hym a lewed man in this   *base*
> That he wol putte his wyf in jupartie.
> Herkneth the tale er ye upon hire crie.
> She may have bettre fortune than yow semeth;
> And whan that ye han herd the tale, demeth. (V, 1493–8)   *judge*

To justify a questionable decision by the happy outcome may appear as a cheap excuse. But the point of the plot is surely that a noble act generates another: the young lover is so impressed by Dorigen's faith that he releases her from her promise, thus demonstrating that a 'squire' is capable of a 'gentil dede' as well as a knight (ll. 1543–4), and since in the context of the story 'gentillesse' is a contagious virtue, the clerk, at the lower end of the scale, cannot but imitate his betters and waives his financial claim on the youth. Dorigen is spared the fate of the Roman martyr Lucrece, not because there is any softening of the tale's moral rigour, but because of the – perhaps naive – optimism of the story and of its teller.[64] He trusts that there is a perfect answer to every moral dilemma, if only you let yourself be guided by the rules of 'gentillesse'.

Of course, Chaucer the poet does not claim to offer an ideal solution to all the moral problems raised by the plot; he presents a 'case' and invites discussion, very much in the manner of the French *demande*-convention, a favourite technique in writings on courtly love.[65] The controversial critical response to the 'Franklin's Tale' only proves that Chaucer has succeeded in provoking an interesting debate. It is doubtful whether there is a single, satisfactory answer to the *demande* the Franklin puts to his audience:

> Lordynges, this question, thanne, wol I aske now,
> Which was the mooste fre, as thynketh yow? (V, 1621–2)   *generous*

The question is more important than any simple response. Whether Chaucer agrees with the Franklin or whether he wants us to smile at his unworldly idealism is really beside the point. His intention is to juxtapose different tales and different ways of telling them, each with a distinctive moral and literary profile.

This basic principle shapes the whole collection, regardless of its fragmentary transmission. Each of the extant 'groups' may have its own theme and its own kind of unity; in addition, there are a number of loose ends and stray stories without a final location in the account of the pilgrimage. This is why many critics have chosen to treat the *Canterbury Tales* not as a book to be commented on in its proper order from begining to end, but as an anthology of narrative material to be classified by genre or other systematic criteria. A convenient and helpful arrangement, often tried with some success, is the division into 'Romances', 'Comic Tales and Fables' and 'Religious Tales'.[66] This helps to gain a kind of clear, serviceable overview, but it also introduces an element of deceptive tidiness and order, clearly at odds with the reader's impression and Chaucer's purpose, which is, above all, plenty and variety.

Each of the three groups contains stories that share only some very superficial literary qualities: the four tales that could loosely be described as romances have very little in common except a familiarity with the European chivalric literature and some popular notions of what a romance should be like: 'The Knight's Tale' combines elements of the classical epic, patterns of courtliness and chivalry, philosophic debate and rhetorical virtuosity. There is nothing quite like it in all medieval English romance literature. 'The Franklin's Tale', as we have seen, is quite different, concentrating on the moral choices often highlighted in romance, but lacking most of the paraphernalia of chivalry, such as tournaments, battles, especially in the service of Christianity, and colourful adventure. It has more of an elaborate domestic drama than an exciting and eventful romance. The unfinished 'Squire's Tale', in contrast, picks out the very ingredients of romance the Franklin is least interested in: the strange, the marvellous and the exotic, without any apparent moral or psychological interest. The fragment, popular with later poets and connoisseurs, seems little more than a glittering display of scraps from many conventional stories and pickings from rhetorical set-pieces, and yet, the exhibition is so skilfully presented that the Franklin's envious admiration for the accomplished aspiring young man is perfectly understandable. Finally, the tale of Sir Thopas, told by the author himself, is a hilarious parody of all that is most ridiculously trite in popular romance. As a most transparent joke it has not much in common with the other three stories, especially since its target is quite different from the kind of romance they, in various ways, represent. It is the silliness of mindless adventure and praise of empty heroism that provokes Chaucer's scorn.

The second category, 'comic tales and fables', is, if anything, even more heterogeneous than the first. Eight (or nine, if we include the comic opening that is all that was apparently written of the 'Cook's Tale') tales can, very roughly, be classed together under this heading, although it would be very easy to find glaring differences between them. Perhaps the only obvious thing they have in common is that they are neither romances nor religious tales and that there is a certain unserious irresponsibility in the way they are told and in the way society is viewed.[67] Trickery, satire and aggression often play a major part, and this also applies to the narrative situation. Many of these tales are used as instruments of hatred or contempt; they are meant to hurt or to shame some of the listeners in the eyes of the others. Storytelling thus turns out to be a complex speech-act, most notably in the tales of such occupational antagonists as the Miller and the Reeve or the Friar and the Summoner. Their four tales are powerful and effective enough to be savoured on their own, but they can only be fully appreciated in their social context, as part of a peculiarly double-edged form of communication. 'The Miller's Tale' glances back at the noble rhetorical canvas unrolled by the Knight, using several of his basic situations as well as stylistic conventions, translating them into an incongruous setting and an unrefined state of mind. In the Reeve's embittered retort we have lost sight of the courtly world and its ideals altogether and the tale seems merely concerned with nasty revenge and humiliation, but since none of the actors have any claim to the audience's sympathy, there is no element of human loss or suffering; even the traditional moment of pathos at the lovers' parting is exploited for comic purposes. The miller's daughter, though grossly abused by the Cambridge undergraduate, does not let him go without some tears as well as useful information about the hiding-place of the stolen flour. The moment seems like a faint reminiscence of the courtly *aubade*, seen through a distorting mirror:

> Right at the entree of the dore bihynde
> Thou shalt a cake of half a busshel fynde
> That was ymaked of thyn owene mele,
> Which that I heelp my sire for to stele.
> And, goode lemman, God thee save and kepe!'
> And with that word almoost she gan to wepe. (I, 4243–8)

The crude joke played on the miller will make listeners laugh, but presumably not all of them. The point is brought home by the Reeve's conclusion, which neatly sums up the narrative confrontation:

> And God, that sitteth heighe in magestee,
> Save al this compaignye, grete and smale!
> Thus have I quyt the Millere in my tale. (I, 4322–4)

The Miller's humiliation greatly amuses the Cook who slaps the narrator's back to express his delighted approval and announces another libellous tale, apparently against innkeepers. We do not know what story Chaucer had in mind, but even the brief fragment shows that one more personal altercation was in preparation.

Similarly, the Friar's tale is prefaced by a rude attack on the Summoner and his profession that leads to a peacekeeping intervention of the Host. The quarrel is continued by the Summoner's defiant announcement that he will 'quiten' the Friar's 'every grot' (III, 1292) and by his furious anger after he has heard the Friar's polemical tale.

This kind of aggression by narration has no parallel in the *Decameron*; in some other cases, however, Chaucer follows the example of Boccaccio and others in presenting tales as part of an argument or supporting instance, such as the tale of the Merchant. His prologue makes explicit reference to the Clerk's tale of Griselda, and his own story is a biting satire on unequal marriages and resourceful women. In this instance, the context is not quite as essential for the story's impact and the tale is not addressed to any particular member of the audience; yet it is certainly part of an argument that connects several of the pilgrims' contributions, not in the sense of a definite 'marriage group', as earlier critics used to call it, but as a clear allusion to other stories on the subject of love and marriage.[68] The consultation between the besotted old wooer and his friends on his marital project is so obviously in a different key from Griselda's story or the Franklin's idealism that it can hardly be taken as a serious answer or part of the same debate. The comedy is in many ways even more aggressive and disillusioning than that of the coarser jokes because it is less superficial and the humour is more sophisticated. The social setting as well as the light-hearted and inventive use of literary topoi place the story well outside the conventional *fabliau*-genre and create a new type of comic tale, combining learned wit and devastating satire.

The Nun's Priest's rich elaboration of the animal fable again extends the range of narrative forms offered within this amazing anthology of stories and, told by a priest with a clearly homiletic purpose, takes comedy away from satire and invective and reminds the audience of the dual use of all literary art and the rules of the game laid down by the Host: 'Tales of best sentence and moost solaas' (I, 798). The narrator has no intention of hurting anyone; his humour ('folye') only wants to make the 'moralite' more acceptable and teach the difference between 'fruyt' and 'chaf' (VII, 3443).

The other representatives of the clergy and some other pilgrims offer religious or more narrowly moral tales. It is a rather mixed group again, connected mainly by the absence of comedy or romantic adventure and by a claim to religious or moral edification.[69] The Prioress and the Second Nun contribute simple, but not necessarily naive saints' legends, pious examples of miracle and martyrdom. The 'Second Nun's Tale', in particular, has been called 'inappropriate to a pilgrim narrator' and, in Derek Pearsall's view, 'demonstrates Chaucer's power to write well in an un-Chaucerian and maybe even uncongenial vein'.[70] It is clear from the Prologue to the *Legend of Good Women* (F, 426) that the legend, or a version of it, existed before the *Canterbury Tales* were conceived, and it is doubtful whether Chaucer took any trouble to adapt it to the larger project. There is no portrait of the narrator in the *General Prologue* and, beyond an unspecified impression of simple piety, there seems to be no very close correspondence between tale and teller. However, the unadorned conventional account of the martyr's irrepressible profession of faith and the gentle humility of style are entirely appropriate to an attitude of untroubled belief in divine intervention and the ultimate victory of the Christian message. The Nun's prologue explicitly refers to the *Roman de la Rose*, perhaps even to Chaucer's own translation of it,[71] and she offers the legend of St Caecilia as the fruit of her 'feithful bisynesse' to avoid sinful 'ydelnesse' (VIII, 22–4). The modest term 'translation' need not be taken as proof that Chaucer had a single source which he faithfully turned into English.[72] Rather it is a reflection on the humility of the narrator and her contribution. If Chaucer here 'grasps the essence of the hagiographical approach',[73] he has deliberately included this unsophisticated, devotional statement in his display of narrative possibilities.

Whether the same applies to 'The Prioress's Tale' is a more difficult question. Interpretations of this legend in praise of the Virgin have differed considerably and, though some of them seem misguided or at least ahistorical, the controversial reactions are an indication of Chaucer's less than straightforward method. The deeply emotional tone of the narrative and confrontational piety suggest that Chaucer here wanted to portray another aspect of contemporary religious discourse, not just one more simple miracle.[74] Though it would be wrong to read the tale as a satire directed against the Prioress's sentimental piety, it is difficult to avoid the impression that there is something inadequate in her account of the divine miracle and especially in her primitive anti-Semitism. The story flaunts the most unattractive aspects of medieval devotion and its repulsive, vengeful aggressiveness is clearly at odds with the Christian spirit that informs other religious tales in this collection. On the other hand, the Prioress's prologue expresses genuine seriousness and prevents a satirical reading of the whole performance. There is no doubt about the narrator's true sincerity, but neither is there any pretence that a really full and generous view of the Virgin and her cult is here presented.

Chaucer often underlines the intended impact of the stories by adding the listeners' reactions to them, be it approval or criticism.[75] The Prioress's tale is greeted with respectful silence, only broken by irreverent (or embarrassed?) joking from the Host:

> Whan seyd was al this miracle, every man
> As sobre was that wonder was to se,   *serious*
> Til that oure Hooste japen tho bigan, (VII, 691–3)   *joke*

Since he had earlier addressed her 'As curteisly as it had been a mayde' (VII, 446) his merriment can hardly be a sign of disrespect, especially as he has a sure sense of the pilgrims' social positions and the kind of deference expected of him.

Chaucer makes clear, though, that the Host is not the most reliable of guides when it comes to literary judgement and we are by no means encouraged to agree uncritically with his verdicts. In the case of the Physician's tale, for instance, it is questionable whether we should share the Host's emotional reaction:

> Oure Hooste gan to swere as he were wood;   *mad*
> 'Harrow!' quod he, 'by nayles and by blood!
> This was a fals cherl and a fals justise.
> As shameful deeth as herte may devyse
> Come to thise juges and hire advocatz! (VI, 287–91)

More likely, this outburst is a gentle hint alerting us to the tale's limitations as well as the Host's inability to grasp the finer points of moral dilemma. Very different reactions to this tale are, of course, possible and the Host's comment is evidently meant to provoke them.

The 'Physician's Tale' can only be classified among the 'religious tales' with some reservation. It is told as a moral *exemplum*, after an episode related by the Roman historian Livy and retold in the *Roman de la Rose* (5589–658) where Chaucer found it. There is none of the elevated tone that the rhyme-royal stanza lends to the religious *exempla* told by the Clerk and the Man of Law. The story is set in a pagan world, but with clearly Christian overtones, and it is possible that it was written before *The Canterbury Tales* were planned. No attempt appears to have been made to adapt the tale to the Physician. Many critics have felt that it is one of the less sucessful items in the collection because there seems to be a lack of focus or recognisable moral point.[76] What

Chaucer adds to the stern plot is the curiously digressive and, in the context, rather irrelevant adhortation to parents and governesses and the domestic scene between father and daughter that greatly adds to the pathos of the situation and accounts for the Host's noisy commiseration. Again, it would be much too simple to read the tale as a satire on cheap moralising; yet it is hard to overlook the jarring and provocative contrast between the seemingly untroubled narration and the disturbing brutality of the action. Few readers will be satisfied that the tale's harsh moral is unquestioningly endorsed by the poet, but, unlike Griselda's story, it is presented without comment and it is left to the audience to draw their own conclusions.

The collection of 'tragedies' recounted by the Monk introduces another type of medieval narrative, the catalogue of 'cases' to support a particular view of existence. The idea was borrowed partly from the *Roman de la Rose* and partly from Boccaccio's *De casibus virorum illustrium*, acknowledged in the subtitle. Chaucer hints at the bookishness of the project by the Monk's announcement that he has a hundred 'tragedies' in his cell and he evidently wishes to spare his audience the tedium of having to listen to the whole library. It is interesting to note the different reasons given by the Knight and the Host for their unwillingness to hear any more of the Monk's stories. The Knight objects to the relentless repetition of human misery and would prefer happy endings, whereas the Host is bored by the dullness of the *exempla* and asks for something more entertaining, like some hunting anecdote. He is evidently more in sympathy with the Monk's pastime than with his proper vocation.

The rude interruption of the performance does not mean that we are not to take the 'cases' seriously. They come from a variety of sources and show Chaucer's familiarity with many medieval commonplaces, with recent history as well as Dante's *Divina Commedia* and books he has used elsewhere. He obviously enjoyed collecting this kind of miscellaneous information and it was probably Boece who provided him with the definition of tragedy that serves as a frame for the portraits. The Knight's intervention may imply criticism of a somewhat monotonous series of similar patterns that do not really engage our sympathy, and it is also an effective way of putting a stop to a recital that might otherwise go on for ever. Chaucer's own handling of tragic material in *Troilus and Criseyde* and the 'Knight's Tale' shows that he himself did not try to achieve tragic effects by mere accumulation, but by concentration on a single story of genuine human interest. The context of the 'Monk's Tale' sufficiently demonstrates the inadequacy of this method of dealing with tragic experience.

Two of the *Canterbury Tales* are in prose and they clearly mark the outer limit of the work's narrative territory. The 'Tale of Melibee', offered by the poet himself in reply to the failure of 'Sir Thopas', has only a minimum of action, barely an excuse for a collection of moral commonplaces, but the 'Parson's Tale' deserves its name even less. It is a straightforward penitential treatise, probably translated by Chaucer from an unknown original and placed at the conclusion of the pilgrimage, as if the original frame and the narrative contest had been forgotten.[77] The Host announces that there is only one more tale due, and the Parson offers not only to honour his part of the bargain, but to lead the pilgrims into Canterbury and at the same time, spiritually speaking, into the celestial city of Jerusalem:

> I wol yow telle a myrie tale in prose
> To knytte up al this feeste and make an ende.
> And Jhesu, for his grace, wit me sende
> To shewe yow the wey, in this viage,
> Of thilke parfit glorious pilgrymage
> That highte Jerusalem celestial. (X, 46–51) *is called*

This is not the conclusion the Prologue had led us to expect, but in its own way it is just as appropriate and fitting. It seems indeed possible that Chaucer had by this time changed his mind about the whole design of his collection and, since the 'Parson's Tale', together with the 'Retraction', appears in all manuscripts of the complete work, it can be assumed that this ending is Chaucer's last word on the subject of the pilgrimage, unless we believe with Derek Pearsall that the General Prologue reflects a later addition to the plan and that the 'Parson's Prologue and Tale' is part of a structure that had already been superseded.[78]

Leaving speculation aside, the present closure is the only one we have. Its effect is particularly unsettling, as an unprepared–for transition from fiction and illusion to the unpoetical reality of our own presence as Christians and sinners, a presence that includes the author in his own person. This sudden change of direction seems like an unprecedented denial of fiction and a radical questioning of everything that has gone before. However, it is important to keep in mind that the Parson's treatise is part of the *Canterbury Tales* as fiction and so, even, is the 'Retraction', in which Chaucer revokes and asks Christ's forgiveness for 'the tales of Caunterbury, thilke that sownen into synne' (X, 1086), along with the bulk of his love poetry. If this is a 'denial of art' and an act of penitence outside the poet's art, it is yet a denial of something that cannot be revoked because it is inseparable from the book, which, in turn, is part of the 'auctoritee' so cherished by Chaucer and part of the 'key of remembrance'. If Chaucer had really planned to cancel this ending and replace it by another design, it would only have reaffirmed this impossibility of retracting a work of art and, for better or worse, the enduring life of Chaucer's world of fiction in all its inclusive vitality.

Notes

1. See William Shakespeare, *A Midsummer Night's Dream*, ed. R. A. Foakes, The New Cambridge Shakespeare (Cambridge, 1984), p. 12.
2. Ed. W. F. Bryan and Germaine Dempster (New York, 1941, reissued 1958).
3. Ed. Geoffrey Bullough, 8 vols (London, 1957–75).
4. See Caroline F. E. Spurgeon, *Five Hundred Years of Chaucer Criticism and Allusion, 1357–1900* (Cambridge, 1925), i, 14. On Lydgate's estimation (and imitation) of Chaucer see Derek Pearsall, *John Lydgate* (London, 1970), pp. 49–82.
5. Spurgeon, i, 58.

6. See the invaluable collection by Martin M. Crow and Clair C. Olson, *Chaucer Life-Records* (Oxford, 1966).

7. All quotations from, and references to, Chaucer's works use *The Riverside Chaucer*, ed. Larry D. Benson (Boston, 1987).

8. See Derek Pearsall, *The Life of Geoffrey Chaucer: A Critical Biography* (Oxford, 1992), especially 'Introduction: Writing a Life of Chaucer', pp. 1–8.

9. See Pearsall, *The Life*, p. 5. Pearsall rightly draws attention to poets like Machaut, Froissart, Deschamps and Christine de Pizan as well as Thomas Hoccleve, a true 'Chaucerian'. On Hoccleve see chapter 6, below.

10. Pearsall, *The Life*, p. 16.

11. She was the wife of Edward's second surviving son Lionel (1338–68). For details see Pearsall's biography and *Chaucer Life Records*.

12. See Pearsall's biography for a less genial, but perhaps more plausible view of Chaucer's character.

13. See *Chaucer and the Italian Trecento*, ed. Piero Boitani (Cambridge, 1983). This is a valuable collection of essays by different authors on many aspects of Chaucer's Italian connections. A new look at Chaucer's Italian connections and more fundamental implications is taken by David Wallace's wide-ranging study *Chaucerian Polity: Absolutist Lineages and Associational Forms in England and Italy* (Stanford, 1997).

14. There is a good account of Chaucer's indebtedness – in some cases mutual – to his French courtly contemporaries in James I. Wimsatt, *Chaucer and His French Contemporaries: Natural Music in the Fourteenth Century* (Toronto, 1991).

15. This is a dangerous and in some ways untenable position, as Alastair Minnis, in his very helpful account of the *querelle* points out: 'who among us would give universal consent to the principle that a statement in a literary text, no matter how offensive or repugnant it may be, must be allowed its say if it is put in the mouth of a character who may not express the personal views of the author?' 'Theorizing the Rose: Commentary Tradition in the *Querelle de la Rose*', in: *Poetics: Theory and Practice in Medieval English Literature*, ed. Piero Boitani and Anna Torti (Cambridge, 1991), pp. 13–36; the quotation is from p. 22.

16. See David Lawton, *Chaucer's Narrators* (Cambridge, 1985), pp. 62–75.

17. See Pearsall, *The Life of Geoffrey Chaucer*, pp. 77–82. Pearsall sees adequate explanation for Chaucer's translation 'in his practice to appropriate major texts of the European tradition to himself and to his literary imagination by translating them' (p. 81), but it seems hard to imagine that he did not have some more specific reason and some audience in mind.

18. See Pearsall, *The Life*, p. 164.

19. Though there was, of course, also the French translation by Jean de Meun. Most scholars agree that Chaucer used it side by side with the Latin text for his own translation.

20. Lee Patterson, *Chaucer and the Subject of History* (London, 1991), pp. 167–8.

21. See the account by D. W. Robertson in *Companion to Chaucer Studies*, ed. Beryl Rowland (Toronto, 1968), pp. 403–13, a rather biased review of scholarship. The originality of the poem is convincingly demonstrated in some detail by Wolfgang Clemen in his *Chaucer's Early Poetry* (London, 1963), pp. 23–66. See also my chapter on the poem in *Geoffrey Chaucer: An Introduction to his Narrative Poetry* (Cambridge, 1986), pp. 22–36.

22. For the chronology of Chaucer's works and some discussion of the canon, see Pearsall's biography.

23. The wealth of the poem's literary references and sources is made accessible in the edition by D. S. Brewer: Geoffrey Chaucer, *The Parlement of Foulys* (London, 1960, reissued 1972). Some of the ideas discussed here are developed more fully in my *Geoffrey Chaucer*, pp. 37–53.

24. See Piero Boitani, *Chaucer and Boccaccio* (Oxford, 1977), chapter VI, and, for some easily accessible passages in translation, N. R. Havely, *Chaucer's Boccaccio*: Sources for *Troilus* and the *Knight's* and *Franklin's Tales*. Translations from the *Filostrato*, *Teseida* and *Filocolo* (Cambridge, 1980).

25. Chaucer found this description in the *Planctus Naturae* as well as in the *Roman de la Rose* (ll. 16,782 and 19,507).

26. On the tradition of *fame* see the wide-ranging study of Piero Boitani, *Chaucer and the Imaginary World of Fame* (Cambridge, 1984).

27. See John Burrow, 'Poems Without Endings', *Studies in the Age of Chaucer*, 13 (1991), 17–37, especially 22–3 and 33.

28. The best critical edition of the poem is that by B. A. Windeatt: Geoffrey Chaucer, *Troilus and Criseyde: A new edition of 'The Book of Troilus'* (London, 1984). Its commentary is helpful on almost any aspect of the poem. There is also an excellent guide to the poem by B. A. Windeatt, *Troilus and Criseyde*, Oxford Guides to Chaucer (Oxford, 1992), with bibliographies and a comprehensive account of earlier scholarship, altogether perhaps the most useful single book on the poem.

29. See my 'Chaucer's narrator: *Troilus and Criseyde* and the *Canterbury Tales*', in *The Cambridge Chaucer Companion*, ed. Piero Boitani and Jill Mann (Cambridge, 1986), pp. 213–26, and 'The Audience of Chaucer's *Troilus and Criseyde*', in *Chaucer and Middle English Studies In Honour of Rossell Hope Robbins*, ed. Beryl Rowland (1974), pp. 173–89, repr. in *Chaucer's* Troilus: *Essays in Criticism*, ed. Stephen A. Barney (Hampden, CT, 1980), pp. 211–29.

30. See Jane Austen, *Mansfield Park*, beginning of the final chapter.

31. This is the title of a very sensible section of the chapter 'Themes' in Windeatt, *Troilus and Criseyde* (pp. 215–28).

32. See the fine article by Jill Mann, 'Troilus' Swoon', *Chaucer Review*, 14 (1979–80), 319–35.

33. This, of course, suggests an intriguing affinity between Pandarus and the Wife of Bath, who also knows 'of that art the olde daunce' (I, 476).

34. See the account in Patricia Kean, *Chaucer and the Making of English Poetry*. Volume I: *Love Vision and Debate* (London, 1972), 175–8, and Karl Reichl, 'Chaucer's *Troilus*: Philosophy and Language', in *The European Tragedy of Troilus*, ed. Piero Boitani (Oxford, 1989), pp. 133–52, especially pp. 150–2.

35. On the time-scheme of Chaucer's poem see Windeatt, *Troilus and Criseyde*, pp. 198–204.

36. See iii, 241, 360, and the notes in Windeatt's edition.

37. See ii, 666–86. It is hard to believe that Chaucer was unaware of this discrepancy. The narrator seems over-anxious to refute the impression that 'This was a sodeyn love' (ii, 667) and yet he deliberately shortens the time of the wooing. A very similar contrast has been noted with regard to the time-scheme of Criseyde's betrayal. See my *Geoffrey Chaucer*, pp. 88–9.

38. See E. Talbot Donaldson, 'The Ending of Chaucer's *Troilus*', in *Speaking of Chaucer* (London, 1970), pp. 84–101, and the discussion in Windeatt, *Troilus and Criseyde*, pp. 298–313. Windeatt speaks of the impression 'of deploying as many closing devices and formulas as can be thought of, with shifts and turns, in a way that dramatizes narratorial nervousness and anxiety'. (p. 302)

39. Cf. Lisa J. Kiser, *Telling Classical Tales: Chaucer and the* Legend of Good Women (Ithaca and London, 1983), Donald W. Rowe, *Through Nature to Eternity: Chaucer's* Legend of Good Women (Lincoln, Nebraska, 1988), William A. Quinn, *Chaucer's Rehersynges: The Performability of* The Legend of Good Women (Washington DC, 1994), Sheila Delany, *The Naked Text: Chaucer's* Legend of Good Women (Berkeley,

1994) and, for a particularly sane and helpful reading, Florence Percival, *Chaucer's Legendary Good Women*, Cambridge Studies in Medieval Literature (Cambridge, 1998). See also Robert Worth Frank, *Chaucer and* The Legend of Good Women (Cambridge, MA, 1972). Perhaps the most comprehensive and stimulating appraisal of the poem and its problems is the chapter in A. J. Minnis, *Oxford Guides to Chaucer: The Shorter Poems* (Oxford, 1994), pp. 322–454.

40. Carol M. Meale sees Chaucer's irony mainly directed against the traditional form of the legendary and its undiscriminating piety; see 'Legends of Good Women in the European Middle Ages', *Archiv*, 229 (1992), 55–70.

41. See his translation of the *Aeneid*, i, 449, and below p. 188.

42. Cf. Boitani, 'What Dante Meant to Chaucer', in *Chaucer and the Italian Trecento*, pp. 115–39; of the *Legend's* introduction he rightly says, 'It seems almost certain that these lines contain an allusion to Dante.' (p. 125).

43. See the excellent study by V. A. Kolve, 'From Cleopatra to Alceste: An Iconographic Study of *The Legend of Good Women*', in *Signs and Symbols in Chaucer's Poetry*, ed. John P. Herman and John J. Burke Jr (Alabama, 1981), pp. 130–78.

44. See Minnis, *The Shorter Poems*, pp. 413–16.

45. See the discussion in Minnis, *The Shorter Poems*, pp. 357–66.

46. Again, the most comprehensive and helpful survey of problems and scholarship is the relevant volume of the *Oxford Guides to Chaucer*, Helen Cooper's *The Canterbury Tales* (Oxford, 1989). Among books on the *Canterbury Tales*, Derek Pearsall's *The Canterbury Tales*, Unwin Critical Library (London, 1985) is one of the most stimulating and undogmatic.

47. See the classic collection of source-material, *Sources and Analogues of Chaucer's Canterbury Tales*, ed. W. F. Bryan and Germaine Dempster (New York, 1941, repr. 1958), especially the chapter 'The Literary Framework of the Canterbury Tales', pp. 1–81. It quotes many parallels, but is not as confident about Chaucer's knowledge of the *Decameron* as many more recent scholars. For an indispensable update of this chapter see Helen Cooper, '*Sources and Analogues of Chaucer's* Canterbury Tales: Reviewing the Work', *Studies in the Age of Chaucer*, 19 (1997), 183–210. See also Robin Kirkpatrick, 'The Wake of the *Commedia*: Chaucer's *Canterbury Tales* and Boccaccio's *Decameron*', in *Chaucer and the Italian Trecento*, pp. 201–30.

48. See Jill Mann's seminal study *Chaucer and Medieval Estate Satire: The literature of social classes and the* General Prologue *to the* Canterbury Tales (Cambridge, 1973). The *General Prologue* is probably the most frequently discussed part of the *Canterbury Tales*. For a good overview see Cooper, *The Canterbury Tales*, pp. 27–60, and for a recent stimulating, unorthodox voice, Alcuin Blamires, 'Chaucer the Reactionary: Ideology and the General Prologue to *The Canterbury Tales*, *The Review of English Studies*, 51 (2000), 523–39.

49. See, for instance, Derek Pearsall's book and my own account in *Geoffrey Chaucer*, pp. 157–204.

50. This is persuasively argued by Jerome Mandel in his *Geoffrey Chaucer: Building the Fragments of the Canterbury Tales* (London and Toronto, 1992).

51. For an elaborate, if somewhat speculative reconstruction of the intended structure see Charles A. Owen Jr, *Pilgrimage and Storytelling in the Canterbury Tales: The Dialectic of 'Ernest' and 'Game'* (Norman, 1977).

52. For conflicting accounts see N. F. Blake, *The Textual Tradition of the Canterbury Tales* (London, 1985) and Charles A. Owen Jr, *The Manuscripts of the Canterbury Tales* (Cambridge, 1991). Cf. also the Chapter 'Date and Manuscripts' in Pearsall, *The Canterbury Tales*, pp.1–23. All the manuscript texts will eventually be available on CD-Rom: see *The* Canterbury Tales *Project: Occasional Papers Volume I*, ed. Norman

Blake and Peter Robinson, Office for Humanities Communication Publications, 5 (Oxford, 1993). The booklet has a useful brief essay by Norman Blake, 'Editing the *Canterbury Tales*: An Overview', pp. 5–18, arguing that early readers saw the *Canterbury Tales* as a whole and never referred to the work as unfinished.

53. *The Canterbury Tales*, p. 23.

54. In his preface to the 'Fables' (1700) Dryden states that 'Palamon and Arcite' (i.e. 'The Knight's Tale') 'is of the *Epique* kind, and perhaps not much inferiour to the *Ilias* or the *Æneis*: the Story is more pleasing than either of them, the Manners as perfect, the Diction as poetical, the Learning as deep and various; and the Disposition full as artful' (*The Poems and Fables of John Dryden*, ed. James Kinsley [1961], p. 536).

55. See the edition by Lois Potter, The Arden Shakespeare, third series (Walton-on-Thames, 1997). For a spirited account of Shakespeare's use of Chaucer see E. Talbot Donaldson, *The Swan at the Well: Shakespeare Reading Chaucer* (New Haven, 1985), especially the chapter 'Love, War and the Cost of Winning: *The Knight's Tale* and *The Two Noble Kinsmen*', pp. 50–73.

56. See Cooper, p. 60.

57. See the textual note in *The Riverside Chaucer*, p. 1125.

58. The fact that the Canon's Yeoman's Prologue and his tale are missing in the earliest manuscript (Hengwrt) has persuaded some critics that they were not, in fact, written by Chaucer. It seems very unlikely, though, that the scribe of the Ellesmere manuscript should have copied a text he knew to be by someone else. More importantly, we do not know of any contemporary writer capable of composing a text that looks so unmistakably Chaucerian. See especially N. E. Blake, *The Textual Tradition of the Canterbury Tales* (London, 1985).

59. *The Tale of Beryn*, written a generation or two after Chaucer, gives a lively account of the Pilgrims' arrival at Canterbury and some adventures there. It is evident that the anonymous author was intrigued by Chaucer's portraits as much as by his story collection, to which he adds a lengthy romance. See Cooper, pp. 415–17. The text was edited for the Early English Text Society by F. J. Furnivall and W. G. Stone as vol. 105 of the Extra Series (1909, reprinted 1973).

60. See the helpful survey by Robin Kirkpatrick, 'The Griselda Story in Boccaccio, Petrarch and Chaucer', in *Chaucer and the Italian Trecento*, pp. 231–48.

61. Helen Cooper aptly speaks of 'an approximation of literary criticism' and continues, 'When Chaucer excuses himself, something suspicious is always happening' (p. 310).

62. For analogues see Laura A. Hibbard, *Mediaeval Romance in England: A Study of the Sources and Analogues of the Non-Cyclic Metrical Romances*, new edition (New York, 1963), pp. 3–80.

63. See Romans, xv, 4.

64. See the balanced discussion of the tale and its difficulties in Cooper, pp. 230–45, and the useful account in William Calin, *The French Tradition and the Literature of Medieval England* (Toronto, 1995), pp. 347–56.

65. See Wimsatt, pp. 277–8.

66. These are the labels used by Derek Pearsall; see *The Canterbury Tales*, pp. 46–51. I largely agree with his view of the poet's intentions: 'Chaucer's endeavour is to release narrative from external pressure, and to allow it a self-validating, non-exemplary significance of its own which grows out of its intrinsic nature as an imitation of human life'. (p. 48)

67. See the concise discussion in Pearsall, pp. 166–71.

68. See the balanced summary of the classic debate in Donald R. Howard, 'The Conclusion of the Marriage Group: Chaucer and the Human Condition', *Modern Philology*, 57 (1959–60), 223–32.

69. See the valuable collection of essays, *Chaucer's Religious Tales*, ed. C. David Benson and Elizabeth Robertson (Cambridge, 1990).

70. See *The Canterbury Tales*, pp. 254 and 256.

71. The ministre and the norice unto vices,
      Which that men clepe in Englissh Ydelnesse,
      That porter of the gate is of delices,
      To eschue, . . . (VIII, 1–4)

    See Chaucer's version of the *Romaunt of the Rose*, ll. 531–618, where the lover meets 'Ydelnesse' (l. 593), who allows him to enter the enclosed garden of love's delights.

72. See *Sources and Analogues*, pp. 667–71.

73. See P. M. Kean, *Chaucer and the Making of English Poetry* (London, 1972), vol. II, *The Art of Narrative*, p. 201.

74. See Pearsall, *The Canterbury Tales*, pp. 246–52, for a spirited account of the differences in interpretation, and the balanced account in Cooper, pp. 292–8.

75. In the *Decameron*, too, the tales are often discussed among the company, but since there is nothing like the same degree of social differentiation, such debates are not very controversial.

76. Cf. Pearsall's somewhat dismissive account in *The Canterbury Tales*, pp. 277–9, and Anne Middleton's more sophisticated plea in 'The *Physician's Tale* and Love's Martyrs: "Ensamples mo than ten" as a Method in the *Canterbury Tales*', *Chaucer Review*, 8 (1973–4), 9–32.

77. See Lee W. Patterson, 'The "Parson's Tale" and the Quitting of the "Canterbury Tales" ', *Traditio*, 34 (1978), 331–80.

78. See *The Life of Geoffrey Chaucer*, p. 233.

Chapter 3

John Gower

Chaucer's friend, as he is generally considered, respectfully referred to by him at the end of *Troilus and Criseyde* as 'moral Gower' (v, 1856–7), to whom he dedicates his poem, has for centuries been the victim of more or less unfair comparisons, as if he had tried and failed to achieve what Chaucer accomplished much more successfully. In fact, John Gower is in many respects a very different kind of writer, with a different temperament, different interests and, as far as can be judged from his impressive œuvre, different ideas about poetry.[1]

Gower's life is even less well documented than Chaucer's; we know of no important office he held and no regular patronage. Though he tells us at the beginning of *Confessio Amantis* that it was King Richard II himself who personally charged him to write 'Som newe thing' (Prologue, 51*), it would be more than rash to take this as evidence of more intimate royal favour. In any case, the tribute to Richard was removed from the text some time later and Henry Lancaster, the future King Henry IV was inserted as dedicatee.[2] Instead of 'A bok for king Richardes sake' (Prologue, 24*), the *Confessio Amantis* is now announced as 'A bok for Engelondes sake' (Prologue, 24). Since, at the time, there was yet no question of Henry Lancaster becoming king of England, it is not easy to draw very definite conclusions as to Gower's political allegiance or closeness to the seats of power. There is, however, the record of a ceremonial collar given to Gower in 1393 by Henry, Earl of Derby at the time, shortly after the revised dedication, and, five weeks after Henry's coronation in 1399, a grant for life of two pipes of wine of Gascony yearly in the Port of London, a gift Gower gratefully acknowledged in a poem.[3]

For most of his earlier career the poet seems to have led a comparatively inconspicuous life. It is very probable that he was involved in one or two legal actions concerning property in Kent, though, like most of the details of his biography, this is a matter of inference rather than of reliable documentation.

Among the established facts, however, there is Gower's marriage to Agnes Groundolf, licensed by the bishop of Winchester in 1398, when Gower was described as a resident of St Mary Overeys Priory in Southwark, just across the river from the Temple. There is some likelihood that Gower had lived there from about 1377, when the Priory was restored, but again this is a matter of inference rather than documented fact. In May 1378, however, Geoffrey Chaucer, embarking on one of his diplomatic journeys to Italy, gave his power of attorney to Gower, together with a Richard Forester (who in 1386 took over Chaucer's house in Aldgate). This is the first documented association of the two poets. Gower outlived Chaucer by about eight years. His will was proved in 1408; he left a number of bequests to the Priory, to several churches and hospitals in Southwark, and the bulk of his property to his wife.

The Gower canon

Though Gower in his later work refers to 'foolish love songs' composed in his immature youth, none of his surviving poetry can with any certainty be assigned to that period. The most explicit account the poet gives of himself and his writing is in a letter, or colophon, appended to some twenty manuscripts of the *Confessio Amantis* and one of the *Vox Clamantis*, written probably around 1392–93, where the poet gives a list of the three major works still associated with him.[4] They are written in the three languages more or less current and in all likelihood accessible to most educated men in England at the time. The letter, in Latin, is a rare early instance of an English author providing a list of his principal writings in his own name. There are two versions of it composed in Gower's lifetime. They reflect the author's change of political allegiance: the earlier version makes excuses for the young King Richard's youth and inexperience in connection with the Peasants' Revolt, whereas the later one puts heavy blame on him (*crudelissimus rex*).

Gower introduces his account with the conventional explanation that one should share the gifts received from God with others. Therefore he, wanting to lighten the debt put on him by God's bounty, between labour and leisure composed three books for the instruction of others.

The first work, written in French, called *Speculum hominis* in its earlier state, *Speculum meditantis* in the revised version, according to Gower deals with the vices and virtues of estates and tries to teach the sinner the proper way back to recognition of his creator. It was only in 1895 that Macaulay identified this poem in a French manuscript acquired by Cambridge University Library. It lacks beginning and end, but it is the only text of *Mirour de l'omme* now extant, a poem of nearly 30,000 lines, composed, most scholars assume, between 1376 and 1378.

The second work described by Gower, named by him *Vox clamantis*, is in Latin verse (hexameter and pentameter). Its subject, according to the author, is the Peasants' Revolt in 1381, its causes and effects. It is likely, however, that the larger part of it (books II–VII) was written earlier than the events described in the first book. The poem is preserved in eleven manuscripts; four of them are elaborate presentation copies, commissioned by Gower himself and including poems written specially for Henry's coronation in October 1399. In addition, these manuscripts contain the *Cronica tripartita*, an account of the events following the peasants' uprising up to the death of Richard in February 1400. This cannot have been begun much earlier than 1399 or finished before Richard's death. It looks like an explicit defence of Henry's usurpation and a final verdict on Richard.

Confessio Amantis: transmission and genesis

The third book listed by Gower, written in English, is briefly described as a treatise on love and the passions of lovers, with examples taken from various historical chronicles, as well as the writings of poets and philosophers. This is the *Confessio Amantis*, Gower's only major work in English and the only text discussed here in more detail. It is, however, closely linked to Gower's other poems, not only in its major moral and philosophical concerns,[5] but also, as we have seen, by direct references to the author's political sympathies, clearly reflected in the revisions of the text.[6]

There are 49 manuscripts of *Confessio Amantis* extant, transmitting three distinct versions differing in a number of details and, more significantly, in their dedications, prologues and conclusions. These differences suggest that between about 1385 and 1400 Gower repeatedly returned to the poem, adapting it to the current political situation and, probably, preparing specific presentation copies. The textual changes do not, however, amount to a wholesale revision of the whole work, as in the case of Langland and his *Piers Plowman*, but are mostly local alterations, in particular some additions.[7] It appears from the evidence of the manuscripts that Gower was more closely involved in the production of copies than his friend Chaucer, probably because of his near associations with the Priory of St Mary Overeys and its scriptorium. A number of the manuscripts are more carefully and expensively executed than the majority of Chaucer manuscripts.

Gower's account of himself, especially his own brief bibliography suggest that he was, at least superficially, more anxious to lay claim to his writing and present himself as an author than Chaucer. Though we know much less about his day-to-day duties and occupations than we know of Chaucer's public life, he tells us more about his political and philosophical position and his patrons. The changes in the text of the *Confessio Amantis* indicate that from a devout admirer of Richard II he turned into a critical and finally a disappointed observer and, in the end, a loyal follower of Richard's successor, Henry IV. His early work in French and Latin shows that he was chiefly interested in moral questions, relating to contemporary events as well as to the life of the individual, and that he saw himself as a poet with a clearly didactic mission.

The *Confessio* must be approached in this context. It is misleading to read it as if it were, so to speak, a companion piece to Chaucer's *Canterbury Tales*. Gower never attempted anything like the kind of experimental collection of competing tales and tellers. His intention, as stated in the prologue, especially in its revised form, is clearly to present a variety of exemplary tales, taken from antiquity and held together by a firm moral purpose. This does not mean that there should not be 'solace', as demanded by Chaucer's Host, but it is not of the kind of entertainment provided by the 'low' characters among the Canterbury pilgrims, but is strictly subordinated to the overall instructive scheme. This is stated in traditional terms, sometimes quoted as a general description of Gower's narrative method and his poetic style in the *Confessio*:

Bot for men sein, and soth it is,   *say*
That who that al of wisdom writ
It dulleth ofte a mannes wit
To him that schal it aldai rede,   *all the time*
For thilke cause, if that ye rede,
I wolde go the middel weie
And wryte a bok betwen the tweie,
Somwhat of lust, somwhat of lore,   *knowledge*
That of the lasse or of the more
Som man mai lyke of that I wryte: (Prologue, 12–21)

'middel weie' has been used as a convenient label for Gower's unpretentious
rhetoric and lack of flamboyant virtuosity.[8] It also suggests a change from
Gower's previous, predominantly didactic kind of writing. It is difficult to say
whether it was, in fact, the King's personal instigation that caused the poet to
undertake 'Some newe thing' (Prologue 51*), as he himself claims, or whether
this is just a flattering tribute to his patron at the time. In any case, Gower
makes a point of the new direction taken by his activity as author by explicit
reference to a deliberate difference:

Forthi the Stile of my writinges
Fro this day forth I thenke change
And speke of thing is noght so strange,
Which every kinde hath upon honde,   *creature, is concerned with*
And wherupon the world mot stonde,   *must*
And hath don sithen it began,
And schal whil ther is any man;
And that is love, of which I mene
To trete, as after schal be sene. (i, 8–16)

The most obvious difference, of course, stated near the beginning of the Prologue,
is the fact that the work is written in English. When, at the outset, Gower gives
as a reason that 'fewe men endite / In oure englissh' (Prologue, 22–3) he can only
mean that there was not a great deal of the kind of writing he favoured available in English and that the majority of serious authors, like himself up to this
time, preferred to use Latin or French. Chaucer apparently did not feel that such
an explanation was necessary for him; there is nothing apologetic about his use
of English. Gower's statement, in contrast, almost sounds like a concession to
such readers as might be bored by undiluted instruction. It is, at any rate, clear
that his poetic temperament tended towards serious instruction rather than to
relaxed entertainment and humour.[9] The 'lust' he promises appears to have no
other justification than to make the 'lore' more palatable. This is confirmed by
the Prologue, that 'to wisdom al belongeth', as the revised version has it (l. 77).
The earlier version, though unchanged in substance, at least suggests that, in
obedience to the King's request, the book should appeal to different readers:

So as I made my beheste,   *promise*
To make a bok after his heste,
And write in such a maner wise,
Which may be wisdom to the wise
And pley to hem that lust to pleye. (81–5*)   *like to be amused*

63

When Gower revised the Prologue he had also introduced a number of significant changes at the conclusion of his work. One that has provoked a great deal of speculation concerns an intriguing tribute to Chaucer, left out in revision. At the very end of the lover's vision, as Venus leaves him, she asks him to 'gret wel Chaucer whan ye mete, / As mi disciple and mi poete:' (viii, 2941–2*) and, in particular, to tell him from Venus that he should now in his old age follow Gower in turning away from love poetry and make his 'testament of love' (2955*). There is no need to account for the omission of this affectionate pastoral advice by a conjectured estrangement between the two authors. It is just as plausible that in revising the conclusion Gower felt that the personal note was not quite appropriate within the serious context of the new 'Epilogue'; he might even have taken note of Chaucer's 'Retraction' at the end of the *Canterbury Tales* and concluded that his admonition was no longer called for. The dramatic effect of Venus' sudden departure is, if anything, heightened by the cancellation of the topical reference.

When Gower rewrote the last section of the *Confessio*, apart from the Epilogue proper, he replaced Venus' message to Chaucer by exactly the same number of lines, as he did in revising the prologue, probably to facilitate the work of copying the text or even to encourage a physical exchange by scratching out the first version. This is, in fact, what happened in the production to the Fairfax manuscript, the basis of Macaulay's edition,[10] where the original version was partly erased and partly replaced by new leaves. Instead of the reference to Chaucer and the poet's prayer 'For hem that trewe love fonde' (viii, 68*), there is now a moving passage, showing the lone poet left to his own meditation, without illusion or hope, and finally resolved to spend the rest of his life in prayer (viii, 2951–65). We will return to this conclusion.

More important as a document of Gower's political commitment is the long concluding prayer for the state of England and the King, completely recast in the final version. In the early text the poet pays generous and lavish tribute to Richard II, to whom the book is dedicated. He bids a last farewell to love, a subject he will, in his feeble old age, no more treat in his writing, since it is best left to those who can still enjoy it.

Like the revised prologue, the new ending reflects Gower's changed allegiance. There is no explicit mention of Richard, but a general sermon on the duties of a King and the dangerous evil of pride and false pomp. In place of the King the author now seems to seek the approval of 'lered men' (3113) to whom he offers his apologies for the lack of elaborate rhetoric and knowledge of the world, since he himself is now feeble and without vitality. Even the admission that song and dance are appropriate for the young lovers has gone; instead, the poet takes a final leave of 'love and of his dedly hele, / Which no phisicien can hele' (3155–6).

The frame and the tales

The frame of the *Confessio* is a distinctly more closely integrated part of the work's overall design than Chaucer's Canterbury pilgrimage; it is clearly more than a conventional device for telling stories, for it describes a mental progress and a lesson in spiritual wisdom more like Boece's *Consolatio Philosophiae* than the majority of love allegories. Throughout the whole poem Gower is very explicit in stating his moral intention, his 'testament of love'. At the end of the vision, the narrator, *Amans*, in pointed contrast to the 'I' of the *Roman de la rose*, will find that old age has turned love into an illusion and that he has wasted his time in futile desire and hope. This sudden realisation is not just a pious afterthought, but an essential part of the poem's whole structure. It also accounts for the most dramatic and emotionally powerful section of the *Confessio*.

As the title suggests, Gower's ambitious collection of stories is cast in a frame-work of a penitential treatise, following the traditional pattern of the mirrour of deadly sins as, for instance, represented in the 'Parson's Tale', at the conclusion of the Canterbury pilgrimage.[11] Gower brilliantly combines the familiar confes-sional scheme with the convention of the encyclopedic analysis of love estab-lished by the *Roman de la rose*. From the start, however, the text leaves no doubt as to the author's serious moral intention and his own idea of 'ernest and game' (viii, 3109). It is only after a long introduction on the world's evils and their cause that we enter the private scene of the poet–lover's sorrows and his love vision. The socio-political theme of the prologue and its intensity establish a context of authorial concerns far beyond the scope of any *ars amandi*, ranging from the duty of worldly rulers to the state of the clergy and the empires of the world. The first exemplary story quoted and explicated at some length is that of Nebuchadnezzar's dream, with Daniel's prophecy about the kingdoms of the earth and the end of the world (Book of Daniel, ii, 1–45). The eschatological view of history provides a new perspective on the subject of love, since discord and division, the cause of all the world's evil, can only be overcome by the principle of love and universal concord, as illustrated by the myth of Arion, whose harp set every creature at peace with the other (Ovid, *Fasti*, ii. 79–118). The Prologue concludes with a sigh for a new Arion who could end all strife within the community:

> And if ther were such on now,
> Which cowthe harpe as he tho dede,
> He myhte availe in many a stede   *succeed in many places*
> To make pes wher now is hate;
> For whan men thenken to debate,
> I not what other thing is good. (Prologue, 1072–7)   *do not know*

Only after this long homily the poet confesses to his own inability to set everything right himself and therefore decides to change the subject.[12] Before embarking on his own story, however, 'my woful care' (i, 74), he meditates on the universal power of love, its inconstancy and unreasonableness. He himself wants to provide an example of this 'unsely jolif wo' (i, 88)[13] so that after his death the world may learn from it.

Unlike Chaucer, who invariably presents himself as a detached observer, unfit for love's service, the narrator of the *Confessio* introduces himself as the traditional stock-figure of the unhappy lover bewailing his ill fortune, wishing for death and appealing to the classical deities of Love:

> O thou Cupide, O thou Venus,
> Thou god of love and thou goddesse,
> Wher is pite? wher is meknesse?
> Now doth me pleinly live or dye,   *it is clearly for me to live or die*
> For certes such a maladie
> As I now have and longe have hadd,
> It myhte make a wisman madd,
> If that it scholde longe endure. (i, 124–31)

There is no explicit indication in the text that the lover falls asleep at this point, as do nearly all the lovers in the wake of the *Roman de la rose*, though some of the inevitable traditional attributes are there, almost like a quotation, to announce a poem on love, after all the serious matter of the Prologue:

> And that was in the Monthe of Maii,
> Whan every brid hath chose his make   *bird has chosen his mate*
> And thenkth his merthes forto make   *jubilation*
> Of love that he hath achieved; (i, 100–3)

The poet deliberately puts himself in the conventional situation of the un-happy lover, familiar to his audience, but unspecified here and without any particular courtly context. We hear less than usual about the poet's personal story. Love is treated as a universal malady, threatening every individual, and the lover's symptoms are generalised, with no specific reason, even before the God of Love shoots his fiery dart through his heart.

With the appearance of Venus, however, the situation is given a new turn by the unexpected switch to penitential terminology. It is part of the time-honoured convention of love allegory that the lover is encouraged to tell his own story,[14] since sharing one's grief is one of the classic remedies recom-mended in all discussions of 'courtly' love. But Gower's Venus requires more than this, and it is here that the discourse enters what appears to be religious territory when the idea of confession and shriving is introduced:

> Mi will is ferst that thou be schrive;   *confessed*
> And natheles how that it is
> I wot miself, bot for al this   *I know myself*
> Unto my prest, which comth anon,
> I woll thou telle it on and on,
> Bothe all thi thoght and al thi werk. (i, 190–5)

This is clearly 'the master-stroke which organises the whole of Gower's mater-ial'.[15] Venus' priest, 'this holy man' (i, 203), is an ambiguous figure.[16] On the one hand he is the servant of the Goddess of Love and his office is evidently to hear the lover's confession and prepare him for absolution. On the other hand he is also the voice of reason, responsibility and, in the end, of a higher wisdom that knows of the 'idle dreams and feigned consecrations of human infirmities'.[17] Thus, the confessional debate continually ranges beyond the traditional subject of an anatomy of love. At any rate, the idea of love is constantly extended to include the whole field of individual and social morality. The debate introduced in the Prologue remains a kind of moral subtext throughout the entire work.

The lover himself is a more interesting figure than many first-person narrators of medieval love-visions, though we never see him in any other capacity than that of AMANS. Being continually questioned by Genius he has to confess a number of minor sins in love's service, but he also firmly protests his innocence of many more serious crimes.[18] It has been a matter of debate whether he is from the start shown as an old man believing himself still capable of young love, traditionally a ridiculous figure, or whether this revelation comes as a dramatic surprise at the end. It is quite possible – perhaps even more so for Gower's contemporaries – to detect an element of veiled tragical irony throughout the whole dialogue, but this does not detract from the powerful effect of Amans' sudden realisation that he has all the time been the victim of a fond illusion.

Earlier criticism of the *Confessio Amantis* often concentrated on the stories that make up the bulk of the poem, but this ignores the overall structure of the work and the evident didactic intentions of its author,[19] who seems to have attempted a synthesis of his political and historical treatises and a lighter narrative discourse. For the modern reader, much of it may at first give the impression of an uneasy compromise, a strenuous effort of having it both ways. What Gower has achieved, however, is no less than a compendium of biblical, classical and medieval story material for his English readers, together with a moralising, but not narrowly restrictive commentary. The first book is a good example. Genius, as confessor, briefly explains his office and his authorisation which, as he points out, is not strictly confined to matters of love, but includes 'othre thinges' (i, 240) as well. In particular, the sins against Love are here understood as sins in a much wider sense, and the examination of the lover–narrator begins with a general catechism on the five senses and the seven deadly sins.

The first *exemplum*, quoted from Ovid's *Metamorphoses* (iii, 131–252) and used to impress the sins of the eye, is the story of the hunter Actaeon who happened to see Diana bathing, was turned into a hart by the angry Goddess and torn to pieces by his own hounds. Genius next proceeds to expound the sin of pride, subdivided into five chapters ruled by 'ministers' and illustrated by episodes from the myth of Troy, natural history, the *Metamorphoses*, from various romances and from the Old Testament. To trace the precise source of each tale is not always possible; some of them were widely disseminated and available in a large number of different versions. The collection as a whole gives ample proof of Gower's wide reading and impressive learning as well as of his narrative skill.

Perhaps the most successful and accessible of the stories retold in Book i is that of Florent: it has several times been reprinted in selections and anthologies[20] and was probably known to Chaucer. The tale is offered by Genius as a warning against disobedience to Love's commands, especially 'murmur and complaint', and it is characteristic of the way Gower adapts his source material to the particular situation within the adopted system of vices and virtues.

The story is set in a world of romance and chivalry, of 'daies olde', though its plot rather suggests a folk-tale origin. Riddles and the precarious task of finding the right answer to an apparently impossible problem are ancient devices, yet, in this case, the solution seems humorous or satirical rather than ingenious. Chaucer, who has basically the same story told by his Wife of Bath, has suited the plot to his (anti)feminist context and, unlike Gower, has left it within the world of the Arthurian court. It is instructive to compare the two versions, especially if one does not merely try to demonstrate Chaucer's superior narrative art. Gower's effects are quite different and not necessarily inferior: he is not reaching for dramatic or comic surprises, but his even and careful account has an appeal of its own, and it is clear that he is by no means blind to the subtler psychological and social implications of his plot, even though the application to Genius' confessional argument seems somewhat unfocused.

What Gower evidently found particularly interesting was the knight's dilemma between the courtly obligation to be true to his word and the repulsive ugliness of the lady who claims him as husband. His pained hesitation before he agrees to her bargain and his secret reflection that, at her age, she cannot last long and he therefore intends to hide her from the world until her death, create a minor psychological drama, intensified by the changes of scene between court and forest forced on him by his promises. At the first climax, he saves his life by producing the right answer, but is morally bound to face his second 'penance'. Gower effectively combines drama and moral choice:

> And whan that this Matrone herde
> The manere how this knyht ansuerde,
> Sche seide: 'Ha treson, wo thee be,
> That hast thus told the privite,   *intimate secret*
> Which alle wommen most desire!
> I wolde that thou were afire.'   *be burnt*
> Bot natheles in such a plit   *danger*
> Florent of his answere is quit:
> And tho began his sorwe newe,
> For he mot gon, or ben untrewe,   *must go, unfaithful*
> To hire which his trowthe hadde.
> Bot he, which alle schame dradde,   *dreaded*
> Goth forth in stede of his penance,
> And takth the fortune of his chance,
> As he that was with trowthe affaited. (i, 1657–71)
>   *bound by his faithful promise*

The special stress laid on the knight's 'trowthe', not necessarily demanded by Genius' reason for telling the story, might suggest a connection, if only an indirect one, with the theme of *Sir Gawain and the Green Knight*. It is also worth noting in this context that the two closest analogues (apart from the Wife of Bath's Tale), the ballad *The Weddynge of Sir Gawene and Dame Ragnell* and *The Marriage of Sir Gawain*, have Gawain as the hero. Whether Gower originally adapted a Gawain-story or whether he found Florent already in his source we cannot know. He certainly made the most not only of the knight's moral test, but also of the comedy of the wedding night, when courtesy and his 'bond' oblige him not to turn away from his loathly wife in the marriage bed, but to face 'his penance' bravely. Magically, the bride turns out to be the most beautiful young lady, to whom it is easy enough to surrender love and sovereignty.

When Gower decided to fit this tale into the scheme of the deadly sins against love, he did not press every detail into an abstract system, but evidently followed his poetic programme of mixing instruction and entertainment. Florent may not be the ideal pattern of obedience in love, but he is certainly a model of chivalry, true to his ideal of trowthe and gentillesse.[21] Yet Gower's narrative does not merely present him as an *exemplum*; for him, he is also the hero of an enjoyable courtly adventure, even though at the end he has Genius return to his didactic purpose:

> And clerkes that this chance herde
> Thei writen it in evidence,
> To teche how that obedience
> Mai wel fortune a man to love
> And sette him in his lust above,   *achieve the top of his happiness*
> As it befell unto this knyht. (i, 1856–61)

As in many other story collections, 'cases' from history, classical literature or folklore are re-told to support certain observations on human behaviour or illustrate particular moral concepts. Gower uses different methods of fitting the 'chances' gleaned from his extensive reading into his penitential scheme, though in the process of adapting plots he generally appears to put his master-plan first and change the stories accordingly, in some cases quite radically.

The tale of Albinus and Rosemund, towards the end of the first book, is a typical instance. Genius has explained to the lover the vice of 'avantarie', i.e. vain boasting, of which Amans feels perfectly innocent and in no need of repentance. Nevertheless, the confessor repeats his warning and supports it with an 'ensample' he has found in 'the bokes write' (i, 2458). It is first related in the *Gesta Langobardorum* of Paulus Diaconus (*c.* 720–99) and frequently retold; Gower probably had it from the late twelfth-century *Pantheon sive Memoria Saeculorum* of Godfrey of Viterbo, where it is presented as a demonstration of cruelty punished. Albinus, the first King of the Lombards, has married the daughter of the enemy he had killed in battle; at a feast he asks her to drink out of a precious cup he has caused to be made from her father's skull. When he tells her what he has done she decides on a conspiracy to have him killed. In the end, none of the main actors survive.

Gower, though retaining the outline of the action, completely altered the motivation and the moral to be drawn from it.[22] What, in his source, is a story of political intrigue and wilful cruelty avenged, is transformed into an illustration of proud showing-off in love. This is why the narrator dwells on the first part of the episode in new detail, while passing over the rest of the action rather briefly. Albinus has the richly decorated cup made not out of contempt for his defeated enemy, but rather in his memory as well as to celebrate his own victory, and he marries his daughter because he has genuinely fallen in love with her ('His herte fell to hire anon', i, 2484). For a long time they live together in mutual affection ('Thei love ech other wonder wel', i, 2489), until Venus, acting as *Fortuna*, turns her wheel and prepares for the Lovers' tragic downfall:

> Bot sche which kepth the blinde whel,
> Venus, whan thei be most above,
> In al the hoteste of here love,
> Hire whiel sche torneth, and thei felle
> In the manere as I schal telle. (i, 2490–4)

It is the classic definition of medieval tragedy, and in this sense Fisher is right when he calls the tale 'a genuine love tragedy in spite of its clerical descent'.[23] It is the lover's overweening pride that causes the catastrophe, when at the climax of the lavish entertainment he produces the cup and in full audience boasts of his success in battle and in love:

> So that the lordes knowe schulle
> Of his bataille a soth witnesse,
> And made avant thurgh what prouesse   *boasted*
> He hath his wyves love wonne,
> Which of the Skulle hath so begonne. (i, 2558–62)

None of this motivation is found in the sources, where the deliberate use of the cup seems an act of cynical cruelty: the splendid feast and the public boast are Gower's own addition to the plot. It is almost a secular version of the much more famous feast of Belshazzar (Book of Daniel, v), often quoted by medieval writers as an example of pride before fall.

Here, as elsewhere, the freedom Gower allows himself in adapting his sources is hardly less remarkable than Chaucer's, though exercised in a very different direction. If Gower appears to lack Chaucer's sheer delight in narrative role-playing and creative exuberance he can, in his own way, surprise the reader by the persistence of collecting material from an astonishing range of sources and fitting it into his ambitious moral scheme. Derek Pearsall persuasively argues that 'It is in the stories that Gower's imagination receives its final and fullest release',[24] but as the ambitious design of the *Confessio* makes clear, the stories are hardly told for their own sake. They are, throughout the whole work, offered as part of a moral argument, regardless of their particular origin.

Thus, in the second book, devoted to the sin of envy, Gower gathers a variety of examples from very different sources to illustrate several subspecies of this deadly sin, the most important being defined as grief for another person's joy. The first supporting story is an episode Gower found in Ovid's *Metamorphoses*, where it forms the substance of Galathea's complaint (xiii, 750–897). Gower's version is much abbreviated (ii, 104–200), reducing the plot to Polyphem's jealous rage and cutting out his most eloquent wooing speech, in which he tries to impress her by promises of all the riches in his power (xiii, 799–858). It is only at the end of this impressive plea that he turns to the favoured Acis and threatens revenge. Gower's Polyphem knows all out about Galathea's lover after the first six lines, and the rest of the tale is a study in mad jealousy. All that makes Ovid's tale such a moving account of divinely ordered metamorphosis and has made Galathea a favourite subject of later artists, especially Renaissance painters, is omitted in order to press the episode into the service of Genius' argument.[25] Instead, Polyphem's fury is described in vivid detail. When he discovers the happy lovers he experiences the agony of the despised lover and becomes a victim to the deadly sin of envy:

> The place wher as he hem syh,   *saw*
> It was under a banke nyh   *near*
> The grete See, and he above
> Stod and behield the lusti love
> Which ech of hem to other made
> With goodly chiere and wordes glade,
> That al his herte hath set afyre
> Of pure Envie: (ii, 143–50)

Unlike Ovid's wooer, he runs off, 'As he that was for love wod' (153), roaring like a bear, behaving like a wild beast and roaming round hell, 'Wher nevere yit the fyr was oute' (164). No wonder Gower's *Amans* feels quite innocent of such passion and begs Genius to proceed with his analysis of envy's manifestations. A little later, however, he has to confess that he feels envy when he sees his lady, of whom he himself is unworthy, beset by deceivers who might beguile her trusting innocence. In this situation he admits to being tempted into saying things that might cast blame on his lady:

> Therof I wol me wel avise,
> To speke or jangle in eny wise   *joke*
> That toucheth to my ladi name,
> The which in ernest and in game
> I wolde save into my deth;
> For me were levere lacke breth   *I would rather*
> Than speken of hire name amis. (ii, 525–31)

It is a conventional maxim of courtly behaviour, even if its application to the deadly sin of envy seems less obvious; however, it is used by Genius as an opportunity to retell the homiletic romance of Constance. This is one of the most successful demonstrations of Gower's narrative art, though it has more than once been unfavourably compared with Chaucer's use of the same material in 'The Man of Law's Tale'.[26] The immediate source of both poets is Nicholas Trivet's early fourteenth-century Anglo-Norman chronicle, but the story is evidently the product of a long process of combining elements of Greek romance, chronicle and hagiography. The English versions belong to the type of exemplary romance bordering on saints' lives that enjoyed particular popularity for several generations.[27] The heroine does not die a martyr's death and she is no saintly virgin; as wife and mother she has to suffer calumny, persecution and separation, but under God's protection she comes out of all temptations sinless and as a model of virtue and Christian patience and an instrument of converting two pagan monarchs. Where Gower departs from his sources is in the particular emphasis on the three acts of cruel treachery committed against the innocent heroine, motivated by envy and, in the last instance, executed by means of slander. Thus, Genius can draw a moral not necessarily evident from the other versions of the legend, but fitting for its place in the *Confessio*:

> And thus the wel meninge of love
> Was ate laste set above;
> And so as thou hast herd tofore,
> The false tunges weren lore,   *lost*
> Whiche upon love wolden lie.
> Forthi touchende of this Envie
> Which longeth unto bacbitinge,
> Be war thou make no lesinge   *tell no false lies*
> In hindringe of an other wiht: (ii, 1599–1607)

Nevertheless, Gower retells the pious romance without striving for pointed brevity or dramatic effects, with careful attention to detail. He is much less interested in emotional intensity and pathos than Chaucer's narrator, nor does he consistently comment on the action, except for regular reminders of God's providence and the innocence of Constance. There is no need to justify a narrative method so different from the *Canterbury Tales*. Gower's narrator is neither a professional entertainer nor a self-conscious author or any of the *personae* Chaucer slips into, but a moral guide, a spiritual father instructing his son, as he persistently addresses him. His unadorned style, consciously avoiding rhetorical virtuosity, gives the impression of merely wishing the events to speak for themselves, which, of course, is only another form of highly disciplined rhetoric. The homiletic romance of Constance is a remarkable instance of Gower's personal and by no means artless style.

The discussion so far has started from the observation that Gower deliberately, and possibly with a royal patron in mind, produced something like an inventory of classical or traditional stories to support his catechism of a moralised *ars amandi* in the course of which he developed his personal version of courtly love conventions and, in the way of many medieval preachers, made the miscellaneous fruits of his extensive reading serve his didactic purpose. Illustrations could be multiplied: it is obvious that some tales lend themselves more easily to this kind of treatment than others, and every reader will easily find examples where the moral application seems to fit uneasily and others where it seems all too simple, but no other Middle English author has left us such wealth of traditional tales in plain versions that have inspired other authors, most famously William Shakespeare, who in *Pericles, Prince of Tyre* (printed 1609) makes Gower the Chorus introducing the story of Pericles (Apollonius in all previous versions).[28] For many of these plots, Gower was for generations the most authoritative and convenient source.

The lover's shrift and the closing of the frame

In Gower's *Confessio*, as in many penitential treatises and manuals from the times of the Church Fathers, the Deadly Sins are discussed in the traditional

'Gregorian' order: after the discussion and illustration of Pride and Envy, Genius proceeds in the third book to analyse the sin of Wrath, divided into five separate vices (melancholy, evil speech, hate, *contek* [rash hostile action] and homicide). The fourth book is devoted to the manifestation of Sloth, the fifth to Avarice, the sixth to Gluttony, which is bracketed with *luxuria*.[29] Genius confines his homily to specific warnings against love-drunkenness and 'delicacy', with a final caveat against sorcery, with cautionary examples from the story of Ulysses, the Egyptian king Nectanabus and Saul. Genius then, in Book Seven turns to an exposition of the Aristotelian principal areas of philosophy, the liberal arts and the chief social virtues, culminating, not surprisingly, in the praise of chastity, illustrated by the famous stories of Lucrece and Virginia, often retold and painted by later artists.

At this point, disagreement arises between the confessor and the lover, who has listened to all the stories, but still suffers from love's pain:

> The tales sounen in myn Ere,   *sound*
> Bot yit myn herte is elleswhere, (vii, 5411–12)

This opens a new stage in the spiritual admonition, ending in an all but wholesale rejection of love and a meditation on last things.

The eighth book of the *Confessio* is the most original section of the whole work and the one in which the poet's deepest concerns about the entire subject of courtly versus divine love are most expressively dramatised. Throughout the confessional exchange between Genius and Amans there have been hints of Genius dissociating himself from his traditional role and even from the goddess he is supposed to serve. The first clear hint comes about halfway through the poem, at the conclusion of the story of Rosiphelee; it is told as an *exemplum* against 'idleness in love' and shows the miraculous conversion of a beautiful princess whose only fault is sloth in matters of love. Venus and Cupid decide to take action:

> For thei merveille how such a wiht,
> Which tho was in hir lusti age,
> Desireth nother Mariage
> Ne yit the love of paramours,
> Which evere hath be the comun cours
> Amonges hem that lusti were. (iv, 1266–71)

When the two immortals have chastised the independent lady as a warning to all despisers of love, Genius intervenes to make a clear distinction between the 'love of paramours' demanded by Venus and 'honeste' love, the only kind he can seriously approve of:

> Mi ladi Venus, whom I serve,
> What womman wole hire thonk deserve,
> Sche mai noght thilke love eschuie   *avoid such love*
> Of paramours, bot sche mot suie   *follow*
> Cupides lawe; and natheles
> Men sen such love sielde in pes,   *see, seldom in peace*

> That it nys evere upon aspie   *on the lookout*
> Of janglinge and of fals Envie,   *quarrel*
> Fulofte medlid with disese: *Most often*
> Bot thilke love is wel at ese,
> Which set is upon mariage;
> For that dar schewen the visage
> In alle places openly. (iv, 1467–79)

Genius evidently feels some embarrassment in view of the story's moral implications and wants to affirm the orthodox view. He continues with a particular piece of advice to young girls to make sure of marriage before they lose valuable years in which they could have borne children (iv, 1488–1501). Though at this point Genius' arguments seem to be mainly of a practical nature, a paternal warning to avoid inconvenient gossip and loss of time for a safe marriage, there is little doubt that he has no sympathy for the conventions of 'courtly' love, but tries to instil into his pupil the ideal of 'love honeste'.[30]

The concluding book of the *Confessio* leaves no doubt about the author's moral position and the lesson for the lover, who is a long time grasping the fundamental finality of what has been revealed to him by Venus' servant and his treasury of tales. The last and longest of them, the romance of Apollonius of Tyre (viii, 271–2008), is evidently meant as the climax of the collection and the clinching *exemplum* of a love that is free from 'lust' and in complete accordance with the precepts of reason. In this instance, Gower makes no attempt to shorten the long and fairly intricate plot, and he follows Apollonius' adventures in more detail than his alleged source.[31] In contrast to earlier exemplary tales, he is not conspicuously concerned with adapting the plot to a moral thesis, but appears to be enjoying the colourful world of romantic adventure and the bustling succession of scenes. The narrative is presented in the manner of a circumstantial account by a chronicler who wants to hold the attention of his audience and to satisfy their interest in exotic, even improbable adventure, without obtrusive moralising or the simpler formulas of popular romance.

At the same time, Gower (and Genius) is using the ancient romance to serve his overall poetic and didactic intention.[32] There are, for one thing, serious issues recurring in the course of the eventful narrative. Genius introduces the story as a warning against incest, like the preceding examples, briefly related, of Caligula and Lot, and the opening episode of Antiochus raping his daughter is the cause of all the complications to follow. The first sequence of events comes to an end when Apollonius is told by his subjects that Antiochus and his daughter have both been destroyed by God's vengeance 'With thondre and lyhthnynge' (viii, 1000). After this, the romance of shipwreck, separation, trial and reunion takes its traditional course towards 'perfect felicity',[33] virtue rewarded and the final vindication of 'love honeste'. Throughout all wanderings and tribulations, Apollonius represents a 'cultural ideal' which is far removed from the accepted conventions of chivalry, and all the more exemplary for being pagan.[34] It combines constancy in love with a gentleness of conduct in a variety of trials, apt to win hearts and loyalties, without any of the more glamorous heroic exploits. His wife and daughter, likewise, impress their surroundings by a civilised humanity that prevents their coming to any harm. The theme of love is kept present by Apollonius' memories, his grief and unquestioned faith.

At the end, there is a brief, but important reminder of Antiochus, whose unnatural love is held up as a warning and contrast to the happy outcome of the main plot. For Genius, the moral of Apollonius' history is clear:

> Lo, what it is to be wel grounded:
> For he hath ferst his love founded
> Honesteliche as forto wedde,
> Honesteliche his love he spedde   *pursued*
> And hadde children with his wif,
> And as him liste he ladde his lif;   *as he pleased*
> And in ensample his lif was write,
> That alle lovers myhten wite
> How ate laste it schal be sene
> Of love what thei wolden mene.
> For se now on that other side,
> Antiochus with al his Pride,
> Which sette his love unkindely,   *against nature*
> His ende he hadde al sodeinly,
> Set ayein kinde upon vengance,
> And for his lust hath his penance. (viii, 1993–2008)

In simple terms, this is the quintessence of the *Confessio* and its doctrine of wedded love as opposed to all the aberrations of lust and incest.

Amans still fails to see the full implications of what is presented to him even when Genius attempts to impress on him the necessity of choice in no uncertain terms:

> For love, which that blind was evere,
> Makth alle his servantz blinde also.
> My Sone, and if thou have be so,
> Yit is it time to withdrawe,
> And set thin herte under that lawe,
> The which of reson is governed
> And noght of will. (viii, 2130–6)
> . . .
> For I can do to thee nomore
> Bot teche thee the rihte weie:
> Now ches if thou wolt live or deie. (viii, 2146–8)

When Amans, still unable to follow his reason, writes a complaint to Venus, the Goddess herself appears again, promising, with a touch of Chaucerian irony, to cure him of 'thilke unsely jolif wo' (viii, 2360).

Her 'medicine' takes the form of a vision that is one of Gower's most brilliant inventions. A long procession of famous lovers, from Tristan and Isolde to Cleopatra and Antony, demonstrate the unhappy end of love's passion, followed by a small group of four faithful wives (Penelope, Lucrece, Alceste and Alcyone). At the climax of the pageant Venus presents him with a mirror through which he at last comes to understand the passing of the seasons and his own old age. This finally makes him deny all thoughts of love, to the undisguised amusement of Venus who advises him to leave her court:

> Venus behield me than and lowh,   *laughed*
> And axeth, as it were in game,
> What love was. And I for schame
> Ne wiste what I scholde ansuere;   *knew*
> And natheles I gan to swere
> That be my trouthe I knew him noght;
> So ferr it was out of mi thoght,   *far*
> Riht as it hadde nevere be. (viii, 2870–7)

It is an unexpected tragi-comic finale to his confession, which began with the hope for a much more comforting answer from the Goddess of Love. Her parting gift is a black rosary and the admonition to be guided by reason and by his own earlier books, 'ther vertu moral duelleth' (viii, 2925). The poet is left feeling that he has wasted his time on an illusionary pursuit and had much better go home to spend the remainder of his life in prayer:

> And y was left with outen helpe.
> So wiste I nought wher of to yelpe,   *boast*
> But only that y hadde lore
> My time, and was sori ther fore.
> And thus bewhapid in my thought,   *bewildered*
> Whan al was turnyd in to nought,
> I stod amasid for a while,   *amazed*
> And in my self y gan to smyle
> Thenkende uppon the bedis blake,   *beads*
> And how they weren me betake,   *given*
> For that y schulde bidde and preie.
> And whanne y sigh non othre weie   *saw*
> Bot only that y was refusid,
> Unto the lif which y hadde usid
> I thoughte nevere torne ayein: (viii, 2951–65)

It is a form of 'retraction', such as Chaucer and other poets put at the end of their work; but in this case it is undeniably an essential part of the complete conception. It is not that all the entertaining stories are in the end rejected because, in Chaucer's words, they might 'sownen into synne',[35] but rather that we should read them all in the light of the inevitable conclusion. Both poets wish to put on record that an important part of their literary output is a morally unassailable achievement they need not repent of. Gower explicitly refers to his earlier work, before he changed his style (see i, 8–9). It is only consistent, therefore, that the last word belongs to a resumption of the social and political concerns voiced in the prologue, and throughout the entire *confessio*, in particular the proper duties of the several estates and, above all, the King, whose authority alone can secure unity and peace. This, as Fisher rightly concluded a generation ago, 'is the real conclusion of the *Confessio Amantis*, not the withdrawal from romantic love. And this is the context in which the Lover's confession must itself be viewed.'[36] Later critics have confirmed this estimate of Gower's real interest, especially his negative view of courtly love conventions and the chivalric code.[37]

When Chaucer referred to his friend as 'moral Gower' he almost certainly meant nothing like disrespect or even gentle mockery for a seriousness different from his own, but only recognition of Gower's earnest concern for a moral and social order he saw threatened by the political events of his time and for the true office of poetry.[38] Though his literary fame and influence soon fell behind that of Chaucer, he still rewards a reader's attentive consideration by the unpretentious retelling and thus preserving of many classical plots and by his moving portrayal of an immature lover's conversion.

Notes

1. The best and still generally quoted edition of Gower's English poems is *The English Works of John Gower. Edited from the Manuscripts, with Introduction, Notes and Glossary*, ed. G. C. Macaulay, 2 vols, EETS, ES, 81, 82 (1900–1). *Selections from John Gower*, with useful notes, were edited by J. A. W. Bennett in the Clarendon Medieval and Tudor Series (Oxford, 1968).

2. See the section on 'Date and Circumstances' in Macaulay's edition, pp. xxi–xxviii.

3. See the informative and unbiased account in John H. Fisher, *John Gower: Moral Philosopher and Friend of Chaucer* (New York, 1964), chapter 2, 'Life Records', pp. 37–69.

4. See Macaulay's edition, II, 479–80.

5. This is emphasised by Fisher: 'the architectonic development of Gower's major themes embraces the *Mirour, Vox* and *Confessio*', *John Gower*, p. 115.

6. Described in detail by Fisher, *John Gower*, pp. 116–27. My account is greatly indebted to his. For a stimulating discussion of Gower's political allegiance, sometimes taken for opportunism, see Hans-Jürgen Diller, ' "For Engelondes sake": Richard II and Henry of Lancaster as Intended Readers of Gower's *Confessio Amantis*', in *Functions of Literature. Essays presented to Erwin Wolff on his sixtieth birthday*, ed. Ulrich Broich, Theo Stemmler and Gerd Stratmann (Tübingen, 1984), 39–53.

7. See Fisher, pp. 120–1 and notes, and Macaulay's description of the manuscript and different versions in his edition, pp. cxxxviii–clxvii.

8. See the valuable study by Götz Schmitz, *the middel weie. Stil und Aufbauformen in John Gowers 'Confessio Amantis'*, Studien zur englischen Literatur, 11 (Bonn, 1974), and the excellent treatment of many aspects of Gower's style by R. F. Yeager, *John Gower's Poetic: The Search for a New Arion* (Cambridge, 1990).

9. The opposite kind of concession is provided by the Latin poems and marginal notes accompanying the text in most manuscripts, rarely taken into account by critics, but reaffirming the moral backbone of the whole project. A valuable tool is provided in Siân Echard and Claire Fanger, *The Latin Verses in the* Confessio Amantis. *An Annotated Translation* (East Lansing, 1991). There is a useful preface by A. G. Rigg.

10. See Macaulay, pp. clvii–clvix.

11. For a more elaborate example of such systematic treatment of sins and virtues see the Latin *Fasciculus Morum. A Fourteenth-Century Preacher's Handbook*. Edition and translation by Siegfried Wenzel (Pennsylvania State University Press, 1989), extant in twenty-eight manuscripts.

12. See the lines i, 8–16, quoted above.

13. See Pandarus' 'joly wo' in Chaucer's *Troilus*, ii. 1099.

14. Cf. Chaucer's *Book of the Duchess* for a typical example. The *Roman de la rose* is the most influential model.

15. See C. S. Lewis, *The Allegory of Love. A Study in Medieval Tradition* (Oxford, 1936; many times reprinted), p. 200. Lewis' chapter on Gower still seems to me one of the sanest and most sympathetic accounts.

16. See the appendix in Lewis, *The Allegory of Love*, pp. 361–3.

17. See Lewis, p. 219.

18. See the excellent essay by John A. Burrow, 'The Portrayal of Amans in *Confessio Amantis*', in *Gower's* Confessio Amantis: *Responses and Reassessments*, ed. A. J. Minnis (Cambridge, 1983), pp. 5–24. See also the stimulating and wide-ranging chapter 'John Gower', by Winthrop Wetherbee in *The Cambridge History of Medieval English Literature*, ed. David Wallace (Cambridge, 1999), pp. 589–609.

19. See *Gower's* Confessio Amantis: *A Critical Anthology*, ed. Peter Nicholson (Cambridge, 1991). Nicholson's Introduction gives a brief outline of criticism from 1900 to 1982; pp. 1–4.

20. E.g. in *Selections from John Gower*, ed. Bennett, and in *Sources and Analogues of Chaucer's Canterbury Tales*, ed. W. F. Bryan and Germaine Dempster (New York, 1958; first published, 1941).

21. See especially i, 1511–13:

> This knyht hath levere forto dye   *had rather*
> Than breke his trowthe and forto lye
> In place ther as he was swore,   *bound by his oath*

When he takes the loathly lady to the court, it is 'for pure gentilesse' (i, 1721).

22. See Arno Esch, 'John Gower's Narrative Art', in: *Gower's* Confessio Amantis, ed. Nicholson, pp. 81–109; first published in German as 'John Gowers Erzählkunst' in *Chaucer und seine Zeit. Symposium für Walter F. Schirmer* (Tübingen, 1968), 207–39. My account of this tale is much indebted to Esch.

23. *John Gower*, p. 195.

24. Cf. Derek Pearsall, 'Gower's Narrative Art', *PMLA*, 81 (1966), 475–84, reprinted in *Gower's* Confessio Amantis, ed. Nicholson, pp. 62–80.

25. To be sure, the Latin summary of the tale in the margin of the best manuscripts provides a slightly more accurate account of Ovid's story, especially the end; but it also omits Polyphem's wooing.

26. Cf. the verdict in *Sources and Analogues of Chaucer's Canterbury Tales*: 'his [Gower's] rather mediocre narrative shows no sign of demonstrable influence by Chaucer's more original and moving tale' (pp. 154–5). See also the detailed interpretation in Esch, 'John Gower's Narrative Art', pp. 96–108. Many critics feel a need to apologise for Gower's unpretentious narrative style.

27. See the chapter on 'Homiletic Romances' in Dieter Mehl, *The Middle English Romances of the Thirteenth and Fourteenth Centuries* (London, 1969), pp. 120–58.

28. See the story of Apollonius of Tyre in book viii and Shakespeare's *Pericles, Prince of Tyre*, ed. Doreen Delveccio and Antony Hammond, The New Cambridge Shakespeare (Cambridge, 1998), especially pp. 27–36.

29. See the important study by Morton W. Bloomfield, *The Seven Deadly Sins* (Michigan, 1952).

30. See also iv, 2296–315. There is also a marginal Latin note opposite iv, 1454 in which the author wants to make clear that he is not to be identified with the character of Amans: '*Non quia sic habet veritas, set opinio Amantum.*'

31. Genius claims that he has the story (like that of Albinus and Rosemund) from Godfrey of Viterbo's *Pantheon*; but this is a briefer version, and many details come from a Latin prose version, *Historia Apollonii Tyrii*, the translation of a Greek original. See the brief account of the sources in Macaulay's edition, vol. II, pp. 536–8 and *passim*. The estimate of Gower's success has differed greatly among critics. See the collection of verdicts in the indispensable reference work by Peter Nicholson, *An Annotated Index to the Commentary on Gower's* Confessio Amantis (Binghamtom, New York, 1989), pp. 500–2. For other versions, in particular the sources of Shakespeare's *Pericles*, see Geoffrey Bullough, *Narrative and Dramatic Sources of Shakespeare*, vol. VI (London, 1966), pp. 347–564.

32. For a more sophisticated discussion of the tale and Gower's poetics see William Robins, 'Romance, Exemplum, and the Subject of the *Confessio Amantis*', *Studies in the Age of Chaucer*, 19 (1997), 157–81.

33. Jane Austen's phrase in the last chapter of *Northanger Abbey*.

34. See Wetherbee, 'John Gower', p. 605. Wetherbee draws attention to the parallels between the stories of Appolonius and Constance.

35. *The Canterbury Tales*, X, 1086.

36. See *John Gower*, p. 192. Yeager very aptly describes the *Confessio* as 'a love poem designed to outgrow itself. It is a poem of conversion . . .', *John Gower's Poetic*, p. 265.

37. Cf. Wetherbee, 'Chivalry is in effect the villain of the *Confessio*, at odds with Genius' teaching in virtually every area', 'John Gower', p. 602.

38. See the important study by Alastair Minnis, ' "Moral Gower" and Medieval Literary Theory', in *Gower's* Confessio Amantis: *Responses and Reassessments*, ed. Minnis, pp. 50–78.

Chapter 4

William Langland

William Langland, Geoffrey Chaucer's contemporary, is a much more shadowy figure, yet his life-work, *Piers Plowman*, in the words of one of his most recent editors, 'has a good claim to be the greatest English poem of the Middle Ages. It was certainly one of the most popular.'[1] More than fifty manuscripts survive, and the all but impossible task of establishing something like a 'reliable' or 'authentic' text has exercised generations of scholars.[2] Indeed, the debates about authorship, possible versions, revisions and transmission of the poem have been at the very centre of Langland studies for the last century. This, of course, could only happen because the text itself, in whatever editorial guise, is so startlingly original and full of urgent uncertainties, concerning religious, theological, social and poetic issues, that it has provoked continuing discussions from the time of its first being composed down to this day.

Text, texts and poem

It is difficult to discuss what the poem actually wants to say without first making some basic assumptions about its genesis and, moreover, about the poet's own share in the complex textual situation. The ordinary reader, whether an undergraduate studying Middle English or anyone just interested in English literature and fourteenth-century religion, wishing to find out more about *Piers Plowman*, is confronted by a bewildering choice of texts and editions, much more so than in the case of Chaucer or any other work of Middle English literature. This is due mainly to the evident popularity of the poem, attested by well over fifty manuscripts, containing complete or fragmentary versions that demonstrably are merely the fortunate survivors of a much greater number of original witnesses.[3] If there is anything most *Piers Plowman* scholars would probably agree on it is the fact that many more copies of the poem must at one time have existed and circulated than are now extant and that those we know do not enable us to draw up a simple stemma that would account for the innumerable differences between them. The variants range from thousands of changes in single words or phrases to wholesale deletion, substitution, addition or rewriting of large passages and complete episodes.

From the time of W. W. Skeat, the first serious editor of *Piers Plowman*, until fairly recently there seemed to have been general consensus that the poem exists in three distinct versions, A, B and C, produced in that order, B being a thorough expansion and revision of A, and C being an extensive though uncompleted revision of B. A very brief version of the poem, designated as Z-version is considered by many to be an even earlier first draft, though this has not been generally accepted.[4] The theory of the three texts, first established by W. W. Skeat, has for generations been taken as an undisputed dogma, as has the general chronology of these versions, implying a conscientiously revising author who produced three complete poems, one after the other, without any mutual interference or piecemeal correction.[5] Recently, however, the universally accepted chronology has been contested and reasons have been shown for the assumption that the shorter A-text is not a first attempt but an abridged version, omitting Latin quotations, sexual material, criticism of clergy and secular authority and reducing metaphor.[6]

Another assumption, and one that is no longer seriously questioned, is that all the extant texts and versions are the work of a single author whose name is William Langland.[7] This is, however, where certainty ends and hypothesis must begin. It is very difficult for the modern reader to imagine a situation in which the kind of textual multiplicity attested by the extant manuscripts could arise. George Kane, the most influential modern editor and textual critic of the poem, who masterminded the Athlone edition, single-handedly produced its first volume and a large part of the second, gives the most thorough account of the textual data and editorial problems, though his own methods and solutions are clearly controversial and have been frequently criticised.[8] They are principally based on the assumption that Langland produced three versions of his poem, and only three, and that we should try to recover a text as near as possible to what the author originally wrote or intended. This, for Kane and his collaborators, involves not just a choice of the 'best' manuscript, but a critical decision about 'authorial' readings in each single case of variant readings. As a result, the Athlone edition presents a distinctly eclectic text, with meticulous documentation as to the possible groups of variants and the provenance of every editorial decision.

Perhaps the most serious objection to a neat definition of the three texts (or four, if we include the Z-version) comes from the great diversity of individual readings cutting across clearly defined boundaries between assumed versions and making it all but impossible to distinguish between authorial revision and scribal 'improvement' or error with any confidence. Even if the editor believes that Langland revised the poem systematically more than once in succession, as D. H. Lawrence twice rewrote *Lady Chatterley's Lover* in its entirety, he or she has to explain why there is such lack of consistency in verbal variants – supposed A readings resurfacing in C or Z readings appearing in B. This makes it difficult to believe in the existence of a systematically revising author and in strictly progressive or 'linear' revision. It seems much more likely that the poet revised and altered his text in a more haphazard way, that he sometimes produced inferior alternatives and that, on the other hand, some scribes came up with equally successful alternatives. All this makes it practically impossible to produce a readable text that yet incorporates all the options presented by over fifty 'versions'. So far, however, the traditional solutions, single critical editions of each version or parallel-text editions including three or four versions, still offer the only workable method of making available the poem to the reader, other than just reproducing any one manuscript in facsimile.[9] With the advent of electronic editions, there will eventually be a generally accessible database, making it possible for every reader to create his own edition or at least to produce a full survey of variants of any given passage.[10] Still, it is likely that even in the foreseeable future readers will prefer the page to the screen and for the majority of them any good working edition of one of the three versions, with some explanatory notes and commentary, will provide the most accessible entrance into the world of *Piers Plowman*.

Piers Plowman in its time

To be fascinated with *Piers Plowman* requires, I suggest, initially no very sophisticated linguistic, historical or philosophical competence. Having said that, however, it has to be added immediately, as the text soon makes clear, that the poem is deeply rooted in the political and theological upheavals of its period and Langland, whatever his exact professional and material circumstances, takes up some very explicit and by no means impartial positions in a number of controversial issues.[11] The most obvious ones are the abuses of the established church, the corruption of the high clergy and the overbearing arrogance of mendicant friars, which Langland cannot stop himself castigating wherever he sees an opportunity. More radical is his passionate insistence on the crucial importance of true contrition, spiritual renewal and simple Gospel precepts, rather than academic argument, and confident trust in God's grace above formal conformity to clerical doctrine or institutional rules. His angry criticism and satire of the decline from the apostolic discipline and selfless humility of the church's basic ideals is not particularly original, but his probing into some fundamental theological issues shows that he is not afraid of confronting hotly contested areas to the very limits of traditional answers. The poem offers no direction or recipe for a pilgrim's progress to Dobest, but it is unambiguous in its general position within the contemporary controversies and in its homiletic message.[12] It also shows the poet responding either to political and spiritual movements he observed around him or to explicit criticism. This is confirmed by the revisions, especially in the C-version.[13] One can, with Kerby-Fulton, see the movement from the A-version to B as a reflection of Langland's mental progress from the basically rural West Midlands to the more sophisticated world of London, though this assumes that the traditional chronology and order of revisions is accepted.

It is evident that the poet was alive to the intellectual and political debates of his time and anxious to take them up in his own work. A particularly interesting example is the long addition in C to B's passus VII at about line 100, where the text of B might suggest that a life of contemplation, wandering about the world and begging is more valuable than the active work of the plowman. Langland here inserts a long digression on hermits, where he makes a sharp distinction between true hermits and those who use the habit as an excuse for idling and exploiting the charity of their fellows. In this connection Langland deliberately uses the term 'lollar', which does not occur in A or B and was apparently a new word, soon becoming fashionable as a, mostly derogatory, name for the followers of Wyclif.[14] For Langland, it appears to describe any 'lolling' vagrant beggars who discredit the Christian notion of not caring about provisions and bodily needs by their lazy dependence on those who work for their living. Langland's addition makes clear that poverty and beggary was not only a social but a theological problem. Most of his brief autobiographical hints suggest that he was well acquainted with the life of the poor. Their plight is of genuine concern to him, but he is equally intolerant of sponging parasites who pervert one of the Church's ideals closest to Langland's heart. This is why his attitude towards the image of pilgrimage is oddly wavering. It remains the perfect metaphor of the Christian quest for Dowel, Dobet and Dobest, but at the same time it must not be used as an excuse for neglecting the active life.

Another instance of the poem's political implications is the use made of it during the Peasants' Revolt of 1381, when Piers was used as a rallying cry for the plebeian uprising, although the poem demonstrably speaks out on the side of the traditional feudal structure.[15] At the same time, its explicit protest against the abuses of the ruling powers could well be understood as an encouragement to rebellion. The fate of several protesters, who were persecuted, excommunicated or put to death, however, is an eloquent reminder of the precarious position of any too outspoken author. Langland was writing in a period when political and ecclesiastical censorship was by no means uncommon and he was obviously treading on dangerous ground, if only because his 'passionate, genuinely exploratory poem'[16] could be read in different ways.[17] His revisions in B and C may well be a reflection of that. Langland was evidently familiar with an impressively wide range of the political and theological thinking of his time, with university debates,[18] monastic interests and with very different circles of readers as well as possibly illiterate craftsmen and labourers. It is this unconventionally broad scope of his interests, literary techniques and even points of view that has been explored and emphasised by recent criticism. There seems to be no end to the discoveries still in store for the modern reader of this astonishing poem.

Structure and narrative discourse

Like the *Roman de la Rose* and many poems of Chaucer and his contemporaries, *Piers Plowman* begins as a dream vision, but, unlike the conventional dream poems, it develops unexpectedly into a series of dreams, including even dreams within dreams, that may well confuse the reader at first, especially if he is looking for strict narrative or fictional consistency. It soon becomes clear, however, as we follow the poem's visions, that the narrative surface, the 'literal' level of the fiction, is only very lightly sustained, and the reader, or listener, is appealed to by images and arguments that should make him disregard any idea of a realistic or strictly consistent story line, insofar as there is a coherent story line other than the narrator's vision and his search for spiritual guidance and instruction.

The poem begins with a conventional formula claiming, without particular narrative preliminaries and with only the most perfunctory sketch of the traditional May morning, landscape and river-bank, to introduce a wondrous vision:

In a somer seson, whan softe was the sonne,   *mild, sun*
I shoop me into shroudes as I a sheep were,   *dressed myself, shepherd*
In habite as an heremite unholy of werkes,
Wente wide in this world wondres to here.   *hear*
Ac on a May morwenynge on Malverne Hilles
Me bifel a ferly, of Fairye me thoghte.   *A marvellous thing, fairyland*
I was wery [of]wandred and wente me to reste
Under a brood bank by a bournes syde;   *a brook's edge*
And as I lay and lenede and loked on the watres,
I slombred into a slepyng, it sweyed so murye.   *sounded*
   Thanne gan [me] to meten a merveillous swevene –   *dream*
That it was in a wildernesse, wiste I nevere where.   *knew*
(Prologue, 1–12)[19]

This dream occupies the Prologue and four passus. In the midst of the action the poet awakes, deeply dissatisfied with the interruption of his vision and anxious to have more of it. Almost immediately he falls asleep again for another instalment of his revelation:

Thanne waked I of my wynkyng and wo was withalle   *sleep*
That I ne hadde slept sadder and yseighen moore.   *more soundly, seen*
Ac er I hadde faren a furlong, feyntise me hente,   *faintness, seized*
That I ne myghte ferther a foot for defaute of slepynge, *proceed further, lack*
And sat softely adoun and seide my bileve;   *Creed*
And so I bablede on my bedes, thei broughte me aslepe.
        as, mumbled, prayers
   And thanne saugh I muche more than I bifore tolde –   *related*
For I seigh the feld ful of folk that I before of seide,
And how Reson gan arayen hym al the reaume to preche,
        prepared himself, realm
And with a cros afore the Kyng comsede thus to techen. (V, 3–12) *began*

The second dream thus continues the first without more than a very brief break. Something similar happens, with variations, seven times in the course of the poem, except that the time scheme becomes more complicated and the sequence of dreams appears to span almost the whole of the poet's adult life. In addition, there are two dreams within dreams, suggesting an even higher degree of vision at points where even the dreamer is at a loss and seems to be granted some extra revelation to help his deficient comprehension. This 'gathering of dreams' appears to be unprecedented in English literature.[20] There is no doubt that the poet was familiar with dream allegories such as the *Roman de la Rose* and that he depends on the reader's knowledge of the convention, but he evidently chose to depart from the tradition in order to express something of the developing scope of his subject and its close relation to the mental and spiritual growth of the dreamer himself.

The series of dreams is effectively combined with brief, but suggestive glimpses of the poet's own biography. This is emphatically underlined by one of the most famous additions to the text in the 'C-version', where the poet describes himself as a man disappointed in his hopes and the hopes of his family, who sent him to school and obviously expected a more reputable career than his present dwelling in Cornhill, not a very distinguished quarter of London at the time, with a wife and no regular occupation, except irregular spiritual jobs as an unbeneficed cleric for his livelihood (C, V, 1–108).[21] It is not particularly profitable to speculate whether this biographical sketch has any real basis in Langland's own life, though it is very unlikely that it has not. What evidently concerns the poet at this point is the dreamer's own sense of idling away his time instead of honest labour, and thus being in dire need of forgiveness and spiritual support.

The interlude ends with a penitential prayer and tears of contrition which induce sleep and thus set the scene for the second vision. An additional line in this version recalls the scene of the first:

> And to þe kyrke y gan go, god to honoure,
> Byfore þe cross on my knees knokked y my brest,
> Syȝing for my synnes, seggyng my *pater-noster*,　　　　*sighing, saying*
> Wepyng and waylyng til y was aslepe.
> 　And thenne mette me muche more then y byfore tolde
> Of þe matere þat me mette furste on Maluerne hulles.
> 　　　　　　　　　(C, V, 105–10)

The whole episode replaces the brief transition from the first vision to the second in the B-version and thus makes the dreamer a more explicit presence after the first vision. This may have something to do with the fact that by the time Langland kept revising his poem, his identity could be assumed to be familiar enough to his readers. At least the poet seems deliberately to toy with the suggestion that he, as the creator of the poem, is to be associated with the dreamer[22] and that his vision has a direct bearing on his personal life. This teasing relationship between author, narrator and dreamer seems to me a deliberate part of the poem's rhetoric and its homiletic urgency.

At the climax of the second dream, the poet is awakened by the noisy dispute of two of the dream characters and finds himself without food and without money among the Malvern hills, where he began, reflecting on his vision and its significance to the end of the passus (VII, 140–201). He then starts on a new quest for spiritual guidance and explanation of what he has experienced in his vision, until he once more finds himself in a 'wilde wilder-nesse' (VIII, 63), near a woodside, with some of the familiar properties of dream allegory. This time, the scenery is sketched in a little more detail:

> Blisse of the briddes abide me made,　　　　　　　　　*Joy, birds*
> And under lynde upon a launde lened I a stounde　*clearing, reclined, a while*
> To lythe the layes that the lovely foweles made.　　*listen, songs, birds*
> Murthe of hire mouthes made me ther to slepe;　　　*cheerful sound*
> The merveillouseste metels mette me thanne　　　　　*dreams*
> That ever [wight dremed] in world, as I wene. (VIII, 64–9)

This, the third, vision, gives him even more food for thought and keeps his mind occupied for years:

And I awaked therwith, witlees nerhande,	*nearly mad*
And as a freke that fey were, forth gan I walke	*man, bewitched*
In manere of a mendynaunt many yer after,	*mendicant*
And of this metyng many tymes muche thought I hadde: (XIII, 1–4)	*dream*

The frame of the dream-series begins to assume a life of its own and it is clear that the poet is asking the reader not only to share his dreams, but to join the dreamer in meditating on the spiritual issues discussed in his visions and to accompany him on his pilgrimage through life. The quest for spiritual certainty turns out to be an ongoing process, inside the dream and, almost simultaneously, in the poet's waking existence. The visions almost appear as another level of the poet's consciousness, troubling and supporting him all through his life. In the end, the poem has assumed the form of a spiritual auto-biography, charting the lifelong search for ultimate answers to basic existential questions on which individual and communal salvation depends.

As the poem proceeds, the dreamer seems to be increasingly disturbed by his dream-experience and almost out of his mind with worry about the conflicting claims on his intellect and on his spiritual allegiance. The visions become shorter as the text progresses, and the intervals more desperate. After the fourth vision, the disconsolate poet appears to lose his wits and is taken for a fool and a spendthrift by those around him, until at last Reason takes pity on him and sends him sleep, with another dream vision (XV, 1–11).[23] The following (fifth) vision hardly leaves him in a happier state: aimlessly he wastes his lifetime, until again he falls asleep, snoring till Palm Sunday, where a new vision awaits him (XVIIII, 1–6). This time, awakening does not throw him back into desolation and despair, but he finds himself stirred by hymn-singing and bell-ringing for Easter morning, and instead of continuing spiritual uncertainty he actively joins the service, calling on his wife and daughter to do the same:

'Ariseth and go reverenceth Goddes resurexion,	
And crepeth to the cros on knees, and kisseth it for a juwel!	
For Goddes blissede body it bar for oure boote,	*salvation*
And it afereth the fend – for swich is the myghte, (XVIII, 429–32)	*frightens*

The penultimate passus and the (seventh) dream it recounts begins and ends with the poet telling us that on awaking he wrote down what he saw in his vision (XIX, 1 and 485). Thus he explicitly makes the dreamer lay claim to the poem.[24] The literary activity becomes part of the fiction, just as the visions and the spiritual quest of the dreamer themselves. The two visions he claims to have chronicled are also the most closely related to the gospel account of our redemption and the life of the church, beyond detached and non-committal speculation and intellectual debate at last.

The last passus, though, once more returns, first to the desperate poet, wandering aimlessly till he is reproached by 'Need' who justifies his own existence and spiritual usefulness till the dreamer again falls asleep and meets a vision of Antichrist and the ultimate struggle of the Church with the forces of Evil. Nothing seems to be finally resolved, however, and the poems ends with the beginning of a new quest:

> 'By Crist!' quod Conscience tho, 'I wole become a pilgrym,
> And walken as wide as the world lasteth,
> To seken Piers the Plowman, that Pryde mighte destruye,
> . . .
>
> Now Kynde me avenge,
> And sende me hap and heele, til I have Piers the Plowman!
> And siththe he gradde after Grace, til I gan awake.   *cried out*
> (XX, 381–3, 385–7)

Thus, in a way, the poem seems to end where it began, and, as readers and critics have found, it describes a circle rather than a linear progress.[25] But, of course, the quest was not futile, even though there is nothing like the arrival at the Heavenly City, as in Bunyan's *Pilgrim's Progress*, or an intellectual resolution of all spiritual uncertainties, but a final need to rely on God, the Father (Kynde), the Son (Piers Plowman) and the Holy Ghost (Grace).[26] 'All that remains for the wakened Dreamer is to go on, like Conscience, "walking the world".'[27]

The very last phrase of the whole poem is 'til I gan awake' (XX, 387). Thus the dreamer presents himself not only as a person whose troubled sense of unanswered need for reliable instruction haunts him and never leaves him satisfied throughout his mortal existence, but also as an author who reveals his literary and homiletic motivation. His poem is the record of a long spiritual as well as intellectual struggle and at the same time a homily and an urgent appeal to the reader or listener. This is, in a way, confirmed by the fact that, for all we can infer from the work's transmission, Langland spent the best part of his lifetime composing and revising it. He does not seem to have written anything else of any significance.

Allegorical method, homiletic criticism and theological argument

Though the different dreams follow a continuous pattern of discourse and progressive knowledge, they do not all exactly belong to the same fictional world, but they employ varying kinds of allegorical method and different species of dramatis personae. It is unrewarding to look for consistency in characterisation or complete logical conclusiveness of argument. More important than theological orthodoxy and flawless reasoning is the imaginative richness and integrity of aspiration, whether the poet makes use of narrative material, philosophical disputation or biblical and liturgical vision, with surprising transitions and an emotional and sometimes dramatic intensity that gives relevance even to seemingly dry or theoretical issues. Unlike the author of the *Roman de la Rose* and many allegorical fictions in its wake, Langland does not even vaguely conform to one or two particular conventions of narrative discourse, but seems to be blithely unpredictable in his choice of literary method. As Pearsall has admirably put it: 'Langland moves with breathtaking abruptness between these different allegorical modes, and intrudes the literal into all of them . . . and seems most characteristically active in exploring the borderland of the literal and the allegorical, where the allegorical is endorsed by the realities of the literal and the literal vivified by the possibilities of the allegorical.'[28] This is more helpful than elaborate definitions or classifications of Langland's allegorical procedures, but some of his principal strategies can be singled out.

In all three versions of *Piers Plowman*, the first section, named 'Prologue' in one A-manuscript and in most editions, introduces the dreamer to a most lively panorama, combining symbolic scenery with a realistic overview of contemporary society made up of fleeting glimpses of various trades, occupations and activities, mixed with personified moral qualities (Kynde Wit, Conscience) and, added to B and C, dramatis personae from a traditional animal fable (Prologue, 146–208). This already raises the problem of explication, but the poet retreats from interpreting his oblique message with a joke:

> (What this metels bymeneth, ye men that ben murye,   *dream means*
> Devyne ye, for I ne dar, by deere God in hevene)! (Prologue, 209–10)
>   *Explain, I dare not*

At the beginning of the following passus we are again reminded of the need for didactic assistance by the poet in his own voice:

> What this mountaigne bymeneth and the merke dale   *dark*
> And the feld ful of folk, I shal yow faire shewe. (I, 1–2)   *clearly*

This is followed (now back within the dream) by the appearance of a fair lady, revealing herself as Holy Church and explaining to the bewildered dreamer the visionary scene in some detail. The reader is thus introduced to the pressing subject of indirect discourse and hidden meaning waiting to be disclosed. At first, homiletic aid is freely given, and Holy Church acts as a beneficient teacher in the tradition of what has been described as 'vertical debate' literature, where the dreamer is granted straightforward instruction by some superior authority, not without stern reproof for his ignorance and lack of comprehension:

> 'Thow doted daffe!' quod she, 'dulle are thi wittes.   *stupid fool*
> To litel Latyn thow lernedest, leode, in thi youthe: *Too, fellow*
> *Heu michi quod sterilem duxi vitam iuvenilem!* (I, 140–141a)
>   *Alas, what a fruitless life I have led in my youth*

Examples of this kind of dream revelation are the *Consolatio Philosophiae* by Boece, one of the most widely read and influential books of the Middle Ages, and Alan of Lille's *De Planctu Naturae*. In the *Roman de la Rose*, Lady Reason descends from a tower to give advice to the dreamer, and there can be little doubt that Langland was aware of and influenced by this tradition. Here, however, after some preliminary explanation and instruction, there is a complete change of method with the end of the first passus: the instructress takes leave of the dreamer and directs his attention to a new scene, with an implicit appeal to his own powers of exegesis. In fact, Holy Church has reminded him in plain words and with supporting biblical quotation of the basic principles of the Christian faith and the one thing needful for salvation. There is a clear echo of the gospel in her insistence, three times repeated, that Truth is the one treasure that passes every other consideration:

> Whan alle tresors arn tried, Truthe is the beste.
> Lereth it th[u]s lewed men, for lettred it knoweth –
> *Teach, without education, educated*
> That Treuthe is tresor the trieste on erthe.' (I, 135–7)   *most tried*

In a way, this could end any further instruction, but, like other dreamers in this genre, Langland's cannot be satisfied with simple home truths, but insists on questioning every plain statement and demanding answers to his ever more sophisticated and speculative and yet urgent uncertainties. On his knees, he implores to continue her teaching, to 'Kenne me bi som craft to knowe the false' (II, 4). Yet, instead of further explanation, the dreamer is treated to a dramatic scene, representing the universal law of social unrest by the corrupting power of money and human greed. This is one of the subjects that runs through the whole of the poem in constantly changing guise. It is closely related to the dreamer's disgust with the abuses of the established church and its most eloquent representatives, especially corrupt priests and the friars.

The first episodes (Vision I, passus I-IV) attempt to explore the working of society and government within a framework of dramatic action and debate. On the literal story-level, this is a political fable, describing a ruler's problems in choosing his advisers and the potentially corrupting power of money. Lady Meed obviously represents all that money and wealth can effect, particularly in the way of influencing and perverting men and women. The intended marriage of the Lady to the egregious villain 'False Fickle-Tongue', like much of the allegory at this stage, hardly needs any gloss. It is evident that the vision is concerned with the dangerous liaison between civil authority and money, with the accompanying vices of bribery, nepotism and injustice. It also becomes clear enough that Conscience, and later Reason, represent the opposing forces of Christian integrity and responsible clear sense, within a framework of unquestioned biblical authority. Both parties use scriptural quotations for argument, both in English and in Latin, especially where phrases or passages familiar from homiletic and liturgical practice are employed. What is, perhaps, most original here, is the fusion of vivid narrative and intellectual debate and the simultaneous appearance of personifications representing political functions and those that speak for certain social, moral or theological concepts. I think that much of this eclectic use of allegory poses fewer problems to the unsophisticated reader than, perhaps, to the scholar interested in analysing the conventions and the functions of allegory. But it is clear that the poet seems less concerned with established poetical and rhetorical conventions than with his search for a rhetoric that best conveys his particular questions, uncertainties and hopes.[29]

The same applies to the second vision, divided from the first by the brief waking episode already quoted (V, 3–12), and introducing a new aspect of the general state of the community. More important, or at least no less urgent, than the political situation is the moral and spiritual attitude of the individual, his personal determination and commitment to achieve his salvation. The first step is confession and repentance, prefaced by a penitential sermon preached by Reason, but more powerfully and poetically dramatised by a famous episode, the confessional procession of the Deadly Sins. Here again, a familiar homiletic convention is transformed into a most original and expressive pageant, combining vivid character-sketches with pungent satire and memorable scenes of vice and debauchery. Some of the personifications, like Wrath, Envy and Avarice, describe their activities, others act them out before the reader's eyes, like Gluttony. His performance shows Langland's brilliant ability to create dramatic scenes, rich with comic and colourful domestic detail: the Glutton is diverted from his walk to church by the innkeepers' soliciting, and his first attempt at confession ends in bed, where he has to be conveyed by his wife and the servant and where he snores all through the weekend until Sunday sunset. His first words on waking up are 'Where is the bowl?', but his wife and his own conscience bring him to a sense of sin: he listens to 'Repentance' and he promises to reform and to obey his aunt 'Abstinence' whom he has hated all his life (V, 297–385).

The techniques used here are largely traditional, though employed with unusual gusto and unorthodox freedom.[30] There is no apparent consistency in the conception of some of these personifications: are they just typical examples of the sins they personify, or are they meant to be the general, abstract principle behind them, like the protagonists of the *Psychomachia* of the early Christian poet Prudentius? It is not untypical of the medieval preacher or spiritual demagogue, like Chaucer's Pardoner, to blur the lines of demarcation between quite different rhetorical strategies. The homiletic drive behind the text is clear and poignant enough.

The poet's method, at first comparatively lucid and hardly unfamiliar to the contemporary reader, gradually moves into more unconventional and exploratory areas, as the dreamer's journey continues. Thus, the discourse proceeds from the pageant of the sins to more general questions of confession and contrition and from picturesque personification to more abstract concepts. The combination is often at first sight surprising, but, I believe, hardly ever confusing as regards its direction. A typical example occurs at the end of the Deadly Sins' procession:

> Roberd the robbere on *Reddite* loked,   *'Give back'*
> And for ther was noght wher[with], he wepte swithe soore.   *most pitifully*
> And yet the synfulle sherewe seide to hymselfe: *wretch*
> 'Crist, that on Calvarie upon the cros deidest,
> Tho Dysmas my brother besoughte thee of grace,   *At that time,*
> And haddest mercy on that man for *Memento* sake,
> So rewe on this Rober[d] that *Reddere* ne have.   *have pity, means to restore*
> Ne nevere wene to wynne with craft that I knowe;   *imagine, earn, skill*
> But for thi muchel mercy mitigacion I biseche:
> Dampne me noght at Domesday for that I dide so ille!'
>   What bifel of this feloun I kan noght faire shewe.

Wel I woot he wepte faste water with hise eighen,	
And knoweliched his [coupe] to Crist yet eftsoones,	*revealed, guilt, again*
That *Penitentia* his pik he sholde polshe newe	*pikestaff, freshly polish*
And lepe with hym over land al his lif tyme,	*accompany him*
For he hadde leyen by *Latro*, Luciferis Aunte. (V, 462–77)	*lain, Robbery*

The sense of the passage is perfectly clear, although there is such a puzzling mixture of poetic and homiletic conventions. The underlying action suggests a dramatic scene of confession and contrition, with clear references to the Crucifixion and to the vital problem of restitution, an important issue in confessional theory and practice. The use of Latin might point towards a more clerkly audience, but for the most part it does not go beyond relatively familiar homiletic terminology or biblical quotation from liturgical manuals.[31] Nevertheless, the technique is highly original, though it does not seem to have stood in the way of the text's enormous popularity.

This applies, too, to the poem's most stunning image, the figure of Piers the Plowman, emerging suddenly out of nowhere and soon assuming a commanding position of spiritual authority. Much has been written about him,[32] but again, there is no real indefiniteness as to his overall significance and function in the poem, though he appears in different guises and seems to change shape and substance in the course of the dreamer's quest.

On his first entrance into the vision, he seems merely another character in the poem's social panorama, a representative of the labouring community, as opposed to those that make religion their profession. Moved by contrition, everyone starts for a pilgrimage to Truth, but nobody knows the way, least of all the professional pilgrim who has visited all the traditional Holy places (V, 515–36). This is evidently not where salvation can be achieved. At this moment, Piers makes his unexpected entry:

'Peter!' quod a Plowman, and putte forth his heved,	*head*
'I knowe hym as kyndely as clerc doth hise bokes.	*intimately*
Conscience and Kynde Wit kenned me to his place	*showed*
And diden me suren hym [siththen] sikerly to serven hym for evere,	
	made me assure him
Bothe to sowe and to sette the whyle I swynke myghte.	*plant, work*
I have ben his folwere al this fourty wynter – (V, 537–42)	

It hardly needs any explanation that there is a deliberate opposition between demonstrative religious routine and simple day-to-day practical duty and humble activity. Langland was certainly not the first to celebrate the ploughman's station as the model of Christian humility and selfless service,[33] but the way he elevates this figure into a position as the chief representative of the perfect Christian, even the Christ-like mediator between man and God and the sole guide to salvation, makes this a unique creation and one that soon became popular beyond the actual familiarity of the text as a whole.

At first, Piers offers practical instruction and guidance to the people, teaching plain moral precepts according to Christian tradition and the Gospels. Soon, however, the conflict between simple home truths and prescriptive clerical thinking once more erupts, in the famous episode of the Pardon sent from Truth. This, again, has more than one layer of meaning and need not confuse the unsophisticated reader, though it touches more complicated issues and invites closer scrutiny. As in many other parts of the poem, dramatic action is fused with debate on larger concepts. The pardon Piers receives seems, at least in one respect, rather a denial of official pardon than an effective document and a promise that practical obedience to biblical teaching and dutiful activity is more important than indulgences granted by clerical authority. This is why it divides the recipients and provokes a heated discussion between a priest and Piers. The actual content of the message seems no more than a truism, but this only serves to cast doubt on the whole concept of pardon as a legal document rather than a reward for active Christian service.[34] This is why the priest denies that it is a pardon at all, and Piers, after tearing the document in a spontaneous gesture of anger, decides that he will turn his plough into prayers and penance. The fact that this brief dramatic incident is missing from the C-version suggests that it was liable to be misunderstood by early readers or that the author himself had doubts about its intended effect. The C-text also omits a brief passage in which Piers explains to the contemptuous priest where he acquired his 'learning':

> 'Abstynence the Abbesse,' quod Piers, 'myn a.b.c. me taughte,
> And Conscience cam afterward and kenned me muche moore,'   *taught*
> (VII, 133–4)

The C-text, instead, has a long passage on true and false hermits, a spirited specimen of the author's vigour as satirist and social critic. This is in line with that version's tendency to leave out possible obscurities and be more explicit in its verdicts on true or false, right or wrong.

It is likely, if we attach due weight to the witness of the Z-version, that the poem in its earliest form ended here, with an assertion of the importance of dream-visions and an appeal to call on God's mercy and to work for 'Do-well' to vouch for us on the Day of Judgement. In several manuscripts, this first part is described as *visio*, to distinguish it from the following sections. The division has little authorial sanction, but it certainly helps to grasp the poem's overall structure, in addition to the rather loose division into passus. The second vision clearly concludes an important argument, the need for social and spiritual reform and penitence, in society as well as in the individual, and it is likely that at this point something like a new beginning and an expansion of the whole plan was projected.[35]

The third vision noticeably introduces a somewhat different discourse, beginning with the dreamer's search for Do-wel and leading into much more theologically sophisticated and intellectually demanding debate through changing encounters with personifications of mental faculties and spiritual guides. Another concept that from now on plays a major part in the dreamer's quest is the three-part gradation of the Christian's ultimate destination into Do-wel, Do-bet and Do-best, in other words, degrees of perfection and a hierarchy of aims on the passage to salvation. It is first spelt out by Thought, a representation of the dreamer's own intellectual faculty and its groping for helpful insight. It is Thought who suggests the first definition of the three steps towards complete realisation of God's will. From the first, however, the three are not offered as a choice of careers, as simple honest labour, humility and charity, or contemplation and holiness, but essentially they are inseparable 'in that Dowel and Dobet must always be inspired by the possibility of Dobest'.[36]

After the first mental sketch presented by Thought, the Dreamer is passed on to Wit, a further aspect of his own mind, understanding by reflection and experience through the senses. The three days in discussion with Thought, before Wit is met, are a graphic description of intellectual development and progress of understanding. Wit provides further insight into the nature of Dowel, Do-bet and Do-best, partly by introducing new personifications to illustrate the moral hierarchy, such as 'Kynde', as the creative power of God and his beloved *Anima*, who is pursued by Satan and has been placed by 'Kynde' under the protection of Do-wel and his daughter Do-bet.

Wit has hardly developed his particular answer to the dreamer's inquiry and offered one further explanation of the proper path to perfection, when he is interrupted and berated by his wife, 'Study', who tells him that he has been casting pearls before swine and proceeds to discuss questions of true and false learning. She evidently believes that the dreamer should do some intellectual homework before aspiring to any higher knowledge, and, as a reward for his humility, directs him to her cousin 'Clergy' and his wife 'Scripture'. It is difficult to discover a consistent philosophical system behind this rambling sequence of didactic encounters, but there is an obvious progression in the way various traditional lines of argument are explored.

Argument is constantly supported by glimpses of allegorical narrative, drawing on images of family relationship, social bonds or political rank. The reader is time and again forced to switch from one kind of discourse to another. One can only wonder whether this caused problems to the less educated medieval reader or listener, unfamiliar with theological terminology; but then, unsophisticated attention to the underlying story of a desperate quest and concentration on the homiletic message will make the text sufficiently arresting and relevant. On one level the narrative resembles that of one of those interminable romances whose evident appeal lay in their inexhaustible wealth of incident and whose structure, at least for the modern reader, is anything but orderly or symmetrical. On another level, we have a repeated recurrence of question, answer, reproach and instruction, as in many didactic dream allegories or fictional disputations. There is more than one point where an element of impatience or frustration informs the dreamer's reaction to all these conflicting voices offering advice, as in his retort to 'Scripture':

'This is long lesson,' quod I, 'and litel am I the wiser!
Where Dowel is and Dobet derkliche ye shewen.   *obscurely*
Manye tales ye tellen that Theologie lerneth,   *teaches*
And that I man maad was, and my name yentred   *entered*
In the legende of lif longe er I were,   *Book of Life*,[37] *before I existed*
Or elles unwriten for som wikkednesse, as Holy Writ witnesseth:
Nemo ascendit ad celum nisi qui de celo descendit. (X, 371–6a)[38]

On the other side, the dreamer is almost constantly rebuked by the figures he questions, either for his dullness, his lack of perseverance, or his refusal to act in obedience to the simple will of God instead of indulging in fruitless intellectual speculation. At the same time, the series of debates makes ample use of bookish wisdom and scholastic method, in a continuous effort not to leave any tried means of obtaining further wisdom unattempted. The whole quest thus assumes a distinctly dramatic character, due to the dreamer's passion for knowledge, his anger at the glaring abuses of the clear Gospel truth and the arrogance of so many of the Church's representatives who ought to know better.

The extant manuscripts do not allow us to be quite certain at what precise point the A-version – and, if we assume the traditional order, Langland's first complete attempt – broke off, but it is likely that the poet came to a first halt when the dreamer had been instructed about the need for penance and for striving after Do-best. The B-version continues the debate and first explores the possibility of salvation without the old law, not by formal obedience to any rigid commandments, but through God's mercy alone. This raises a number of fundamental theological issues, fervently discussed during the thirteenth and fourteenth centuries, in particular predestination, the effect of good works and the question of salvation by merit or grace.[39]

After another rough rebuke by Scripture, the dreamer, weeping and angry with her speech, falls asleep again and at a deeper level has another dream, a vision within his vision, a device unique in Middle English literature. This dream includes a new image of the dreamer's whole life within a world seen through a mirror, a deceptive apparition promising a life based on false values. His progress is at first governed by Fortune and two of her handmaids, '*Concupiscentia carnis*' and 'Coveitise of Eighes' who induce him to waste more than forty years of his life and to forget about Do-wel and Do-bet, until Elde (Old Age) and Holyness catch up with him and return him to a sense of his sinfulness and need for repentance. But because of his poverty the Friars are not interested in him, which provokes the question of the use of learning for achieving salvation and, ultimately, the relative values of individual effort and redemption. More guidance comes from 'Lewte' (Loyalty), a personification already introduced as early as the Prologue (126) and embracing, within the poem, a variety of virtues, even Christ himself. He points out the misuse of learning by the Friars and implicitly justifies the poet's criticism of them on the grounds that we should correct, not hate, our erring brethren. There is an explicit reference to Christ's eschatological parable of the royal wedding, related in the Gospel of St Matthew (xx, 1–24), ending in the harsh verdict, 'many are called, but few are chosen'. It frightens the dreamer and makes him fear for his own salvation. The theological question suddenly becomes a very personal matter of life and death:

> Al for tene of hir text trembled myn herte,   *distress*
> And in a weer gan I wexe, and with myself to dispute   *became perplexed*
> Wheither I were chose or noght chose; on Holy Chirche I thoughte,
> That underfonged me atte font for oon of Goddes chosene.[40]   *received*

> For Crist cleped us alle, come if we wolde –   *called*
> Sarsens and scismatikes, and so he dide the Jewes: (XI, 115–20)   *Pagans*

This leads to another fundamental question, in particular the salvation of the unbaptised and the heathen, and to renewed doubt as to the authority and efficacy of book-learning. For once, a personification of spiritual authority, 'Scripture', actually assents to the dreamer's conclusion that contrition can win mercy in spite of a sinful life. But even 'Scripture', affirming 'what our bokes telleth' (XI, 139), is overruled and corrected by a new character who breaks in:

> 'Ye, baw for bokes!' quod oon was broken out of helle
> Highte Troianus, a trewe knyght, took witnesse at a pope   *Called Trajan*
> How he was ded and dampned to dwellen in pyne   *torment*
> For an uncristene creature: 'Clerkes wite the sothe –   *unbaptised*
> That al the clergie under Crist ne myghte me cracche fro helle   *snatch*
> But oonliche love and leautee of my lawful domes.   *justice, judgements*
> (XI, 140–5)

The legend of the Roman Emperor Trajan (AD 98–117), who was released out of Hell by the intercession of Pope Gregory (AD 590–604), was often told as an example of that great Pope's power and charity. The surprising appearance of the legend's subject is a typical illustration of Langland's narrative method, proceeding by sudden changes of dramatis personae and startling entrances, without particular attention to consistency of illusion or levels of reality. The Roman emperor clearly belongs to a different category of fictional character from the other personifications in this episode; yet there is no real confusion as to what he stands for. Once the reader has been absorbed by the world of the poet's vision, he or she will surely accept the simultaneous appearance of figures from dissimilar modes of discourse. It is the absence of the comparative lucidity and precision of the allegories in the tradition of the *Roman de la Rose* that is perhaps the most distinctive feature of *Piers Plowman*, but this evidently has not been an obstacle to its wide appeal.

The testimony of Trajan is a powerful argument in the debate about the surest way to salvation, but it is also a most controversial one because of the claim that the observance of Christian duties and eccleciastic discipline are neither necessary nor unfailing remedies:

> . . . I saved, as ye may see, withouten syngynge of masses,
> By love and by lernyng of my lyvynge in truthe,
> Broughte me fro bitter peyne ther no biddyng myghte. (XI, 150–2)   *praying*

Within the context of the whole poem, this does not, of course, suggest that baptism and all the authority of the Christian Church can be dispensed with. Langland is nothing less than an advocate of a general religion of benevolence. He is, however, uncompromising in his insistence on priorities and impatient with self-assured legalism and false securities, especially by superior learning. Trajan himself, who was baptised immediately after his rescue from Hell, turns out to be a most eloquent spokesman of true Christian values:

'Lawe withouten love,' quod Troianus, 'ley there a bene –
                                                            not worth a bean
Or any science under sonne, the sevene arts and alle!
– But thei ben lerned for Oure Lordes love, lost is al the tyme,   *Unless*
For no cause to cacche silver therby, ne to be called a maister,   *earn*
But al for love of Oure Lord and the bet to love the peple.'
                                            (XI, 170–4)[41]

The dream within the dream continues with a lively vision of God's creation and an exchange between the dreamer and Reason on the difference between man's position, confronted with existential choices, and the rest of the creation, ordered by Reason in complete harmony. Once more the dreamer is chided for his lack of understanding, and he awakens, deeply disappointed and angry for having missed the rest of the dream. He believes that now at least he has learnt what Do-wel is, until he is questioned by another character he has not met before, who tells him that his rash impatience has prevented him from receiving more instruction by Reason and Clergy. This new personification introduces himself as 'Imaginatif', and explains that he has followed him for forty-five years, to warn him against wasting time and think more of his old age and amend his life. The name of this new teacher derives from what Medieval psychology defined as the *vis imaginativa*, the faculty of making images and abstract ideas out of what our senses experience.

'Imaginatif' first objects to the dreamer's writing poetry on the grounds that there are enough books to teach us what is necessary for salvation. The dreamer's defence, after a hasty excuse, adducing poetry's recreational function, seems to me the most explicit justification of the whole poem, not because it claims to be original poetry or an indispensable record of the past, but because it tries to do what apparently no other form of instruction has achieved so far. There are not, the poet retorts, books sufficient to tell us the essential truths:

... if ther were any wight that wolde me telle
What were Dowel and Dobet and Dobest at the laste,
Wolde I nevere do werk, but wende to holi chirche   *go*
And there bidde my bedes but whan ich ete or slepe.' (XII, 25–8)   *prayers*

It seems certain to me that the dreamer here says what Langland himself would describe as the purpose of his writing, borne out by the form of his poem. From the start, he has made it clear in no uncertain terms that he disapproves of frivolous entertainment, of 'japeres and jangleres, Judas children, / Feynen hem fantasies, and fooles hem maketh' (Prologue, 35–6)[42] and he evidently felt the necessity for an apology for poetry, even the kind of poetry he himself is writing. This is why he mentions Cato's familiar line about the need for some pleasure between daily cares (XII, 21–2: 'as I do whan I make [*write poetry*]') only in passing, with the feeble admission, 'somwhat me to excuse', even though he agrees with Imaginatif's objections. His real justification is the lack of genuinely helpful instruction in fundamental questions of faith. There is no doubt that he is conversant with the classical arguments in favour of poetry, yet for his own activity he accepts practically only the use of poetry for instruction and correction, including satire. The contrast to Chaucer's poetics could hardly be more radical. Learning, as the following debate with 'Imaginatif' insists, is only useful to the extent that all books are, in the last resort, inspired by God himself.

Imaginatif, then, is one way of arriving at knowledge through imaginative observation of life and reading the scripture, and he leaves the dreamer with the decided assurance that just action will be recognised and rewarded by God. It is significant that in parting, Imaginatif reminds the Dreamer of the psalmist's confident belief: *Si ambulavero in medio umbre mortis* [*Ne timebo mala, quoniam tu mecum es*].[43] This had been quoted defiantly by Piers in the face of the provocative 'pardon' in Passus VII (116–17). The whole debate in vision three has confirmed this need for unquestioning trust in God's mercy, above the letter of academic learning.

Between 'Imaginatif's' sudden disappearance and the next vision, there is a brief interlude, suggesting a period of 'many yer', in which the dreamer wanders about like a mendicant and reflects on what has been revealed to him. Without taking this passage literally, as an autobiographical document or the like, it is clear that the author wants to suggest that the best part of a lifetime can be (and has often been) spent pondering on the mysterious relationship between God's free grace and the law requiring justice and truth in our own lives. What follows in the text is therefore not an immediate continuation of the previous vision, but something like a new start, underlined by a change in allegorical method. After the predominantly discursive progression of the third vision, the new dream returns to a more narrative mode. The fourth vision (Passus XIII and XIV) contains two vivid scenes, the dinner with 'Clergie', 'Patience', the 'Doctor' and 'Conscience', and the encounter with Haukyn, a new character, evidently a representative of the sinful layman seeking grace.

The dinner at the house of 'Conscience' provides a telling context for the academic conversation concerning the nature of Dowel. The allegory speaks by graphic images and social parable. Will and Patience are placed at some distance from the High Table, where the Doctor and Clergy are feasting by themselves at the place of honour, and though they are served with food prepared from the writings of the Church Fathers and the Evangelists, they eat the choicest morsels and refined dishes, whereas Patience and the dreamer are only offered simple bread and drink, the ordinary pilgrim's fare. Langland has returned to an allegorical mode that seems completely unconcerned with consistency, deliberately and unashamedly conflating literal and metaphorical items, even English and Latin expressions, homely images and learned terms, in a bold if not entirely unconventional homiletic simile:

> Conscience ful curteisly tho commaunded Scripture
> Bifore Pacience breed to brynge and me that was his mette.   *bread, companion*
> He sette a sour loof toforn us and seide, '*Agite penitenciam,*'   '*Do penance*'
> And siththe he drough us drynke: '*Dia perseverans* –
>   then, '*Long persevering*'[44]
> As longe,' quod he 'as lif and lycame may dure.'   *body, last*
> 'Here is propre service,' quod Pacience, 'ther fareth no prince bettre!'
>   (XIII, 46–51)

Again, there is nothing obscure about this method. To the unsophisticated reader it may even be more persuasive than mere learned discourse. The phenomenal success of John Bunyan's allegorical narrative *The Pilgrim's Progress* (1676–84) demonstrates the popular appeal of such didactic narrative. Both the message and the satire are to a large extent self-explanatory. Will wants to protest against spiritual arrogance, but is calmed by Patience, who advises against emotional refutation or rudeness. Still, he cannot refrain from giving the doctor a piece of his mind, when he smugly explains that Do-wel is the same as loving your neighbour:

> 'By this day, sire doctour,' quod I, 'thanne be ye noght in Dowel!
> For ye han harmed us two in that ye eten the puddyng,
> Mortrews and oother mete – and we no morsel hadde. . . .   *stews*
> I wolde permute my penaunce with youre – for I am in point to   *exchange*
>   dowel.' (XIII, 106–8, 111)

Conscience intervenes to strike a conciliatory note and (unsuccessfully) tries to get a more satisfactory explanation from the doctor, but failing, she turns to 'Clergie', addressed more familiarly in the singular ('Now thow, Clergie', XIII, 119) who evidently stands for the more formal and academic aspect of church doctrine. He, surprisingly, has to concede that there are limits to his own knowledge and authority. It is another instance of Langland's singularly creative imagination that at this point there is a reminder of Piers Plowman as the ideal mediator between man and God, clerkly learning and simple Christian practice. It is Clergie who presents this new description of Piers:

> For oon Piers the Plowman hath impugned us alle,   *found fault with*
> And set alle sciences at a sop save love one;   *worthless thing, alone*
> And no text ne taketh to mayntene his cause
> But *Dilige Deum* and *Domine quis habitabit* . . .[45]
> And seith that Dowel and Dobet arn two infinites,
> Which infinites with a feith fynden out Dobest,
> Which shal save mannes soule – thus seith Piers the Plowman.'
>   (XIII, 124–30)

Even Conscience cannot add to this, but looks forward to another meeting with Piers who alone can offer a final solution to the most existential questions. Thus, Conscience, with Patience and Will, leave the dinner circle and the three embark on a new pilgrimage rather than engage in more theoretical debate. In parting, Conscience tells 'Clergie',

> 'Me were levere, by Oure Lord, and I lyve sholde,   *I would prefer, if I*
> Have pacience parfitliche than half thi pak of bokes!' (XIII, 201–2) *perfectly*

'Clergie', however, is not repudiated, and the parting is in a conciliatory spirit suggesting a division of tasks. James Simpson has expressed it very well: 'a reconciliation takes place which imaginatively represents the fundamental, ideal relation between formal education and experiential knowledge in the poem'.[46] 'Clergie' is left to look after his duty and to see to the instruction of children 'and oothere folk' (XIII, 214).

Once more, the pilgrims set out, like the courtly knights in a romance of chivalry, on a never-concluded quest for the ideal goal rather than a clearly defined destination, and, as one would expect, there is immediately another strange encounter, one more of Langland's brilliantly puzzling inventions. As in the first part of this (the fourth) vision, academic debate is supported, if not replaced, by dramatic action and visual, almost emblematic images. The person the pilgrims meet next is a curious blend of abstract personification and vaguely individualised character with a Christian name, Haukyn. He calls himself *Activa Vita* and thus stands for the practical aspect of Christian activity, as opposed to sinful idleness. He represents a 'profession' (if it can be called that) very low in the social scale, a 'minstrel', as he appears to the pilgrims, who is yet unable or unwilling to perform the tasks usually associated with minstrels, musical entertainment, singing, dancing, jesting and juggling, but sells wafers, light refreshment, to make a precarious living for himself and his family.[47] Yet, it soon becomes evident that the active life is anything but sinless: Haukyn's coat is soiled and dirty, full of clear signs of an unclean life, and the discourse once more returns to the question of penitence and the still unresolved problem of human effort and the achieving of salvation by the power of Dowell. The dramatic quality of the encounter and the visual sign-language of the scene suggest that Langland has deliberately chosen another strategy to approach the central subject of his poem, not necessarily changed direction. The crucial part allotted to Patience in this vision, however, gives a new emphasis to the life of devotion and prayer, as opposed to ceaseless activity and effort. When Haukyn begins to recount his sinful life, we are conspicuously reminded of the Deadly Sins' confession in Passus V, but, this time, all the sins committed by the active person are concentrated in one figure, whose confession thus takes on a far more personal and urgent character and whose tears of contrition appear more emotionally charged than in an allegorical representation of sin and repentance. There is also a change of tone when the personification of Patience offers his remedy against the afflictions of sin, available to every human being, not through any formal compliance with clerical prescriptions, but through strict observance of patient poverty and avoiding all temptation by worldly possessions. It is a distinctly more emotional than didactic appeal: the fourth vision ends with Haukyn bewailing his offences against God's love and the dreamer awaking to a life of lone hopelessness. He literally arrives at the end of his wit and despairs of ever truly knowing Do-wel. In the end, Reason sends him another sleep, with a new vision and a new guide in the figure of 'Anima', another aspect of the human soul.

The terminology in this sequence seems to have troubled the author himself, because in the C-version the same speaker is renamed *Liberum Arbitrium*, i.e. 'free will', man's freedom to make moral choices.[48] His appearance in C follows immediately on Patience's last speech (B XIV, 319), without Haukyn's tearful contrition. In both versions, however, the new character explains that he goes by different names, according to his various functions within the complete person. The speech is, in fact, a paraphrase and partly literal quotation of a famous passage from Isidore of Seville's *Etymologiae*, where the names of *anima* are listed as *mens* (Thought), *memoria* (Memory), *ratio* (Reason), *sensus* (Sense), *amor* (Love), *conscientia* (Conscience) and *spiritus* (Spirit). *Anima* then treats Will to a long sermon on the authority and the history of the Church, with liberal use of supporting quotation from the Church Fathers and Holy Scripture. In contrast to what has gone before, *anima* hardly engages in theological subtleties and scholarly controversy, but endeavours to bring the listener to a sense of what is essential to a life of Christian humility and devotion. Once more, the emphasis seems on instruction rather than on showing or on action. The discourse turns on the subject of charity and the office of the Church, whose duty it is to instil charity, not to offend by the example of avaricious priests and friars.

In the course of Anima's exposition, Charity seems to change from an abstract concept of mere spiritual quality into a character whose actions express what he stands for; when Will wants to meet this perfect creature, he is told that it is impossible to know Charity without the help of Piers the Plowman. It is a puzzling statement, made even more mysterious by Anima's further insistence that this is the only way, apparently repudiating all rhetoric, academic discourse and even formal rite:

> 'Therefore by colour ne by clergie knowe shaltow hym nevere, *appearance*
> Neither thorugh wordes ne werkes, but thorugh wil oone, *alone*
> And that knoweth no clerk ne creature on erthe
> But Piers the Plowman – *Petrus, id est Christus.*[49] (XV, 209–12)

Again, this is a passage Langland apparently decided to omit when revising the poem. The C-version only has the briefest reference to Piers, without suggesting his near-identity with Christ, the rock and the foundation of the Church. There is much to be said for the suggestion that Langland, when revising his text and creating the C-version, was attempting to straighten up potentially obscure or misleading passages, perhaps even at the expense of poetic intensity and rich suggestiveness.

The fifth vision (Passus XV–XVII) is particularly difficult in this respect, yet at the same time astonishing by the boldness of its imagery and the daring juxtaposition of scriptural characters, homiletic personifications and animated visual demonstration.[50]

Again, Piers the Plowman appears in person, omitted in the C-version, and the mere mention of his name makes Will swoon with joy. It is Piers who in this version explains to Will, in an inner dream, the vision of the Tree of Charity – a poetic evocation that would require a chapter of its own[51] – and the meaning of the strange episode, combining hints of Old Testament anticipations of Christian beliefs and culminating in the appearances of Abraham ('*Fides*' [Faith]), Moses ('*Spes*' [Hope]), and, last, the Good Samaritan, perfect embodiment of practical Charity and the most moving teacher-guide so far, whose call to repentance ends this vision. The dreamer, once again, is left alone for an indefinite period, metaphorically described as 'al my lif tyme' (XVIII, 3), till, 'wery of the world', at the approach of Lent he falls into a long sleep and hears the cries associated with Palm Sunday.

The instruction Will has been receiving in the course of his visions so far has steadily grown in intensity and at the same time moved further away from theological discourse. With the sixth vision, the poem reaches the heart of the gospel narrative and, simultaneously, of the liturgy appropriate to the approaching passion of our Lord, perceived through a veil of seemingly contradictory images, almost mystically enigmatic in their determined disregard of consistency. Will's bewildered request for some explanation is answered in a hardly less obscure manner, in particular by the unprecedented fusion of the good Samaritan, Piers the Plowman and Christ himself – perhaps the most daring image so far:

> Oon semblable to the Samaritan, and somdeel to Piers the Plowman,
>   *resembling, somewhat*
> Barefoot on an asse bak bootles cam prikye,   *riding*
> Withouten spores other spere; sprakliche he loked,   *lively*
> As is the kynde of a knyght that comes to be dubbed,   *manner*
> To geten hym gilte spores on galoches ycouped.   *slashed shoes*
>   Thanne was Feith in a fenestre, and cryde 'A Fili David!'
>   *window, Son of David*[52]
> As dooth an heraud of armes when aventrous cometh to justes.
>   *adventurous knights, joust*
> Olde Jewes of Jerusalem for joye thei songen,
> *Benedictus qui venit in nomine Domini.*
>   *'Blessed is he that comes in the name of the Lord'*
>   Thanne I frayned at Feith what al that fare bymente, *asked, business meant*
> And who sholde juste in Jerusalem. 'Jesus', he seide,
> And fecche that the fend claymeth, Piers fruyt the Plowman.'   *the fruit of*
>   'Is Piers in this place?' quod I, and he preynte on me.   *winked*
>   'This Jesus of his gentries wol juste in Piers armes,   *in his nobility*
> In his helm and his haubergeon, *humana natura.*   *mail coat, human nature*
> That Crist be noght biknowe here for *consummatus Deus,*
>   *acknowledged as fully God himself*
> In Piers paltok the Plowman this prikiere shal ryde;   *jacket, horseman*
> For no dynt shal hym dere as *in deitate Patris.'*
>   *blow, hurt, in his divine capacity as the Father* (XVIII, 10–26)

The stunning vision and Will's predictable questions are the poet's attempt to present and simultaneously explain the miracle of Christ's passion as a historic event, perceived through the metaphor of a courtly tournament, and at the same time, as a divine mystery, to be described only in theological (Latin) terms, but, without scholarly definition, accepted in simple belief. It is clear that Piers the Plowman has by now assumed the status of an ideal representative of humankind who, symbolically speaking, lends his human form to the Son of God, Christ, for decisive, literally 'crucial' single combat with our Fiend. The simile, though unexpected, is not really obscure. It is difficult to think of a more accurate and poignant description of what Christianity has always called our redemption through the vicarious sacrificial death and victory of Christ. The Gospel account of Jesus' entry into Jerusalem (Matthew xxi, 1–10), used in the liturgy of Lent and Eastertide, is intertwined with the dramaturgy and the language of courtly romance. Piers appears as a knight in a scene that has all the properties of a chivalrous combat, familiar enough to Langland's audience to convey a sense of immediate intelligibility and relevance. Such comparisons are, of course, not new in the homiletic discourse of the Middle Ages; what is so startlingly original in *Piers Plowman* is the almost imperceptible transition from one kind of reality into another, from the world of romance to the world of the Gospel, from the fiction of dream allegories to that of sermon rhetoric.

At the end of the sixth vision, when Will is woken by Easter bells and calls his wife and daughter to join him on the way to worship the resurrection of our Lord, the poem seems to assume a new degree of personal directness and immediacy. It is at this stage, all of a sudden, that Will is concerned with producing a record of his vision before himself going to church, only to meet another overwhelming and bewildering dream:

> Thus I awaked and wroot what I hadde ydremed,
> And dighte me derely, and dide me to chirche,   *dressed neatly, went*
> To here holly the masse and to be housled after.   *receive communion*
> In myddes of the masse, tho men yede to offryng,   *when, went, offertory*
> I fel eftsoones asleepe – and sodeynly me mette   *again, dreamt*
> That Piers the Plowman was peynted al blody,
> And com in with a cros before the comune peple,
> And right lik in alle lymes to Oure Lord Jesu.   *all his shape*
>   And thanne called I Conscience to kenne me the sothe: *teach*
> 'Is this Jesus the justere,' quod I, 'that Jewes dide to dethe?   *jouster, killed*
> Or it is Piers the Plowman! Who peynted hym so rede?'
>   Quod Conscience, and kneled tho, 'Thise arn [hise] armes –
> Hise colours and his cote armure; ac he that cometh so blody   *coat-of-arms*
> Is Crist with his cros, conquerour of Cristene.' (XIX, 1–14)

Again, at the end of this, the penultimate, passus, Will writes down what he has seen. This seems to give particular prominence to this passus, with its emphasis on Christ's role in the gospel account of our salvation. In an important way, therefore, this vision marks the climax of what is ultimately revealed to Will, the very centre of the Christian faith. In Langland's world, however, it is a message that cannot be communicated and received without the medium of the Church and its ordained servants, whether they be bishops, monks or simple priests. It is only natural, therefore, that the vision of Christ's suffering and resurrection leads straight into the brief account of Pentecost and the birth and growth of the Christian Church. It is made clear at this stage that Piers the Plowman is closely related to Christ's promotion of St Peter as the first of the apostles and the rock upon which the Church is to be built. Once more, Piers seems to be actually identified as the recipient of Christ's command and rightful substitute on earth, with the power 'To bynde and unbynde bothe here and ellis, / And assoille men of alle synnes save of dette one' (XIX, 190–1). At the same time, Piers is not only spiritual leader, but a model of humility and lack of avaricious ambition. He expects neither honour nor worship, neither wealth nor glamorous authority. In complete accordance with the teaching of Jesus, he leads the lowly life of a ploughman, in the spiritual as well as in the literal sense. Langland describes his activity as one where preaching and doing go hand in hand; traditional images and metaphors suggest the particular dignity of manual labour, especially farm-work, by equating it with pastoral duty and sowing the word of God. There is no slighting of Gospel authority or the teaching of the church fathers, but these texts are not to be revered as formal laws, propping up any spiritual church hierarchy; they are valuable only in so far as they support the virtuous life of the community.

Soon Langland again throws himself into the midst of practical issues, religious controversy and Church politics. Though he is evidently a firm believer in the primacy of scriptural authority, some of his most passionate concern is with the dangers and abuses manifested in the realities and afflictions of the Christian community, and it is not long before he returns once more to the particular threats to harmony and obedient faith. The remainder of passus XIX describes Piers' efforts to protect the crop yielded by his fourfold seed, building a barn 'Unite – Holy Chirche on Englissh' (XIX, 331) and defending it against Pride and his army. In the end, the vision dissolves in a general exchange of hostilities, the Church being, hopefully, supported by a king, governing in a spirit of reason and truth, and fearfully threatened, on the other side, not only by the company of Pride, but, even more dangerously, by church potentates who care more for their own aggrandisement than for the common people and false prophets. There is a powerful impression of a church surrounded, tempted and beset by a multitude of enemies from the outside and from within. Moreover, Piers the Plowman mysteriously disappears after he has sown his seeds and built the barn, to leave Christendom to fight for itself. Grace leaves at the same time 'As wide as the world is, with Piers to tilie truthe / And the lo[nd] of bileve, the lawe of Holy Chirche' (XIX, 336–7).[53] Both are pursuing the missionary work to the far corners of the earth, and the poem loses sight of them for the time being, until, at the very end, Piers is envisioned as the ultimate goal and desperately needed support of the Christian pilgrimage. Throughout the poem, he has not been a continuous presence, but only put in an appearance at a few crucial moments. When he leaves, the community of Christians seems to be back, almost at the scenario of the first visions; but the position is entirely different after the poetic (and homiletic) recapitulation of Christ's mission on earth and its effect on his disciples, including Piers.

When Will awakes after this climactic vision, however, he finds himself in a position that seems in sharp contrast to the confidently forward-looking mood at the Barn of Unity, desolate and depressed by the simple necessities of life: 'I ne wiste wher to ete ne at what place' (XX, 3). The poem has returned from the general to the individual, from the history of the church to the lone dreamer, threatened by need and old age. When Need lectures him on the virtues of poverty, he falls asleep for the last time, to be thrown into the midst of an apocalyptic scenario, with Antichrist besieging the Church and with opposing forces collecting on both sides. The worst enemies of the Church in this closing confrontation are not the obvious vices and temptations of the fiend, but the hypocritical professors of the faith, in particular deceiving friars who overcome even Conscience for a time. The last victory of the Antichrist concerns the sacrament of confession and contrition, a crucial issue throughout the whole poem. When 'Frere Flaterere' (XX, 326), posing as surgeon, gains entrance into the Barn of Unity and 'heals' Contrition so that he ceases to be afraid of sin, Conscience can do nothing but take refuge in another pilgrimage to seek Piers.

The end of the poem is, in fact, a new beginning. There is no final vision of Paradise, as in *Pearl*, and there is remarkably little talk of God's promises and the rewards in store for the just. Throughout his poem, Langland seems far more concerned with the uncertainties, doubts, dangers and temptations of the Christian life than with the joys in store beyond. It is only one of the fundamental differences between this extended vision and Dante's *Divine Comedy*, though both of these monumental poems are firmly rooted in the religious and political controversies of their times, so much so that, at first sight, they seem to offer little spontaneous pleasure to the modern reader without extensive historical and theological commentary. On the other hand, their sheer poetic brilliance and inventive exuberance should be accessible as soon as one has achieved a certain familiarity with their language and is prepared to enter into their world of biblical, theological and moral discourse. Not many poets have engaged so intensely in the fundamental intellectual and spiritual convictions and controversies of their generation.

Notes

1. William Langland, *The Vision of Piers Plowman. A Critical Edition of the B-Text Based on Trinity College, Cambridge, MS B.15.17*, second edition, ed. A. V. C. Schmidt (London, 1995), p. xix. This is, at present, the most useful and affordable edition for the student as well as for the general reader. Equally valuable is Derek Pearsall, *Piers Plowman by William Langland. An Edition of the C-Text* (London, 1978), with excellent commentary. The most thorough critical edition is the Athlone Press edition: *Piers Plowman: The A Version* (London, 1960; second edition 1988), *Piers Plowman: The B Version*, ed. George Kane and E. T. Donaldson (London, 1975; second edition 1988), *Piers Plowman: The C Version*, ed. George Russell and George Kane (London, 1997).

   There are prose translations into modern English, with useful commentary, by J. F. Goodridge, William Langland, *Piers the Plowman*, Penguin Classics (Harmondsworth, 1959), and A. V. C. Schmidt, William Langland, *Piers Plowman. A New Translation of the B-Text*, World's Classics (Oxford, 1992).

2. See the detailed and engrossing account by Charlotte Brewer, *Editing* Piers Plowman. *The evolution of the text*, Cambridge Studies in Medieval Literature, 28 (Cambridge, 1996).

3. The manuscripts are listed and described in the editions by Schmidt and the three volumes of the Athlone edition. A valuable inventory is provided by *The Manuscripts of* Piers Plowman: *The B-Version*, ed. C. David Benson and Lynne Blanchfield (Cambridge, 1997).

4. See *Piers Plowman: The Z Version*, ed. A. G. Rigg and Charlotte Brewer (Toronto, 1983), and *Piers Plowman. A Facsimile of the Z-Text in Bodleian Library, Oxford, MS Bodley 851*, introduced by Charlotte Brewer and A. G. Rigg (Cambridge, 1994), and Brewer, *Editing* Piers Plowman, pp. 420–6.

5. At least this is the general assumption behind the editions by Kane and Kane-Donaldson, cautiously questioned by Charlotte Brewer and others.

6. See Jill Mann, 'The Power of the Alphabet: A Reassessment of the Relation between the A and the B Versions of *Piers Plowman*', *The Yearbook of Langland Studies*, 8 (1994), 21–50. For Mann, A is 'a simplified version, stressing the practical duties of Christian living, reducing the text's metaphoric complexities, and toning down its social criticisms' (p. 46). Her dating of the revisions is briefly refuted by Kathryn Kerby-Fulton: 'the pattern of Langland's inclusion and deletion of historical allusions in revision makes Mann's theory untenable'. See '*Piers Plowman*', in *The Cambridge History of Medieval English Literature*, ed. David Wallace (Cambridge 1999), p. 515, n.7.

7. See George Kane, *Piers Plowman. The Evidence for Authorship* (London, 1965). This closely argued essay collects and appraises all the external and internal evidence for Langland's authorship of the three versions. Its basic conclusions seem to have been generally accepted.

8. See Brewer's chapter V, 'The Athlone Press Edition' in her *Editing* Piers Plowman, pp. 343–408. For a critical assessment of Kane's principles see also Tim William Machan, *Textual Criticism and Middle English Texts* (Charlottesville and London, 1994), pp. 56–60.

9. See *Piers Plowman. A Critical Edition of the A Version*, ed. T. A. Knott and David Fowler (Baltimore, 1952), and the editions by Kane, Kane-Donaldson, Kane-Russell, Pearsall and Schmidt quoted above. For parallel-text editions see *The Vision of William Concerning Piers Plowman in Three Parallel Texts . . .* , ed. W. W. Skeat, 2 vols (Oxford, 1986), and William Langland, *Piers Plowman. A Parallel-Text Edition of the A, B, C and Z Versions*, volume I: *Text*, ed. A. V. C. Schmidt (London, 1995). Schmidt's parallel-text edition enables the reader to compare the four versions at a glance, though it silently endorses the notion that there are, in fact, these distinct versions. A second volume, containing a full commentary, is promised.

10. See Hoyt N. Duggan, 'The *Piers Plowman* Electronic Archive', 1994. Mosaic (World Wide Web). http://jefferson.village.virginia.edu/piers/report94.html. and Hoyt N. Duggan, 'The Electronic *Piers Plowman*: A New Diplomatic Critical Edition', Æstel 1 (1993), 1–21.

11. See the chapter on *Piers Plowman* by Kathryn Kerby-Fulton in *The Cambridge History of Medieval English Literature*, pp. 513–38, and the still very useful survey in Robert Adams, 'Langland's Theology' in *A Companion to* Piers Plowman', ed. John A. Alford (Berkeley, Los Angeles, London, 1988), 87–114; see also, more generally, F. R. H. Du Boulay, *The England of* Piers Plowman. *William Langland and His Vision of the Fourteenth Century* (Cambridge, 1991).

12. I agree with Simpson's general conclusion that 'Langland has exhausted the discourses of both the conservative and radical wings of the Church, and it is unclear to me what discourse the poem could possibly adopt, or what institutional form it could imagine'. James Simpson, *Piers Plowman. An Introduction to the B-Text* (London, 1990), p. 243. However, I do not quite share his radical view of the Church's 'total failure' and 'disintegration'.

13. See Malcolm Godden's chapter on the C-version in his *The Making of Piers Plowman* (London, 1990), pp. 171–203, and Kerby-Fulton, '*Piers Plowman*', pp. 520–34, both with bibliographies of earlier criticism.

14. See Pearsall's note on V, 2 in his edition of the C-text. Chaucer's Host seems to use the term in the later, more specific sense (*The Canterbury Tales*, II, 1173), though the *Riverside Chaucer* rather vaguely glosses it as 'Lollard, a heretic'.

15. See David Aers, '*Vox populi* and the literature of 1381' in *The Cambridge History of Medieval English Literature*, pp. 432–53, and Anna Baldwin, 'The Historical Context' in *A Companion to* Piers Plowman, ed. Alford, 67–86, with useful bibliography.

16. Aers, '*Vox populi* and the literature of 1381', p. 439.

17. This is reflected in the provenance and ownership of the manuscripts, a subject of which it would be very important to know more. See Ralph Hanna III, 'Studies in the MSS of *Piers Plowman*', *The Yearbook of Piers Plowman Studies* 7 (1993), 1–25.

18. An interesting area, one of many, is pointed out by Janet Coleman, *Piers Plowman and the Moderni*, *Letture Di Pensiero e D'Arte* (Rome, 1981).

19. All quotations are from Schmidt's Everyman edition, unless otherwise indicated.

20. See John Burrow, *Langland's Fictions* (Oxford, 1993), chapter 1 ('A Gathering of Dreams', pp. 6–27). For Burrow, '*Piers Plowman* represents, in the tradition of dream poetry, a radically original development' (p. 8). His book is one of the most lucid and stimulating introductions to many aspects of the poem.

21. All quotations from the C-version are from Pearsall's edition (see above, note 1).

22. See the chapter 'Signatures' in Kane, *Piers Plowman: The Evidence of Authorship*, pp. 52–70.

23. The passage is remodelled in the C-version and the waking episode lost; see C, XVI, 157 and Pearsall's note. Pearsall suggests that 'For convenience, the fifth vision may be said to begin at [XVIII] 182' (note on C, XVIII, 179). It seems that the poet inadvertently failed to make clear the transition from sleep to waking at this point, perhaps a sign that he did not always pay very close attention to the exact consistency of the dream fiction.

24. See Kane, *Piers Plowman: the Evidence for Authorship*, p. 62.

25. See, for instance, Burrow, *Langland's Fictions*, pp. 26–7.

26. See the notes on the poem's conclusion in Schmidt's edition and his translation of the B-text.

27. *Piers Plowman. A New Translation of the B-Text*, p. 351.

28. Pearsall, *Piers Plowman by William Langland*, p. 16.

29. In a still very interesting and valuable essay Priscilla Jenkins has argued that Langland is 'deliberately frustrating the desire for allegorical tidiness'. Cf. 'Conscience: The Frustration of Allegory', in *Piers Plowman: Critical Approaches*, ed. S. S. Hussey (London, 1969), pp. 125–42; the quotation is on p. 128.

30. Cf. the influential book by G. R. Owst, *Literature and Pulpit in Medieval England: A Neglected Chapter in the History of English Letters & of the English People* (Cambridge, 1933), especially the chapter 'Scripture and Allegory', pp. 56–109. Owst's comment on the Deadly Sins in *Piers Plowman* seems rather too dogmatic: 'the pioneer at so experimental a stage, Langland finds himself compelled apparently to leave some of these characters quite inadequately harmonized or unified' (p. 88).

31. See my '*Piers Plowman* and Intertextuality', *Poetica* (Tokyo), 32 (1990), 8–24.

32. See the stimulating study by Margaret E. Goldsmith, *The Figure of Piers Plowman. The Image on the Coin*. Piers Plowman Studies, 2 (Cambridge, 1981).

33. A well-known example is Chaucer's Ploughman (*Canterbury Tales*, I, 529–41). See in particular Jill Mann, *Chaucer and Medieval Estates Satire* (Cambridge, 1973), pp. 67–74, for the traditional background.

34. Cf. the thoughtful essay by Rosemary Woolf, 'The Tearing of the Pardon', in *Piers Plowman: Critical Approaches*, pp. 50–75. There is also a brief but helpful and sensible note on the Pardon in Pearsall's edition of the C-text, p. 174. For a fuller, more recent interpretation of the episode see Simpson, *Piers Plowman: An Introduction to the B-Text*, pp. 71–85.

35. On the problems of revision and rewriting at this point see Godden, *The Making of Piers Plowman*, pp. 78–100.

36. See Pearsall's edition of the C-text, p. 182.

37. See Revelation, xx, 12: 'And I saw the dead, small and great, stand before God; and the books were opened: and another book was opened, which is *the book* of life.'

38. 'And no man hath ascended up to heaven, but he that came down from heaven' (St John, iii, 13).

39. See Simpson, *Piers Plowman: An Introduction to the B-Text*, pp. 117–28.

40. This seems to refer back to Passus I, 76, where Holy Church tells the dreamer that she 'underfeng thee first and the feith taughte'. The implication is not the same, however. Baptism does not automatically make him one of the chosen.

41. There is some doubt as to where Trajan's speech ends. Like Schmidt and others, I believe that it extends to line 318.

42. The C-version is even more uncompromising in its criticism of minstrels; cf. Pearsall's edition of the C-text, note on Prologue, 35. It is also worth noting that the C-version omits the whole passage about the justification of Langland's own writing. On the autobiographical value of this and other passages in *Piers Plowman* see the excellent chapter 'Fictions of Self' in Burrow, *Langland's Fictions*, pp. 82–108.

43. 'though I walk through the valley of the shadow of death, I will fear no evil: for thou *art* with me' (Psalm xxiii, 4).

44. See Matthew x, 22: 'but he that endureth to the end shall be saved'.

45. 'Love God' and 'Lord, who shall dwell . . .'. Cf. Matthew xxii, 37: 'Jesus said unto him, Thou shalt love the Lord thy God with all thy heart, and with all thy soul, and with all thy mind', and Psalm xv, 1: 'Lord, who shall abide in thy tabernacle? who shall dwell in thy holy hill?'

46. *Piers Plowman. An Introduction to the B-Text*, p. 151. A page later, Simpson puts it admirably: 'this is a leave-taking which represents a transition of intellectual and emotional allegiance, a moment when sympathies for a culture are expressed, but, in leaving it, judgement is made about its limitations' (p. 152).

47.
Ac for I kan neither taboure ne trompe ne telle no gestes,	*tales*
Farten ne fithelen at festes, ne harpen,	*fiddle*
Jape ne jogele ne gentilliche pipe,	*Joke, juggle, skilfully*
Ne neither saille ne saute ne synge with the gyterne,	*dance, jump*
I have no goode giftes of thise grete lordes	*from*
For no breed that I brynge forth – (XIII, 231–6)	*bread, offer for sale*

48. The text of the C-version differs noticeably from B at this point. The division into passus is omitted and so is the waking episode at the beginning of B, Passus XV. See Pearsall's edition, note on XVI, 157. On the whole rearrangement of the Haukyn material in C see Pearsall's note on XV, 194 and *passim*.

49. *Petrus, that is Christ*. A particularly enigmatic, or rather poetically suggestive passage. Peter, according to the New Testament, is the rock on which the church is built. See Matthew xvi, 18: 'thou art Peter, and upon this rock I will build my church', and 1 Corinthians x, 4: 'that Rock was Christ'.

50. The change in method is well described by Burrow: 'It is not difficult to see how, from Passus XVI on, salvation-history dictates the order of events – though not without some characteristic delays and diversions on the way.' (*Langland's Fictions*, p. 53). The whole chapter, 'Fictions of History' (pp. 53–81), provides an excellent introduction to this aspect of the poem.

51. See the important study by Peter Dronke, 'Arbor Caritatis' in *Medieval Studies for J. A. W. Bennett*, ed. P. L. Heyworth (Oxford, 1981), pp. 207–43.

52. See Matthew xxi, 9 (Christ's entry into Jerusalem on Palm Sunday): 'And the multitude that went before, and that followed, cried, saying, Hosanna to the Son of David: Blessed *is* he that cometh in the name of the Lord.' See also line 17a below.

53. As Burrow has noted, Piers' disappearance has a parallel in the Acts of the Apostles, a book intimately known by Langland. See *Langland's Fictions*, pp. 78–80.

Chapter 5

The *Gawain*-Poet

The '*Gawain*-Poet' or '*Pearl*-Poet', as he is sometimes called, is, after Gower and Langland, the third of Chaucer's best-known poet-contemporaries, and it is no wonder that this astonishing quartet of authors has given rise to attempts to find some kind of common literary, philosophical, or temperamental denominator that could serve as a convenient label. John Burrow's stimulating book on *Ricardian Poetry*[1] has pointed out several important features that seem to unite these four poets, but, quite apart from obvious differences in dialect, subject and poetic idiom, the works of the *Gawain*-poet, four uniquely original poems, *Pearl, Cleanness, Patience* and *Sir Gawain and the Green Knight*, form a very distinct group. They seem to belong to a different literary tradition, address a different audience and in many ways enrich our picture of Middle English literature immeasurably. It appears little short of a miracle that the unpretentious little volume that contains the single extant text of these poems has survived the ravages of time; without this modest, crudely illustrated manuscript our estimate of the whole period and its literary achievement would be substantially poorer. Very little is known about this collection, preserved in the British Library under the signature Cotton Nero A.x.[2] It dates from about the last quarter of the fourteenth century and is written in a West Midland dialect, probably the language of the author. The poems were all copied by the same hand, almost certainly not the hand of the poet, but this is where certain knowledge ends and conjecture has to begin. Most scholars agree that the four poems were all composed by the same person, whose identity and individual character must remain a matter of speculation, though to most readers he speaks as a very distinct personality, certainly very different either from Geoffrey Chaucer or William Langland.[3] Derek Brewer, in his magisterial introduction to *A Companion to the Gawain-Poet*, puts it with admirable clarity:

> Like Langland he writes in alliterative verse, is deeply devout, has a sardonic humour, is not interested in romantic ('courtly') love. Unlike Langland, he is very courtly. Like Chaucer he is courtly, but in a different style. He is not ironic, or flippant, and does not tell secular comic tales, but he is more attracted to courtly festivity than is Chaucer, who is dismissive, not to say *blasé*, about feasts, and who mocks Arthurianism.[4]

As far as the poetic form of his writing is concerned, the poet's close links with the 'alliterative revival' is perhaps the most striking feature. He handles the alliterative style and metre with consummate mastery and an evidently intimate knowledge of formulaic techniques,[5] but he is also perfectly able to use intricate forms of end-rhyme and stanzaic patterns, as in *Pearl* and, partly, in *Sir Gawain and the Green Knight*. He is familiar with biblical and exegetical traditions, but also with courtly manners and courtly language. It seems very likely that he was in holy orders and that he had connections with the court or some major aristocratic household, but most of such guesses come from our reading of the poems and not, as in the case of Chaucer, from any documented facts. The poet himself is remarkably silent about his own person, his domestic environment or professional background and, in particular, his status as an author.[6] Most of the references to his role as the 'I' of his poems are to an immediate relationship between speaker and audience, not to a book and to readers. Thus, in *Patience*, after the introductory passage, the audience is addressed and prepared for the following homily:

> Wyl ȝe tary a lyttel tyne and tent me a whyle,   *moment, attend*
> I schal wysse yow þerwyth as holy wryt telles. (ll. 59–60)[7]   *inform, about it*

Similarly, at the end of the third 'fytte' of *Sir Gawain and the Green Knight*, when Gawain has retired to his bed on the eve of his ordeal, we are told:

> Let hym lyȝe þere stille;
> He hatz nere þat he soȝt.   *nearly what*
> And ȝe wyl a whyle be stylle,   *If you*
> I schal telle yow how þay wroȝt. (ll. 1994–7)   *fared*

More problematic is, perhaps, the author's reference to his source at the outset of the narration:

> If ȝe wyl lysten þis laye bot on littel quile,   *tale*
> I schal telle hit astit, as I in toun herde,   *immediately*
>   With tonge.
> As hit is stad and stoken   *set down, fixed*
> In stori stif and stronge,
> With lel letteres loken,   *true letters interlocked*
> In londe so hatz ben longe. (ll. 30–36)

Scholars have disagreed about whether this refers to the truth of the story or to the verse technique, to faithful narration or to the written text.[8] In view of the fact that the poet nowhere claims that he is the author of a literary work, it seems more likely that he is talking about the subject of his performance, not the manuscript in front of him. The four poems consistently avoid any implication of authorial or bookish activity, though this is in fact contradicted by the very existence of the collection, with its clearly self-conscious literacy.

There is no other Middle English manuscript of this period that similarly assembles poems by one poet – if that is what he is – and this is emphasised by the unusual illustrations. Altogether, we have here a striking co-existence of fictitious orality and distinctly literary artifice.

The closer one looks at the four texts, the more one is impressed by the unprecedented, easy mastery of verse and poetic idiom, the highly wrought metrical and numerical patterning and the independent treatment of traditional material. This is hardly less true of the two overtly homiletic poems than of the brilliant poetic jewellery of *Pearl* and the stunning dramatic characterisation in *Sir Gawain and the Green Knight*. Each of the four items seems to establish an original poetic genre of its own, independent of any particular model or literary programme, unless the collection itself can be read as a kind of consciously designed poetic and homiletic statement.

Patience

Of the four poems, *Patience* (531 lines) is the shortest and the least pretentious or intricate in form as well as in its subject, but the simplicity is deceptive. The leap from the New Testament and the Beatitudes to the Old Testament story of Jonah may not be as original as it seems to the modern reader,[9] but the dramatic retelling of the biblical account and the psychological insight revealed in the characterisation of the prophet make *Patience* one of the most remarkable homiletic poems in Middle English. Like the other three poems, it is circular in its structure, which is underlined by the clear echo of the beginning in the last line: 'pacience is a nobel poynt' (l. 531, referring back to l. 1). This also draws attention to the argumentative character of the poem. It begins with a pointed statement that is supported and illustrated by the body of the work and repeated for confirmation at the end. The poet's concept of patience is unfolded in detail and dramatically exemplified by God's dealings with Jonah.

At the outset, however, the poet introduces himself as a member of a congregation, listening to a passage from the Gospel of St Matthew, which he then proceeds to present in his own, rather faithful, but nevertheless personal translation. He evidently does not wish to pose as a preacher, but puts himself on a level with his listeners, as one who is himself far from perfect: he modestly does not claim to be in possession of those eight Blessed States that are praised and promised heavenly rewards in the words of Christ. The only 'virtue' he humbly and perhaps half-humorously claims for himself, is poverty, which, in turn, asks for the Christian virtue of patience, and this brings him to the subject forming the central concern of the poem, which is the problem of suffering and of endurance without grumbling or open rebellion against God's providence:

> Pacience is a poynt, þaȝ hit displese ofte.   *virtue*
> When heuy herttes ben hurt wyth heþyng oþer elles,   *derision*
> Suffraunce may aswagen hem and þe swelme leþe,
>   *long-suffering can assuage them, heat, ease*
> For ho quelles vche a qued and quenches malyce;
>   *she (Patience) kills everything bad*
> For quoso suffer cowþe syt, sele wolde folȝe,
>   *if one can suffer sorrow, happiness will follow*
> And quo for þro may noȝt þole, þe þikker he sufferes.
>   *resentment, endure, heavier*
> Þen is better to abyde þe bur vmbestoundes   *put up, just from time to time*
> Þen ay þrow forth my þro, þaȝ me þynk ylle.
>   *always, resentment, though* (ll. 1–8)

First, however, the Beatitudes are translated into the image of eight ladies, personifying the eight blessings praised in Christ's Sermon in the Mount. At first sight, it is not quite clear which of the Beatitudes is meant to be represented by each particular lady; in some cases the correspondence is evident, as with Poverty, Meekness, Cleanness and Peace, even though the poet's paraphrase does not always agree entirely with the sense of the Gospel's words. For instance, the poet's translation of 'pauperes spiritu', as 'in hert pouerté' (l. 13) seems to prepare the shift of meaning twenty lines on, when he applies 'poverty' to himself.[10] His way of arguing for a close companionship of Poverty and Patience shows a particular fondness for verbal subtlety and word-game. By clever sleight of hand he makes the two words first and last in the series of Beatitudes; he proposes to 'play' with them (and with those two ladies) and he reasons till they become 'nedes playferes' (l. 45). The pattern established by the poet is certainly not in the Gospel text, but it provides him with a theme for his narrative. In the Gospel of St Matthew, the eighth Beatitude is addressed to those who suffer persecution for their righteousness, perhaps also the first Christian martyrs, but the *Gawain*-poet apparently seizes on the etymological kinship of *patiuntur* and *patientia* which he uses as a handle for his subject.

Patient Poverty is also an important concept in the C-version of *Piers Plowman* (especially in Passus XII and XIII), where, however, Poverty is treated more literally and explained at greater length: in *Patience* it appears to stand for any kind of hard fate or affliction, and lastly, indeed, for a burdensome task commanded by God, such as a hazardous and possibly futile journey to Rome.[11] The narrator seems to be deeply pre-occupied with his own troubles; his is not the voice of a superior, complacent preacher, but rather that of a sympathetic fellow-Christian who has been through some trials and has found his own solution.

The poet then proposes to illustrate the need for patience by the story of the prophet Jonah. There is something unexpected and distinctly individual in this transition. Jonah's story is offered as a useful and entertaining precedent: 'Did not Jonas in Judé suche jape sumwhyle?' (l. 57); 'jape' clearly anticipates the slightly humorous perspective from which the following story will be told. Like the Beatitudes, this is announced not just as a divine text, to be accepted reverentially as unquestioned authority, but also as a good yarn and as an experience the speaker wants to share with us: Jonah, in the eyes of the poet, was trying to pull a fast one on God.

It is fascinating to watch the poet producing his own version of the biblical source, sometimes translating whole verses almost *verbatim*, at other times expanding a brief sentence into a lively passage of his own invention, as happens with verse three, where the book merely tells us that Jonah rose up to run away from the face of the Lord. The poet adds a vivid interior monologue, thus creating a memorable character sketch of a prophet fooling himself that he can escape God's commission. In his mind there arises a frightening picture of the hostile reception he is certain to meet, and of the likely martyrdom awaiting him at Nineveh. In his imagination, God turns into an enemy who must be outwitted or frustrated, an authority whose protection or even notice is not to be relied on. Jonah envisages no less than his own crucifixion, thus unknowingly suggesting to the reader a reflexion on Christ's patient acceptance of *his* passion.

The traditional association of Christ's three days' period in the tomb with Jonah's sojourn in the belly of the fish is powerfully restated,[12] but this symbolic reading of Jonah's story is hardly more unusual than the imaginative addition of dramatic detail. The tempest raised by the omnipotent creator, the frantic despair by the seamen and fellow-travellers and the horrible journey into the infernal regions of the fish's stomach, visualised with uncomfortable concreteness, are expanded by the consummate art of the story-teller. Among the many unexpected touches in the poet's version are the references to classical mythology: Eurus and Aquilon, two of the winds raised by the *pater omnipotens* in Virgil's *Aeneid* (I, 60) are immediately at God's command,[13] and when the terrified men invoke their several gods ('clamaverunt viri ad deum suum', Jonah 1,5), the poet adds the names of several heathen deities, some of them familiar from the Charlemagne romances ('Vernagu, Mahoun, Mergot') and two ('Diana, Neptune') from Roman mythology. Another suggestive and original image occurs in the description of Jonah's passage into the whale's stomach: the throat is compared to 'a munster dor' (l. 268), but the place where he arrives 'stank as þe deuel' and 'sauoured as helle' (ll. 274–5), adding a spiritual dimension to the extreme desolation of the place.[14]

The prophet's moving prayer from the bottom of this hell, evidently the spiritual centre of the biblical account, is given a rich context and the emphasis is significantly redirected by Jonah's promise of strict obedience to God in the event of his safe escape from this divine punishment:

> Bot I dewoutly awowe, þat verray betz halden,   *which faithfully is kept*
> Soberly to do Þe sacrafyse when I schal saue worþe,
>   *Earnestly, will be saved*
> And offer Þe for my hele a ful hol gyfte,   *rescue*
> And halde goud þat Þou me hetes: haf here my trauthe.' (ll. 333–6)
>   *keep truly, command, my faithful word*

The poet's particular concern with 'trouthe' as a binding commitment gives added strength to Jonah's obligation: he enters into a contract with God, an idea hinted at in the Latin text, but not expressed in the same legal terminology.[15]

The second and concluding part of Jonah's story is told with equal gusto, and again it is the prophet's all too human weakness that receives the most shrewdly critical yet sympathetic attention. What appears to exercise him most is the undermining of his reputation as the messenger of God's wrath by the Creator's mercy. Jonah feels discredited by the unexpected success of his mission: his own satisfaction and his belief in the justice of God's revenge are evidently stronger than pity for the victims. God's method of exposing the folly of his anger shows a kind of humour clearly appreciated and savoured by the poet, who only adds a brief moral to God's rhetorical victory, a moral directed as much at himself as at his audience.

Throughout his spirited commentary on the prophet's career we are aware of the narrator's own relationship with God. For him, he is 'my lege lorde' (l. 51), 'oure mercyable God' (l. 238) or 'oure Fader' (l. 337) and 'oure Lorde' (l. 340),[16] whereas Jonah speaks rather dismissively of 'Oure Syre' (l. 93) or reproachfully as 'Þou Maker of man' (l. 482). The narrative point of view persistently reminds us of the simple fact that it is *our* God Jonah is so fool-ishly misjudging, treating him like another fallible human being. The poet is emphatic in his condemnation of Jonah's stupidity: 'Lo, þe wytles wrechche!' (l. 113) and he quotes the psalmist as another witness to the plain truth that it is madness to expect the creator of ears to be deaf or the maker of eyes to be blind (ll. 123–4). For him, Jonah is a powerful proof of the utter imbecility of any attempt to escape the 'destiné' (l. 49) sent by God.

The poem ends, as it began, with an acknowledgement of Patience as the key to contentment in the face of suffering and affliction, a lesson first applied by the speaker to himself:

> Forþy when pouerté me enprecez and paynez innoȝe *oppresses*
> Ful softly with suffraunce saȝttel me bihouez; (ll. 528–9) *be reconciled*

The conclusion drawn from Jonah's story seems so personal that the reader may well suspect some individual tragedy behind the touching sermon, some impoverished cleric or member of a congregation deriving new strength and spiritual support from the Old Testament account.[17]

As a small masterpiece, *Patience* combines some of the characteristic and original literary achievements of its poet, in particular, an almost unique jux-taposition of biblical faith, realism and humour and an astonishing sense of form and symmetry matched by very few of his contemporaries.

Cleanness

Cleanness or *Purity,* as it is called by some editors, is a more elaborate and, at first sight, less unified version of the poetic biblical commentary, so success-fully achieved in *Patience*.[18] It is a much more ambitious poem in that it discusses its declared theme through a whole series of biblical 'exempla' and homiletic commonplaces, showing an impressive familiarity with biblical commentary and sermon literature while at the same time taking remarkable liberties with the canonised texts. What critics, before the appearance of Lecklider's seminal study, had not fully realised, is the way the poet's selec-tions from the scripture deliberately follow the course of the church calendar and, moreover, make use of established exegetical traditions, especially the church fathers and contemporary preachers.

The poet begins by stating his theme, 'Clannesse' and its opposite, 'fylþe' and, as in *Patience*, he embarks on his disquisition by way of the parable of the wedding banquet as related by Matthew (xxii, 1–14) and Luke (xiv, 16–24), a traditional lesson for Pentecost. Naturally, the poet lays particular emphasis on the episode of the wedding-guest who appears in dirty clothes and is thrown into the dungeon by the lord's executioners. It is interesting to watch the poet conflate the two New Testament accounts of the parable, which shows him a close reader of the Bible as well as the commentary tradition. Also he has opted for a strategy that seeks to impress the reader with an idea of God's wrath and vengeance in the face of man's disobedience and uncleanness, rather than his patience and forgiving mercy. This is why the three most notorious and frightening Old Testament accounts of God's judgement constitute the poem's centre. They all contain instances of divine pity as well as promise, but the dramatic power and poetic zest is clearly on the side of wrath and punishment. The narratives chosen by the poet all parallel assigned biblical readings, or pericopes, and the transitional passages between them also reflect the traditional order of the liturgical year, but at the same time are deliberately selected so that they serve as an extended gloss on the one Beatitude singled out here from the eight listed in Christ's Sermon on the Mount, as in *Patience*:

> 'Þe haþel clene of his hert hapenez ful fayre,   *man, has good fortune*
> For he schal loke on oure Lorde with a leue chere';
>   *delighted countenance* (ll. 27–8)

The structure of the poem is governed by the progression of Old Testament precedents and warnings, linked by passages of commentary and homiletic application. A brief table will illustrate the poet's plan and may help to show that there is no question of 'failure' here:[19]

Introduction
1–22	Praise of 'clannesse'
23–32	Beatitude: 'Þe haþel clene of his hert hapenez ful fayre'
33–48	Application and transition
49–160	**Parable of the marriage feast**
161–192	Exegesis: God's wrath against unclean sinners

Three exempla
193–204	Introduction to the three exemplary stories
205–234	The Fall of Lucifer
235–248	The Fall of Adam
249–540	**The Flood**
541–600	Transitional passage: God's repugnance of filth
601–1048	**Abraham, Lot and the destruction of Sodom**
	God's visit to Abraham and Sarah (601–780)
	Lot and his family (781–890)
	God's judgement of Sodom and Gomorrah (891–1048)
1049–1148	Application: penance as ablution; imitation of God's love; Christ's incarnation; image of the pearl (1069–1108)
	Imitation of God's 'clannesse' (1109–1148)
1149–1804	**Nebuchadnezzar, Daniel and Belshazzar's feast**
	Seizure of the sacred vessels (1149–1332)
	Belshazzar's feast and punishment (1333–1804)

Conclusion
1805–1812	Brief summary: þrynne wyses (1805–12)

The whole plan is firmly rooted in biblical texts. As in the case of *Patience,* the poet appears to make very little use of non-scriptural source material, though he claims at one point that he has done a great deal of diligent reading in books of 'hyʒe clerkez' (l. 193) for more information about God's judgement. His method of dramatisation is very similar in both poems, though the homiletic passages occupy a larger proportion of the text. The vivid concreteness of the descriptions, in particular the Flood, with the desperate panic of the victims, God's dealings with Abraham and his wife, and Belshazzar's feast have impressed many modern readers, and this may account for some critics' dissatisfaction with the homiletic application, although this is obviously the very purpose of the scriptural examples. There is no arguing about poetic unity where the speaker's intention is so clear. His forceful condemnation of all manner of uncleanness and filth hardly needs any defence on grounds of literary polish or modern concepts of unity.

The only point in the poem where the author openly betrays his familiarity with more secular reading is his digression on the art of love, with a direct reference to the *Roman de la Rose* (ll. 1057–64), paraphrasing the Friend's advice to the Lover to study the ways and manners of the Beloved and adapt his own accordingly.[20] Earlier in the poem, there is an equally surprising passage, where God himself, resolved to destroy Sodom, explains his own 'construction' of human love and procreation in terms of secular love discourse:

> I compast hem a kynde crafte and kende hit hem derne,
> > *devised for them a lawful art and taught it them in secret*
> And amed hit in Myn ordenaunce oddely dere,
> > *esteemed, singularly valuable*
> And dy3t drwry þerinne, doole alþer-swettest,
> > *set love within, sweetest part of all*
> And þe play of paramorez I portrayed Myseluen,
> And made þerto a maner myriest of oþer:
> When two true togeder had ty3ed hemseluen, *joined each other together*
> Bytwene a male and his make such merþe schulde come,
> Welny3e pure paradys mo3t preue no better;
> Ellez þay mo3t honestly ayþer oþer welde,
> > *Provided, in honesty, possess each other*
> At a stylle stollen steuen, vnstered with sy3t,
> > *secret contract, undisturbed by sight*
> Luf-lowe hem bytwene lasched so hote *love-flame, blaze*
> Þat alle þe meschefez on mold mo3t hit not sleke.
> > *evils, earth, quench* (ll. 697–708)

Both passages have attracted some comment because they seem to stand out from a poem based so deliberately on biblical authority. It is evident, however, that the poet was acting on the conviction, quoted (and practised) by Chaucer, that 'al that writen is, / To oure doctrine it is ywrite, ywis' (*Canterbury Tales*, VII, 3441–2). He felt free to make use of wisdom drawn from unorthodox sources and to apply it to his own homiletic purposes, without being troubled by the non-scriptural context. He clearly expected his audience to pick up his allusions to more contemporary issues.

From the author's literary references in all four poems it seems possible to draw some conclusions as to his reading; it is hardly more unconventional than could be expected from a member of a larger household, connected with a religious community, whether monastic or attached to a cathedral.[21]

Whether *Cleanness* was written before or after *Patience* is impossible to say, but there is no doubt that the two poems are closely related in their method of explicating moral and theological key issues by way of dramatised scriptural episodes.

Pearl

This poem, which comes first in the *Gawain*-manuscript, is an even more remarkable literary achievement and evidence of an astonishing sense of poetic form and symmetry. It demonstrates the author's consummate mastery of rhyme and stanza technique as well as his familiarity with literary conventions, in particular the dream vision,[22] although no direct model has been found. In a general way, the poem is clearly in the tradition of the *Roman de la Rose* and, in its thematic concerns, of Boece's *Consolatio Philosophiae*. Like the author of this influential treatise, the dreamer in *Pearl* has to come to terms with the experience of losing his most valuable treasure and of being tormented by fundamental doubts in the existence of a benign providence.

At the outset he seems merely to bewail the fact that in an arbour this precious pearl slipped from him and tumbled away into the grass:

Allas! I leste hyr in on erbere;	*lost her, arbour*
Þur3 gresse to grounde hit fro me yot. (ll. 9–10)	*Through the grass, went*

But when, 'In Auguste in a hy3 seyson' (l. 39), he revisits the ground where he lost her to lament his bereavement, it soon becomes clear that behind the image of the pearl there is a human being whose loss he mourns. No other English dream-poem has anything like this almost imperceptible transition from a general experience to a clear and definite vision, from a vague impression of sad emptiness to an individual encounter with the departed person.[23]

The dream-character of the vision is tellingly conveyed by the poet's incomprehension and his gradual recognition of who it is he has before him, as the apparition comes closer:

More meruayle con my dom adaunt.	*judgement, overwhelm*
I se3 by3onde þat myry mere	*saw, pleasant water*
A crystal clyffe ful relusaunt:	*dazzling*
Mony ryal ray con fro hit rere.	*magnificent, reflect*
At þe fote þerof þer sete a faunt,	*child*
A mayden of menske, ful debonere;	*grace, beautiful*
Blysnande whyt watz hyr bleaunt;	*Gleaming, mantle*
I knew hyr wel, I hade sen hyr ere. (ll. 157–64)	*before*

He is puzzled and afraid to call her: 'I se3 hyr in so strange a place' (l. 175), and it is only when she herself hails him that he dares address her, still only half comprehending her present state:

'O perle,' quoþ I, 'in perlez pyȝt,   *pearl of pearls*
Art þou my perle þat I haf playned,   *bewailed*
Regretted by myn one on nyȝte?   *at night*
Much longeyng haf I for þe layned,   *longing sorrow, hidden*
Syþen into gresse þou me aglyȝte. *Since, grass, slipped from me*
                                   (ll. 241–5)

Still there seems no clear indication who she is, though a few lines earlier he states that 'Ho watz me nerre þen aunte or nece' (l. 233). It is reasonable to conclude that she was his daughter who died in her infancy, but this is never stated in so many words. We are clearly not encouraged by the poem to read it as an autobiographical document and to enquire too closely for the story behind the vision.[24] The ensuing debate between the dreamer and his pearl turns on the disquieting issues of God's justice, heavenly reward and that state of the Blessed. No explicit consolation is offered beyond the assurance that his pearl, regardless of her tender age, is one of the Blessed Brides of Christ and has her full share of his glory. What consolation there is, must come from a contemplation of God's grace and the heavenly city, not from any human or secular arguments. The little girl, who evidently did not even live to reach the age of two,[25] and therefore was never old enough to learn about God and about prayer, has become his teacher, but it is not any abstract doctrine she expounds to him, but, more than anything else, her visible example as one of the chosen.

Pearl combines instruction, illustration by scriptural narrative, and vision in an unprecedentedly persuasive fusion of homely, biblical and apocalyptic imagery.[26] The circular structure, adopted to some extent in the other poems of the *Pearl*-manuscript, is here refined to the point of preciousness, in evident analogy to the subject of the vision. The symmetry extends from the intricate rhyme-scheme and the carefully patterned number of stanzas to the structure of the argument and the architecture of the whole poem. Some of these symmetries may be glanced from the following table:

Introduction: Loss of the pearl
    I   '. . . pryuy perle withouten spot' – poet visiting the place where he lost the pearl and falls asleep
Vision of earthly paradise and apparition of his pearl
    II '. . . adubbement' – waking up in a precious landscape
    III '. . . more and more' – approaching a borderline; an apparition which he recognises
    IV '. . . perle . . . pyȝte' – pearl beyond all description
The dreamer's errors corrected by her
    V '. . . joylez (gentyl, no kynde, joyfol) jueler' – his illusions corrected by her
    VI '. . . deme' – her reproaches; human and divine judgement
    VII '. . . grounde of alle my blysse' – dreamer asks for forbearance and for instruction
    VIII '. . . quene (kyng) of cortaysye' – her high rank and his doubts
Parable of God's grace: the labourers in the vineyard
    IX '. . . date' – question of time, rank and limit; the parable told

    X   '. . . more' – the problem of measure; the same wage for every labourer
   XI   '. . . þe grace of God is grete inoghe' – God's grace without proportion
  XII   '. . . by ryȝt' – God's justice without measure; Jesus and the children
The Blessed in Heaven
 XIII   '. . . perle . . . maskelles' – pearl as the supreme treasure and path to redemption; Pygmalion and Song of Songs; image of mystical marriage
 XIV   '. . . Jerusalem' – the 144,000 virgins, his pearl as one of them; Jerusalem as the scene of Christ's work on earth and as heavenly city; the revelation of John
  XV   '. . . neuer þe lesse' – description of the heavenly city; the dreamer's question
 XVI   '. . . withouten mote (þat myry mote)' – heavenly and earthly Jerusalem
Vision of earthly paradise
 XVII   '. . . þe apostel John' – vision of heavenly Jerusalem; dreamer has confirmation of the Apostle's revelation
XVIII   '. . . (sunne and) mone' – further description; number twelve: 12 tribes in Israel, 12 gates, 12 pearls, 12 months; shines brighter than sun and moon
 XIX   '. . . (with gret) delyt' – adoration of the Lamb; his pearl among the blessed; the dreamer's longing
The dreamer's awakening and new knowledge
  XX   '. . . (Pryncez) paye' – awakening in the arbour; the folly of rebellion against God's plan; resignation in the face of suffering; bread and wine as the means of approaching Christ

Looking at the progression of the dream, it is clear that the parable of the vineyard stands at the centre of the dreamer's vision and the theological argument, enclosed in the eschatological and apocalyptic revelation in answer to his grief and his uncertainties. His incredulity and scepticism in the face of her undeservedly exalted state is answered by two passages from the gospel of Matthew, the parables of the vineyard and of the pearl, and by the immediate sight of the Lamb and the redeemed souls. As in the other two scriptural poems, it is again the Bible that is upheld as the surest means of approaching God, available to all men, and it is the scriptural account of God's incommensurable grace that is confirmed by the dream vision, first by the pearl's own teaching and then by what he is allowed to see for himself.

Both argument and vision are neatly highlighted by the concatenation phrases and key words that act as refrains to each group of five stanzas, sometimes repeated *verbatim*, but, more often than not, ingeniously taken through a set of variations to enrich the meaning of certain important terms and crucial ideas. Thus, in the ninth set of stanzas, it is the multiple meanings of 'date' that serve to press home the radical differences between God's standards and measurements and the limitations of human ideas. In group XVI, the concatenation turns on a clever punning with 'mote', as 'place, dwelling, city' and 'flaw, stain, speck'. In group III, the phrase 'more and more' is used to give a sense of gradual approaching and comprehending, whereas, in group X, 'more' appears in the context of measurement and God's immeasurable grace. Other concatenation terms ('Jerusalem', XIV; 'apostle John', XVII) underline thematic concerns and others, like 'adubbement' (II), 'perle' (I, IV, XIII), 'delyt' (XIX) mainly harp on the heavenly splendour and preciousness of the vision.[27]

At the end, the poet finds himself in the same spot where he fell asleep, praying to Christ for comfort,[28] certain that he has been granted a 'veray avysyoun' (l. 1184) and he is prepared to believe in it as in a 'ueray and soth sermoun' (l. 1185). In contrast to Chaucer's dreamers, he has been changed and educated by the dream experience and appears a different person from the mourner of the beginning.

Unlike the two homiletic poems, *Pearl* is in the form of a dialogue. The dream vision enables the poet to describe an experience that cannot be conveyed in any other form. One would like to know whether he had actually read Dante when he thought of his beatific vision. There are no demonstrable verbal borrowings, but there is little doubt that no other English poet comes as near to the splendour and the ravishing sight of the *Paradiso*.

Sir Gawain and the Green Knight

Sir Gawain and the Green Knight, the most famous item of the manuscript, clearly claims to be something quite different from the other three poems. It is announced by the poet as 'an outtrage awenture of Arthurez wonderez' (l. 29) and recorded 'As hit is breued in þe best boke of romaunce' (l. 2521). Indeed, it has often been praised as the finest of all Middle English romances and there is no reason to differ from this high estimate.[29] If we read the poem in the context of the whole collection, it becomes even clearer that the author wants to emphasise the historical or legendary nature of the story, to celebrate the heroic British past as well as traditional values that may provide models for the present. At the same time, it is evident that he is deeply interested in the moral and spiritual basis of courtly ideals. He is full of admiration for the ceremonial and the ethical aspects of true chivalry, which he is anxious to distinguish from popular views of errant warriors and amorous knights of romance.

At the poem's moral centre is the testing of Arthurian claims and aspirations in the person of their most famous representative. The poet goes out of his way to establish Gawain as the most prominent member of Arthur's court and, moreover, as the knight with the highest moral demands on himself. The elaborate description of the pentangle as emblem of perfection in all courtly and spiritual virtues is a vital part of his portrait and defines his 'adventure' as a journey towards existential choices and judgements. When the Green Knight descends on the Christmas revels at Camylot, it is the 'renoun' of the Round Table he is determined to try, and though in the beginning it appears as a mere test of courage and daring, an extravagantly joyful 'Crystemas gomen' (l. 283), it becomes clear, as the action unfolds, that the real issue is 'trawþe' in the widest meaning of the word, embracing faithfulness, honesty, integrity and cleanness in a moral as well as a spiritual sense. This does not make *Sir Gawain and the Green Knight* a religious poem in the same way as *Pearl* or *Patience*, but it clearly puts the Arthurian world and Gawain's adventure in a more Christian and spiritual framework. Not only are the two households where Christmas is celebrated ruled by Christian observations and liturgical timetables, but Gawain himself is also presented as a deeply religious person who cannot envisage the Christmas season without attending Holy Mass and whose self-questioning leads to penitential tears and disillusioned mortification in the end. Most readers would agree with the Green Knight who tells him:

> I halde þe polysed of þat ply3t and pured as clene
> > *consider you freed from that failure, made pure*
> As þou hadez neuer forfeted syþen þou watz fyrst borne.
> > *As if you had never transgressed* (ll. 2393–4)

But the poem also wants to persuade us to respect Gawain for his sad dissatis-faction: it shows the ethical standard he has set himself to be so much higher than that of most of his fellow men, including the rest of the Round Table. He must learn that he has fallen short of his own perfectionist aspirations and has come out of his trial with a blot on his pentangle, for all the cheerful applause and friendly laughter of the whole Arthurian Court. This adds a deeply religious seriousness to the ending and, at the same time, gives us a more convincing picture of Gawain's excellence as a Christian knight than the majority of popular romances celebrating unrealistically superlative exploits and perfections.[30]

Like the other poems in the *Gawain*-manuscript, *Sir Gawain and the Green Knight* has a carefully designed circular structure. The end brings us back to the beginning: the adventure taken on by Gawain in the poem's opening scene is concluded when he returns at the end, and we are once more reminded of British chivalry's Trojan descent. More important is the intricate, yet symmetrical progression from Gawain's ceremonial agreement with the Green Knight to his arrival at Bertilac's castle. There, a new Christmas pact is concluded, before he departs again to the Green Chapel, where the outcome of both bargains is resolved. There it is revealed that both adventures have been closely dependent on each other – as they have been all the time in Gawain's mind. All through the temptation scenes in his bedroom he has really been preoccupied with his dangerous mission, and it was his concern with the threatened return-blow that made him susceptible to the lady's parting gift. Nothing but the thought of this mortal danger could have persuaded him to accept and to hide the magic girdle; the moral irony of the poem and one of its most brilliant touches consists in the discovery that 'if Gawain . . . had lived up to the ideal of the pentangle – he would have been better protected than by a thousand magic girdles'.[31]

The metrical form of the poem also shows the author's brilliant craftsman-ship: the *Gawain*-stanza is a most effective narrative unit, unlike most other stanza forms in Middle English, compact and flexible at the same time. While the body of each stanza, a variable number (between 12 and 37) of alliterative long lines is skilfully adapted to the tempo and the stylistic register demanded by each episode, the rhyming conclusion ('bob and wheel') creates a clear-cut caesura between stanzas and a metrical refrain, providing either a bridge to the next stanza or a pithy summary, a witty comment or a surprising piece of information, as at the Green Knight's entrance into the hall:

For wonder of his hwe men hade,
Set in his semblaunt sene;
He ferde as freke were fade,   *behaved, man, bold*
And oueral enker grene. (ll. 147–50)   *intensely*

In the delicate exchanges between Gawain and Bertilac's lady, the 'wheel' perfectly matches the tone of the speakers. When she teasingly refers to his own 'lemman', he courteously wards her off:

Þe knyȝt sayde, 'Be Sayn Jon'
(And smeþely con he smyle)   *gently*
'In fayth I welde riȝt non,   *have none at all*
Ne non wil welde þe quile.' (ll. 1788–91)   *for the time*

The alliterative long lines, too, show an astonishing range of variation; they can be extended or shortened, slowed down or speeded up according to the character and mood of the context. The metre allows elaborate description (e.g. of the 'pentangel', ll. 640 ff.) as well as quick and pointed dialogue (e.g. ll. 1208–89). The variable length of of the individual stanza effectively avoids monotonous repetition. Sometimes descriptive passages cut across the stanza-pattern, as in the account of the deer hunt (ll. 1319–71), and sometimes the scene changes in the middle of a stanza (as at l. 1731), another means of reducing the prominence of the stanza pattern. Throughout, the poet success-fully combines the solemn heroic tone of traditional alliterative epic poetry with the urbane elegance and polish of courtly novels in verse.

The poem's tensely woven narrative is supported by the sophisticated treat-ment of perspective and point of view. Most of the events are described through the mind of Gawain. The three hunting scenes are an obvious exception, but they only establish a colourful background and thematic counterpoint and do not immediately contribute to the inner action of the poem. From the moment Gawain leaves Arthur's court – 'And gef hem alle goud day – / He wende for euermore' (ll. 668–9) – we are for the most part alone with him, except that now and then we are told about the voice of society, the grieving and wondering sighs of the knights watching his departure (ll. 672–86) and the joyful murmuring of Bertilac's court when the identity of the guest is revealed (ll. 915–27). Most moving, however, are the moments of wintry loneliness and spiritual desolation, when the knight, having left the sociable warmth of Arthur's court behind him, realises that Christmas is approaching without the prospect of a Christian community, and he begins to say his 'Pater and Aue / and Crede':

He rode in his prayere
And cryed for his mysdede.
He sayned hym in syþes sere   *crossed himself each time,*
And sayde, 'Cros Kryst me spede.' (ll. 758–61)

At this point, care for his spiritual obligation is more important to him than concern for his safety or any imminent danger. It is only when he is resting in his warm bed at Bertilac's castle that the thought of the Green Chapel begins to trouble him. During the first encounter with Bertilac's wife it is suggested that Gawain is immune against sexual temptation because he is mentally preoccupied with the thought of the return-blow.[32] This becomes more insistent during his last, sleepless night in the castle when the voice of the cock reminds him of the appointment: 'Bi vch kok þat crue he knwe wel þe steuen' (l. 2008).[33] Earlier, as the poet tells us in so many words, it was the thought of his danger that had persuaded him to accept the lady's gift, not its material value.[34]

The deliberate concentration on Gawain's point of view is an important factor in our understanding of his moral dilemma. Perhaps the most brilliant example comes on the first morning when the slumbering knight is surprised by the lady's early-morning visit to his bedside and quickly has to think 'in his conscience' of the most effective and at the same time courtly strategy (ll. 1179–1203). This prepares the reader for the important force of Gawain's consciousness, especially towards the end, when it becomes clear that, in contrast to the majority of romances, it is not his reputation that is most precious to Gawain, but his personal integrity. The point is explicitly brought home by the guide episode immediately before the last encounter with the Green Knight, when Gawain refuses to back out although his mortal danger is once more presented to him and secrecy is promised (ll. 2089–2139). There is no suggestion of the guide being an accomplice of Bertilac, like his wife (though he might well have turned out to be, if Gawain had given in), and Gawain certainly does not suspect it. It is his last temptation and it leaves him finally to encounter the Green Knight all on his own.

Again, the decisive moment is experienced from his point of view: he becomes aware of the uncanny 'chapel' and associates it with some satanic ceremony:

> Here myȝt aboute midnyȝt
> Þe Dele his matynnes telle!' (ll. 2187–8)   *Devil, matins*

The knight's soliloquy is interrupted by terrifying noise, an ultimate test of his resolution and a cue for his final determination. Again, when the Green Knight's battleaxe descends on him, we are made to follow his eyes, as he watches it, aware of its deadly force, and we share the fright that makes him shrink before the blow. His natural human reactions are thus conveyed most vividly by the narrative technique, not unlike Jonah's experience on his way to Nineveh.

The drama of Gawain's testing is set in a familiar world of romance, but it is very soon clear that the poet is not interested in the traditional paraphernalia of chivalry, but in its moral and religious ideals. He deliberately plays down the expected marvels and love-problems in order to point at more fundamental choices and decisions beyond. When Gawain rides through the 'ryalme of Logres', i.e. Arthur's Britain, he encounters, so we are told, all the conventional perils and adventures of romance, but the poet suggests that it is not worth his while to do more than name them because more important trials lie ahead:

At vche warþe oþer water þer þe wyȝe passed	*ford, hero*
He fonde a foo hym byfore . . .	
Hit were to tore for to telle of þe tenþe dole.	*difficult, part*
Sumwhyle wyth wormez he werrez and with wolues als,	*dragons, fights*
Sumwhyle wyth wodwos þat woned in þe knarrez,	*satyrs, live, crags*
Boþe wyth bullez and berez, and borez oþerquyle,	
	bears, boars at other times
And etaynez . . . (ll. 715–6, 719–23)	*giants*

Without his allegiance to the Lord, he would have been killed many a time, but, the poet adds with characteristic realism, the hardships of winter were worse, and he proceeds with an impressive description that is the very opposite of the conventional *locus amoenus* of many dream allegories: falling ice forces him to sleep in his armour and the birds suffer as much as the hero: 'pitosly þer piped for pyne of þe colde' (l. 747).

Another aspect of traditional romance is rejected with similarly uncompromising sense of true values when Bertilac's lady tries to remind him of the rules of courtly chivalry and love. The programme outlined by her evidently describes a popular idea of what knighthood and adventure is about:

For to telle of þis teuelyng of þis trwe knyȝtez,	*endeavour*
Hit is þe tytelet token and tyxt of her werkkez	*rightful, title, their deeds*
How ledez for her lele luf hor lyuez han auntered,	*knights, loyal, ventured*
Endured for her drury dulful stoundez,	*love, painful times*
And after wenged with her walour and voyded her care	*avenged, removed*
And broȝt blysse into boure with bountées hor awen – (ll. 1514–19)	*bower*

The difference is that this neat description of romance-love is part of her strategy, 'to haf wonnen hym to woȝe' [*harm*] (l. 1550) and has to be courteously refuted by Gawain whose behaviour clearly does not conform to the expectations of Bertilac's party: 'I hope þat may hym here / Schal lerne of luf-talkyng' (ll. 925–6). For all the gaiety and laughter of the two Christmas feasts, the poet leaves us in no doubt about the hollowness and the moral dangers of some literary clichés and the real obligations of Christian chivalry. The portrait of his hero unmistakably corrects the widely current medieval reputation of Gawain as courtly lover of women, and attempts to replace it by a new pattern of perfection epitomised in the figure of the pentangle.

Nevertheless, the poet delights in courtly 'nurture' and rhetorical artifice and he evidently enjoys displaying his expert knowledge of aristocratic accomplishments, as shown in the passage on the breaking of the deer (ll. 1325–64) or the descriptions of festive entertainment. An audience trusted with the sophisticated theological argument of *Pearl* and the lively scriptural exegesis of *Patience* and *Cleanness* could surely be expected to appreciate the moral and literary subtleties of *Sir Gawain and the Green Knight*, where the frequently outworn genre of popular Arthurian romance is raised to a level of moral seriousness and consummate artistry not found in any other Middle English romance.

Notes

1. *Ricardian Poetry. Chaucer, Gower, Langland and the* Gawain *Poet* (London, 1971).

2. For a succinct account of the manuscript see A. S. G. Edwards, 'The Manuscript: British Library MS Cotton Nero A.x.' in Derek Brewer and Jonathan Gibson, eds, *A Companion to the Gawain-Poet*, Arthurian Studies, 38 (Cambridge, 1997), pp. 197–219 (subsequent references are to *Companion*). This collection of essays provides an excellent up-to-date introduction to practically every aspect of the *Gawain*-poet's work.

3. See Malcolm Andrew, 'Theories of Authorship', in *Companion*, pp. 23–33, and A. C. Spearing, 'Poetic Identity', in *Companion*, pp. 35–51.

4. *Companion*, pp. 5–6.

5. See the ground-breaking study by J. P. Oakden, *Alliterative Poetry in Middle English*, 2 vols (Manchester, 1930, 1935).

6. See Spearing's excellent summary in *Companion*, pp. 37–41.

7. All quotations, unless otherwise indicated, are from *The Poems of the Pearl Manuscript*, ed. Malcolm Andrew and Ronald Waldron (London, 1978, rev. edn Exeter, 1987).

8. See the notes to the passage in Andrew and Waldron's edition and in the classic edition by J. R. R. Tolkien and E. V. Gordon, rev. Norman Davis (Oxford, 1967); also Spearing, 'Poetic Identity', p. 38, n. 7.

9. The prophet Jonah is repeatedly referred to in the New Testament; see Matthew xii and Luke xi. To quote Jonah as a symbolic precursor of Jesus was a commonplace of medieval commentators and preachers.

10. See A. C. Spearing, *The Gawain-Poet. A Critical Study* (Cambridge, 1970), p. 75. Andrew, commenting on line 25, says, 'as in 17, the English rendering is an interpretation rather than a direct translation' (p. 186). The correspondence does not seem to be very close in each case; even if 'penaunce' is applied to the second beatitude, 'meekness' (l. 32, perhaps placed here because of the rhyme) appears to fit as well and rather better than for those 'þat hungeres after right'.

11. See Malcolm Andrew, ' "Rome-runners" and *Patience*, line 52', *Archiv für das Studium der Neueren Sprachen und Literaturen*, 219 (1982), 116–18.

12. See Christ's crucial prophecy: 'For as Jonas was three days and three nights in the whale's belly; so shall the Son of man be three days and three nights in the heart of the earth' (Matthew xii, 40).

13. See *Aeneid* I, 85 and 103. The whole account of the storm and of the terror among the men returning from the siege of Troy might well have been in the poet's mind.

14. See Malcolm Andrew, '*Patience*: the "Munster Dor" ', *English Language Notes*, 14 (1976–7), 164–7.

15. On the importance of 'trouthe' as a crucial issue in *Sir Gawain and the Green Knight* see below.

16. At other times the poet draws attention to God's omnipotence, 'þat Wyȝ þat al þe world planted' (l. 111) and 'þe Welder of wyt þat wot alle þynges' (l. 129).

17. On the *Gawain*-poet's concept of 'patience' see Ad Putter, *An Introduction to the Gawain-Poet* (London, 1996), pp. 143–6.

18. The poem is criticised for lack of unity in W. A. Davenport, *The Art of the Gawain-Poet* (London, 1978), 55–6; for a more thorough and substantiated account of the poet's achievement and purpose see Jane K. Lecklider, Cleanness: *Structure and Meaning* (Cambridge, 1997).

19. There are similar tables in the edition by Andrew and Waldron (p. 25) and in the books by Spearing (p. 43) and Davenport (p. 56) among others. Davenport's verdict, 'The

failure of *Purity* is a failure satisfactorily to integrate the vivid tales with one another and with the poem's framework, which consists of intermittent assertions of God's hatred of human impurity' (p. 55), seems to me to rest on his inability to recognise the liturgical structure of the poem and the poet's individual method of blending biblical narrative with personal application.

20. See Lecklider, pp. 163–5, for possible precedents.

21. Cf. Lecklider, pp. 25–7.

22. See the valuable study by A. C. Spearing, *Medieval Dream-Poetry* (Cambridge, 1976), with a good account of *Pearl* (pp. 111–29). Readers of *Pearl* are particularly indebted to the most helpful commentary notes in Malcolm Andrew's edition.

23. Chaucer's *Book of the Duchess* is perhaps the closest parallel, but then it is a distinctly secular treatment of bereavement and loss.

24. Spearing, *Medieval Dream-Poetry*, p. 120: 'We do not have to choose whether or not to see the poem as genuine autobiography, because that question is not raised in the poem itself.'

25. 'Þou lyfed not two ȝer in oure þede' (l. 483).

26. Cf. Putter, *An Introduction to the* Gawain-*Poet*, pp. 168–83, on the linguistic artistry of the poem.

27. For further examples see Andrew's commentary.

28. The circular structure is underlined by the location:

> Þen wakned I in þat erber wlonk;
> My hede vpon þat hylle watz layde
> Þeras my perle to grounde strayd. (ll. 1171–3)

29. There is a good and sensible chapter on the poem in W. R. J. Barron's *English Medieval Romance*, Longman Literature in English Series (1987), pp. 166–73. See also my *The Middle English Romances of the Thirteenth and Fourteenth Centuries* (London, 1969), pp. 193–206. The literature on the poem is of an inexhaustible and delightfully controversial variety. Perhaps the most stimulating introduction is still John Burrow, *A Reading of* Sir Gawain and the Green Knight (London, 1965). For accounts of older criticism see Malcolm Andrew, *The* Gawain-*Poet: An Annotated Bibliography, 1839–1977* (New York, 1979) and Robert J. Blanch, *Sir Gawain and the Green Knight: A Reference Guide* (Troy, New York, 1983).

30. See the lucid comments in Appendix A to Andrea Hopkins's study *The Sinful Knights. A Study of Middle English Penitential Romance* (Oxford, 1990), pp. 204–18.

31. Hopkins, p. 215.

32. Cf. the often discussed lines 1283–7:

> Þaȝ ho were burde bryȝtest þe burne in mynde hade,   *woman*
> Þe lasse luf in his lode for lur þat he soȝt   *danger*
>   Boute hone –
> Þe dunte þat schulde hym deue,   *stroke*
> And nedez hit most be done.

Andrew and most critics accept this amended version; see his note. The manuscript reading, 'Þaȝ I were burde bryȝtest þe burde', makes this an aside by the lady. It has been defended by some authors, e.g. Larry D. Benson in *Art and Tradition in* Sir Gawain and the Green Knight (New Brunswick, NJ, 1965), pp. 45–6 and note 46, and Davenport, *The Art of the Gawain-Poet*, pp. 166–7. For the opposite view see the note on the passage in the edition by Tolkien and Gordon (rev. Davis) and Burrow, p. 84. I agree with his note: 'I doubt whether we should be told at this point what the lady is thinking'. The emended reading is clearly more consistent with the poet's handling of point of view.

33. See the gloss in Andrew's edition. Though 'steuen' often means 'voice' in the poet's vocabulary, it is often, especially in this poem, used with reference to an appointment; see especially ll. 2194, 2213, 2238.

34. See also ll. 1750–4, where his mental preoccupation with the ordeal at the Green Chapel is stressed.

Chapter 6

John Lydgate and Thomas Hoccleve

To present-day readers, John Lydgate often appears not so much as an original poetic talent, let alone a creative innovator, but rather as a most industrious and influential collector and preserver of literary traditions, conventions and story-materials. He is, like many writers in the century after Chaucer's death, a pupil of Chaucer's, but also a successor in his own right, whose impact on later poets was significantly more powerful than is often realised, if only as a rich storehouse of traditional material. For several generations he belonged with Chaucer and Gower to the trio of supreme masters of English poetry and models for later writers. By the time of Shakespeare, however, his reputation had begun to fall behind and it has never recovered since. This is partly due to the size of his output, about 145,000–150,000 lines,[1] but chiefly to major changes in literary taste, in particular a general prejudice against prolixity and suspected dullness, which is a historical phenomenon rather than a valid criterion of quality and poetic achievement.[2]

Lydgate has often been described as a typical respresentative of the culture of his age, and it is true that for a just appreciation of his contribution to medieval literature we have to try and read him within his religious, social and literary environment. Unlike Chaucer and Gower, he did not grow up in the immediate vicinity of the city of London or the Royal court, but in a monastic context. Much of his life was spent within the Benedictine abbey of St Edmund's at Bury in Suffolk. This establishment did not, by any means, confine the monks to a life of physical or intellectual seclusion. As Derek Pearsall has pointed out,

> it may be helpful to think of an abbey in the fifteenth century as something like Oxford or Cambridge colleges in the eighteenth century – wealthy, privileged, celibate, rich in books and heavy with tradition, learned and scholarly, though often in an antiquarian way, close in the counsels of the great yet devoted to their own self-justifying interests and their own intricate manoeuvring: a rich soil, but fat with weeds.[3]

Such was the world into which Lydgate was received at a fairly young age. Born about 1370, he was, according to the earliest records in which his name appears, ordained in 1389, and in 1397 took the full orders of priesthood. St Edmund's was one of the wealthiest abbeys in the country, housing in Lydgate's time about 60–70 monks, with probably the same number of servants, and great estates in Suffolk and neighbouring counties. There was evidently a great deal of contact with the court, with aristocracy and gentry, and Lydgate very early enjoyed the patronage of influential magnates, not least the king himself. The order to which Lydgate belonged even had its own college at Oxford, and we know that he was sent there to pursue his studies: around 1406–8 the Prince of Wales and future King Henry V wrote to the abbot and chapter of Bury to ask for an extension of leave for Lydgate of whom he had received favourable reports. We do not know how long he actually stayed there, but there is no doubt that the relative freedom he must have enjoyed during this period partly accounts for his evident familiarity with matters secular. In his later years, Lydgate seems to have moved between Bury and the court, in London and Windsor, and in the years around 1426 and 1429 he spent some time in Paris, accompanying the Duke of Bedford, brother to Henry V and uncle to Henry VI. From 1423 to 1432 he was prior at Hatfield in Essex, and by 1434 he had returned to Bury for good. He died there in 1449.

At Bury, Lydgate had access to a large library that not only contained a rich collection of devotional literature and patristic bible commentaries, but also a surprising variety of classical writing from Horace, Virgil and Ovid to medieval Latin authors, such as Bartholomeus, author of the widely used *De Proprietatibus Rerum*, and Guido delle Colonne who wrote the *Bellum Troianum* (*c.* 1287).[4] This was Lydgate's principal source for his *Troy Book*, written between 1412 and 1420 and, as the author claims, undertaken at the invitation of Prince Henry.

Unfortunately, we have not many details about Lydgate's association with Henry, apart from the intervention on his behalf during his stay in Oxford and Lydgate's own references. It seems a little rash to link him too narrowly with Lancastrian concerns, especially their problems of legitimacy and succession,[5] but it appears that he impressed the heir to the Crown by his learning and was therefore entrusted with a rather formidable literary labour. Before that, he had written a number of minor poems, mainly in emulation of Chaucer, whose courtly love allegories apparently provided his chief secular poetic model. The disciple's imitations are revealing for their borrowing as well as for the differences.

Courtly love poems

A Complaint of a Loveres Lyfe is an interesting example.[6] The poem, 681 lines in seven-line rhyme-royal stanzas, is obviously modelled on Chaucer's *Book of the Duchess*, his 'Complaint unto Pity', *Troilus and Criseyde*, and Guillaume de Lorris's part of the *Roman de la Rose*. In fact, the poem was included in editions of Chaucer in the sixteenth century and for over a hundred years counted as one of Chaucer's most successful shorter poems. This alone shows that early readers were appreciating other things in Chaucer than later critics and were more impressed by what the two authors have in common than by the differences that strike us so forcefully today.[7] Lydgate seems to have been interested mainly in the demonstration of rhetorical formulae, not in the psychology of the lovers or any more complex moral problems connected with the experience of courtly love. It is therefore not quite fair to compare it with Chaucer's love poems expecting to find the same experimental curiosity and dramatic unpredictability. Neither is it just to call Lydgate's poem merely a conventional set piece, although there is an element of five-finger exercise and a tendency to go beyond the model mainly in the number of rhetorical figures and 'colours', as he and the rhetoricians of his age would have called them.

At the centre of the poem is a love-complaint, overheard and reported by the narrator, just as in Chaucer's *Book of the Duchess*, except that there is no dream vision and no actual contact between listener and mourner, nor are there any particularly individual touches to the love-story. The poet, like Chaucer, portrays himself as one who is himself suffering from the pangs of love, without any personal details:

And wyth a sygh [I] gan for to abreyde	*start*
Out of my slombre and sodenly [vp]-stert	
As he, alas, that nygh for sorow deyde,	
My sekenes sat ay so nygh myn hert.	
But for to fynde socour of my smert,	*suffering*
Or attelest sum relesse of [my] peyn	*at least*
That me so sore halt in euery veyn,	

I rose anon and thoght I wol[de] goon	
Vnto the wode to her the briddes sing	*birds*
When that the mysty vapour was agoon	
And clere and feyre was the morw[e]nyng. (ll. 15–25)	

The traditional morning landscape is presented in more detail than it usually is in Chaucer, and Lydgate's tendency to double and treble effects soon becomes evident. He cannot resist bringing in classical examples, such as Daphne, Diana and Actaeon, when describing the trees and the well (ll. 64–70, ll. 94–8), or mentioning two of the chief villains from the *Roman de la Rose*, Daunger and Disdain when referring to his own sickness (l. 106). The clear water relieves his own burning heartache, but presently he stumbles on one lying between a holly and a woodbine and complaining so piteously that 'Hyt was a deth for to [her] him grone' (l. 140). The narrator tells us that he is going to record his complaint for the benefit of all lovers. Again he makes use of a number of clichés he could easily have picked up from Chaucer or some other writer of the period, but it is worth noting that his emphasis is on his modest role as a reporter. Moreover, he echoes Chaucer in denying any knowledge, let alone experience of his own, such as a love-poet ought to possess:

For vnto wo accordeth compleynyng	*is fitting*
And delful chere vnto heuynesse:	*doleful*
To sorow also, sighing and wepyng	
And pitous mo[u]rnyng vnto drerynesse;	
And who[so] that shal write[n] o[f] distresse	
In party nedeth to know felyngly	*To a certain extent*
Cause and rote of al such malady.	

But I, alas, that am of wit but dulle
And no knowyng haue of such mater
For to discryve and write[n] at the fulle

> The wofull compleynt which that ye shul here,
> But euen like as doth a skryuener
> That can no more what that he shal write   *knows*
> But as his maister beside doth endyte: (ll. 183–96)

Another thought borrowed from Chaucer almost verbatim is the appeal to the lovers among his listeners to whom his report is addressed.[8] The emphasis, however, seems to be chiefly on their suffering from wicked gossip, and there is no mention of the importance of sympathy and pity for others:

> And yf that eny now be in this place
> That fele in love brennyng or fervence   *burning heat*
> Or hyndred were to his lady grace
> With false tonges that with pestilence   *slander*
> Sle tr[e]we men that neuer did offence   *Kill*
> In word ne dede, ne in their entent, –
> If eny such be here now present
>
> Let hym of routhe ley to audyence   *out of compassion*
> With deleful chere and sobre contenaunce
> To here this man, by ful high sentence,
> His mortal wo and his [grete] perturbaunce: (ll. 204–14)

There is no communication between the narrator and the despairing stranger, who exits as soon as he has finished bewailing his misery. We are only told that he is off to another wood, to continue his solitary complaint, as he apparently has done 'For yer to yer' (l. 588). Thus the situation is quite different from *The Book of the Duchess*. The narrator is an unintentional witness of the lover's complaint and an author who is producing a record of the stranger's words and his suffering. He neither interrupts nor directly comments on what he has heard, but immediately stops to set it all down:

> And while the twilyght and the rowes rede   *rays*
> Of Phebus lyght wer deaurat a lyte,   *lost their golden glow*
> A penne I toke and gan me fast[e] spede
> The woful pleynt[e] of this man to write,
> Worde by worde as he dyd endyte:
> Lyke as I herde and coud him tho reporte
> I haue here set, youre hertis to dysporte. (ll. 596–602)   *delight*

The literary document and the pleasure derived from it by the audience seem to be as important as the individual human situation that caused it.

While composing his poem, the author has a vision of Venus, evening star and goddess, to whom he prays for the unhappy lover and for all true lovers. It is difficult to be sure as to the degree of seriousness and the presence of tongue-in-cheek humour, when the poet reminds Venus of the joy she had lying with Mars and of her love for Adonis. These are not very fortunate precedents, and Lydgate can hardly have been unaware of the dissonance, especially since Venus' fatal love for Adonis and her comical escapade with

Mars has already been referred to earlier in the course of the knight's complaint (ll. 389–92), with rather unhappy associations. The irony is compounded by the speaker's parting wish that before sunrise each faithful lover should have 'His ovn lady in armes to embrace' (l. 658).[9]

The 'complaint of the Black Knight'[10] at the centre of the poem is usually described as thoroughly conventional. This is only partly true, however, because the sheer accumulation of familiar rhetorical devices, typical of Lydgate, creates a new effect, either of demonstrative virtuoso craftsmanship or – which to me seems more important – of a half-serious indulging in an essentially meaningless convention – enjoyable, but not really relevant to actual life or to serious moral debate.[11] The monologue hardly succeeds as an expression of genuine suffering, and the listener's reaction suggests indignation with the general injustice of Love's favours and the evil forces of society, rather than personal sympathy and compassion. The unfortunate lover paints a scenario that seems applicable to a whole society, not only to his personal love affair:

> 'And Male-bouche gan first the tale telle   *Wicked-mouth*[12]
> To sclaundre Trouthe of Indignacion,
> And Fals-Report so loude rong the belle
> That Mysbeleve and Fals-Suspecion   *Disbelieve*
> Haue Trouthe brought to hys damnacion:
> So that, alas, wrongfully he dyeth
> And Falsnes now his place occupieth
>
> 'And entred ys into Trouthes londe
> And hath therof the ful possessyon. (ll. 260–8)

The dramatis personae are old acquaintances from the *Roman de la Rose*, but they have become figures of speech rather than substantial personifications. The story behind the allegorical campaign is not particularly original or individualised and it is moved even further away from actuality by the string of classical examples that suggest either the speaker's ignorance of the tradition behind them or wilful misinterpretation for the sake of making them fit the subject of the complaint. A typical instance is the stanza about the lovers of Venus:

> 'For trwe Adon was slayn with the bore
> Amyd the forest in the grene shade:
> For Venus love he felt[e] al the sore.
> But Vulcanus with her no mercy made,
> The foule cherle [ha]d many nightis glade:
> Wher Mars her [worthy] knight, her [trewe] man,
> To fynde mercy comfort noon he can. (ll. 386–92)   *no comfort of pity*

Neither Adonis nor Mars seem to be very happily chosen as examples of faithful lovers betrayed by wicked tongues. The Black Knight's lady apparently has withdrawn her favour from him under the impression of false lies against him, for which he blames Venus and Cupid as the rulers over the fortune of

131

lovers. Altogether, the wretched lover strikes an accusing tone; he is more angry at all those forces that have worked together to frustrate his love than grieved about her lack of pity. Hers is not the conventional reluctance to accept his love, nor is Daunger his worst enemy, though that traditional opponent to love is denounced as well, but the evil counsellors of suspicion and slander which the Goddess of Nature has given her:

> '. . . – and altherlast Dysdeyne
> To hinder Trouth she made her chambreleyne,
>
> 'When Mystryst also and Fals-Suspecion   *Distrust*
> With Mysbeleve she made for to be   *Disbelieve*
> Chefe of counseyle, to this conclusion,
> For to exile Routhe and eke Pite:
> Out of her court to make Mercie fle
> So that Dispite now haldeth forth her reyn   *Contempt*
> Thro hasty beleve of tales that men feyn. (ll. 503–11)   *falsely invent*

The complaint ends without reproach for the lady and with 'no demaunde' (l. 565), affirming the lover's willingness to die in her service if she so chooses, bequeathing her only the lasting testimony of his *trouthe*.

Unless we are satisfied to read the poem only as a superficial collection of outworn formulae, we should stop to look for signs of a less conventional attitude towards the familiar complaint. What the Black Knight appears to accuse is not so much vicious gossip and calumny, but the whole system of values and social obligations behind the tradition of courtly love. The radical choice offered to the lady – her lover's life or death – is presented without any tangible context, except for the abstract quality of his 'trouthe'. This recurs in the closing section of the double frame, when the poet first prays for 'ye louers al[le] that be trewe' (l. 653) and then addresses his dedicatee or patroness, repeating his message that a true lover deserves mercy and pity because 'hit is ayen[e]s kynde / False Daunger for to occupie his place' (ll. 672–3). The very last stanza, recommending his little book to his 'verry hertes souereigne' (l. 675), once more bemoans the exile of 'Mercie, Routhe, Grace and eke Pite' (l. 679) that leaves the poet without any cure for his suffering.

It is hard to believe that Lydgate did not know what he was doing when he composed this ostentatiously conventional poem. It seems to conform to all the rules of the game, yet by seemingly indiscriminate piling on of over-used poetic devices and by largely depersonalising the situation it becomes a literary exercise and at the same time an implicit criticism of a code that has lost the vital connection with the life of the individual. If there is any explicit moral drawn from the text it is the value of truth in a society that does not respect it, within a discourse that borrows its terms and references from the tradition of courtly love, but without subscribing to its values or pretending to be rooted in actual experience. For a monk in full orders to slip into the mask of an unhappy lover is not an unusual phenomenon in the Middle Ages – many a sorrowful love lyric was composed by clerics – but in this case it does suggest a critical distance from the conventions used with such intimate knowledge and artistic expertise.

The Temple of Glass is a more ambitious and more difficult poem. It is more than twice as long as *The Complaint of a Lover's Life* (1403 lines)[13] and divided into three sections by changes in metre. Three narrative passages in rhyming couplets introduce three groups of rhyme-royal stanzas, consisting mainly of speeches by a lady caught in an unhappy marriage and her unrewarded lover, with Venus as arbiter. The text is extant in eight manuscripts and was evidently very popular in the fifteenth century. Lydgate revised it more than once, changing the character of the lady and her situation and thereby introducing some ambiguity in the relationships implied.[14]

The Temple of Glass again starts with a scenario that combines elements and near-quotations borrowed from Chaucer, the *Roman de la Rose* and other such literary quarries. The poet goes to bed 'For thou3t, constreint and greuous heuines, / For pensifhede, and for hei3 distres' (ll. 1–2), on a cold winter night, to be surprised by a vision of a temple of glass which turns out to contain a gallery of lovers, from Dido to Adonis, from Griseldis to Philomene and including even Philologia, married to Mercury according to Martianus Capella's often quoted fifth-century poem *De Nuptiis Philologiae et Mercurii*. The catalogue reads like an inventory of classical love stories, most of them familiar to readers of Chaucer, who is mentioned as the author of 'The Knights Tale', but has also furnished several examples and other materials in *The Legend of Good Women*, *The House of Fame*, *Troilus and Criseyde* and several of the *Canterbury Tales*. Moreover, the dreamer finds in the temple

> Ful mani a þousand of louers, here and þere,
> In sondri wise redi to complein
> Vnto þe goddes, of hir wo and pein,
> Hou þei were hindred, some for envie,
> And hou þe serpent of fals Ielousie
> Ful many a louer haþ iput obak   *aback*
> And caus[e]les on hem ilaid a lak. (ll. 144–50)   *put a blame on them*

Once again the chief culprits are, besides Ielousie, 'wikkid tungis and fals suspecioun', Daunger and Disdain. Another, more unusual group encountered in the temple is made up of young girls married, against nature, to old men,[15] forced 'into religioun' (l. 201) before the age of discretion and doomed to a life of complaining in feigned perfection, or married 'Wiþoute fredom of eleccioun' and without love at a tender age. This provides the background for the poem's heroine, a lady the dreamer finds kneeling before the statue of Venus. His description, a conventional rhetorical set piece, celebrates her as the most perfect specimen Nature could create. Her motto, *De Mieulx en Mieulx*, could suggest an association with the Paston family, who had chosen it as theirs, but the phrase was evidently common at the time and does not prove any personal application. This is even less likely when the substance of the lady's complaint to Venus is taken into account. It is supported by a 'litel bil' (l. 317) in her hand, which lends a formal, almost judicial quality to her plea. The lady suffers from hopeless love, but what is unconventional in her situation is that she is not free to speak of her affection:

> 'For I am bounde to þing þat I nold: *do not want*
> Freli to chese þere lak I liberte,   *choose*
> And so I want of þat myn hert[e] would,
> The bodi knyt, alþouȝe my þouȝt be fre;   *joined (by marriage)*
> So þat I most, of necessite,
> Myn hertis lust outward contrarie –
> Thogh we be on, þe dede most varie. (ll. 335–41)   *are one, be different*

After what has been said before there can be little doubt that the lady is the victim of a forced marriage. Her dilemma is almost wittily put in a nutshell:

> For þat I nold is redi aye to me,   *do not want*
> And þat I loue, forto swe I drede: *I fear to desire*
> To my desire contrarie is my mede. (ll. 351–3)   *reward*

Though extramarital affairs are by no means uncommon in continental courtly love poetry, indeed, they are, according to an older school of criticism, essential to *fin amour*, the case is different here because a poet like Lydgate could not possibly sanction an adulterous relationship or turn a serious complaint into a farcical *fabliau*. He seems to have struggled with the subject because he replaced four stanzas of his first version, where the lady complains bitterly about old men ('krokede fer in age') 'couplid with ȝouthe'.[16] This was evidently too explicit and the poet decided to tone it down, which modifies or at least clouds the whole issue. At any rate, Venus pities the lady and promises a happy outcome.

The second part of the poem starts again with a narrative passage in couplets, introducing a new suitor to Venus, the unhappy lover of the lady who, after a soliloquy expressing his sorrow, makes his formal complaint in rhyme-royal stanzas. He seems unaware of the reasons that prevent the lady from granting him her favour, but Venus encourages him to confess his love and sue for grace, holding out a prospect of success.

At this point the poet steps in once more, protesting his inability to do justice to the Knight's suffering and calling on Thesiphone, one of the Furies, to help him.[17] This part, a kind of invocation, is again written in couplets (ll. 932–69). Through Venus' intercession the knight's humble suit succeeds, but the solution is so ambiguous that earlier scholars have taken the poem as a work written for a particular wedding,[18] while Pearsall calls it 'not a poem about love' but 'a poem about suffering'.[19] Within the time-honoured triangle the lover's 'trouthe' can, for Lydgate, only be rewarded spiritually, by a union founded on honesty, constancy and all the virtues associated with love, excepting physical fulfilment. For that the lovers must wait in hope and they appear to be satisfied without reserve. At least this seems implied in the lady's condition:

> 'For vnto þe time þat Venus [list] prouyde   *is pleased to*
> To shape a wai for oure hertis ease,
> Boþe ȝe and I mekeli most abide,   *meekly to suffer*
> To take agre and not of oure disease   *accept graciously*
> To grucch agein, til she list to appese   *grumble against*
> Oure hid[de] wo, so inli þat constreyneþ
> From dai to day and oure hert[is] peyneþ. (ll. 1082–8)

Earlier, Venus had warned the knight that all the favours he can expect must be 'grovndid opon honeste' (l. 870) and must not give occasion for any misconstruction by society. This sounds almost like the language of Chaucer's Criseyde and her anxious care for her good name, but Lydgate steers clear of any suggestion of an illicit affair, and Venus bestows her blessing on a bond with a golden chain (l. 1106), as if all problems were solved by mutual affection and constant 'trouthe'. After all we know (and the poet has reminded us of it) about Venus' previous loves, she seems an unlikely patroness of chaste affection, but there is no doubt about Lydgate's determination to extract all the positive moral qualities fostered by an honest attachment, by constancy and devotion to an ideal human being. This explains why the actual story, if there is one, seems hardly relevant in view of Venus' celebration of this marriage of true minds and the imperatives of moral perfection.

Perhaps there is a connection between the ambiguity of the conclusion and the poet's grief when he awakes from the dream and finds that he has forgotten it. This appears rather inconsistent at the end of a poem that has given such a detailed account of the dream, but it creates an additional distance between the reader and what we have been told. The poet has described an idealised vision of love inspired by his December-dream, of which he intends to give a more faithful account when it comes back to his memory. The *envoi* to his own lady adds a conventional conclusion to this neatly constructed and, for all its borrowed phrases, quite original poem.

There is some justification for devoting so much space to Lydgate's comparatively slight love visions, because they were so popular with the generations after Lydgate and even today are probably the most accessible part of his immense output. The bulk of his canon consists of translations and adaptations that are remarkable chiefly as documents of European literary traffic and the receptivity and taste of a class of English readers. From the number of surviving manuscripts, *Troy Book*, the *Siege of Thebes* and, above all, the *Fall of Princes,* were widely esteemed, the last apparently more in the form of excerpts than as a complete work.

Major translations and adaptations

Lydgate's *Troy Book* was the first major order, began in 1412 for Prince Henry and completed in 1420. As in a number of works written during the previous century, one of the declared reasons given for the project is the demand for English rather than French or Latin versions of prestigious stories.[20] The 'matter of Troy' was, for the Middle Ages and the Renaissance, the most famous classical myth and a compendium of true chivalry. It had been translated from Guido delle Colonne twice, shortly before Lydgate, but the two anonymous works are only preserved in unique manuscripts, whereas the *Troy Book* is extant in twenty-three.[21] Lydgate's version, in rhyming couplets, is over 30,000 lines long. The author is evidently anxious to give a faithful English version of the whole history, following his source without any major omission, alteration or rearrangement, but with a great deal of expansion and rhetorical flourishes. From the evident favour the book enjoyed we can only conclude that Lydgate's decorated rhetorical style met exactly the taste of his audience, at least the wealthier patrons and customers who paid for the expensive copies that were made of several of his poems.

When Chaucer approached the matter of Troy, he preferred to choose one episode out of this huge panorama, basing his *Troilus and Criseyde* on Boccaccio, while pretending to follow a Latin source. Lydgate's order was entirely different. He did not feel free (nor, probably, willing) to create his own, personal version of the historic events and his ambition was obviously towards rhetorical showmanship rather than psychological depth or complexity. It is therefore inappropriate to measure his endeavour against Chaucer's poetic masterpiece. Lydgate's stylistic aims can be judged from his excessive praise of Guido, whom he, in vain, as he admits, attempts to emulate:

> For he enlvmyneth by crafte & cadence   *illumins, skill and art of metre*
> This noble story with many fresche colour
> Of rethorik, and many riche flour
> Of eloquence to make it sownde bet
> He in the story hath ymped in and set,   *engrafted*
> That in good feythe I trowe he hath no pere,   *trust*
> To rekne alle þat write of this matere,
> As in his boke 3e may beholde and se. (Prologue, 362–9)

The *Troy Book* is divided into a Prologue of 384 lines and five books. The first is almost completely taken up with the story of Jason and the Argonauts, the love of Jason and Medea and the winning of the Golden Fleece. The second book tells the story of Priam and his family, the rebuilding of Troy, the expedition of Paris to Greece, his abduction of Helena and their wedding, Cassandra's prophetic warnings, the Greeks' decision to collect an army and their encampment before the walls of Troy. The third book describes the battles around Troy, the story of Troilus and Cressida and the death of Hector. Book four continues the account of the war, with the death of Troilus and Achilles, to the betrayal of Troy by Anchises, Eneas, Antenor and Polydamas with the scheme of the Horse of Brass and the destruction of the town. The last book follows the fates of the surviving Greeks and Trojans, ending with the death of Ulysses and a summary of the war.

Lydgate's effort to excel his model often has the unfortunate result that it leads him into prolixity. There is, for the most part, a competent sameness, with very little gradation of effects and hardly any climax or startling surprises. Lydgate's method of 'illumination' is often mere addition or multiplication of conventional devices, without a gain in complexity. However, Benson is right when he claims that 'Lydgate's amplifications of his source often show real intelligence and craft, even by modern standards'.[22]

Only a few of these amplifications can be illustrated here. If they often seem to be no more than commonplace observations or almost mechanical padding, they evidently reflect the taste of the period and have to be judged within the context of the whole project. Some of Lydgate's most frequent expansions consist of added moral commentary at important points of the action and the insertion or rhetorical lengthening of elaborate speeches. An instance of the first occurs when in Book ii the Trojans celebrate their fatal triumph of winning Helena. Here the English translator steps in with an observation not found in his source, but not exactly original:

The vnhappy tyme & þe same while	
Þat Fortune falsly gan to smyle	
Vp-on Troyans & bad hem [to] be merye,	
For whiche hiȝly þei gan her goddis herie,	*praise*
Wenyng in Ioye to haue ben assured wele,	*Believing*
No þing aduerting þe turnyng of þe whele	*paying attention to*
Of hir þat lastiþ stable but a throwe –	*moment*
Whan men most trust, sche can make a mowe,	*move*
Turne hir forhed, & hir face writhe,	*distort*
(Suche Ioye sche haþe hir doubilnes to kiþe,	*doubleness, make known*
And to wrappe hir clernes vnder cloude),	*clear aspect*
Ageyn whos myȝt no man may hym schrowde –	*protect*
Whan sche most flateriþ þan sche is lest to trist:	*least to be trusted*
For in her Ioye þe Troyans litel wist	
What sche ment to her confusioun. (ii, 4255–69)	

This may seem superfluous to the informed reader, but it marks an important turning point in the history of Troy, and one can sympathise with the chronicler who wants to draw the audience's attention to such opportunities for serious reflection.

The expansion of speeches is another conventional device recommended by rhetoricians. A typical example comes soon after the passage just quoted, when Agamemnon tries to cheer up his brother Menelaus, who is lamenting the loss of his wife. In Guido this is a rational address of about a dozen lines. In Lydgate, Agamemnon's speech of consolation takes up ninety lines like these:

With word & wepyng for to venge oure peyne,	*revenge*
Be no menys to worschip to attayne;	*to achieve glory*
Lat vs with swerde & nat with wordis fiȝt,	
Our tonge apese, be manhod preve oure myȝt:	
Word is but wynde, & water þat we wepe,	
And þouȝ þe tempest and þe flodis depe	
Of þis two encresen euere-mo,	
Þei may nat do but augmente oure wo – (ii, 4379–86)	

Lydgate was writing in good faith when he claimed that he was true to his source in all essential points. His high regard for Guido's rhetoric must have persuaded him that any stylistic embellishment would be an act of reverence rather than of schoolmasterly correction and would not interfere with the substance of the history.

There is, however, one subject where Lydgate appears to be at odds with his predecessor: his attitude to women. This has often been commented on, but with uncertain results. It is at first puzzling that Lydgate regularly translates and even expands Guido's anti-feminist attacks and then leaps to women's defence or pretends to do so. The description of Medea's love for Jason is a characteristic example. Guido has only one, not violently offensive sentence of some three lines, which Lydgate takes 25 (short) lines to 'translate' (i, 2072–96) and about forty to 'refute' (2097–135). After the enthusiastic amplification of Guido's comparatively routine exclamation Lydgate's apology sounds like hypocritical irony or heavy-handed humour, as well as a rather feeble imitation of Chaucer's infinitely lighter touch:

Þus liketh Guydo of wommen for tendite.	*write poetry about*
Allas, whi wolde he so cursedly write	*hatefully*
Ageyne[e]s hem, or with hem debate!	*quarrel*
I am riȝt sory in englische to translate	
Reprefe of hem, or any euel to seye;	*Reproof*
Leuer me wer for her loue deye. (i, 2097–102)	*I would prefer to*

He goes on with exaggerated praise for women and somewhat ludicrous defence of their changeable nature. In the end he protests that he is going to despair of Guido's salvation, unless he died repentant, and offers to shrive him in person if he were still alive and willing to recant.[23]

When it comes to Cryseyde's betrayal of Troilus, Lydgate, without support from Guido and paying no heed whatever to Chaucer's compassionate portrait of his heroine, indulges in a particularly unsympathetic and hostile view of the tragedy. His cynical humour has more in common with the bitter Merchant of the *Canterbury Tales* or Shakespeare's Thersites than with Chaucer's sorrowful narrator. When, even against the advice of her father,[24] Cryseyde visits Diomede in his tent and within ten lines gives him her heart ('Hooly hir herte', iv, 2147), without any effort on his part, the translator adds some thirty, clumsily satirical lines to Guido's far more factual account:

Loo! what pite is in wommanhede,	
What mercy eke & benygne routhe –	
Þat newly can al her olde trouthe,	
Of nature, late slyppe a-syde	*let slip*
Raþer þanne þei shulde se abide	
Any man in meschef for hir sake!	
Þe change is nat so redy for to make	
In Lombard Strete a crowne nor doket	*ducat*
Al paie is good, be so þe prente be set: (iv, 2148–56)	*ever, printing*

He cannot even blame Guido at this point.

It is difficult for a reader of a different age to be sure whether Lydgate's elaborate defence of women against his source is meant to be light-heartedly humorous or as a particularly vicious confirmation of Guido's diatribes against women. Rather than deciding where the author personally stands, one should, I believe, take his teasingly confrontational intervention at this point, as on several others where the reputation of women is concerned, as an invitation to a literary debate on an always popular issue.[25]

For all his truthfulness in respect to the history he is Englishing, Lydgate never hesitates to interrupt the flow of the narrative with personal comments or remarks on his own literary labour. For instance, Chaucer, his chief model, is invoked more than once: Lydgate laments his loss since he could have advised him:

> And Chaucer now, allas! is nat alyue
> Me to reforme, or to be my rede, *counseller*
> For lak of whom slou3er is my spede – (iii, 550–2) *clumsier*

Earlier, when introducing Cryseyde, he inserts a long eulogy of Chaucer (ii, 4677–729), whose golden rhetoric transformed the rude English of his day and whose excellence he can never hope to equal. When he comes to Cryseyde's departure from Troy and Troilus' grief, Lydgate again refers the reader to Chaucer's account, repeating his praise of Chaucer's service to the English tongue and comparing him with Petrarch as worthy of the laurel crown (iii, 4195–263). On the last pages of the work, asking for the reader's indulgence, the translator again pays tribute to Chaucer who, Lydgate says he has been told, was a gentle judge of other men's work (v, 3521–39).

The book concludes with a dedication to Henry V who commissioned the work eight years earlier and who is celebrated as the conqueror of Normandy and future King of France, his rightful inheritance. Finally, there are a conventionally fulsome *envoy* of thirteen rhyme-royal stanzas addressed to his prince and patron and another two stanzas ('Go, litel bok') to his poem asking for criticism and correction. With somewhat exaggerated modesty the poet protests that the work is 'enlumined w*ith* no floures / Of rethorik, but white & blak' (100–1), which is contradicted by nearly every page. Nevertheless, as a skilfully presented repository of the medieval Troy myth, the book was very succesful and gratefully exploited by several generations of authors and readers.

The Siege of Thebes was begun soon after completion of the *Troy Book* in 1420 and finished in 1422, before Henry's death in August of that year, but there is no record of any commission or patronage in this case. Twenty-nine manuscripts are extant; in three of them the poem is copied together with the *Troy Book*.[26] The two stories often occur together in French manuscripts and are closely related in other ways, which may account for Lydgate's choice. *The Siege of Thebes* is more readable than the *Troy Book*, if only because it is much shorter (only 4716 lines) and less ambitious in the use of rhetorical amplification and surface embellishment.

Perhaps the most interesting part of it is the Prologue, in which Lydgate introduces himself as one who has made a pilgrimage to Canterbury, where he encounters the company Chaucer has already described in his *Canterbury Tales*. They are about to return to London, and the newcomer is invited by the host to join them on their way home. After a short while, a tale 'of myrth or of gladnesse' (Prologue, 168) is demanded by the host and Lydgate readily obliges. The fiction is transparent and not quite consistent: Lydgate tells the host his name and age ('Lydgate, / Monk of Bery / ny3 fyfty 3ere of age'

Prologue, 92–3), which has been taken as proof of his real birth-date, but he appears to know all about the pilgrims and the stories that have already been told on the way. More important, however, than this minor problem of fictional realism is Lydgate's novel tribute to Chaucer and to the popularity of his Canterbury pilgrims.[27] Chaucer himself does not appear, and of the company only the host is sketched with some attempt at Chaucer's humour and realism; but the reader is evidently expected to recognise old friends.

The story itself, about twice as long as the 'Knight's Tale', seems almost conceived as a rival to it: it contains the whole history of Thebes from the city's foundation to the point where the 'Knight's Tale' begins. Lydgate's source is an Old French prose romance based on the verse narrative *Roman de Thebes*, and the context of the pilgrimage is soon lost sight of, except for the end of the first part and the beginning of the second (1044–60), where the geography of the road back to London and the time of day are recalled. All the pilgrims ride near him when he continues his tale. Towards the end, when the narrative almost runs parallel with the 'Knight's Tale', Lydgate reminds his audience that they have already heard this part of the story 'at Depforth in the vale, / In the bygynnyng / of the knyghtys tale' (ll. 4523–4), where, as a matter of fact, within his own fiction, he had not been present. There is no attempt to connect the remainder of the story with the Canterbury fiction. Like the 'Knight's Tale', but infinitely less structured and unified, the *Siege of Thebes* is a self-contained narrative with a distinctly literary attitude. The amount of material Lydgate presents is not organised in such a way as to form a coherent story, and the poem remains a rather loose sequence of episodes with no firm thematic thread. Much of it is competently recounted, and there are some impressive moments, but it is hard to differ from Pearsall when he speaks of the 'colossal irrelevance of the Oedipus-story as Lydgate tells it'[28] or from Cooper's verdict: 'Lydgate did not have the advantage of knowing Sophocles, but it is still hard to forgive a man who can read the story of Oedipus as (*a*) a warning to princes against incest, and (*b*) an exemplum of a man cast off Fortune's wheel'.[29]

Yet when all has been said against Lydgate's treatment of a myth ennobled for us by the Greek tragedians, one should also do justice to the more successful sections of the tale, e. g. the characters of Eteocles and Tydeus, and to Lydgate's earnest endeavour to extract some consistent moral out of this famous sequence of events.

The next major commission Lydgate undertook was the translation of the *Pélerinage de la Vie Humaine* of Guillaume de Deguileville, a Cistercian monk who wrote the work in the first half of the fourteenth century.[30] The translator's Prologue says that the work was begun in 1426 at the command of the Earl of Salisbury; the authorship of the translation is not certain, but there is no reason to doubt the sixteenth-century ascriptions of the poem. Earlier scholars believed that John Bunyan (1628–88), the author of the popular *Pilgrim's Progress* (1678) was influenced by it; but it is not likely that he ever heard of the book.

The Pilgrimage of the Life of Man, like its French original, is a dream-vision clearly modelled on the *Roman de la Rose*, describing in allegorical guise man's progress through life, from birth to approaching death, with encyclopedic information and discussion of the history of the church, temptation, deadly sins, heresy and many related topics. The work is presented as a dream, beginning with a vision of the heavenly city Jerusalem, where the dreamer meets many pilgrims who have already come to the end of their journey through life and is received by a lady, *Grace Dieu*, who offers to guide him on his pilgrimage. This familiar image is also introduced by the translator:

> Trusteth ther-for, ye folk of euery age,
> That yowre lyff her ys but a pylgrymage;
> ffor lyk pylgrymes ye passë to & ffro,
> Whos Ioye ys euere meynt A-mong with wo. (Prologue, 45–8)   *mixed*

The translation, though rather longer than the original (24,832 against 18,123 lines), keeps very close to the French text; there are no major additions or changes and not as much prolix rhetorical decoration (or padding) as in the *Troy Book*. The writer modestly declares at some length that he is 'bareyn of all eloquence' (l. 166) because none of the nine Muses has befriended him, and he therefore asks the reader to pay attention to the 'sentence' and not to 'the makyng' (ll. 164–5). Furnivall, the first editor, is scathing in his verdict on the work's literary merits, but he is not wrong in judging that the chief interest for the modern reader is its value as a linguistic, religious and theological document: 'Of the literary quality of the rest of the verse, the less that's said, the better; but of course the text is of worth for its words, metre and grammar, and its gauge of religious folks' minds in the 14th and 15th centuries'.[31] Nevertheless, it is to scholars like Furnivall that we owe the majority of editions that have made these texts accessible.

The other major work of Lydgate's to be discussed here is a translation, or rather adaptation of a particularly influential and popular work, Boccaccio's *De Casibus Virorum Illustrium*, in Latin prose, finished around 1358, a collection of tragic 'cases' of famous personalities brought down by Fortune through their own ambition and sinful pride. The English version was commissioned by Humphrey, Duke of Gloucester in *c.* 1431, when Lydgate was about to return to Bury for the rest of his life. The duke was a younger brother of Henry V and protector of England during the minority of Henry VI who was crowned 1429. He had been to the continent on several occasions, both military and political, and had brought Italian scholars to England. In a still basically medieval England he tried to act as a patron of Humanist studies; he was a great collector of books, many of which he gave to the University of Oxford.

The Fall of Princes, Lydgate's longest work (36,365 lines), is extant in over 30 manuscripts containing the complete poem; but the 'more characteristic dissemination is in the form of collections of extracts, particularly the envoys'.[32] This is not surprising since *The Fall of Princes* is an encyclopedic compendium or comprehensive collection rather than a definitively structured book, even more so than the other major works Lydgate had translated. Its source material as well as its afterlife show that the plan allowed for constant revision and addition. This is confirmed by its most famous and influential descendant, the Tudor classic *Mirror for Magistrates* (first edition 1559).[33]

Boccaccio's work, used by Lydgate in a French prose translation, already generously amplified, consists of a long series of individual 'tragedies' mostly drawn from biblical and classical accounts and presented as cumulative warning against the instability of Fortune and the end of overweening human ambition and pride. Sometimes the author tells their story and often they tell it themselves. Lydgate, as is usual with him, amplifies his source to produce a work so unwieldy that it was more often anthologised and quoted than read in its entirety. In his prologue, he quotes the French adapter Laurence de Premierfait who maintained that one should not be brief in such a case, but add to one's material for the readers' instruction. Throughout the work, however, the English translator refers to his author as 'Bochas', though there is no evidence that he ever consulted the Latin text. His own translation is in seven-line rhyme-royal stanzas, a metre that seems to act as stimulus to his prolixity. The Prologue of 469 lines repeats at some length the moral purpose of the work:

> Do plesance to the comon profit,
> Off noble stories to make rehersaile,   *rehearsal*
> Shewyng a mero*ur* how al the world shal faile,
> And how Fortune, for al ther hih renou*n*,
> Hath vpon pryncis iurediccio*un*. (Prologue, 157–61)

As in the *Troy Book*, there is elaborate praise for Chaucer who, Lydgate says, 'whilom made ful pitous tragedies; / The fall of pryncis he dede also compleyne' (ll. 248–9). He gives an interesting long list of Chaucer's works, including the 'Monk's Tale', a kind of humorous short-hand version of the *Fall of Princes*:

> And how the Monk off stories newe & olde
> Piteous tragedies be the weie tolde. (ll. 349–50)[34]

The Prologue concludes with an enthusiastic tribute to the Duke of Gloucester, who is praised as a lover of scholarship and languages and a protector of the church who will not tolerate any Lollards in his country.

Lydgate's patron not only paid for the commission, though apparently in fits and starts,[35] he also took some active interest in the progress of the translation and suggested additions, as in the case of Lucrece's story, which the poet, though he at first refers the reader to Chaucer's account, had to enrich by translating a version from a book suggested, and probably provided by Humphrey. The insertion is fair sample of Lydgate's verbose style and his lavish use of Latinate vocabulary:

> But at Lucrece stynte I will a while,   *stop*
> It were pite hir story for to hide,
> Or slouthe the pen*ne* of my reude[e] stile,   *prevent, rude*
> But for his sake alle materis set a-side.
> Also my lord bad I sholde abide,   *take the time*
> By good auys at leiser to translate   *advice, leisure*
> The doolful processe off hir pitous fate.
>
> Folwyng the tracis off Collucyus,
> Which wrot off hir a declamacio*un*

> Most lame*n*table, moost doolful, most pitous,
> Where he descryueth the dolerous tresou*n*   *deplorable*
> Off hir constreyned fals oppressiou*n*,   *forced*
> Wrouht & compassid bi vnwar violence,   *unforeseen*
> The liht ontroublid off hir cleer conscience. (ii, 1002–15)[36]

In retelling the tragedy of Lucrece, Lydgate shows no sign of being aware of her (and her commentators') moral dilemma. For him, her story is a simple tale of cruel tyranny and rape. Chaucer's less 'aureate' version in *The Legend of Good Women* is infinitely more subtle and compassionate in comparison.

The most revealing document of Humphrey's active interest in the progress of Lydgate's commission is the addition of 'envoys' to many of the individual tragedies. The poet's own account of the Duke monitoring the progress of the translation and actual interference in the text suggests an unusually close relationship between patron and writer, even if some of it may be fictionally embellished:

> Anon afftir, I off entenciou*n*,   *with full intention*
> With pen*n*e in hande faste gan me speede,   *hasten*
> As I koude, in my translaciou*n*,
> In this labour ferthere to proceede,
> My lord com forbi, and gan to taken heede;   *pay attention*
> This myhti prynce, riht manly & riht wis,
> Gaff me charge in his prudent auys,   *counsel*
>
> That I sholde in eueri tragedie,
> Afftir the processe made menciou*n*,   *story*
> At the eende sette a remedie,
> With a lenvoie conueied be resou*n*,
> And afftir that, with humble affecciou*n*,
> To noble pryncis lowli it directe,
> Bi othres fallyng [thei myht] themsilff correcte.
>
> And I obeied his biddyng and plesau*n*ce,
> Vnder support off his magnyficence.
> As I coude, I gan my penne auau*n*ce,   *drive forward*
> Al-be I was bareyn off eloquence,   *barren*
> Folwyng myn auctou*r* in substau*n*ce & sentence:
> For it suffised, pleynli, onto me,
> So that my lord my makyng took at gre. (ii, 141–61)   *with good will*

This is quite different from Gower's brief gestures currying royal favour, and nothing like Chaucer's apparent independence of any such consideration. This can be seen as evidence of Lydgate's different social and political position, but also as a document of a far-reaching change in the poetic climate.

Lydgate's envoys were evidently valued out of their context by later readers and collectors. They are mostly conventional rhetorical set pieces, moralising the tragedies and lamenting the fall of another great man and admonishing 'noble princes'. Sometimes Lydgate makes an attempt at imitating Chaucerian irony, as when he caps his pathetic complaint of Dido's suicide with another envoy warning matrons not to follow her example, but make sure to be always provided with lovers (ii, 2171–233). There is also plenty of unsubtle irony in Lydgate's rendering of Boccaccio's notorious long anti-feminist invective (i, 6511–734), reminiscent of his interventions on the same theme in the *Troy Book*.

The prologues provide further evidence of Lydgate's anxious glances at his patron, by flattery, by learned name-dropping and by appeals to his generosity.[37] But, above all, like his numerous additions, digressions and asides, they amply testify to his impressive reading and easy command of rhetorical commonplaces. His memory or else his ready access to texts and references is astonishing and as good as unprecedented in Middle English poetry. It has made *The Fall of Princes* for a century a most valuable source book for other writers. For the modern reader, however, the interest of this massive compilation is historical rather than literary, much as one must respect the dedicated industry of the translator and adapter.

A monastic hack-writer?

In conclusion, I will briefly return to Lydgate's 'minor' poetry because it is here that, at a glance, we get an idea of his versatility and his usefulness as a writer who could be employed on all kinds of occasions and turn his hand at any subject where a few lines or a longish poem would be required or be appropriate. MacCracken's collection of religious and secular short poems not only contains some of Lydgate's more successful poetry, it also provides an instructive survey of contemporary themes and concerns. It is perhaps not untypical that of all of Lydgate's verse, the most frequently copied is also one of the least remarkable 'as literature'. The 'Dietary' is a collection of platitudinous rules for healthy and moral living, probably designed for schoolchildren or adolescents to learn by heart as a practical guide. One can only agree with Pearsall: 'Literary criticism has no part here, except to say that what had to be done is well done, and with assurance, and that the manner is well suited to the matter.'[38] Nevertheless, 'literary criticism' has to take note of the poem's striking dissemination, if only for the sake of a sense of proportion as to the actual use and function of texts. It is likely that this kind of short, practical rhyming was copied and transmitted even much more frequently than the number of extant texts suggests. Many others of Lydgate's minor poems are of such practical nature, occasional pieces, entertainments, political homage or religious devotion, often more or less loosely translated from Latin or French. It is evident that during the fifteenth century and beyond, a large body of literature on various prosaic topics was being turned into English verse and prose because its audience was no longer conversant with Latin lore.[39]

The range of subjects is remarkable. There are poems on particular occasions, like the famous 'On the Departing of Thomas Chaucer', or the begging letter to the Duke of Gloucester, apparently composed while Lydgate was translating the *Fall of Princes*.[40] More political are the poems in honour of King Henry VI, whose title and pedigree, coronation and triumphal entry into

London are the subject of translations, ballads and roundels; other pieces are dedicated to Humphrey, Duke of Gloucester. Of particular interest among the 'minor' poems are seven 'mummings', poems written to be recited with pageants or dumb shows, for the court or on public occasions, commissioned either by guilds, civic officials or the Royal Household. These mummings are often described in connection with the early history of English drama, though most of Lydgate's texts are at best semi-dramatic in form.[41] The 'Mumming at Windsor', presented before Henry VI at Christmas on the eve of his departure for his coronation as King of England and France, is a characteristic example. The speech, delivered perhaps by Lydgate himself, describes the miracle at Rheims that led to the fleurs de lis being chosen as the device of the French kings. The final stanza introduces a visual representation or show:

> Nowe, Royal Braunche, O Blood of Saint **Lowys**,
>   So lyke it nowe to Þy Magnyfycence,
> Þat þe story of þe flour delys   *fleur de lis*
>   May here be shewed in þyne heghe presence,
>   And þat þy noble, royal Excellence
> Lyst to supporte, here sitting in þy see,   *Will be pleased to*
> Right as it fell þis myracle to see. (ll. 90–8)[42]

It is neither great poetry nor has it the inventive ingenuity of later Tudor and Stuart masques, but it illustrates once more Lydgate's useful talent and apparent readiness to oblige his noble patrons.

A large part of Lydgate's shorter poems are religious and, again, the variety of topics is more impressive than the artistic quality or the individuality of inspiration. Lydgate wrote on a great variety of religious subjects, biblical, liturgical and devotional, prayers, saints' legends and poems on the Virgin Mary. Between religion and politics, there are verses like the impressive 'Defence of Holy Church' against Lollards, one of Lydgate's more original poems. It is not easy to date with certainty because the 'Most worthi prince' to whom it is addressed might be either King Henry V or Humphrey, Duke of Gloucester, though the first seems more likely.[43] The poem skilfully combines biblical and historical allusions, using the imagery of flood and sea-voyage, together with Old Testament precedents to admonish the present ruler to arm against the enemies of the church. The context leaves no doubt that it is the Lollards that present the immediate threat:

> Slouh nat Helye in all his holinesse   *Did not Elijah slay*
> The fals prophetis longyng vnto Baal?
> O noble prynce, exaumple of rightwisnesse,
> Off God preservid to be the myghty wall
> Of Hooly Churche in thyn estate royall,
> Distroye hem tho, that falsely now werrey   *make war against*
> Her own modir, to whome thai shulde obeye.
>
> And namely hem that of presumpcyoun
> Dispraven hir, and hir ornamentes   *Corrupt*
> And therwithall, of indignacioun

Withdrawe wolde hir rich[e] paramente₃.
O prudent prynce, thynke what her intent is,
Who falsely the Hooly Churche accuse,
For thay hemsilff the riches wolden use. (ll. 120–33)

The last line of the poem refers to the writing on the wall at Babylon, one of the most urgent biblical warnings against presumption. The brevity and concentration of the poem, homiletic and political at the same time, make it a characteristic example of Lydgate at his best. He remains the most prolific and influential representative of fifteenth-century English literature and its culture.

Thomas Hoccleve

Lydgate's contemporary Thomas Hoccleve, born around 1368, perhaps a year or two before Lydgate, followed a very different career, yet he is closely associated with him through their common sympathies with the Lancastrian court, their anxiously cultivated patronage of Humphrey, Duke of Gloucester and the complicated relations with the various rulers under whom they lived.[44] His reputation, however, never approached that of Lydgate, and he was, neither by contemporaries nor by later authors, ever cited alongside Chaucer, Gower and Lydgate, though his only major work, *The Regement of Princes*, survives in no less than forty-three copies and he is, personally and in terms of literary influence, as closely associated with Chaucer as any of them.

Unlike Lydgate, Hoccleve spent the best part of his working life, nearly forty years, as clerk in the royal office of the Privy Seal, an environment he describes with gusto and evident truth in some of his poems.[45] The clerks formed a fairly close community, lived together at the Privy Seal Hostel and shared the precarious experience, the professional temptations, deceptions and uncertain rewards of their influential office. Their daily routine involved dealing with all kinds of clients, petitioners and hangers-on and the remuneration was evidently a matter of luck rather than reliable income. At least, in Hoccleve's own poetry he repeatedly presents himself as petitioner in need of money, seeking regular payment and patronage, apparently without great success.[46]

Much of Hoccleve's writing has an unusually frank autobiographical tenor, less sophisticated and ironical than Chaucer's, but considerably richer in observed detail and, one is inclined to believe, candour;[47] his daily drudgery, for instance, is described with graphic realism:

¶ 'This artificers, se I day be day,   *artisans*
   In þe hotteste of al hir bysynesse
Talken and syng, and makë game and play,
   And forth hir labour passith with gladnesse;
   But we labour in trauaillous stilnesse;
      We stowpe and stare vp-on þe shepës skyn,   *i.e. parchment*
      And keepë muste our song and wordës in.[48]

There are, however, compensations; at least the author seems to be able to take time off, when he has had enough of pen and parchment:

> And if it happid on the Som*er*es day
> Þ*at* I thus at the tauerne hadde be,
> Whan I departe sholde / & go my way
> Hoom to the priuee seel / so wowed me   *invited*
> Heete & vnlust and superfluitee
> To walke vn-to the brigge / & take a boot /
> Þ*at* nat durste I contrarie he*m* all three,
> But dide as þ*at* they stired me / god woot.[49]

Among the most typical and accessible of Hoccleve's minor poems are the *Complaint* and *Dialogue*, the first two items in the group of linked writings now designated his *Series*. The sequence is extant in six manuscripts, of which the most authoritative, copied by Hoccleve himself, unfortunately lacks the *Complaint* and first 252 lines of the *Dialogue*.[50] According to the author, the poems of the *Series* were begun after Humphrey's return from France in 1419 in order to please him with some poetry suitable to his taste. The *Complaint* and *The Dialogue* together provide an introduction to the whole series, which includes two stories from the *Gesta Romanorum*, a moral poem on *How to Learn to Die* and prose moralisations of the two tales.

The *Complaint* introduces the poet on a sleepless November night, troubled in his mind by thoughts of life's unstableness: he then begins a moving account of a period of mental illness, during which he lost contact with the world and was avoided by all acquaintance, till by God's grace he was restored to health:

> Right so / thogh þ*at* my wit / were a pilgrym   *mind*
> And wente fer from hoom / he cam agayn.
> God me voidid / of the greuous venym   *poison*
> Þ*at* had infectid / and wyldid my brayn.   *confused*
> See how the curteys leche / souerain
> Vnto the seeke / yeueth medecyne
> In neede / and him releeueth / of his pyne.[51]

Many, however, do not believe in his recovery, though they enquire after his health from 'my felawes / of the privee seel' (296). In his despair he finds consolation in the 'lamentation of a woful man' discovered in a book,[52] and he decides to trust in God's judgement and make good use of his newly given health:

> He yaf me wit / and he took it away   *reason*
> Whan þ*at* he sy / þ*at* I it mis despente,   *saw, misused*
> And yaf ageyn / whan it was to his pay.   *advantage*
> He grauntid me / me giltes to repente
> And hens forward / to sette myn entente
> Vnto his deitee / to do plesance
> And tamende / my synful gouernance. (ll. 400–6)   *to amend*

The *Complaint* passes into the *Dialogue* without a break when a friend from long ago knocks at Hoccleve's door to enquire after his present state and to ask for his confidence. It is a tone of domestic privacy and personal heart-to-heart contact very rare in medieval English literature. Hoccleve reads his complaint to the visitor, who then strongly advises him, as a friend, not to publish it, but keep silent about his past illness and trust that people will forget all about it and treat him as they had before. Hoccleve, however, protests that he wants to publish the nature of his recovery just as he would advertise the name of a good physician. He insists on his determination to serve God by composing and translating edifying texts and he rejects the friend's suggestion that it was hard study that deranged his mind in the first place. He then discusses with his friend his plans of producing some work to please Humphrey of Gloucester who, apart from being a brilliant soldier and knight, enjoys 'For his desport / & mirthe in honestee / With ladyes / to haue daliance' (ll. 705–6) and is likely to show them anything Hoccleve might compose in the defence of women. There is a reference to an earlier work by Hoccleve, *The Letter of Cupid to Lovers, his Subjects*[53] that apparently was understood, wrongly, Hoccleve claims, to contain a slur on women, and there is also a witty brief mention of the Wife of Bath who is quoted as witness to the fact that women dislike men's criticism of their sex (ll. 694–6).

The whole *Dialogue* contains much traditional material, especially the poet's defence of his own work and apologies to women; yet it sounds more personal and truthful than most similar confessions, if only because it includes more details that can be verified independently. No other writer in Middle English has written at such length and in such personal terms about the difficulties and aspirations of his own literary activities. Even conventional arguments, the writer's infirmity, old age, modesty or anxious regard of his patron, are given an unexpected and individual twist that seems to invite a confidential glimpse of the poet's workshop.

The author's unusually intimate exchange with his friend, combining personal confidence with literary reflection and planning, continues after he has finished the story of Jereslaus's wife, when, after 'a wike or two' the friend returns, looks at what Hoccleve has written and critisises him for omitting the 'moralizynge' which he then goes home to fetch for him to translate.[54] Hoccleve then adds a prose moralisation, with an allegorical interpretation of the romantic story. The whole episode gives a convincing fictional portrait of the creative process and author's writing methods, framing his *Series* and, hopefully, supporting the dedication to his wished-for patron.

The *Series* continues with a free translation or adaptation from the second part of the second book of Heinrich Suso's *Horologium Sapientiae* (1334) on the art of dying.[55] It is the earliest Middle English version of an *Ars Moriendi* in verse, a subject that reflects the obsession of the century with death. The poem, in 131 rhyme-royal stanzas, is twice as long as the original, partly because of Hoccleve's versifying and partly through several additions and the adaptation to his typical form of didactic dialogue.

The theme of the poem relates to the poet's own complaint about his mispent life: Wisdom lectures her disciple on the pains of death and on the need to make adequate preparations; he presents a fictional monologue of a dying man who confesses his guilt and laments the thirty years of his life that have slipped from him. The poem concludes with an appeal to be ready for the end:

¶ 'Right as a Merchant stondynge in a port,
his ship þat charged is with marchandyse
To go fer parties / for confort
Of him self / lookeþ / þat it in sauf wyse   *safe manner*
Passe out / Right so, if thow wirke as the wyse,
See to thy soule so / or thow hens weende,   *before*
Þat it may han the lyf þat haath noon eende.
                          Amen!' (ll. 911–17)

The poet adds that he has not bothered to translate the rest of the book because 'swich a fool as me' (l. 921) feels overcharged by such high labour, but ends with a prose translation of the ninth lesson for All Hallows Day about the pains of Hell and the joys of Heaven. He then comes forward with another addition, again suggested by the friend who made him change the plan by proposing another tale he wants Hoccleve to translate for the benefit of the friend's fifteen-year-old son who is in danger of running wild. Since the story is about wicked women, Hoccleve fears it might be inconsistent with his original plan and his intention to regain women's favour, but the friend pleads for this tale as a mirror for virtuous women because it shows the cruel end of a wicked one. Hoccleve then asks for the friend's copy of the tale which is sent to him the next morning. The translation, 96 rhyme-royal stanzas, is again allegorically 'moralised' in prose, and the book ends with a dedication to Joan, Countess of Westmoreland, for whom Hoccleve evidently copied the manuscript of the *series*; her name does not appear in the other copies.

The Regement of Princes, written about 1412, is Hoccleve's most ambitious and in his time most popular poem. It consists of 5,463 lines, more than a third of them taken up by an autobiographical prologue which many readers may well find the most interesting part of the whole work. It introduces the poet in a somewhat conventional state of unhappiness, depressed by thought of Fortune's unstableness and his own poverty and low expectations. He knows from his reading and his own experience that a pensive man ('inly pensif', l. 85) wants most to be alone, and he is not particularly pleased when in this mood he encounters an old beggar who offers to cure the young man of his sorrow and listen to his complaint. There are some interesting echoes of Chaucer, e.g. of the poet consoling the Black Knight in the *Book of the Duchess*, or Pandarus trying to cheer up the love-sick Troilus. Hoccleve, like Chaucer's 'pensive men', at first rejects any attempt to relieve him and tells the beggar to leave him in peace, since he is not even able to help himself.[56] In the end, however, he listens to the beggar's experience and reveals his own grievance to him. As in some of Hoccleve's other works already quoted, what his complaint is not about is the traditional worries of love or general misfortune, but the specific grievances of a neglected civil servant moaning about his work and the damage it does to one's health, in particular his eyesight:

¶ 'What man þat *thre & twenti* yeere and more
  In wrytyng hath continued, as haue I,
I dar wel seyn it smerteth hym ful sore   *hurts*
  In euere veyne and place of his body;

And yen moost it greeveth trewëly	*eyes, injures*
Of any crafte þat man can ymagyne:	
ffadir, in feth, it spilt hath wel ny myne.[57]	*has ruined*

The beggar offers plenty of traditional lore, quoting many familiar classical authorities, mixed with practical experience and examples taken from life. It is clear, though, that the speakers move in a different world than Chaucer's, a more private world of the writing desks and of domestic worries rather than public affairs and urbane cosmopolitanism. In this context it is another interesting personal touch that the beggar asks Hoccleve at the beginning of the conversation whether he is 'lettred', and when the poet answers in the affirmative, he notes with satisfaction that such people are easier to deal with:

¶ 'Lettered folk han gretter discreciou*n*,	
And bet conceyuë konne a mannes saw,	*man's wisdom*
And ra*þ*er wolle applië to resou*n*	
And from folyë sone hem wi*th*-draw,	
Þan he þat no*þ*er reson can, ne law,	
Ne lerned ha*þ* no man*er* of lettrure:	*literacy*
Plukke vp þin herte! I hope I schal þe cure.' (ll. 155–61)	

In the end, Hoccleve is prepared to acknowledge the Beggar's moral authority and to accept his advice not to beg or flatter, but to present Prince Henry with a book of useful counsel gleaned from various sources. After the beggar's parting admonition: '"Sharpë thi penne, and write on lustily; / Lat se, my sonë, make it fresh and gay' (ll. 1905–6), Hoccleve returns home, not without a regretful glance at Chaucer and Gower who are no longer able to help him, and the next day begins his poem to Prince Henry. It is not often that the prologue of a literary work is more than half as long as the whole text.

The treatise itself, evidently much valued during the fifteenth century, combined conventional material with plenty of contemporary references and original additions addressed to the young prince.

One of the best-known and most original passages of the *Regement of Princes* occurs towards the end when Hoccleve, telling the Prince about the value of experienced counsellers, returns to the subject of Chaucer, 'The firstë fyndere of oure faire langáge' (l. 4978), whom he wants to recommend to the Prince, but also to all posterity. To support his anxious desire that those who had not seen the poet in person should be put 'in rémembraunce / Of his persóne' (ll. 4994–5) he has his 'likeness' inserted in the manuscript copy: 'Þat þei þat haue of him lest þought & mynde, / By þis paynturë may ageyn him fynde' (ll. 4997–8). It is probably the first time in English literature that a portrait was used, not to suggest an idealised image of a great person, but to provide an actual likeness that, in 1410, could be seen and compared by many who remembered Chaucer when he was still among them. Derek Pearsall, who has made the most thorough study of Chaucer portraits claims that 'Hoccleve seems . . . to have "invented" English portraiture, and invented it for the purpose of imprinting on his readers an image of Chaucer the man'.[58] Hoccleve goes on to put this portrait on a level with the representation of saints in church and their religious function; it is a daring comparison applied to a poet who died only a decade earlier, and it says much about the over-arching position accorded to Chaucer by his fellow:

> ¶ The ymages þat in þe chirchë been,
>   Maken folk þenke on god & on his seyntes,
> Whan þe ymáges þei be-holden & seen;
>   Were oft vnsyte of hem causith restreyntes   *lack of an image*
> Of þoughtës godë: whan a þing depeynt is,
>   Or éntailëd, if men take of it heede,   *carved, take note*
>   Thoght of þe lyknesse, it wil in hem brede. (ll. 4999–5005)

Hoccleve adds four polemical lines on heretics (i.e. the Lollards) who are against images, which may have been an extra reason for his unconventional inclusion of the portrait,[59] but whoever executed the likeness for him had created the earliest portrait of an English poet that has a just claim to be a recognisably accurate representation. It is quite in keeping with Hoccleve's unprecedented frankness in making his own biography and observation part of traditional literary material. Though his stature as a poet and his literary influence are immeasurably less than that of Lydgate, he is in some respects a truer 'Chaucerian' than many who refer to him as their master, not least in that he can be called 'the only inheritor of Chaucer's well-bred low vernacular'.[60]

Notes

1. On a rough estimate, this is about twice as much as Shakespeare's complete works and three times as much as Chaucer's. On the Lydgate canon see Walter F. Schirmer, *John Lydgate. A Study in the Culture of the XVth Century* (London, 1961; first published in German 1952), Appendix III, pp. 264–86. See also John Lydgate, *The Minor Poems*, ed. H. N. MacCracken, Part I, *EETS, ES*, 107 (1911), pp. v–lviii ('The Lydgate Canon').
2. See discussion in Derek Pearsall, *John Lydgate*. Medieval Authors (London, 1970), pp. 1–21. I am much indebted to this sensible and helpful account of Lydgate's literary career and poetic achievement within the context of fifteenth-century culture.
3. *John Lydgate*, p. 27.
4. See Pearsall, *John Lydgate*, pp. 32–5.
5. This is the chief interest of Paul Strohm in his chapter on 'Hoccleve, Lydgate and the Lancastrian Court', *The Cambridge History of Medieval Literature*, ed. David Wallace (Cambridge, 1999), pp. 640–61.
6. In John Lydgate, *The Minor Poems*, ed. H. N. MacCracken, Part II, *EETS*, 192 (1934), and in John Lydgate, *Poems*, ed. John Norton-Smith, Clarendon Medieval and Tudor Series (Oxford, 1966), pp. 47–66; with good commentary. Quotations are from this text.
7. See Norton-Smith's headnote, pp. 160–2, in his selection, where he lists the Chaucerian features he finds lacking in Lydgate's poem. Pearsall also puts emphasis on the conventionality of the poem he calls 'a mosaic of Chaucerian themes and phrases', *John Lydgate*, p. 84.
8. Cf., for instance, the beginning of *Troilus and Criseyde*, i, 15–49.
9. The succeeding stanza hastens to explain that nothing improper is meant, but this hardly alters the impression of a certain levity and lack of full commitment to the courtly love-service.

10. This is the traditional title of the poem.

11. When Pearsall speaks of 'the profusion of surface ornament at the expense of inner significance' (*John Lydgate*, p. 86) he probably means the same thing, though readers' reactions will differ as to the ultimate intention and effect of this kind of verbal artistry.

12. A character from *Roman de la Rose*, translated by Chaucer as 'Wikked Tonge' in his translation; see 3027 ff.

13. The number refers to the text of Norton-Smith, pp. 67–112 of his selection, with valuable commentary (pp. 176–91), where several passages cancelled or altered by Lydgate in revision are reproduced. Pearsall gives a sympathetic account of the poem (*John Lydgate*, pp. 104–15).

14. See Pearsall, *Lydgate*, pp. 107–9. He regards the revisions as less than significant, because for him the poem is 'an anthology of set pieces', not 'an allegorical narrative' (p. 109). The alternative implied here seems to me a little too rigid.

15. There is an unmistakeable allusion to 'The Merchant's Tale', when the poet comments:

> For it ne sit not vnto fressh[e] May   *it is not fitting*
> Forto be coupled to oold Ianuari. (ll. 184–5)

16. See stanza 5a in Norton-Smith's selection, p. 184.

17. See Chaucer's *Troilus and Criseyde*, i, 6–7 and iv, 22–4. Lydgate is clearly echoing his predecessor, but the context is as different as Venus is from Pandarus.

18. 'It was probably designed as a festive poem for some wedding celebration', Schirmer, *John Lydgate*, p. 37. See also the thorough edition by J. Schick, *EETS, ES*, 60 (1891).

19. *John Lydgate*, p. 109. C. S. Lewis confessed that he did not quite know what Lydgate meant and he was not sure whether the poet himself knew 'how his story ended': cf. *The Allegory of Love* (Oxford, 1936), pp. 241–2.

20. This is stated in the Prologue at some length, e.g.:

> ... Henry ek, the worthy prynce of Walys,
> To whom schal longe by successiou*n*   *belong*
> For to gouerne Brutys Albyou*n* –
> Whyche me comaunded the drery pitus fate   *sad, piteous*
> Of hem in Troye in englysche to translate,
> The sege also and the destrucciou*n*,   *siege*
> Lyche as the latyn maketh menciou*n*,   *Just as*
> For to compyle and after Guydo make,
> So as I coude, and write it for his sake,
> By-cause he wolde that to hyȝe and lowe
> The noble story openly wer knowe
> In oure tonge, aboute in euery age,
> And y-writen as wel in oure langage
> As in latyn and in frensche it is;
> That of the story þe throuth[e] we nat mys   *lose*
> No more than doth eche other naciou*n*:
> This was the fyn of his entenciou*n*. (ll. 102–18)

Here and in a number of other quotations, individual letters are printed in italics, where in the manuscript they are indicated by flourishes or other forms of abbreviation.

21. See *Lydgate's Troy Book*, ed. H. Bergen, *EETS, ES*, 97 (1906), 103 (1906), 106 (1910), 126 (1935, for 1920). Nineteen manuscripts and three prints are described and analysed in part iv, pp. 1–91. The volume also has generous excerpts from Guido delle Colonne's work. See also Schirmer, *John Lydgate*, pp. 42–51, Pearsall, *John Lydgate*, pp. 122–51 and C. David Benson, *The History of Troy in Middle English Literature: Guido delle Colonne's Historia Destructionis Troiae in Medieval England* (Woodbridge, 1980). Benson usefully compares the three major English versions, the anonymous alliterative

The Destruction of Troy, the *Laud Troy Book* and Lydgate's *Troy Book*. His account of Lydgate's major work (pp. 97–129) is particularly sensible and sympathetic.

22. *The History of Troy in Middle English Literature*, p. 102. Benson rightly insists that Lydgate's intention to follow his source truthfully has to be respected as has Lydgate's genuine, if necessarily limited sense of history.

23. H. Bergen in his edition early commented on this passage: 'It would seem, in view of the evident pleasure with which Lydgate amplified Guido's remarks, that his apology is not to be taken very seriously' (IV, p. 105). See also Pearsall, *John Lydgate*, pp. 134–6 and Benson, *The History of Troy*, pp. 103–4, for comment on Lydgate's sense of humour. A number of similar instances of antifeminist invective occur throughout the *Troy Book*: e.g. i, 1840–1904 (Medea); ii, 3536–631 (Helena); iii, 4264–417 (Criseide); iv, 2148–77 (Criseide). At ii, 3555–8 he repeats his reluctance to translate what he has just amplified with evident relish:

Þus Guydo ay, of cursid fals delit,	*with wicked enjoyment*
To speke hem harme haþ kauȝt an appetit,	*has taken pleasure*
Þoruȝ-oute his boke of wommen to seyyn ille,	*speak*
Þat to translate it is ageyn my wille.	

Towards the end of his poem, praising Penelope's faithfulness, the translator cannot resist another swipe at his predecessor:

And, o Guydo, þou shuldest ben ashamed
To seyn of wyves any þing but wele: (v, 2198–9)

24. Lydgate has this from Guido ('contra sui patris voluntatem'; cf. Bergen's edition, *EETS, ES*, 126, p. 168); though he refers the reader to Chaucer's version of Criseyde's story (see iii, 4410–48), he completely ignores Chaucer's defence of her; the only excuse he pretends to know is women's changeable nature ('kyndes transmutacioun, / Þat is appropred vn-to hir nature', iii, 4442–3).

25. This certainly applies to Lydgate's first readers: Pearsall notes that 'there is more marginal annotation in MSS of these passages about women than of any others'. Commenting on Lydgate's broadly humorous treatment of Medea, he adds: 'it is a trick he has caught from Chaucer, but the heavy playfulness is all his own, and not unwelcome' (*John Lydgate*, p. 136).

26. Ed. Axel Erdmann, *EETS, ES*, 108 (1911) and (ed. A. Erdmann and E. Ekwall) 125 (1930).

27. This is the first but not the only attempt to claim a share in that popularity. *The Tale of Beryn* is perhaps the most successful example, at least as far as the continuation of Chaucer's frame and the description of the pilgrim's adventures in Canterbury are concerned. See Helen Cooper, *The Canterbury Tales*, Oxford Guides to Chaucer (Oxford, 1989), pp. 413–27, and *The Tale of Beryn, with A Prologue of the merry Adventure of the Pardoner with a Tapster at Canterbury*, ed. F. J. Furnivall and W. G. Stone, *EETS, ES*, 105 (1909).

28. See *John Lydgate*, p. 153.

29. *The Canterbury Tales*, p. 417.

30. See the edition by F. J. Furnivall, *The Pilgrimage of the Life of Man*, ed. F. J. Furnivall and K. B. Locock, *EETS, ES*, 77 (1899), 83 (1901), 92 (1904), reprinted as one volume 1970; see also Schirmer, *John Lydgate*, pp. 120–6, and Pearsall, *John Lydgate*, pp. 172–9.

31. *EETS, ES*, 77 (1899), p. vi. On Furnivall see the excellent article by Derek Pearsall in *Medieval Scholarship: Biographical Studies on the Formation of a Discipline*. Volume 2: Literature and Philology, ed. Helen Damico (New York, 1998), pp. 125–38.

32. Pearsall, *John Lydgate*, 250. Pearsall has a sensible and informative account of the work (pp. 223–54), usefully supplemented by Schirmer, *John Lydgate*, pp. 206–27. See the edition by E. Bergen, *EETS, ES*, 121–4 (1918–19).

33. See the edition of the *Mirror for Magistrates* by Lily B. Campbell (Cambridge, 1938, repr. New York, 1960; supplementary volume, Cambridge, 1946), and the classic study by Willard Farnham, *The Medieval Heritage of Elizabethan Tragedy* (Oxford, 1936, several times repr.), especially pp. 160–70.

34. Like his source, he gives the concise definition of tragedy he could also have found in Chaucer or Boece:

> Wherfore Bochas for a memoriall,   *Boccaccio*
> Consid[e]ryng the greete dignitees
> Off worldli pryncis in ther power roiall,
> Grete emperours, estatis and degrees,
> How Fortune hath cast hem from ther sees;   *thrones*
> Namly such as koude hemsilff nat knowe,
> Ful sodenly to make hem lyn ful lowe. (ll. 64–70)   *lie*

35. Cf. Pearsall, *John Lydgate*, pp. 227–30.

36. See Pearsall, *John Lydgate*, pp. 244–5 and Eleanor P. Hammond, 'Lydgate and Coluccio Salutati', *Modern Philology*, 25 (1927), 49–57.

37. Of particular interest is the prologue to book iv, where Lydgate explains the use of writing, with a brief account of the most famous Roman authors, Petrarch and Dante. Some of the other prologues (e.g. to books vi and viii), are skilfully adapted, occasionally even abridged.

38. *John Lydgate*, p. 220. The poem is preserved in over fifty manuscripts. The text is in *The Minor Poems of John Lydgate*, pp. 703–7. A different version is included in *Secular Lyrics of the XIVth and XVth Centuries*, ed. Rossell Hope Robbins (Oxford, 1952), pp. 73–6 and 251.

39. See the verse ranged under 'Didactic Poems' in MacCracken's volume, pp. 702–44. MacCracken's categories are perhaps more formal than is quite justified by the diversity of the poems themselves, but they give an idea of the range of material: 'Poems of Courtly Love', 'Satirical Poems', 'Narrative Poems', 'Political Poems', 'Occasional Poems', 'Didactic Poems', 'Little Homilies with Proverbial Refrains'. Paul Strohm also rightly draws attention to Lydgate's stylistic range; see 'Hoccleve, Lydgate and the Lancastrian Court', *The Cambridge History of Medieval English Literature*, p. 653 n. 27.

40. See MacCracken, *Minor Poems*, 657–9 and 665–7 and, with useful commentary, Norton-Smith, *Poems*, pp. 1–6; Schirmer and Pearsall also offer additional comment on these and other occasional poems.

41. See especially Glynne Wickham, *Early English Stages 1300–1660*, vol. I: 1300–1576 (London, 1959), pp. 191–207. Texts in MacCracken, *Minor Poems*, 668–701.

42. MacCracken, *Minor Poems*, p. 694.

43. See Norton-Smith, *Poems*, pp. 30–4 and 150–4. He gives good reasons for dating the poem around 1413–14, when there were serious Lollard risings in London. In the 'Ballade to King Henry VI upon His Coronation', Lydgate wants Henry to resemble his father, 'Heretykes and Lollardes for to oppresse' (MacCracken, *Minor Poems*, p. 627).

44. See the well documented account by Paul Strohm, 'Hoccleve, Lydgate and the Lancastrian Court', in *The Cambridge History of Middle English Literature*, pp. 640–61, and Jerome Mitchell, *Thomas Hoccleve. A Study in Early Fifteenth-Century Poetic* (Urbana, 1968), with a useful account of Hoccleve's possible association with Chaucer, pp. 110–23. For a brief comparison with Lydgate see the useful *Selections from Hoccleve*, ed. M. C. Seymour (Oxford, 1981), pp. xxx-xxxii; his final verdict, 'Lydgate's greyness throws Hoccleve's brightness into a sharper relief' (p. xxxii) seems somewhat unjust.

45. On the question of 'truth' in Hoccleve's autobiographical writings see especially J. A. Burrow, 'Autobiographical Poetry in the Middle Ages: The Case of Thomas Hoccleve', *Proceedings of the British Academy, London*, volume 68 (1982), 389–412 and *Thomas Hoccleve*, Authors of the Middle Ages, 4 (Aldershot, 1994); see also Stephen Medcalf's section 'Allegory of the mind: Thomas Hoccleve', in *The Later Middle Ages*, The Context of English Literature, ed. Stephen Medcalf (London, 1981), pp. 123–40.

46. See John Burrow, 'The Poet as Petitioner', *Studies in the Age of Chaucer* 3 (1981), 61–75, reprinted in *Essays on Middle English Literature* (Oxford, 1984), pp. 161–76.

47. 'Hoccleve's greatest debt to Chaucer concerns the creation of his poetic *persona* which is the basis of much of his verse', *Selections from Hoccleve*, ed. Seymour, p. xxv.

48. *The Regement of Princes*, in *Hoccleve's Works*, ed. Frederick J. Furnivall, vol. III, *EETS, ES*, 72 (1897), ll. 1009–15.

49. 'La Male Regle de T. Hoccleve', ll. 185–92; *Hoccleve's Works*, vol. I, *The Minor Poems*, ed. Frederick J. Furnivall, *EETS, ES*, 61 (1892).

50. Durham, University Library MS Cosin V.iii.9. See *Thomas Hoccleve's Complaint and Dialogue*, ed. J. A. Burrow, *EETS*, 313 (1999); a parallel-text edition of the (scribal) MS Selden Supra 53, Oxford, Bodleian Library and a reconstructed edited text, based on the extant part of the Durham MS in Hoccleve's own hand, with thorough and up-to-date introduction and commentary.

51. *Compleynt*, ll. 232–8, from Burrow's 'Edited Text' in *Thomas Hoccleve's Complaint and Dialogue*, ed. J. A. Burrow. All quotations from the *Complaint* and *Dialogue* are from this edition.

52. Hoccleve's source is reprinted by Burrow in *Excursus II* of his edition, p. 119. See also his note 'Hoccleve's *Complaint* and Isidore of Seville Again', *Speculum*, 73 (1998), 424–8.

53. Furnivall's title in *Hoccleve's Works*, vol. I, pp. 72–91, and by Sir Israel Gollancz in *Hoccleve's Works*, vol. II, *EETS, ES*, 73 (1892), pp. 20–34. In the text itself, the poem is dated 1402. It is a free adaptation of Christine de Pisan's *Epistre au Dieu d'Amours*. See note on *Dialogue*, l. 754 in Burrow, p. 107. The poem was included in some sixteenth-century editions of Chaucer.

54. See Furnivall's edition, *Hoccleve's Works*, vol. I, p. 174.

55. *Hoccleve's Works*, ed. Furnivall, vol. I, pp. 178–212.

56. Cf. Hoccleve's retort when the beggar tells him 'I hope I schal þe cure':

'Curë, good man? ya þow art a fayre leche!	*physician*
Curë þi self, þat tremblest as þou gost,	
ffor al þin art wole enden in þi speche;	
It liþ not in þi power, porë gost,	*lies*
To helë me; þou art as seek almost	*sick*
As I; first on þi self kyþë þin art;	*apply*
And if aght leue, late me þanne hauë part. (ll. 161–8)	*any left*

Troilus uses practically the same argument against Pandarus: 'Thow koudest nevere in love thiselven wisse. / How devel maistow brynge me to blisse?' *Troilus and Criseyde*, ii, 622–3.

57. *The Regement of Princes*, ed. Furnivall, ll. 1023–9.

58. *The Life of Chaucer*, p. 288; the whole of Appendix I The Chaucer Portraits, is relevant to assess the importance of the portrait in British Library MS Harley 4866.

59. See also Hoccleve's polemically orthodox poem addressed to Sir John Oldcastle, written 1415, about two years before Oldcastle's execution as a heretic; see *Hoccleve's Works*, ed. Furnivall, vol. I, pp. 8–24. The poet urges the knight to turn from his heresy, to repent and come to a reconciliation with his King. Refuting Oldcastle's false opinions he

also defends the use of images which the Lollards objected to. Hoccleve insists on their emotional effect:

> Right as a spectacle helpith feeble sighte,
> Whan a man on the book redith or writ,
> And causith him to see bet than he mighte,
> In which spectacle / his sighte nat abit,   *stop*
> Buth gooth thurgh / & on the book restith it;
> The same may men of ymages seye,
> Thogh the ymage nat the seint be / yit   *is not the saint him/herself*
> The sighte vs myngith to the seint to preye. (ll. 417–24)   *causes*

60. Derek Pearsall, 'The English Chaucerians', in *Chaucer and Chaucerians. Critical studies in Middle English literature*, ed. D. S. Brewer (London, 1966), p. 224.

Chapter 7

The Middle English Lyric

A number of middle English lyrics are probably among the best-known remains of poetry we have from this period, most of them, characteristically, in the form of stanzas still sung, either in church or in a secular sociable context. This is a useful reminder of the non-literary, social and basically oral character of a large section of verse that, in many cases, has survived by mere accident and was composed to be performed, not to be fossilised in critical editions. Nevertheless, it is to the effort of enthusiastic collectors and scholarly editors that we owe accessible texts and indispensable commentary.[1] Originally, many shorter poems were probably passed round in a form that left little chance of survival; others were scribbled in free spaces between more important texts or in the margins of larger collections.[2] One of the earliest and frequently anthologised poems, 'Sumer is icumen in', was copied with music among songs in French and Latin in a monks' commonplace book, MS Harley 978, written by several hands at different times.[3] It is just a tantalising glimpse of what was sung and passed on, either orally or in much less carefully written form, without very good chance of survival.

Another frequently quoted little lyric, from the second half of the thirteenth century, again written down with music, illustrates particularly well the allusive and often wistful tone of some of the earlier Middle English poems. It is difficult to say whether it is a fragment or just a plaintive sigh, a kind of shorthand complaint:

Foweles in þe frith,	*birds, wood*
Þe fisses in þe flod,	*fish, river*
And i mon waxe wod.	*must go mad*
Mulch sorw I walke with	*I live in great pain*
for beste of bon and blod.[4]	*because of the best creature*

On occasions, we have snatches from songs quoted in sermons, as a warning against lascivious living or bad company, as in the tantalising refrain:

Atte wrastlinge my lemman I ches,	*lover, chose*
And atte ston-kasting I him forles.[5]	*lost*

It suggests a brief scene from a village fair, a dancing song or a teasing rhyme game. And, more generally, it hints at the existence of a body of texts as part of a popular culture, largely, we may assume, transmitted orally and extant only in accidentally preserved fragments.

Only a minority of lyrical productions was actually gathered in more elaborate manuscript anthologies that have come down to us, such as the famous

Harley Manuscript 2253 from the first half of the fourteenth century, a folio volume of 141 parchment leaves. It is a miscellany of French, Latin and English verse and prose, much of it religious and didactic, including fables, moral instruction and the English romance of *King Horn*. While most of the religious poems have also come down in other manuscript versions, the secular lyrics are only extant in this collection, which illustrates the precarious character of the transmission. The manuscript seems to belong to the Hereford area and has been associated with an aristocratic family, the Mortimers, and with the bishop of Hereford. We can only guess as to the authors, most of them probably clerics with some interest in courtly poetry and more than a nodding acquaintance with the conventions of continental love songs, sophisticated verse forms and traditions connected with important political events. It is one of those precious unique collections 'whose loss would wipe out our knowledge of whole areas of English poetry'.[6]

The subjects of the Harley lyrics, like those of other poems from the thirteenth and fourteenth centuries, range from the passion of Christ, devotion of the Virgin, famous historical exploits and celebrated crises to a variety of love poems, some deliberately simple, others evidently inspired by courtly traditions, such as the dawn song, the *pastourelle* or the more or less stereotyped praise of women. Some give a superficial impression of oral poetry composed by a professional minstrel, but most critics of the last fifty years would reject the older idea of a popular origin or oral transmission of these poems. Rather, they are, in R. L. Greene's apt phrase, 'popular by destination' not by origin, i.e. composed by highly educated men for a popular audience.[7]

Love, fun and day-to-day trouble in the secular lyric

When Geoffrey Chaucer, in his 'Retraction' at the end of the *Canterbury Tales*, reviews his poetic output, he speaks with penitent regret of 'many a song and leccherous lay' he committed,[8] presumably like his Squire, who 'coude songes make and wel endite' (I, 95), and his contemporary and friend John Gower, too, refers to love-ditties he wrote in his youth. Only a small fraction of those works seems to have survived. To compose love-songs was obviously part of being a courtly lover, and Chaucer's own lyrics are again probably only the tip of an iceberg. They clearly show, however, that side by side with 'ditties', or seemingly artless songs, there is also a tradition of elaborate verse-forms and sophisticated rhetoric, largely inspired by Latin and French models.

A telling example is the poem 'To Rosemounde', extant only in one manuscript (Bodley Rawlinson Poet. 163), following Chaucer's *Troilus and Criseyde*, and ascribed to Chaucer in a later hand. Not all scholars have accepted his authorship, though the combination of clever conventionality, detached irony and possible self-mockery seems very much like the author's playful tone elsewhere. It is a combination that tells us much about the Middle English poets' literary resources and their free adaptability:

Madame, ye ben of al beaute shryne	*you are*
As fer as cercled is the mapamounde,	*map of the world*
For as the cristal glorious ye shyne,	
And lyke ruby ben your chekes rounde.	
Therwith ye ben so mery and so jocounde	*cheerful*
That at a revel whan that I see you daunce,	
It is an oynement unto my wounde,	*ointment*
Thogh ye to me ne do no daliaunce.	*will not be friends with me*
For thogh I wepe of teres ful a tyne,	*tub*
Yet may that wo myn herte nat confounde;	
Your semy voys that ye so smal out twyne	*thin, softly, twist out*
Maketh my thoght in joy and blis habounde.	*abound*
So curtaysly I go with love bounde	
That to myself I sey in my penaunce,	*say*
'Suffyseth me to love you, Rosemounde,	
Thogh ye to me ne do no daliaunce.'	
Nas never pyk walwed in galauntyne	*pike, immersed, sauce*
As I in love am walwed and ywounde,	*wound up*
For which ful ofte I of myself devyne	*imagine*
That I am trewe Tristam the secounde.	
My love may not refreyde nor affounde,	*go cold or numb*
I brenne ay in an amorous plesaunce.	*burn*
Do what you lyst, I wyl your thral be founde,	*like, slave*
Thogh ye to me ne do no daliaunce.[9]	

The poem is in the form of a conventional ballade – three eight-line stanzas with a refrain and, unusually, an envoy of four lines – with a demanding rhyme scheme and a refrain that suggests the lady's unaccommodating attitude towards her admirer, who, however, does not seem to be greatly grieved by it. The whole poem seems like a game of playful praise, without any serious desire or earnest wooing. The speaker is quite content to watch the lady, to shed a barrelful of tears and enjoy his 'penaunce', without any reward. The juxtaposition, in the third stanza, of the lover as a pike wallowing in sauce, like a tasty dish ready to be enjoyed, and the famous Tristan, seems ludicrously jarring and surely undermines any sincere pathos the reader might have suspected or experienced at the beginning of the homage to the shrine of all beauty (l. 1). The first stanza appears to employ the clichés of courtly love without any overt mockery. The oxymoron in the second stanza, with the excessive volume of his tears and the jolliness of her voice, then add a note of bathos, and the third stanza confirms the impression that the speaker seems to be in love more with his own witty eloquence than with the lady herself. The whole poem testifies to a poet who is all too conversant with the vocabulary and the conventions of courtly love poetry and evidently can look back on a tradition familiar enough to be gently satirised.

The majority of Middle English love lyrics are less ambivalent in tone and expression, but a surprising number are either light-heartedly humorous or punningly bawdy, particularly those of clerkly or monkish origin. Others, as some of John Lydgate's love poems, read more like five-finger exercises and are clearly derivative, mostly dependent on French types of song and verse forms.[10]

An interesting case, especially as a direct link between French and English poetry of the fifteenth century, is the collection of English verse produced by Charles, Duke of Orleans, who was captured at Agincourt in 1415 and, as an important prisoner, detained in England for twenty-five years. He was kept in comparatively comfortable conditions and was able to preserve and establish contacts with the French and English nobility. He wrote many poems, both in English and in French, mainly love lyrics in the conventional form of the ballade or the roundel – usual form abba abab abba ab, with the ll. 1–2 repeated as ll. 7–8 and ll. 13–14. These forms were used by French court poets like Guillaume de Machaut and Eustache Deschamps and by Chaucer (see his 'Compleynt to Venus' or 'To his Purse'). Many of the poems are evidently Charles's own translations from French originals. They are particularly characteristic witnesses of a literary court culture and a fictional game of love, with standard situations and images that yet allow for fresh expression and original turns of thought and phrase. In a number of ballades, the poet celebrates his love on a May morning, asks for a place in his mistress's heart, urges an exchange of hearts at parting or mourns for her death on Valentine's day. In a roundel, he confesses that he has stolen a kiss, but promises to return it again.[11]

Rossell Hope Robbins, one of the most impressive and influential scholars of Middle English lyric poetry, divides the poems assembled in his magisterial anthology *Secular Lyrics of the XIVth and XVth Centuries* conveniently into 'Popular Songs', 'Practical Verse', 'Occasional Verse' and 'Courtly Love Lyrics'.[12] This at least shows the range of the lyric production in the age of Chaucer, even without the two important groups of political songs and ballads, and religious poetry.

The 'popular' songs are preserved mostly in manuscripts that survived because of other, more edifying or useful items contained in them, such as 'Minstrel Collections', small books probably made for use by a professional entertainer, 'Commonplace Books', flyleaves of religious manuscripts or individual scraps of vellum or paper. Some of the love-songs have a haunting allusive quality, whether by design or by mere brevity is difficult to say, like the often quoted

Al nist by þe rose, rose –	*night*
al nist bi the rose i lay;	
darf ich noust þe rose stele,	*I dare not*
ant ȝet ich bar þe flour away.[13]	*carried*

Other songs are more explicitly about successful courtship or seduction, complaints of betrayed maids or general attacks on women or marriage.

The 'practical' poems, generally of no strictly literary value, provide interesting cultural glimpses of life outside an artificial lifestyle of the gentry or aristocratic fiction. There are rhyming accounts of the occupations of the months, charms against illness or dangerous spirits, calculations of calendar problems (the date of Easter or the weekday of Christmas) or all kinds of medical advice, like the ninety-line poem on the art of bloodletting, which occurs in seventeen manuscripts,[14] or 'Lydgate's Dietary', by far the most

popular of all shorter poems in Middle English, occurring in forty-six manuscripts and apparently used for instruction in schools.[15] The importance of this
kind of mnemonic verse can hardly be exaggerated.

Among the 'occasional verse' anthologised by Robbins and others, there is,
for example, the extraordinary poem against blacksmiths, written about 1440,
complaining in twenty-two onomatopoetic alliterative lines about the excruci-
ating noise made by their work at night (their usual time of business).[16] The
poem seems too sophisticated and stylistically brilliant to be composed on the
spur of the moment. The irritation of the poet, disturbed in his sleep, is most
realistically expressed:

Swarte smekyd smeþes, smateryd wyth smoke,	*black smoky*
dryue me to deth wyth den of here dyntes!	*din*
Swech noys on nyghtes ne herd men neuer:	
What knauene cry, & clateryng of knockes!	*boys'*
þe cammede kongons cryen after 'col, col!'	*crooked bastards, coal*
& blowen here bellewys þat al here brayn brestes. (ll. 1–6)	*bursts*

The skilful use of alliteration and rare vocabulary, especially the virtuoso
reproduction of sense impressions, in particular sounds, connects the poem with
works of the 'alliterative revival', such as *Sir Gawain and the Green Knight*.

Another poem whose realism still appeals to the reader centuries later, is the
venomous exclamation of a schoolboy against a thrashing deputy teacher he
fondly dreams of having his revenge on. He evidently speaks not just for himself:

Wenest þu, huscher, with þi coyntyse,	*usher, cleverness*
Iche day beten us on þis wyse,	*thrash*
As þu wer lord of toun?	*As if you were*
We had leuur scole for-sake,	*We had rather*
& ilche of us an-oþur crafte take,	*each*
þen long to be in þi bandoun.[17]	*power*

The poem is squeezed into the manuscript (Lincoln Cathedral 132) between
didactic items in a later hand, evidently not part of the original programme,
but, like much of the 'occasional verse', it preserves a heartfelt sentiment and
shows what a wide range of actual experience was expressed in verse.

Carols and religious lyrics

There is no doubt that a major part of the Middle English lyric production
was meant to be sung.[18] Most of the poems are composed in stanzas, often
with a refrain, or, in the case of the carol, a 'burden', usually a rhyming
couplet sung at the beginning and repeated after every stanza.[19] The word
originally derives from the Old French *carole*, meaning a ring dance, in which
all the participants join in the 'burden', while the stanzas are sung by a soloist.
The origins of the carol form have been vigorously disputed. Whereas Rossell
Hope Robbins argued that the carols derived from Latin processional hymns,
Richard Leighton Greene was convinced that they had their origin in popular

ring-dances and were at first closely associated with folk customs.²⁰ The two views are not necessarily mutually exclusive, since there are so many different forms of carols that they need not have derived from one single source. Anyway, the carols are the best examples of the fact that a simple distinction between religious and secular lyric is often all but impossible to make. At least there are transitions or exchanges, where it is impossible to say which came first.

An early example is recorded in two lyrics found side by side in the Harley manuscript. Their first lines are practically identical, but then one of the poems turns out to be a secular love lyric, the other a description of Christ's love:²¹

> Lutel wot hit any mon
>   hou derne loue may stonde,   *Little knows it*
> bote hit were a fre wymmon   *secret*
> þat muche of loue had fonde.   *But only*
> . . .   *tried out*

> Lvtel wot hit any mon
>   hou loue hym haueþ ybounde
> þat for vs o þe rode ron   *cross, bled*
> ant bohte vs wiþ is wounde.
> . . .

The refrains, too, are clearly based on each other, perhaps sung to the same melody.²² In this case it seems most likely that the religious version is in fact a 'parody' of the worldly love song, and attempt to convert a popular song into a Christian hymn, though it is just as possible that it was the other way round. More important is the observation that neither in manuscript transmission nor in authorship or audience can a clear-cut division between secular and religious be assumed. The majority of texts up to the time of Chaucer, whether secular or religious, had their origin either in religious communities or in a clerical context. From the turn of the fourteenth century, the importance of educational institutions and lay households grew in importance, but although a very articulate section of the clergy took strong exception to the levity of secular songs and any unchristian habits in their wake, there was a large common area between worldly singing, song-making and religious, liturgical or devotional composition.

Carols, in particular, were adapted to quite opposite uses, as is reflected in the extant texts ranging from irreverent parody to humorous drinking song, amorous wooing and complaint to some of the most delicate devotional lyrics, sometimes with an astonishing yet lightly conveyed doctrinal content, as in the famous 'Adam lay I-bowndyn', which ends in a surprising 'deo gracias' for the fortunate fall.²³ Equally direct and unusual is the carol, sung as part of a nativity play by the mothers whose children were massacred by Herod. The carol is still popular today, although many who sing it during the Christmas season may not quite realise its gruesome background. Its burden is that of any affectionate Lullaby:

> Lully, lulla, thow litel tiny child,
> By, by, lully, lullay

The three stanzas combine the individual grief of a mother for her own baby with a sense of community with all the bereaved mothers and the desire to create a memorial:

> O sisters two,
> How may we do
> For to preserve this day
> This pore yongling
> For whom we do singe
> 'By, by, lully, lullay'?[24]

A much stranger and still not quite explained combination of images occurs in the 'Corpus Christi Carol', preserved in a commonplace book compiled by a London grocer during the first quarter of the sixteenth century (MS Balliol College, Oxford, 354). In 1962 R. L. Greene wrote that 'This carol has been the subject of more discussion than any other in the whole canon'.[25] Its hauntingly mysterious quality almost seems to pose a riddle for which a number of answers have been proposed; yet such is the poetic appeal of the brief stanzas that, even without an entirely satisfactory solution, they stand as one of the most appealing and treasured medieval poems. To understand the problems surrounding the text it needs to be quoted in full:

> Lully, lulley; lully, lulley;
> The fawcon hath born my mak away.   *falcon, mate*
>
> He bare hym up, he bare hym down;
> He bare hym into an orchard brown.
>
> In that orchard ther was an hall,
> That was hangid with purpill and pall.   *rich fabric*
>
> And in that hall there was a bede;
> Hit was hangid with gold so rede.
>
> And yn that bed ther lythe a knyght,   *lies*
> His wowndes bledyng day and nyght.
>
> By that bedes side ther kneleth a may,   *maid*
> And she wepeth both nyght and day.
>
> And by that beddes side ther stondith a ston,
> 'Corpus Christi' wretyn theron.

Again, the burden suggests a lullaby, and the final two stanzas associate the poem with the passion of Christ and the Virgin Mary, the *pietà*, grieving for her son. As in the final section of Langland's *Piers Plowman*, Christ's death and resurrection are imaginatively presented as a chivalric adventure. But there are also suggestions of a Grail legend, with the mysteriously suffering and never dying King waiting for the redeeming question. The idea of the Eucharist may also be present, and it seems possible that the carol was originally intended to be sung on Corpus Christi Day or Good Friday. In addition, a more topical and political interpretation has been proposed; it relates the poem to the replacement of the English Queen Catherine of Aragon in the favour of her husband, King Henry VIII, by Anne Boleyn, whose badge was a falcon. It is just possible that an older poem was adapted to this purpose, though most of the details do not really fit and the poem hardly gains by this personal and short-lived application. It is a fascinating document, provoking, even more immediately, speculation on the relationships between religious ideas, political event, popular practice and poetic imagination.

The Middle English Carols provide the most lively evidence of the constant overlapping of secular and religious emotion and expression. The majority of the extant texts, however, belongs to the large area of religious, liturgical, devotional and practical verse. They evidently had a greater chance of survival than purely secular lyrics, but it is very difficult to be certain about the precise influence the destruction of manuscripts had on the relative preservation of types of poetry. Robbins, who has surveyed the field more thoroughly than most, summarises, 'For every secular lyric there are three or four religious.'[26] This he ascribes less to the survival of manuscripts than to the simple fact that 'religion dominated the scene, and all problems and conflicts had a religious frame of reference'.[27] This is confirmed by the rich variety of themes and images in the Middle English religious lyric, which Douglas Gray describes as 'a rather humble and workaday type of literature, with a practical and devotional bent'.[28] Nevertheless, the number of different kinds of poem mirrors the ubiquitous presence of religious activities, popular and intellectual, as well as the contrasts and conflicts caused by controversial spiritual and theological movements.

One of the most important of these was due to the mendicant orders and the impact of the friars on preaching, education and the use of texts for homiletic purposes. The Franciscans, in particular, who arrived in England in 1224, made a significant contribution to the devotional literature in England, including the lyric. A number of poems are found in friars' miscellanies and books used for preaching. The emotional rhetoric of the friars and their manipulation of the audience was frequently commented on or criticised. Chaucer's host is an eloquent spokesman of popular prejudice in this as in other matters. He warns the Clerk before he has even had a chance to speak:

> But precheth nat, as freres doon in Lente,
> To make us for oure olde synnes wepe,[29]

Like the friars' sermons, the lyrics they wrote or included in their homilies acted on the emotions as much as on the intellect of the audience. They promoted and encouraged a distinctly affective piety which found its most moving expression, apart from the lives and writings of the mystics, in the religious lyric, in particular the songs to the Virgin Mary, the Nativity and the Passion.

Several of the traditional ideas and images connected with the Virgin are brought together in a poem called *Cantus amoris* in the best manuscript (Bodleian MS Douce 322; later fifteenth century). It appears in eight manuscripts and was evidently popular, though the stanza is more demanding than many simpler forms (ababbcbc); the eighth, shorter line is a Latin refrain repeated at the end of each stanza. The poem describes a vision in which the Virgin as crowned queen appears to the speaker, appealing to man, as his sister, mother

and wife, to leave his sinful ways and come to her for everlasting protection
from hell:

> In a tabernacle of a toure,
> As I stode musyng on the mone,
> A crouned quene, most of honoure,
> Apered in gostly syght ful sone.
> She made compleynt thus by hyr one,   *by herself*
> For mannes soule was wrapped in wo:
> 'I may nat leue mankynde allone,
>   Quia amore langueo.[30]   *Because I am burning with love*

A poem with the same stanza form and another Latin refrain appears in two
collections, the important songbook, MS Sloane 2593 (British Library) and,
a better text, in the miscellany of romances, moral pieces and lyrics Edinburgh,
Advocates 19.3.1. The poem has the speaker witness the nativity, the shepherds
and the Magi and immediately join in the adoration of Virgin and child. Like
the previous lyric it is built on a Latin quotation, this time from the Gospel of
St John, skilfully integrated in the syntax of the English text:

> I Passud þoru a garden grene,
>   I fond a herbere made full newe –   *arbour*
> A semelyour syght I haff noght sene,   *more pleasant*
>   O ylke treo sange a tyrtull trew –   *each, turtle dove*
> There-yn a mayden bryȝt off hew,
>   And euer sche sange, & neuer sche sest: *ceased*
> Thies were þe notus þat sche can schew,
>   Verbum caro factum est.[31]   *The word was made flesh*

The refrain, a relatively abstract theological statement by the evangelist, is
made concrete and brought to life by the familiar narrative of the nativity and
experienced by the speaker in his own present situation. The poem is a particularly good example of many Middle English lyrics' emotional and at the
same time doctrinal appeal. Most of them were clearly composed for communal worship and celebration or private devotion and meditation, at any rate,
for practical use, not aesthetic delight and entertainment. The close affinity to
the scripture or liturgy is often stressed by the inclusion of Latin words or
phrases, as in the simple paraphrase of the passion, with a few Latin reminders
of the gospel account. It begins with a personal gesture, involving the individual in the story of our salvation:

> I Hard a maydyn wepe
>   ffor her sonnys passyon;
> yt enterd into my hart full deipe,
>   wyth grete contricion.
>
> Patris sapiencia,   *The Father's wisdom*
>   The sonne off god almyght,
> off fals judas be-trayd he was,
>   The maker off all lyghte.[32]

The brief narrative is punctuated by 'Hora prima, dominus . . .' (l. 13), 'Hora sexta, dominus . . .' (l. 29), 'Ora nona, dominus . . .' (l. 37), and 'De cruce deponitur . . .' (line 49), and the poem closes on a final note of commitment:

> Wyth spices swete in-bracyd,
>   the scrypter to fulfyll –
> Hys passion kynd to haue in mynde,
>   As yt was euermore hys wylle. (ll. 53–6)

Other poems on the Passion, especially those inspired by the image of the *pietà*, dwell on the gruesome suffering of Christ and the grief of his mother with an intensity that may strike later readers as excessive, especially if the poet's rhetorical talent is not up to the extremes of the emotional situation. Yet the expression of such violent compassion in several fifteenth-century poems throws light on the state of affective piety that could unite laymen without any theological training with their spiritual pastors. It also could produce poetry impressive in its imaginative simplicity, like the poem that begins:

> Sodenly afraide, half waking, half slepyng
> and gretly dismayde, A wooman sate weeping,

The poem has the refrain 'Who cannot wepe come lerne at me', and the four stanzas are an affecting appeal to the speaker to join in her grief:

> 'Now breke hert, I the pray, this cors lith so rulye,   *pitifully*
> So betyn, so wowndid, entreted so Iewlye,   *beaten, treated, like a Jew*
> What wiȝt may me behold & wepe nat? noon truly!   *person*
> To see my deed dere soone lygh bleedyng lo! this newlye.' (ll. 19–22)[33]
>   *son lie*

Even more passionate and unusual in painting the despair of the Virgin is a poem that shows the poet's encounter with the lamenting mother, also with a Latin refrain:

> I met a mayde at þe citeys ende,
> snobbynge & syȝynge sche was ny schente,   *sobbing, dead*
> a fayrer foode had y not kende.   *creature*
> hurre herre, hure face, sche all to-rente,   *her hair, tore completely*
> Sche tuggyd & tere with gret turment;
> sche brake hure skynne boþe body & breste,
> and saide þese wordys euer as sche wente,
> 'filius Regis mortuus est.'[34]   *'The King's son is dead'*

Lastly, there is a poem in which the Virgin appeals to all mothers who are enjoying their little children to meditate on her own, much more cruel fate. In a series of touching glimpses the mothers' delight is contrasted with the pitiful image of the *pietà*:

> Therfor, women, be town & strete
> Your childur handis when ȝe be-holde, –
> Theyr brest, þeire body and þeire fete –
> Then gode hit were on my son thynk ȝe wolde,

How care has made my hert full colde
To se my son, with nayle and speyre,
With scourge and thornys many-folde,
Woundit and ded, my dere son, dere. (ll. 49–56)[35]

She then turns her address into a direct homiletic attack:

Wepe with me, both man and wyfe,
My childe is youres & lovys yow wele.
If your childe had lost his life
ȝe wolde wepe at euery mele;   *every time*
But for my son wepe ȝe neuer a del.
If ȝe luf youres, myne has no pere;
He sendis youris both hap and hele   *happiness*
And for ȝow dyed my dere son, dere. (ll. 65–72)

The examples must suffice to give an idea of the kind of lyric vividly commemorating and re-living the most important stages of the church year, in particular
Christmas and the Passion. Most of these poems are directly linked to Church
services, Christian festivals or personal devotion. Some seem artless enough,
but many make use of elaborate verse forms and complicated rhyme-schemes,
not, however, as a demonstration of rhetorical virtuosity, but, more likely, for
mnemonic reasons, i.e. to facilitate memorising and singing or reciting.

Historical and political poems

A considerable section of Middle English lyrics deal with historical events and
popular heroes (or villains). For his splendid collection of many of the best
examples, Rossell Hope Robbins has deliberately used the wider term 'poems'
instead of 'lyrics', since many of these songs have a strong narrative element,
recounting significant events and celebrating or lamenting great personages.[36]
Some of the earliest examples occur in the invaluable Harley manuscript, such
as the ballad relating the execution of Sir Simon Fraser, a Scottish knight
captured and hanged as a traitor in 1306. The poem is an eloquent instance of
the way popular emotion could be stirred up in a particular cause by this kind
of propaganda in verse:

Lystneþ, lordynges, a newe song ichulle bigynne
of þe traytours of scotland þat take beþ wyþ gynne.   *been taken, trick*
Mon þat loueþ falsnesse & nule neuer blynne,   *will never cease*
sore may him drede þe lyf þat he is ynne,
    Ich vnderstonde.[37]

The poem bristles with violent patriotic hatred of the traitors and obviously
tries to appeal to an audience of similar persuasion. The speaker glories in the
gruesome sight of the traitor's head displayed upon London bridge, while the
body remaining on the gallows shall frighten away the Scots. It is a graphic
piece of historiography and at the same time a partisan pamphlet in the form
of a popular song.

In the same manuscript there is also a poem lamenting the death of Edward I (1307), beginning with a similar appeal to the listeners:

> Alle þat beoþ of huerte trewe,
>   a stounde herkneþ to my song,   *listen a while*
> of duel þat deþ haþ diht vs newe,   *grief, inflicted*
>   þat makeþ me syke ant sorewe among;
>   of a knyht þat wes so strong,
>   of wham god haþ don ys wille;   *his*
> me þuncheþ þat deþ haþ don vs wrong,   *I think*
>   þat he so sone shal ligge stille.[38]   *lie*

There is a tradition of similar laments for deceased rulers throughout the fourteenth and fifteenth centuries, from Edward II (1327)[39] to Edward IV (1383), as there is of ballads on famous military exploits. One of the most spectacular was the victory at Agincourt, celebrated by a triumphal entry on the King's return to London, in a ballad, praising 'god omnipotent' in the refrain, and in a popular carol, with the refrain 'Deo gratias'.[40] Some of these poems were used by later historians; most of them are anonymous, and even where the author's name is known, as in the case of Laurence Minot, of whom eleven aggressively patriotic poems on various battles between 1328 and 1352 are extant, we do not know much more than that.[41]

Another type of political poem is concerned with social abuses, criticism of religious factions and the vices of particular estates. Often the tone is clearly partisan, as in some poems referring to the Wars of the Roses (from 1449), when Lancastrians (whose crest was a red rose) and the Yorkists (white rose) agitated and fought against each other. An interesting, if poetically negligible poem describes the state of England immmediately before the outbreak of new hostilities in terms of protagonists' badges (conveniently identified in the margin).[42] Another poem celebrates the – rather short-lived – reconciliation of King Henry VI and the Yorkists (1458), clearly from the position of a Londoner, in eight stanzas, with the refrain: 'Reiose, Anglond, in concorde & vnite.'[43] Almost every significant political event, personality or issue is referred to in one or the other song. Leafing through Robbins's anthology and his commentary is thus like a lively survey of fourteenth- and fifteenth-century English history.

Religious controversy also is a favourite subject of satirical or polemical poems, in particular the abuses of church authorities, complaints about the friars and invective against the Lollards. An early example of spirited satire is a ninety-line poem among the Harley lyrics, where a peasant, charged with immmorality, relates his experience before a consistory court. In the end, to his lively chagrin, he has to marry the woman involved; he evidently feels himself treated most unjustly:

> seþþen y pleide at bisshopes plee,   *since, game*
> ah me were leuere be sonken y þe see,   *I would rather*
>   In sor wiþouten synne.   *grief*
> At chirche ant þurh cheping, ase dogge y am dryue,   *market, like a*
> þat me were leuere of lyue þen so forte lyue,   *I would rather be dead*
>   to care of al my kynne.[44]   *to the grief of*

No less aggressive is 'The Layman's Complaint', written in a fifteenth-century
hand on the flyleaf of a fourteenth-century manuscript, together with the
friar's reply. The verses, though not very remarkable as poetry, provide a
telling glimpse of hostilities treated more eloquently in Chaucer's *Canterbury
Tales* or Langland's *Piers Plowman*:

Þou þat sellest þe worde of god,	
Be þou berfot, be þou schod,	*wearing shoes*
Cum neuere here.	
In principio erat verbum	*In the beginning was the word*
Is þe worde of god, all & sum,	
þat þou sellest, lewed frere.	

The friar defends himself in a poem of 36 lines, with arguments that may well
reflect part of the contemporary situation:

Allas! what schul we freris do,	
Now lewed men kun holy writ?	*uneducated, understand*
All abowte wherre I go	
Þei aposen me of it.[45]	*argue*

The issue could hardly be stated in more specific terms. Similarly, the poem
against Lollards, contained in a manuscript together with *Piers Plowman* and
various other items, explicitly deals with a state of affairs just before 1417,
when Sir John Oldcastle, Lord Cobham, was captured and burnt as a heretic.
Three years earlier, an open revolt by the Lollards had been crushed by the
king's forces. The poem clearly alludes to the name of Oldcastle in terms that
exactly describe the popular view of this movement:

Hit is vnkyndly for a kniȝt,	
Þat shuld a kynges castel kepe,	
To bable þe bibel day & niȝt	*mumble*
In restyng tyme when he shuld slepe;	
& carefoly awey to crepe,	
for alle þe chief of chiualrie.	
Wel aught hym to waile & wepe,	
Þat suyche lust haþ in lollardie.[46]	*has such delight*

Like many of the Middle English lyrics, this polemical piece combines the appeal
and accessibility of a popular song with a certain sophistication of form and
matter. Though there is evidently considerable variation in stylistic competence
and ambition as well as in intellectual originality and independence of thought,
it is hardly possible, apart from some distinct genres, to classify these poems
according to schools, social status or formal development. Yet they form a fairly
distinct body of verse within the history of English poetry; at least it has been
observed that, for a number of reasons, there is little direct influence on later
poets and 'it is rare to find examples of medieval lyrics copied or recorded after
1540–50'.[47] Popular reception, however, has been less negative, and many
medieval lyrics, especially the carols, have found their way into modern song-
books, while a number of ballads have inspired later poets and contributed to
a more lively sense of past history.

Notes

1. For some of the most useful anthologies see *English Lyrics of the XIIIth Century*, ed. Carleton Brown (Oxford, 1932), *Religious Lyrics of the XIVth Century*, ed. Carleton Brown. second edition, revised by G. V. Smithers (Oxford, 1957), *Religious Lyrics of the XVth Century*, ed. Carleton Brown (Oxford, 1939), *Secular Lyrics of the XIVth and XVth Centuries*, ed. Rossell Hope Robbins, second edition (Oxford, 1955), *Historical Poems of the XIVth and XVth Centuries*, ed. Rossell Hope Robbins (New York, 1959).

2. Even in the sixteenth century and long after the invention of the printing press, lyrics mostly circulated in other forms than that of the printed book. For a useful account see Arthur F. Marotti, *Manuscript, Print, and the English Renaissance Lyric* (Ithaca, 1995).

3. Text in *English Lyrics of the XIIIth Century*, ed. Carleton Brown, p. 13, and in the useful anthology *Early Middle English Verse and Prose*, ed. J. A. W. Bennett and G. V. Smithers. With a Glossary by Norman Davis (Oxford, 1966), p. 110.

4. *Lyrics of the Thirteenth Century*, p. 14; also in *Early Middle English Verse and Prose*, p. 111, and *Medieval English Lyrics. A Critical Anthology*, ed. R. T. Davies (London, 1963), p. 52. On the poem and its musical setting see Michael Swanton, *English Literature before Chaucer*, Longman Literature in English Series (London, 1987), pp. 238–41.

5. In *Early Middle English Verse and Prose*, p. 321, and in *Secular Lyrics of the XIVth and XVth Centuries*, p. xxxix, where another version is quoted; it continues:

   allas, þat he so sone fel;
   wy nadde he stonde better, vile gorel?   *why did he not, fat fellow*

6. See Derek Pearsall, *Old English and Middle English Poetry* (London, 1977), p. 120. Pearsall gives a good description of the manuscript and its contents. See also the facsimile edition, ed. N. R. Ker, *EETS*, 255 (1965), with a good introduction, and the edition by G. L. Brook, *The Harley Lyrics. The Middle English Lyrics of MS Harley 2253* (Manchester, 1948). See also *Early Middle English Verse and Prose*, ed. Bennett and Smithers, pp. 111–28 and 320–32.

7. See the useful introduction in *A Selection of English Carols*, ed. Richard Leighton Greene, Clarendon Medieval and Tudor Series (Oxford, 1962), pp. 1–52, p. 13.

8. *The Canterbury Tales*, X, 1087; *The Riverside Chaucer*.

9. *The Riverside Chaucer*, p. 649; for commentary see A. J. Minnis, *The Shorter Poems. Oxford Guides to Chaucer* (Oxford, 1995), pp. 479–80 and *A Variorum Edition of the Works of Chaucer*, vol. V: *The Minor Poems*, ed. George B. Pace and Alfred David (Norman, Oklahoma, 1982), pp. 161–70.

10. On the French element in the poetry of Chaucer (and his contemporaries) see the valuable study by James I. Wimsatt, *Chaucer and his French Contemporaries. Natural Music in the Fourteenth Century* (Toronto, 1991).

11. See *Charles of Orleans: The English Poems*, ed. R. Steele and M. Day, *EETS*, 215, 220 (1941, 1946; reprinted 1970), and M.-J. Arn, *Fortunes Stabilness: Charles of Orleans's English Book of Love*, Medieval and Renaissance Texts and Studies (Binghamton, 1994); selections in *Secular Lyrics of the XIVth and XVth Centuries*, ed. Robbins and in *Chaucer to Spenser. An Anthology of Writings in English 1375–1575*, ed. Derek Pearsall (Oxford, 1999). See also J. Fox, *The Lyric Poetry of Charles d'Orléans* (Oxford, 1969).

12. See his particularly useful introduction, pp. xvii–lv, with a list of types of manuscripts and the distribution of extant poems within them.

13. *Secular Lyrics of the XIVth and XVth Centuries*, p. 12: MS Rawlinson D. 913.

14. *Secular Lyrics of the XIVth and XVth Centuries*, no. 81. The poem begins:

> Maistres! ye that vsen blode-lettynge,
> And therby getten youre lyuynge;
> Here May ye lerne wysdome goode,
> What plase that ye shall letten blode
> In man and in childe,
> ffor euelles that ben wyked & wyld.   *evils*
> Veynes þer ben thirty and ij
> ffor euelles many moste be vndo; (ll. 1–8)   *opened*

15. *Secular Lyrics of the XIVth and XVth Centuries*, no. 78.

16. *Secular Lyrics of the XIVth and XVth Centuries*, no. 118; also in *Chaucer to Spenser*, p. 399. See Elizabeth Salter, 'A Complaint Against Blacksmiths', in *English and International: Studies in the literature, Art and Patronage of Medieval England*, ed. Derek Pearsall and Nicolette Zeeman (Cambridge, 1988), previously published in *Literature and History*, 5 (1979), 194–215. For a blacksmith working at night (very conveniently, in this case) see Chaucer's 'Miller's Tale'.

17. *Secular Lyrics of the XIVth and XVth Centuries*, no. 116.

18. See Swanton, *English Literature before Chaucer*, pp. 237–54, and the important study by John Stevens, *Words and Music in the Middle Ages: Song, Narrative, Dance and Drama, 1050–1350*, Cambridge Studies in Music (Cambridge, 1986).

19. See Greene, *A Selection of English Carols* and his fuller collection *Early English Carols* (Oxford, 1935).

20. See the introductions to Greene's collections and R. H. Robbins, 'Middle English Carols as Processional Hymns', *Studies in Philology*, 56 (1959), 559–82. See also Douglas Gray, *Themes and Images in the Middle English Religious Lyric* (London, 1972), pp. 62–3.

21. See Brook, *The Harley Lyrics*, nos 31 and 32 and notes.

22. Compare

> Euer ant oo for my leof icham in grete þohte;   *always, I am*
> y þenche on hire þat y ne seo nout ofte. (32, ll. 7–8)
>
> *I think of her whom I do not often see*

and

> Euer ant oo, nyht ant day, he haueþ vs in is þohte;
> he nul nout leose þat he so deore bohte. (31, ll. 7–8)
>
> *he will not lose those, dearly bought*

23. *Religious Lyrics of the XVth Century*, no. 83. It is, perhaps, not strictly a carol, but it is preserved in the same songbook with a great number of carols (British Library, Sloane 2593). The manuscript page containing the poem is reproduced in Gray, *Themes and Images in the Medieval English Religious Lyric*, opposite p. 55.

24. Text in *Chaucer to Spenser*, ed. Pearsall, p. 389 and, with original tune of 1591, in *The Oxford Book of Carols*, ed. Percy Dearmer, R. Vaughan Williams and Martin Shaw (Oxford, 1928), no. 22 ('Coventry Carol'). The play was performed by the Coventry Shearmen and Tailors.

25. *A Selection of English Carols*, p. 230, note on no. 67A. Text also in *Chaucer to Spenser*, ed. Pearsall, pp. 393–4 and, with critical commentary on this 'most mysterious and moving of poems', in *Medieval English Lyrics*, ed. Davies, pp. 272 and 363–4.

26. *Secular Lyrics of the XIVth and XVth Centuries*, p. xvii. His calculation is based on Carleton Brown and Rossell Hope Robbins, *The Index of Middle English Verse*, The Index Society II (New York, 1943), supplemented by Rossell Hope Robbins and John L. Cutler, *Supplement to the Index of Middle English Verse* (Lexington, 1965).

27. *Secular Lyrics of the XIVth and XVth Centuries*, p. xvii.

28. *Themes and Images in the Medieval English Religious Lyric*, p. 221. Gray's sensitive study offers an excellent survey.

29. *The Canterbury Tales*, IV, 12–13.

30. *Religious Lyrics of the XIVth Century*, ed. Brown, no. 132, *Medieval English Lyrics*, ed. Davies, pp. 148–51 and 332–3, and *Chaucer to Spenser*, ed. Pearsall, pp. 391–3.

31. 'The word was made flesh' (John i, 14). *Religious Lyrics of the XVth Century*, ed. Brown, no. 78. On the Edinburgh manuscript see Greene, *A Selection of Carols*, p. 183 and Gisela Guddat-Figge, *Catalogue of Manuscripts Containing Middle English Romances*, Texte und Untersuchungen zur Englischen Philologie (München, 1976), pp. 127–30.

32. *Religious Lyrics of the XVth Century*, no. 93 (only in MS Cambridge Univ. Ee 1. 12).

33. *Religious Lyrics of the XVth Century*, no. 9, and p. 298. (Rylands Library, Manchester, Lat. MS. 395). The poem is extant in two manuscripts; the refrain occurs in another, much longer poem extant in three manuscript versions.

34. *Religious Lyrics of the XVth Century*, no. 6. The poem occurs in four manuscripts in different forms.

35. *Religious Lyrics of the XVth Century*, no. 7 and pp. 296–8. This version from Cambridge University MS Ff.5.48 is extant in three manuscripts; a second version occurs in two manuscripts.

36. *Historical Poems of the XIVth and XVth Centuries*, ed. Rossell Hope Robbins (New York and Oxford, 1959).

37. *Historical Poems*, no. 4, ll. 1–5.

38. *Historical Poems*, no. 5, ll. 1–8.

39. See the elaborate lament for Edward II, *Historical Poems*, no. 38. It introduces the speaker walking out 'Opon a somer soneday' (l. 1) and encountering a woman with a wheel, i.e. Fortune, who shows him a king, fallen from high power to a wretched state and death. See Robbins's commentary, pp. 301–3, for the argument that the poem refers to Richard II, as earlier critics thought.

40. *Historical Poems*, nos 27 and 32 and commentary.

41. A number of political poems were, however, written by such recognised poets as Gower, Hoccleve and Lydgate. Robbins includes some of them in his anthology.

42. *Historical Poems*, no. 84; commentary on pp. 363–5. The poem begins, recalling the earlier victorious leaders Bedford, Gloucester and Exeter, referred to by their badges:

    | The Rote is ded, The swanne is goon, | *root* |
    | Þe firy Cresset hath lost his lyght; | *beacon* |
    | Therfore Inglond may make gret mone, | *complaint* |
    | Were not the helpe of godde almyght. (ll. 1–4) | |

43. *Historical Poems*, no. 79; see also the commentary, pp. 357–9.

44. *Historical Poems*, no. 6, ll. 79–84.

45. *Historical Poems*, nos 68 and 69.

46. *Historical Poems*, no. 64, ll. 25–32; see also the commentary, pp. 331–3. The following stanza begins: 'An old castel, & not repaired', and it blames the lord for stirring up riot against the king and his clergy.

47. See Gray, *Themes and Images in the Medieval English Religious Lyric*, p. 221. Gray is concerned only with the religious lyric, affected decisively by the Reformation, whereas ballads and carols lived on, in spite of powerful Continental influences, such as the Petrarchan sonnet and other imports, like the music and poetry of the madrigal and related forms. See the important study by John Stevens, *Music and Poetry in the Early Tudor Court* (London, 1961; revised edition Cambridge, 1979).

Chapter 8

Middle Scots Poetry

The Middle Scots poets of the fifteenth and early sixteenth century form a group whose fresh originality and inventiveness stand out from most of the literary productions of their period. It is more than regrettable that, mainly because of simple linguistic difficulties, this rich chapter of British literary history is usually neglected by all but a small band of devoted specialists. Yet the chief Middle Scots writers have produced a number of poems of extraordinary power and creative energy, texts that also show an impressive familiarity with European literary traditions.[1]

The Middle Scots poets have often been bracketed together under the label 'Scottish Chaucerians'.[2] The term is in many ways misleading, since none of these writers, though they do pay lip-service to Chaucer's towering rank and were, to a considerable extent, inspired by his achievement, particularly his mastery of language and the arts of rhetoric, can in any specific way be called his disciple. These writers lived in a different time, a different cultural climate and drew from many other sources. They developed their own, individual idiom and explored new areas of subject matter as well as new ways of engaging with cultural tradition. That the three most important figures, Robert Henryson, William Dunbar and Gavin Douglas all worked within a space of less than fifty years, can only be explained by the troubled history of the Scottish people during this century, in particular the brief flourishing of an aristocratic culture under James IV (1472–1513), fatally checked by the disastrous defeat of Flodden Field (1513), where the King himself and more than 10,000 men were killed. The cultural life of the country was strongly influenced by the traditional ties with France, an alliance that for centuries poisoned Anglo-Scottish relations, even to the rearguard fights of the last Stuart pretender, finally squashed with the battle of Culloden (1746). At the time of the 'Golden Age' of Scottish poetry (approximately 1450–1550), Scotland, though in social terms far behind the South of England, evidently possessed a cultural elite, three universities, a highly educated clergy and a court that encouraged the arts and furthered the exchange of ideas with the continent.[3]

James I of Scotland: *The Kingis Quair*

This dream vision and love allegory, in 197 rhyme-royal stanzas, best serves to show the close links between the courtly poetry of Chaucer, his successors and the Middle Scots poetic tradition. It is attributed to *Iacobus primus scotorum rex illustrissimus* in the only surviving text, the important manuscript Arch.

173

Selden. B. 24 in the Bodleian Library, Oxford.[4] Since the manuscript was produced some fifty years after the King's death in 1437, the ascription is somewhat uncertain, though it fits in with the known biographical facts. The king spent eighteen years, from 1406 (when he was a boy of eleven), in English custody, partly in the Tower, partly in various castles (e.g. Nottingham and Windsor), until his release and marriage to Joan of Beaufort in 1424. This would explain the mixture of English and Scottish elements in his language, his unprofessional poetic style and his familiarity with poetic conventions made popular by Chaucer and Lydgate.[5] The poem combines philosophical reflection, dream vision and autobiography in an attractively individual manner, beginning with the narrator's reading of Boece, which makes him reflect on the waywardness of Fortune and decide to write 'Sum new[e] thing' (89):

Though nature gave me sufficance in youth,	*sufficient (gifts and means)*
The rypenesse of resoun lak[it] I	
To gouerne with my will, so lyte I couth,	*was able to*
Quhen stereles to trauaile I begouth,	*without steering, began*
Amang the wawis of this warld to driue:	*waves*
And how the case anon I will discriue. (107–12)	

The image of a sea-voyage is especially appropriate here because the narrative proper starts with the poet's capture at sea and his imprisonment, where he bewails his misfortune, like Troilus, 'in my chamber thus allone' (204),[6] until, like Chaucer's prisoners in 'The Knight's Tale', he looks out of the window to see a beautiful maid,

For quhich sodayn abate anon astert	*faintness, rushed*
The blude of all my body to my hert. (279–80)	

In a dream vision that follows, Venus, Minerva and Fortune appear to him and, accepting his protestations of sincere, pure and constant love, promise help and success. Minerva lectures him on the unpredictable power of Fortune and the Boethian question of free will and determination. She sends the dreamer on to Fortune and her wheel, which is described in realistic detail. The Goddess helps him to climb the wheel, admonishing him to hold on fast:

'Ensample', quod sche, 'tak of this tofore	
That fro my quhele be rollit as a ball;	*wheel*
For the nature of it is euermore,	
After ane hicht, to vale and geue a fall –	*a high point, descend*
Thus, quhen me likith, vp or doun to fall.	*it pleases me*
Fare wele', quod sche, and by the ere me toke	
So ernestly that therwithall I woke. (1198–1204)	

The poem thus agrees with the Boethean position, reconciling the capricious nature of Fortune with man's freedom and responsibility.

The poem concludes with a prayer for all lovers who have not yet attained their deserved happiness and a brief envoy, with a homage to Chaucer and Gower, his 'maisteris dere' (1373).

It is easy to see that the work is heavily indebted to Chaucer as well as to Lydgate (who was still living at the time), but there is also a strong sense of spontaneous personal experience, idealised according to the poetic conventions familiar to the author through moving in a courtly environment. There is no reason to question the manuscript's attribution to James I, whose career can best explain the genesis of 'the earliest Scottish poem to acknowledge the influence of Chaucer . . . and also the first Scottish dream-vision poem'.[7]

Richard Holland: *The Book of the Houlat*

This elaborate and witty poem, usually dated about 1445–50, is another instance of Chaucerian influence transformed and combined with quite different traditions, in this case the alliterative 'revival', the beast fable and topical Scottish events.[8] It is written in 77 thirteen-line stanzas, with a demanding rhyme-scheme: abababababcdddc, with the last four short lines forming the wheel or metrical refrain. Each stanza is linked to the following one by concatenation. The third stanza may serve as an example of the poet's rhetorical style:

The birth that the ground bure was browdin on breidis,	*growth, adorned far and wide*
With gers gaye as the gold and granes of grace;	*herbs, beneficient seeds*
Mendis and medicyne for mennis all neidis,	*cure*
Helpe to hert and to hurt, heilfull it was.	*wholesome*
Under the cerkill solar thir savorus seidis	*sphere of the sun, delightful*
War nurist be dame Natur, that noble mastres;	*nourished, mistress*
Bot all thar names to nevyn as now it nocht neid is,	*name, there is no need*
It war prolixt and lang and lenthing of space,	*were tedious, prolonging*
And I have mekle mater in meter to glos	*plenty of*
Of ane nother sentence,	*subject matter*
And waike is my eloquence;	*weak*
Thairfor in haist will I hens	*a hurry*
To the purpos.	

Of that purpos, in the place be pryme of the day	
I herd ane petuos appele with ane pur mane,	*piteous, wretched complaint*
Solpit in sorowe, that sadly couth say:	*Steeped, managed to say*
'Wa is me, wretche in this warld, wilsome of wane!'	
	Woe, distracted in mind (27–43)

The poet walks out on a jolly May morning where he becomes a witness to the lamentations of an owl and his story. The basic plot then follows the traditional fable of the owl complaining of his repulsive appearance. After a ceremonious assembly convened by the pope, the owl is, at the decree of Dame Nature, given a feather by each bird, which makes him so proud that he is immediately stripped bare again by Dame Nature, to serve as a warning against pride. The simple story is greatly elaborated into a general council of spiritual and secular dignitaries in the shape of birds, an allegorical parliament and a banquet attended by lords temporal and spiritual, combined with heraldic representations of the most powerful Scottish families. The beast fable merges into a satirical picture of the contemporary scene, with profusion of references to current events, from the schism of the church to the questionable position of the Holy Roman Emperor and the waning fortunes of the Douglas family, touching on a number of social and political problems. The owl's complaint is almost forgotten, as the poem gets carried away by the description of elaborate festivities, including the grotesque exhibition of an Irish bard and the musical performance of a hymn to the Virgin Mary, with a list of some twenty different instruments.

Very little is known about the author of the poem. It seems that he was a cleric associated with the powerful Douglas family and driven into exile with several others of its members after 1455, when James II broke their power. It is evident, however, that he was well read in Chaucer, whose *Parliament of Fowls* must have been an important model, and familiar with medieval key texts, such as Alan of Lille's *De Planctu Naturae* and Bartholomaeus Anglicus' *De Proprietatibus Rerum*.

Robert Henryson

Of Robert Henryson, perhaps the most original of the Middle Scots poets, very little is known, except that William Dunbar speaks of him as dead soon after 1505 and that tradition associates him with Dunfermline and with the professions of public notary and schoolteacher. The documents also make it very likely that he was admitted to the University of Glasgow and had a degree in canon law.[9] His chief works, the *Moral Fables* and *The Testament of Cresseid*, plainly profess their dependence on the model of Geoffrey Chaucer, yet, at the same time they insist on their difference, almost with a certain defiance. Although we know hardly anything about Henryson's first audience, there is no doubt that it was quite different from Chaucer's. Since all the extant manuscripts and prints postdate Henryson's death by more than a generation we can only speculate about the exact environment or the genesis of his poems.[10]

Henryson's *Moral Fables* have repeatedly been compared with Chaucer's *Canterbury Tales*.[11] The association is suggested by the unorthodox range of stylistic registers, the play on different levels of seriousness and the surprising combination of humour, realism, rhetorical virtuosity and moral earnestness rather than by any marked similarity of form or subject matter. The closest link is, of course, between the fable of the Cock and the Fox and Chaucer's 'Nun's Priest's Tale'. Henryson does not acknowledge his model, and his version is 'selfconsciously independent of Chaucer (though almost exclusively indebted to him)'.[12] His thirteen fables, introduced by a prologue, claim Aesop as their source, but it is obvious that Henryson, in fact, draws on two distinct traditions. One is the animal fable, often vaguely ascribed to Aesop, but handed down over the centuries in countless different versions, continually augmented and adapted. The other is the French epic *Roman de Renart* (thirteenth century), a satiric history of the wily fox, his battle of wits against other animals, especially his traditional arch-enemy, the wolf. Many of the fox's exploits had already been taken out of their context and treated as traditional animal fables, while at the same time Aesopian fables were expanded and turned into little narratives, as in Henryson's collection where all the animal episodes are treated alike regardless of their ultimate origin.

What Henryson seems to have been particularly interested in is the problem of the didactic tale, and he uses the basic form of the animal fable to experiment with various ways of illustrating a moral.[13] The Prologue to the collection makes an eloquent plea for the moral truth of poetry, especially the invented fable:

Thocht fein3eit fabils of ald poetre	*invented*
Be not al grunded vpon truth, 3it than,	
Thair polite termes of sweit rhetore	*noble, rhetoric*
Richt plesand ar vnto the eir of man;	*Very pleasing, ear*
And als the caus quhy thay first began	
Wes to repreif the of thi misleuing,	*reprove, evil living*
O man, be figure of ane vther thing. (1–7)	*by the image of something else*

It is a remarkably concise theory of poetry, in particular the traditional animal fable and the moral justification of fiction. Later he becomes more explicit, and the satirical drive of his work is revealed:

My author in his fabillis tellis how	
That brutal beistis spak and vnderstude,	*beasts*
And to gude purpois dispute and argow,	*argue*
Ane sillogisme propone, and eik conclude;	*also*
Putting exempill and similitude	
How mony men in operatioun	*in their actions*
Ar like to beistis in conditioun. (43–9)	

The message is clear: the poets present animals like humans, to show humans that they behave like beasts. This is illustrated in a series of variations, beginning with the simple fable of the cock and the jewel, extant in many medieval versions, ultimately derived from the Roman poet Phaedrus (*c.* 15 BC–AD 40). Henryson's immediate source was most probably the collection of Gualterus Anglicus of *c.* 1175, extant in over a hundred manuscripts and widely used as a schoolbook. Seven of Henryson's fables are also in Gualterus. The others belong to the beast-epic tradition. One or two may well be his own invention.

Gualterus' version of the first fable has eight lines, plus another six lines of *moralitas*. It is part of a collection of fifty-eight fables, all told with epigrammatic brevity, which was the most common way of assembling and presenting fables. Henryson's treatment is rather unusual; it is not even clear whether he thought of his fables as a distinct group. The witnesses differ in their arrangement; the most complete version has an order, often followed in editions, that might well represent the author's own design and, to some critics, suggests a deliberate pattern.[14] There appears to be a gradual darkening of the vision, beginning with some more light-hearted fables and ending in a rather gloomy view of human society, illustrated by fables that present animals behaving to each other cruelly, like ruthless predators, exploiting tyrants or dissembling friends. In the centre of the collection is a fable ('The Lion and the Mouse' [vii]) framed by a dream vision in which the poet meets Aesop and asks him for a specimen of his fables. The ancient author complies and at the end of his relation, after the 'Moral', urges the author to spread the message:

Quhen this wes said, quod Esope, 'My fair child,	
Perswaid the kirkmen ythandly to pray	*churchmen, constantly*
That tressoun of this cuntrie be exyld,	
And iustice regne, and lordis keip thair fay	*faith*
Vnto thair souerane lord baith nycht and day.'	*both*
And with that word he vanist and I woke;	
Syne throw the schaw my iourney hamewart tuke. (1615–21)	*little wood*

It is a good example of Henryson's varying techniques, his experimenting with the genre and his unmistakable social commitment.

'The Lion and the Mouse' is not necessarily conceived as one item in a series of fables, but might well be a self-contained little poem of its own. It hardly needs a separate prologue since it contains its own introduction and moral explication.[15]

Similarly, 'The Preaching of the Swallow' [viii], the most elaborate and carefully constructed of the fables, does not gain by being part of a cycle. Like 'The Lion and the Mouse', it has its own full prologue, with an eloquent praise of God's omnipotence manifested in his creatures and a traditional, but wonderfully vivid and original description of the seasons. The rhetoric is clearly indebted to the learned Latinate style of academic discourse, yet refreshingly concise and free of Lydgatean prolixity. Complex theological problems are presented as natural facts to be supported by the poet's observation:

The hie prudence and wirking meruelous,	*high, works*
The profound wit off God omnipotent,	
Is sa perfyte and sa ingenious,	
Excellent far all mannis iugement;	*Excelling*
For quhy to him all thing is ay present,	*Because, ever*
Rycht as it is or ony time sall be,	
Befoir the sicht off his diuinitie.	*sight*
Thairfoir our saull with sensualitie	
So fetterit is in presoun corporall,	*prison of the body*
We may not cleirlie vnderstand nor se	
God as he is, nor thingis celestiall;	
Our mirk and deidly corps materiale	*dark*
Blindis the spirituall operatioun,	
Lyke as ane man wer bundin in presoun. (1622–35)	

It is only after twelve stanzas of authorial homily that the poet tells us that on a fine spring day he walked out to become a witness to the events of the fable. It is like a dream allegory without the dream. We are not told that the speaker falls asleep, but the whole situation is obviously indebted to the convention of the dream vision. The fable is related not as a specimen of Aesop's poetic art, as the preceding item, but as a record of the writer's own observation. This is evidently meant to establish the episode as one of God's means to instruct through his creatures. While the prologue to the whole collection admits to fables being invented ('feinȝeit'), 'The Preaching of the Swallow' wants to impress on the reader their actual basis in the world around us. The passing of the seasons is skilfully linked with the narrator's own involvement as he watches the three stages of the action, and these in turn are an illustration of the perennial cycle described in the prologue.

The frame is closed by the *moral*, allegorising the simple fable as a warning against the traps set by the Fiend and an exhortation to listen to preachers.[16]

The fable itself, only twelve lines in Henryson's source, is extended into a colourfully realistic picture of country life, with the coarse brutality of the farmer and the well-meaning, sorrowful swallow as impressive protagonists. It is a dire warning against imprudent lack of foresight and careless disregard of benevolent advice. The swallow's dirge combines genuine humane sympathy with stern moral:

> And quhen the swallow saw that thay wer deid,
> 'Lo,' quod scho, 'thus it happinnis mony syis   *times*
> On thame that will not tak counsall nor reid   *them, advice*
> Off prudent men or clerkis that ar wyis.
> This grit perrell I tauld thame mair than thryis;   *great peril*
> Now ar thay deid, and wo is me thairfoir!'
> Scho tuke hir flicht, bot I hir saw no moir. (1881–7)

It is this rare infusion of personal warmth and genuine fellowship between Henryson's animals that has made his fables so singular.

Almost each one of the thirteen items makes different use of the traditional pattern, which argues against their being conceived as a unified collection, though none of the others are as elaborately self-contained as 'The Lion and the Mouse' and 'The Preaching of the Swallow.' Some begin by mentioning Aesop ('The Two Mice' [ii], 'The Sheep and the Dog' [vi], 'The Fox, the Wolf, and the Husbandman' [x], 'The Wolf and the Wether' [xi], 'The Paddock and the Mouse' [xiii]) or just 'myne authour' ('The Fox, the Wolf and the Cadger' [ix]); some begin with a general wisdom ('The Cock and the Fox' [iii]) and some start immediately with the story itself ('The Cock and the Jasp' [i], 'The Wolf and the Lamb' [xii]). Two are directly linked to the preceding fable ('The Fox and the Wolf' [iv], 'The Trial of the Fox' [v]) and appear to form a little sub-group about the exploits of the Fox.

Each fable is concluded by a *Moralitas* as in the source and many similar collections, but again, these didactic explications vary greatly in length and in method. The particularly lively and realistically told fable of the 'Two Mice' is rounded off with a simple moral, praising domestic contentment in homely terms and with proverbial wisdom:

> Thy awin fyre, freind, thocht it be bot ane gleid,   *own, ember*
> It warmis weill, and is worth gold to the;   *well*
> And Solomon sayis, gif that thow will reid,
> 'Vnder the heuin I can no better se

Than ay be blyith and leif in honestie.' *always, pleasant, beloved*
Quhairfoir I may conclude be this ressoun:
Of eirthly ioy it beiris maist degre, *carries the highest rank*
Blyithnes in hart, with small possessioun. (389–96) *Happiness*

Most of the *moralitates*, however, are more elaborate and defend the moral function of the animal fable, its figurative character and the challenge to the reader to discover significances. Sometimes each character (or animal) is glossed in the manner of medieval preachers, sometimes in such sophisticated detail that the method seems to be employed tongue in cheek. This is especially the case at the end of the last fable ('The Mouse and the Paddock'), where the comic possibilities of talking animals are fully exploited. The mouse, who rightly distrusts the treacherous frog, refers to her own experience of physiognomy, quoting a Latin proverb against him: '*Distortum vultum sequitur distortio morum*' (2832). Henryson's *moralitas* gives a ludicrously literate spiritual application of the fable, concluding with a mock apology to the reader:

Adew, my freind, and gif that ony speiris *enquires why*
Of this fabill, sa schortlie I conclude,
Say thow, I left the laif vnto the freiris, *remainder*
To mak a sample or similitude. (2969–72)

It is an evident satirical dig against the friars with their obsessive 'glosing' and an instance of Henryson's Chaucerian humour.[17]

Most of the *moralitates* are, however, more genuinely serious, and many combine earnest homiletic instruction with compassionate social protest and reproach for all those who misuse their authority to oppress the poor and weak. Henryson's criticism is in substance traditional and does not seem to refer to a very specific historical situation, but the innocent lamb, brutally victimised by the cruel wolf, is treated with sincere sympathy and pity, and the *moralitas* turns into a passionate appeal to lords and governors to beware of becoming tyrannous wolves:

O thow grit lord, that riches hes and rent, *great*
Be nocht ane wolf, thus to deuoir the pure!
Think that na thing cruell nor violent
May in this warld perpetuallie indure.
This sall thow trow and sikkerlie assure: *trust, for certain*
For till oppres, thow sall haif als grit pane *Because of victimisation, pain*
As thow the pure with thy awin hand had slane. *As if*

God keip the lamb, quhilk is the innocent,
From wolfis byit and men extortioneris; *bite*
God grant that wrangous men of fals intent *unjust*
Be manifest, and punischit as effeiris; (2763–73) *is proper*

Here the beast characters are treated without any comic undertone, but even where Henryson is openly relishing the humorous side of the homely animal discourse, he remains true to his conviction that all these actors are instruments of God created for our instruction and salvation. His fables are a rare instance of animals taken entirely seriously as beasts and at the same time as human beings.

For many readers, Robert Henryson is, first of all, the author of *The Testament of Cresseid*, a poem that during the Renaissance was apparently thought to be Chaucer's own sequel to *Troilus and Criseyde*. William Thynne's edition of Chaucer (1532 and 1542)[18] included an anglicised text of *The Testament of Cresseid* and, as Denton Fox claims, 'his edition ensured that it would be accepted as Chaucer's in the sixteenth century'; the attribution also meant that the poem was more widely known, especially in England, than any other Scots poem of the period.[19] One would have thought, however, any attentive reader should have noticed that the narrator is engaging in a critical dialogue with the famous author of *Troilus and Criseyde*, whose veracity he claims to doubt and whose account he attempts to supplement, though it is not entirely inconceivable that Chaucer himself might have indulged in this kind of humorous self-reference.

The introduction is another masterpiece of Henryson's effortless juxtaposition of learned astronomical and mythological reference and homely realism. The traditional spring morning is replaced by a Scottish winter evening, and Chaucer's narrator, using Ovid's tale to help him to sleep, by a freezing author settling down to a fire, a drink and the book of *Troilus and Criseyde*:

I mend the fyre and beikit me about,	*warmed*
Than tuik ane drink, my spreitis to comfort,	*spirits*
And armit me weill fra the cauld thairout.	*armed myself well, outside*
To cut the winter nicht and mak it schort	*night*
I tuik ane quair – and left all vther sport –	*book*
Writtin be worthie Chaucer glorious	
Of fair Creisseid and worthie Troylus. (36–42)	

The distress of Troilus affects him so deeply that he picks up another book, where he finds the continuation of Cresseid's story. This gives rise to his famous question about the credibility of poets, including his own:

Quha wait gif all that Chauceir wrait was trew?	*Who knows, wrote*
Nor I wait nocht gif this narratioun	
Be authoreist, or feinȝeit of the new	*invented for the first time*
Be sum poeit, throw his inuentioun	
Maid to report the lamentatioun	
And wofull end of this lustie Creisseid,	*full of life*
And quhat distres scho thoillit, and quhat deid. (64–70)	*suffered, death*

It seems evident that Henryson was touched by Chaucer's poem and felt the urge to comment on it. Cresseid's cruel punishment by the Gods and Troilus' dim memory of his love as he encounters but fails to recognise her, have given rise to controversial readings. While the majority of earlier critics had taken Cresseid's unprecedented harsh punishment as a sign of Henryson's sternly vindictive morality, others found his version compassionate and much more Chaucerian than it appears at first sight.[20] Another way of looking at the poem is to discover that it 'develops consistently yet in an unexpected way action and character anticipated in *Troilus*, and by so doing evokes pathos and powerful dramatic irony',[21] At any rate, Cresseid is not granted Troilus' vision from the eighth sphere, nor is she put in a position to smile at her own folly. Yet there is none of the traditional clerical antifeminism in the manner of her degradation. It is fortune, not her false nature, the author seems to blame, while echoing Chaucer's plea for pity. Within one single stanza, the poem deals with Cresseid's new lover Diomede, who discards her as soon as he has satisfied his appetite, and 'desolait' she is abandoned to her fate in the Greek camp. Like Chaucer, Henryson reports the most unpleasant news, her decline into a common prostitute, as rumour ('sum men sayis', 77) rather than as a fact, and there is no irony in his sorrowful elegy and the appeal not to judge her maliciously:

O fair Creisseid, the flour and A per se	
Of Troy and Grece, how was thow fortunait	*what was your fate*
To change in filth all thy feminitie,	
And be with fleschelie lust sa maculait,	*defiled*
And go amang the Greikis air and lait,	*at all hours*
Sa giglotlike takand thy foull plesance!	*like a wanton slut, taking*
I haue pietie thow suld fall sic mischance!	*pity, into such misfortune*
3it neuertheles, quhat euer men deme or say	
In scornefull langage of thy brukkilnes,	*frailty*
I sall excuse als far furth as I may	
Thy womanheid, thy wisdome and fairnes,	
The quhilk fortoun hes put to sic distres	
As hir pleisit, and nathing throw the gilt	
Of the – throw wickit langage to be spilt! (78–91)	*On you, ruined*

It is in this spirit that the poet relates Cresseid's blasphemy against the Gods, especially Cupid, and the divine punishment visited on her. As Florence Ridley has pointed out, Henryson takes up various hints from *Troilus and Criseyde*, such as Pandarus' prophetic warnings and, more importantly, the Boethian view of love as a universal life-giving force, experienced by Troilus and betrayed by Criseyde. This is why her refusal to join the public sacrifice in the temple and her rebellious accusation of Venus and Cupid bring down on her the appropriate divine retaliation, with loss of everything that had once made her the flower of Troy. The 'ugly vision' (344) of the Gods' council deciding on her fate is one of Henryson's most original inventions.[22] It leaves Cresseid an utter outcast from society, a leper among lepers. The advice given to her by a fellow leper, to 'mak vertew of ane neid' (478) may be an ironic reference to Criseyde's own parting counsel to Troilus,[23] but it is only when the former lovers have met, without recognising each other, that Cresseid wakes to a sense of her guilt, as her pathetic refrain (546, 553, 560) reveals. Now at last she blames herself, not the Gods, and feels sorry for Troilus, not only for herself and her good name:

All faith and lufe I promissit to the
Was in the self fickill and friuolous:
O fals Cresseid and trew knicht Troilus! (551–3)

To the end, the memory of their love still is alive in both of them, and the reported inscription on the tomb erected by Troilus makes it a monument of grief and reconciliation, not of vindictive defamation.[24] It is one of the most inspired epitaphs to Chaucer's poem and a remarkable early example of an explicit fictitious continuation, an 'offshoot' inspired by a great poem.

The third of Henryson's longer works, *Orpheus and Eurydice*, is much less original and more derivative, yet it also demonstrates his astonishing ability to add surprising new and personal touches to the most conventional subjects. He is never content just to copy, translate or imitate the work of others. The *moralitas* follows the source closely, but the myth itself is rehearsed with some gusto. Henryson's shorter poems belong to various traditional genres, from the lively *pastourelle* 'Robene and Makyne', often anthologised, to the sinister *memento mori* 'The Thre Deid Pollis'. Their most thorough editor, Denton Fox, makes no claim that the ascription to Henryson is in each case justified, and they do not add significantly to his literary stature, but they are typical witnesses of a lively lyric production, with a colourful variety of forms and subjects.

William Dunbar

William Dunbar, a younger contemporary of Henryson's, survived him and many other Scottish poets whose death he lists in one of his most famous poems, the 'Lament for the Makaris'. Instead of any rhetorical complaint or reflection, there is the liturgical refrain *'Timor mortis conturbat me'*. Its monotonous repetition after each of the brief stanzas produces the poem's stark seriousness:

> I se that makaris, amang the laif,   *rest*
> Playis heir ther padʒanis, syne gois to graif.   *pageants, then come to grief*
> Sparit is nought ther faculte: *Spared*
> Timor mortis conturbat me.   *Fear of death disturbs me*
>
> He has done petuously devour   *piteously devoured*
> The noble Chaucer, of makaris flour,
> The monk of Bery and Gower, al thre:
> Timor mortis conturbat me. (**21**, 45–52)[25]

The poem was printed in Dunbar's lifetime (*c.* 1505), as were a number of his other works.[26] He was obviously in a better position than Henryson to see to the publication of his texts. We do not know a great deal about his early life: born about 1460, he obtained a master's degree at St Andrews University in 1479 and travelled to England in 1501. From 1500 to 1513 he received a modest royal pension and was evidently associated with the court until the catastrophe of Flodden Field. He probably died soon after 1513.

Like Henryson, Dunbar experimented with conventional lyric forms and also with Chaucerian material, adapting it with creative independence and in a new personal idiom. The bulk of his poems consists of comparatively brief lyrics on such a variety of subjects and forms that it has proved very difficult to group the poems under convincing headings. The important Bannatyne manuscript, a unique repository of Scottish poetry, completed around 1568 and containing more than forty items attributed to Dunbar, has an arrangement in five sub-groups, 'ballatis of theologie', 'ballatis of moralitie', 'ballettis mirry', 'ballattis of luve' and 'fabillis', but, as the latest editor has shown, the arrangement, like that of other previous editors, is in many ways arbitrary so that she herself simply put the poems in alphabetical order of their first lines.[27] This may seem a counsel of despair, but it gives an adequate idea of the poems' unconventional diversity in form and content and avoids some doubtful interpretations.

Several of Dunbar's poems are directly addressed to events at the royal court. The often quoted 'The Thistle and the Rose' ('Quhen Merche we with variant windis past') celebrates the marriage of King James IV and Margaret Tudor, the sister of the English King Henry VIII (1503), in the form of a dream vision in May, involving the traditional figure of Dame Nature with heraldic animals and plants.[28] The Lion and the Rose are crowned and put above all other animals and plants, with the admonition to 'keip the lawis' and rule justly:

> 'Exerce iustice with mercy and conscience,
> And lat no small beist suffir skaith na skornis   *harm*
> Of greit beistis that bene of moir piscence. (52, 106–8)   *power*

All the birds rejoice at the union, and when the brief vision has dissolved, the poet returns home to write it all down. It is evidently a light-hearted contribution to the occasion, not a very serious attempt to curry favour or offer very serious advice. In fact, most of Dunbar's poems are on a small scale. Even the two longest and most ambitious are more modest than the *Testament of Cresseid*, and the majority are short lyrics.

The poem just quoted is clearly in the tradition of Chaucer's 'Parliament of Fowls'; the more ambitious and general 'The Goldyn Targe' also makes use of the dream convention. The opening, a dazzlingly 'aureate' yet not overloaded description of dawn,[29] introduces a paradisiac vision of Goddess Venus and a train of mythological figures, an opportunity for the poet to display his classical reading and his easy command of classical topoi:

> Discriue I wald, bot quho coud wele endyte   *write*
> How all the feldis wyth thai lilies quhite
> Depaynt war brycht, quhilk to the hevyn did glete? *Painted, glitter*
> Noucht thou, Omer, als fair as thou coud wryte,
> For all thine ornate stilis so perfyte.
> Nor yit thou, Tullius, quhois lippis suete
> Off rethorike did in to termes flete.   *flow*
> Your aureate tongis both bene all to lyte   *weak*
> For to compile that paradise complete. (59, 64–72)

Again, the setting and some of the chief figures are indebted to Chaucer and to Chaucer's sources, the *Roman de la Rose* and Alanus' *De Planctu Naturae*; Dunbar's poem is full of allusions to these texts.[30] 'The Golden Targe', however, is more concise, and there is a more explicit moral message behind the battle between Love's forces and Reason than in Chaucer's love allegories and the *Roman* since the conflict ends with the defeat of Reason, in spite of his golden shield, and the dreamer is 'delyuerit vnto Hevyness' (227). The vision of Love ends in a sense of loss and unreason, but, as the scene suddenly dissolves with a great bang and even the rainbow appears to crack, the poet finds himself once more in the midst of 'mirthful May' (252) and it all seems like a hideous nightmare. The poem ends with a famous tribute to Chaucer, along with Gower and Lydgate, and, again, the highest praise Dunbar can bestow on a 'makar' is his mastery of rhetoric:

O reuerend Chaucere, rose of rethoris all	
(As in oure tong ane flour imperiall)	
That raise in Britane ewir, quho redis rycht,	*understands correctly*
Thou beris of makaris the tryumph riall,	*royal*
Thy fresh anamalit termes celicall	*enamelled, rhetorical devices, heavenly*
This mater coud illumynit haue full brycht.	*brightly*
Was thou noucht of oure Inglisch all the lycht,	
Surmounting ewiry tong terrestriall,	
Alls fer as Mayes morow dois mydnycht? (59, 253–61)	

The images of light and of imperial triumph pick up metaphors used throughout the poem, whose poetic structure is of a density and concentration not often found in this kind of vision.

The Tretis of the Tua Mariit Wemen and the Wedo is the longest poem by Dunbar and, in its own surprising way, the most elaborate and unusual. It belongs to the large and varied chapter of medieval anti-feminist satire[31] and is evidently influenced by the relevant passages in the *Roman de la Rose* and Chaucer's *Canterbury Tales*, in particular the 'Wife of Bath's Prologue' and the 'Merchant's Tale', but it has its very individual inventiveness and gusto. It is written in alliterative long lines, a metre rarely used by the Middle Scots poets at this time, in itself, perhaps, a hint at the satirical spirit of the 'vncouth aventur' (528) to be related. The poem begins, innocently enough, with the poet walking out on an early midsummer morning in search of 'mirthis' (9) when he encounters three elegantly dressed women in a green arbour, drinking wine and indulging in free gossip about their married experience. In his hiding-place, the narrator listens to their uninhibited revelations. The two married women report their suffering from impotent stupid husbands who get what they deserve and who are good for nothing except being cheated, nagged and exploited. The widow then proceeds to a superior lesson in female dissimulation and, to let them profit from her own experience, shares with them her success, first with two husbands, whom she hated, flattered and deceived, and then as a merry widow, enjoying every kind of freedom and entertaining young men galore, apparently by means of her husbands' fortune. It is an outrageous collection of misogynist clichés, presented with such overboard extravagance and relish that the reader cannot help being on the women's side, in spite of their abusive language and their obsession with sexual appetite. The widow's lesson is applauded by the two married women who promise that they will 'exampill tak of her souerane teching / And wirk after he wordis, that women wes so prudent' (507/8), and the conference is concluded with another round of drinks.

The contrast between the coarse behaviour and lewd language of the three ladies and their rich, modish attire, is underlined by the deliberate juxtaposition of low and courtly vocabulary.[32] The widow's drastic confession is called 'hir ornat speche' and she herself 'this eloquent wedow' (505), terms normally employed by Dunbar for the art of rhetoric most admired by him. Throughout the poem this humorous linguistic contrast is used as a means of satiric characterisation. When the three ladies have departed, the narrator retires to another 'plesand arber, / And with my pen did report ther pastance most mery' (525/6). He concludes with the teasing question to his listeners, which of the three 'wanton wiffis' they would choose if they wished to marry one.[33]

In view of Dunbar's rich crop of poems, it may come as a surprise that his most ambitious poem is also his most frivolous. The reason, most probably, has much less to do with the poet's attitude towards women than with his particular interest in poetry and rhetoric, a carnivalesque enjoyment of his own virtuosity and easy command of an unprecedented range of discourse, stylistic contrast and variety of subject. To browse through his collected poems is to be made aware of the almost infinite possibilities and unorthodox freedom of the middle Scots poetic tradition.

Gavin Douglas

Unlike Henryson and Dunbar, Gavin Douglas (1476–1522) is comparatively well documented and we know more about his background and his various activities than those of any other Middle Scots poet.[34] He came from a more prominent family, as the younger son of Archibald, fifth earl of Angus. In 1494 he graduated at the university of St Andrews and in 1515 he was appointed Bishop of Dunkeld. His literary career seems to have ended after the battle of Flodden (1413). He apparently got embroiled in religious as well as political feuds, closely connected with the fortunes of Margaret Tudor, the sister of the English king Henry VIII, who had married Gavin's nephew Angus less than a year after the death of her first husband, James IV, at Flodden. Douglas took part in a diplomatic mission to France in 1517, but later seems to have been associated with Margaret's enemies and had to flee Scotland. Before his efforts at a reconciliation and promotion made any progress, he died of the plague in London, September 1522.

Douglas's chief claim to posterity's attention is his translation of Virgil's *Aeneid*, the first major translation of a classical epic into a variety of English, almost forty years before the version of Henry Howard, Earl of Surrey, who rendered books II and IV in English blank verse.[35] It is a faithful and admirably lively version in rhyming five-foot iambic lines. Virgil's twelve books are preceded by prologues that constitute Douglas's most original work and contain characteristic comments on his own poetic convictions and his ambitious project, beginning with an elaborate praise of Virgil's art of rhetoric and the traditional disclaimer:

Quhy suld I than with dull forhed *and* vayn,	*dull and empty brain*
With rude engyne and barrand emptyve brayn,	*instrument, barren*
With bad, harsk spech and lewit barbour tong	*barbarous*
Presume to write quhar thy sweit bell is rung	*where, sweet*
Or contyrfate sa precyus wordys deir?	*counterfeit*
Na, na, noth swa, but kneill quhem I *th*ame heir.	*not so, kneel*
For quhat compair betwix mydday and ny*ch*t?	*comparison*
Or quhat compair betwix myrknes and ly*ch*t?	*darkness*
Or quhat compar is betwix blak and quhyte?	
Far grettar difference betwix my blunt endyte	*writing*
And thy scharp sugurate sang Virgiliane,	*sugared*
Sa wysly wrocht with nevir a word invane. (Prologue, 19–30)	

The diction justifies Pearsall's verdict that 'Douglas's view of Virgil is not much touched by the Renaissance'.[36] On the other hand, his undertaking itself shows that the whole concept of Renaissance against 'medieval' is an unhelpful simplification.[37] Douglas is not a humanist scholar like many of his contemporaries in Italy and elsewhere, and he does not hesitate to adapt Virgil's heroes and his rhetoric to his own cultural environment, or to include in his translation the thirteenth book, a sequel added in 1428 by Mapheus Vegius and frowned on by some Renaissance scholars. Yet he has a genuine appreciation of Virgil's stature as epic poet and myth-maker. He had no models and not much in the way of linguistic or historical aids, though he made extensive use of a commentary compiled about 1500 by the Dutch humanist Ascenius.[38]

The prologue to the first book explains that the translation was undertaken at the request of Henry, third Lord Sinclair, a distant cousin, who is praised as 'Fader of buk*is*, protectour to sciens *and* lair' (Prologue, 85), and then deals with previous attempts at presenting Virgilian material in English, chiefly William Caxton, whose *Eneydos*, a translation from the French *Livre des Eneydes*, was printed in 1490. Douglas' taunt that it is no more like Virgil than the devil is like St Augustine (143) is not entirely unjust, since the French book is a free retelling of the story rather than a translation, but the ardour of the attack shows the Scots poet's keen commitment and serious concern with the details of the text and the accuracy of the translation. In the end, though, Douglas puts all the blame on the French book, because, as he asserts, he does not wish to enter into a quarrel with any English book or the dead ghost of an author (Caxton had died in 1491); yet he cannot suppress a conviction of his own superiority, when he states his own laws of translation:

Syne I defend *and* forbidd*is* every wight	
*Th*at can no*ch*t spell *th*ar Pater Noster ry*ch*t	
Fortill correct or ʒit amend Virgill,	
Or *the* tra*n*slatar blame in hys wlgar stile;	
I knaw quhat payn was to follow hym fut hait	*immediately*
Albeit *th*ou think my saying intricate.	
Traste weill to follow a fixt sentens or mater	
Is mair practike, deficill *and* far strater,	*more effort, confining*
*Th*och*t thyne engyne beyn elevate *and* hie,	*ingenuity*
*Th*an forto write all ways at liberte. (Prologue, 283–92)	

Douglas is impressively aware of the differences between the two languages he has to bridge and of the injury done to authors by sloppy or deliberately 'improving' translation.[39]

Chaucer is the second main target: though Douglas repeatedly professes his veneration for this 'principal poet but peir' (339), he accuses him of offending Virgil (410) by his characterisation of Aeneas as a traitor, false to Dido, whereas Virgil shows him as obedient to the Gods' command. Douglas' apology for Chaucer has often been quoted, but it seems all but impossible to catch its exact tone with perfect accuracy. Douglas spends more than thirty lines refuting the English poet's aspersions upon the Roman hero in *The Legend of Good Women*, before making his celebrated excuse:

> Bot sikkyrly of resson me behu*fis*　　　　　　　　　*I am obliged to*
> Excuß Chauser fra all maner repruf*fis*
> In lovyng of thir ladeis lylly quhite
> He set on Virgill and Eneas *th*is wyte,　　　　　　　　*reproach*
> For he was evir (God wait) all woma*n*is frend. (445–9)

Whatever one may think of this interpretation, it is a remarkable early instance of historical criticism and genuine literary debate. Douglas clearly reflects on his art and on the particular problems of a great work of poetry and its transfer from one culture to another. None of his contemporaries engages so deeply and knowledgeably with these complex issues.

The prologues to the following books are remarkable for a number of reasons. They deal with a variety of conventional themes, such as the transitory nature of all worldly magnificence, as illustrated by the fall of Troy (three rhyme-royal stanzas before Book ii), the dismal effects of love (38 stanzas, occasionally of eight lines, before Book iv), Virgil's colourful style, adapted to the appropriate mood of each episode (before Book v), his 'Christian' paganism (before Book vi) and, perhaps least conventional, the seasonal changes, evoked in vivid descriptions of nature, have often been picked out for particular praise.[40] Prologue vii is an impressive, sensuous as well as learned portrait of winter, with its effects on the landscape and on living creatures, from the sheep to husbandmen, while Prologue xii pays tribute to the life-giving power of the sun in striking images of creative nature. Again, the poet's close observation of natural phenomena is as impressive as his familiarity with poetic convention.[41] The prologue to the un-Virgilian thirteenth Book is a rather original specimen of the dream-vision convention, where the poet, after a splendid June-day opening, meets the author Maphaeus, who contemptuously asks him to translate his book as well, threatening him with vengance if he should refuse:

> And gif *th*ou haß afortyme gayn onry*ch*t,　　　　　　　*erroneously*
> Followand sa lang Virgill, a gentile clerk,
> Quhy schrynk*is* *th*ou with my schort Christyn wark?
> For *thoch*t it be bot poetry we say,
> My buke and Virgillis morall beyn, ba*th* tway:
> Len me a fourteyn ny*ch*t, how evir it be,　　　　　　　*Grant*

Or, be, *the* fader*is* sawle me gat,' q*uod* he,   *who begot me*
'*Th*ou shalt deir by *th*at evir *th*ou Virgill knew.'   *be sorry*
(Prologue xiii, 138–45)

The humour of this encounter is as remarkable as the skilful justification of this addition to Douglas's ambitious translation and the dexterous adaptation of a convention the closest parallel of which we have met in Henryson's introduction to the fable of the Lion and the Mouse. Unexpected humour is also indulged in the prologue to Book viii, another dream vision, in an elaborate alliterative stanza, quite out of tune with the rest of the translation. This time, the vision, an eloquent invective against the corruption of the times, turns out to be a deceptive fantasy that makes the poet conclude that dreams are only for rascals that cannot sleep well (Prologue viii, 171). In frustration, the narrator returns to Virgil's text, to translate the eighth book, where a much more auspicious and reliable dream is related. It is a bold piece of burlesque comment on dream visions and on Douglas's work of translation which is thus framed by his interventions, drawing attention to his own labour and its moral purpose against the rough attacks of his disgruntled opposite.

On the whole, the prologues have probably been read and discussed much more than the translation itself, for all its unpedantic freshness and vigour. The unfamiliar idiom, of course, acts as a barrier for most readers, but it is worth observing the close and yet creative attention this first translator pays to the sense and the tone of the original. Here is a brief instance from the fourth book, the famous Dido episode, when the queen has a definite suspicion of Aeneas' intended departure:

Bot sone *the* queyn *p*ersavyt al *the* slycht –   *perceived, trick*
Quhay may begile a luffer, day or nyght?   *Who, lover*
Thar departing at hand fyrst sc*h*o aspyis,
Dredyng all sovir thing as is *the* gy*ß*   *secure, custom*
Of eu*e*ry luffar altyme to staand in feir.   *fear*
This ilke cursyt Fame we spak of eyr   *before*
Bair to *the* amorus queyn noy*ß* and gan rown,   *whisper*
'The schippis ar grathand, to pa*ß th*ai mak *th*aim boun.'   *prepared, ready*
Quarfor, impacient and *and* myndles in hir rage,   *out of her mind*
Scho wysk*is* wild throu *the* toun of Cartage,   *rushes wildly*
Syk wy*ß* as quhen *th*ir nu*n*nys of Bachus   *In such a way, women following*
Ruschis and relis our bank*is*, brays and bu*ß*,   *dance over, hillsides*
Quen eu*e*ry thryd ʒeir on *th*ar payane gy*ß*,   *third, after their pagan custom*
*Th*ar goddis feist *th*ai hallow with lowd cryis,   *feast, celebrate, shouting*
That, al *the* nycht, *the* mont of Cytheron
Resound*is* of *th*ar clamo*u*r, whar *th*ai gone.
And at *the* last, ʒit t*h*us, of hir fre will,
Eftir lang musyng, scho spak Eneas tyll:
'With dissymulance wenyt *th*ou, onfaithfull wight,   *you thought*
*Th*ou mycht haue hyd fra me sa fals a slycht,   *hid from, trick*
And, myne onwyttyng, steill furth of my land?   *without my knowledge, steal*
That nothir our gret lufe, promys, no rycht hand   *neither*

Gevyn me vmquhile, may *the* heir withhald,   *formerly, here*
Nor cruel deth of Didois corß so cald! (iv, C. vi, 31–54)[42]   *corpse*

It is not the work of a philologist, but the achievement of a poet, striving to render the words and the meaning of the revered classical poet for an audience unfamiliar with the world of Rome and in need of some assistance, but not at too falsifying a cost to the original.

The only major work confidently ascribed to Douglas is *The Palace of Honour*, finished 1501 and demonstrating his learned familiarity with a great number of texts in the allegorical dream-vision tradition. It is easy to point to vague models, from the *Roman de la Rose*, Chaucer's *House of Fame*, his *Legend of Good Women* and Dunbar's *Golden Targe*, but there is no definite source, and Douglas does not follow any of his predecessors without significant changes and contributions of his own. The poem is an ambitious combination of aureate rhetorical showpiece and moral discourse.[43] The theme is the quality of honour, introduced first in a pageant with processions led by the classical deities, Minerva, Diana and Venus. Similar to the prologue of *The Legend of Good Women*, the poet is accused of blasphemy against the Goddess of Love and tried, but the Muses come to his aid, and there is an interesting discussion about the merits of ancient poets: it is clearly Ovid who is most admired and imitated by Douglas. The third and most elaborate part is devoted to the actual palace of honour, a complicated architectural structure in the tradition of many such allegorical buildings of the poet. In the end, the dreamer is told that 'eirdlie gloir is noch bot vanitie' that will soon come to an end, but 'verteous honour never mair sall end' (1978–80). The poem, written in elaborately rhymed nine-line stanzas, gives the impression of having been written by a young man, eager to show his competence as a master of style, conversant with fashionable poetic conventions and themes. We have no early manuscripts, but the earliest surviving texts, prints of *c.* 1553 (London) and 1579 (Edinburgh), show that there was an audience for this kind of poetry and Douglas's in particular, in spite of the unfamiliarity of the idiom.

Notes

1. See the excellent anthology *Longer Scottish Poems*, Volume I: 1375–1650, ed. Priscilla Bawcutt and Felicity Riddy (Edinburgh, 1987).

2. See Denton Fox, 'The Scottish Chaucerians' in *Chaucer and Chaucerians. Critical Studies in Middle English Literature*, ed. D. S. Brewer (London, 1966), 164–200, and the challenging essay 'Scottish Chaucer, Misogynist Chaucer', by Carolyn Ives and David Parkinson in *Rewriting Chaucer. Culture, Authority and the Idea of the Authentic Text, 1400–1602*, eds Thomas A. Prendergast and Barbara Kline (Columbus, Ohio, 1999), pp. 186–202.

3. See the introduction to *The Middle Scots Poets*, ed. A. M. Kinghorn, York Medieval Texts (London, 1970), pp. 1–50, a useful anthology.

4. There is an excellent facsimile (*The Works of Geoffrey Chaucer and* The Kingis Quair. *A Facsimile of Bodleian Library, Oxford, MS Arch. Selden. B.24*), published by D. S. Brewer, Cambridge, 1997, with an introduction by Julia Boffey and A. S. G. Edwards

and a detailed technical analysis by B. C. Barker-Benfield. The manuscript also contains *Troilus and Criseyde, The Legend of Good Women* and a number of shorter poems by Chaucer. Cf. also Julia Boffey and A. S. G. Edwards, 'Bodleian MS Arch. Selden. B. 24 and the "Scotticization" of Middle English Verse', in *Rewriting Chaucer*, pp. 176–85. For the best scholarly edition of *The Kingis Quair* see James I of Scotland, *The Kingis Quair*, ed. John Norton Smith, Clarendon Medieval and Tudor Series (Oxford, 1971), with good introduction and commentary. Quotations are from this edition.

5. Norton-Smith in his edition speaks of 'the individual, amateurish quality of the author's personality as author – his unsophisticated delight in a direct, easily communicated sense of the enjoyment of experience' (pp. xiv–xv).

6. See Chaucer's *Troilus and Criseyde*, i, 547.

7. *Longer Scottish Poems*, I, 25.

8. See *Longer Scottish Poems*, pp. 43–84, for a full annotated text. The poem is extant in two complete texts (Asloan manuscript, compiled about 1515–30 and the Bannatyne manuscript, written 1568). Quotations are from this edition.

9. See the edition by Denton Fox, *The Poems of Robert Henryson* (Oxford, 1981); pp. xiii–xxv assemble the known and the conjectured facts about his life. See also *The Makars: the Poems of Henryson, Dunbar and Douglas*, ed. J. A. Tasioulas, Cannongate Classics, 88 (Edinburgh, 1999), with introduction, extensive commentary and generous glosses at the foot of each page. The anthology includes the complete poems of Henryson and Dunbar, as well as the full text of Douglas's *Palis of Honoure*, but not the *Enead*.

10. See Fox on the fragmentary and late surviving witnesses in his edition, pp. xxviii–xlii. 'The surviving witnesses, then, are like the few people left alive in a city after a great cataclysm' (p. xxx).

11. See Douglas Gray, *Robert Henryson*, Medieval and Renaissance Authors (Leiden, 1979), p. 161. This is probably the most helpful general study of Henryson's work.

12. Derek Pearsall, ed., *Chaucer to Spenser. An Anthology* (Oxford, 1999), p. 485. This comprehensive and well annotated collection contains four of the *Fables* as well as the whole of the *Testament of Cresseid*.

13. See Dieter Mehl, 'Henryson's Moral Fables as Experiments in Didactic Narrative', *Medieval and Pseudo-Medieval Literature*, The J. A. W. Bennet Memorial Lectures, Perugia, 1982–3, ed. Piero Boitani and Anna Torti (Tübingen, 1984), pp. 131–47. There is a useful edition of the fables with facing prose translation, introduction and notes by George D. Gopen, *The Moral Fables of Aesop: an Edition of the Middle Scots Text, with a Facing Prose Translation, Introduction and Notes* (Notre Dame, IN, 1987).

14. The authority for this order is the Bassandyne print of 1571. See Fox's edition, pp. l–lii, and Gopen's introduction to his edition, pp. 17–24.

15. The fable, however, occupies a special position within the whole cycle, standing exactly in the middle, preceded by six fables and 200 stanzas and followed by the same number of fables and stanzas. See Gopen's introduction, pp. 18–19.

16. See John Burrow, 'Henryson: *The Preaching of the Swallow*', in his *Essays on Medieval Literature* (Oxford, 1984), pp. 148–60; first published in *Essays in Criticism*, 25 (1975), 25–37. Burrow convincingly argues that the whole poem centres on the cardinal virtue of prudence.

17. Chaucer also had made fun of this habit in the more sinister context of the 'Summoner's Tale' when he has the Friar profess: 'Glosynge is a glorious thyng, certayn, / For lettre sleeth, so as we clerkes seyn –' (III, 1793–4).

18. *The Workes of Geffray Chaucer newly printed, with dyuers workes whiche were neuer in print before*. See also Fox's edition, pp. xciv–v and cii–iv.

19. Fox, p. ciii. In his *Animadversions* on Speght's edition (1599) Francis Thynne immediately pointed out that *The Testament* was not by Chaucer, but his warning was not

printed until the nineteenth century, and for most of Shakespeare's contemporaries, Henryson's poem was evidently Chaucer's own sequel to his *Troilus and Criseyde*. Whatever Shakespeare thought about the authorship of *The Testament*, it can hardly be doubted that he knew the poem and was aware of the tradition it gave rise to, namely, Cressida's pitiful fate as beggar and leper, justly punished for her sin of faithlessness. His particular concern with the classical myth's afterlife and Time's verdicts would make him particularly alert to Henryson's pertinent question: 'Quha wait gif all that Chauceir wrait was trew?' (64).

20. See the persuasive defence of Cresseid in Götz Schmitz, 'Cresseid's Trial: A Revision. Fame and Defamation in Henryson's "Testament of Cresseid" ', *Essays and Studies*, 1979, 44–56. Schmitz links the poem with the medieval complaint tradition.

21. See Florence H. Ridley, 'A Plea for the Middle Scots'. *The Learned and the Lewed: Studies in Chaucer and Medieval Literature*, ed. Larry D. Benson, Harvard English Studies, 5 (Cambridge, MA, 1974), 175–96, here 194.

22. Cf. Ralph Hanna III, 'Cresseid's Dream and Henryson's *Testament*', *Chaucer and Middle English Studies. In Honour of Rossell Hope Robbins*, ed. Beryl Rowland (London, 1974), 288–97. He suggests that the vision is a kind of *insomnium*, a vision reflecting her own view of herself 'as an absolutely passive figure, prone and senseless, in the power of baneful forces over which she has no control' (p. 294). Schmitz has convincingly objected that the bias in the description of the trial 'is the author's rather than his heroine's'. ('Henryson's "Testament of Cresseid" ', p. 53, n. 3: 'The trial scene, far from incriminating Cresseid, is a subtly handled means of rehabilitation') ibid., pp. 53–4.

23. See the note on l. 478 in Fox's edition.

24. A very similar conclusion is put very well by Schmitz: 'She comes to accept her fate not as the arbitrary punishment for a venial sin but as a personal act of atonement for betraying her true vocation. In the end she wins the sympathy of Troilus, her true love, and she disgraces the cruelty of her detractors.' 'Henryson's "Testament of Cresseid" ', p. 55.

25. Quotations are from the edition of Priscilla Bawcutt, *The Poems of William Dunbar*, two volumes, published by the Association for Scottish Literary Studies, 27–8 (Glasgow, 1998), by number of poem and line.

26. There are several editions of Dunbar's poems; the most recent and best is that by Bawcutt. See also *The Poems of William Dunbar*, ed. W. Mackay Mackenzie (London, 1932; revised by Bruce Dickins, 1960); *The Poems of William Dunbar*, ed. James Kinsley (Oxford, 1979); there is also a good selection by James Kinsley in the 'Clarendon Medieval and Tudor Series' (Oxford, 1958).

27. See Bawcutt, *The Poems of William Dunbar*, I, 20–1.

28. Almost all titles are non-authorial and were supplied by later editors. See Bawcutt, I, 17–20.

29. See Derek Pearsall and Elizabeth Salter, *Landscapes and Seasons of the Medieval World* (London, 1973), p. 194; the authors justly speak of Dunbar's 'bejewelled landscapes' as 'the most extravagant literary manifestation of decorated Gothic.

30. See Bawcutt's Commentary in her edition, II, 413–21.

31. See the collection of relevant texts, *Woman Defamed and Woman Defended. An Anthology of Medieval Texts*, ed. Alcuin Blamires (Oxford, 1992).

32. See Bawcutt's commentary, *The Poems of William Dunbar*, II, 284–95.

33. Pearsall, who includes more than half of the poem in his anthology, comments, with a sense of humour appropriate to the text: [The narrator] 'deserves all he gets: perhaps they saw him coming'. *Chaucer to Spenser*, p. 509.

34. See the chapter 'Gavin Douglas's Life' in the excellent study by Priscilla Bawcutt, *Gavin Douglas. A Critical Study* (Edinburgh, 1976), pp. 1–22.

35. A number of modern anthologies contain excerpts from Douglas's translation: *Longer Scottish Poems*, vol. I., 233–47, Pearsall, *Chaucer to Spenser*, pp. 519–28 and *Selections from Gavin Douglas*, ed. David F. C. Coldwell, Clarendon Medieval and Tudor Series (Oxford, 1964), with useful introduction and commentary. For a complete edition see *The Poetical Works of Gavin Douglas*, ed. John Small, 4 vols (Edinburgh, 1874) and *Vergil's Aeneid Translated into Scottish Verse by Gavin Douglas*, ed. David F. C. Coldwell, Scottish Text Society, 4 vols (1957–64). Quotations are from this edition.

36. *Chaucer to Spenser*, p. 516.

37. Coldwell rightly concludes his discussion of the translation: 'Terms like "Middle Ages" and "Renaissance" are not of much use in describing a poet': *Virgil's* Aeneid, i, 116.

38. Bawcutt, *Gavin Douglas*, pp. 92–102; and *Selections from Gavin Douglas*, pp. xi–xiii.

39. Douglas is particularly interesting when he draws attention to the untranslatability of many Latin words. He challenges anyone who doubts his words to produce exact equivalents for *animal* and *homo* and to define the differences between *genus*, *sexus* and *species* (Prologue, 359–72).

40. See the fine chapter on the prologues in Bawcutt, *Gavin Douglas*, pp. 164–91.

41. See Pearsall and Salter, *Landscapes and Seasons of the Medieval World*, pp. 139–60, 200–5.

42. Translating the Latin:

> Ac regina dolos – quis fallere possit amantem? –
> praesensit motusque excepit prima futuros,
> omnia tuta timens. eadem inpia Fama furenti
> detulit armari classem cursumque parari.
> saevit inops animi totamque incensa per urbem
> bacchatur, qualis commotis excita sacris
> Thyias, ubi audito stimulant trieterica Baccho
> orgia nocturnusque vocat clamore Cithaeron.
> Tandem his Aenean compellat vocibus ultro:
> 'dissimulare etiam sperasti, perfide, tantum
> posse nefas tacitusque mea decedere terra,
> nec te noster amor nec te data dextera quondam
> nec moritura tenet crudeli funere Dido? (iv, 296–308)

43. See the excellent chapter on the poem in Bawcutt, *Gavin Douglas*, pp. 47–68. For the text of the poem see *The Shorter Poems of Gavin Douglas*, The Scottish Text Society (Edinburgh, 1967); excerpts in *Selections from Gavin Douglas*, ed. Coldwell, pp. 107–15.

Chapter 9

Middle English Prose

Literature in the 'Age of Chaucer' has, so far in this survey, been mainly discussed in terms of its poetry, yet even a superficial look at the extant texts shows that the great majority of writing in his period was actually in prose. To concentrate exclusively on poetical texts posterity has privileged by reprinting, re-editing, anthologising and including in the academic syllabus would give a rather misleading picture of what at the time was actually read, copied and 'used'. Moreover, in the centuries after the Norman conquest, English prose was subject to political forces and to the overruling official status of French and Latin to no lesser extent than English poetry and had to reassert itself in many areas, from political controversy and commerce to philosophical debate, from homiletic instruction to private communication. Naturally, there was an increasing need for translation, and this activity in turn was an essential factor in the development and the shaping of Middle English prose.[1]

One of the more remarkable translators was John Trevisa, who, from 1362 to about 1387 studied and taught at Oxford, first at Exeter College and, from 1369 at Queen's College; later he was installed as Vicar of Berkeley. He died around 1400. His most important translations were of Ranulf Higden's *Polychronicon*, a Latin history of the world down to 1327, and of *De Proprietatibus Rerum*, an encyclopaedia of medieval knowledge by Bartholomaeus Anglicus, written between 1230 and 1250, extant in nineteen, or thirteen, manuscripts and both among the first books printed before 1500. The preface to the translation of the *Polychronicon* is one of the most frequently quoted passages of English prose, because it gives a valuable description of the linguistic situation in England towards the end of the fourteenth century, when French was gradu-ally replaced by English as the dominant language.[2]

More influential and controversial at the same time was the Wycliffite Bible (*c.* 1380–*c.* 1400), a crucial document not only of the emerging importance of English, but also of a religious movement whose repercussions were felt throughout the following century and had a significant share in the English reformation. The translation of the Bible into the vernacular was a project fostered with particular urgency by John Wyclif who felt that this was an essential step towards the reformation of the church and opening the Scripture to laymen. Wyclif's part in the translation was probably small, though he provided the first inspiration. The English Bible became immensely popular, some 250 manuscripts of the text or parts of it are known, but it soon became an object of intense suspicion to the established church and ownership was often considered evidence of heresy, especially after Arundel, Archbishop of

Canterbury since 1396, issued his *Constitutiones* (1409), in which the translation into English 'of any text of holy scripture . . . by means of book, booklet, or treatise' is forbidden on penalty of excommunication. A number of owners of such translations and other Lollard writings were burnt, along with their books.[3]

In more strictly 'literary' terms, too, there is a great deal of Middle English prose writing in a wide variety of genres that deserves attention not only as evidence of rich cultural activity and intense intellectual as well as emotional vitality, but also for aesthetic qualities that still appeal to readers of our own generation.[4]

The present survey has to confine itself to a few particularly characteristic and influential areas of Middle English prose composition while passing by a great amount of literary activity, mainly of religious, homiletic, devotional, educational and practical purpose.[5] Not all of it makes very easy or entertaining reading today, but all of it provides some important insight into essential aspects of medieval culture, forms of religious practice, organisation of spiritual, civic and domestic communities and everyday troubles in various walks of life. From the careful and sophisticated *Ancrene Riwle* (*c.* 1220–30), a prose manual for anchoresses, frequently copied and translated into Latin and French,[6] to the informal *Paston Letters*,[7] prose was, naturally, used for all kinds of written communication, much of it hardly meant for posterity, but none of it negligible for anyone interested in the past.

Mandeville's Travels

The Middle English versions of this immensely popular account of the wonders of the world is an instructive example of the kind of literary commerce that went on between England and the Continent in the centuries following the Norman conquest and the activities of English translators, or adaptors. *Mandeville's Travels*, originally written in French, were translated into most European languages; altogether there are some three hundred manuscripts still extant. For several generations the book was the most comprehensive and accessible source of information about the far regions of the earth, in particular those encountered on a journey to the Holy Land, and what was known or imagined about their geography as well as their inhabitants

What is rather untypical about this particular instance is the unusually large number of witnesses: eighty-one manuscripts of the 'Insular' version are extant, the majority in French or Latin, but also several in English, differing greatly in many details, not least in literary style.[8] There is even a metrical version; it has no particular poetical pretensions, suggesting rather that, at least in this case, verse was considered the more popular or sociably accessible medium than prose. From the outset, the speaker makes clear that he is addressing a listening audience ('this faire gaderinge', l. 6), presenting for their entertainment an abbreviated version of Mandeville's bookish account:

But in þat boke is moch thinge
That nedeth naught in þis talkinge.   *that is unnecessary to relate here*
And þerefor seth hit nedeth nauȝt,   *since it*
As I haue herde men sein offt,   *often say*
Be it in geste othir in songe,
And it be made overlonge,   *If*
Hit maketh men werie and lothe to here
Thouȝ hit be neuer so good matere.
And þerefor this litille tretis
Out of that boke drawe it ys,
That of alle merueilis tellys
That he sawe and some þinge elles. (35–46)   *besides*

The words evidently take it for granted that the 'boke', in this case as prose treatise, would make greater demands on the recipient's mind and his patience than a versified abridgement recited for a particular social group:

Nowe lordis and ladies leve and dere,
Yif ye wolle of wondris here,
A litille stounde yif ye wolle dwelle,
Of grete meruailis I mai you telle. (11–14)

The Latin version on which this may be based merely says:

Nunc in nomine gloriosi dei, si volueris mare transire versus orientem potes per mare et per terram diuersas tenere vias secundum partes diuersas a quibus moueris, vnde multe earum tendunt ad vnum finem.
Et sciend*um* est quod non intendo demonstrare tibi omnes ciuitates, villas, et castella per viam, quia fastidium generaret audientibus, sed solummodo aliquas terras et loca principalia vt possis viam rectam secundum tuum propositum tenere. (I. 6–12)

[*Now, in the name of the glorious God, if you wish to cross the sea towards the East you can take different routes through sea and land, according to the different regions where you set off, from where many of them go to one and the same destination.*
And you must know that I do not intend to show you all societies, villages and castles on the way because this would weary the listeners, but only some particular countries and principal places so that you will be able to find the right way according to your own plan.]

Though the author is speaking of listeners (*audientibus*), who will want no more than a selection of details, he nevertheless sees himself as teacher, offering useful information and facts, rather than an entertainer anxious to divert a specific gathering. Other versions, such as the abridged prose version (Bodleian) extant in two manuscripts, begin, like the Latin text it translates, without further comment with Mandeville's own introduction:

[F]orthy that manye men desyryn to heryn of diuers londis and of the Holy Lond and of the Lond of Beheste and of othere dyuerse reumys beyonde the see in dyuerse partiis of the world, I Iohn Maundevile, knyght, thow I be vnworthi, born and norisched in the reume of Ingeland of the toun of Seynt Albonys passede the see vpon a day of Seynt Michel the Archaungel in the yer of oure lord Iesu Crist m.ccc. and xxii.[9]

The name of the speaker and the precise date of his departure for the 'promised land' ('Lond of Beheste')[10] have given rise to various hypotheses about the identity of John Mandeville, but most scholars now believe that he is an entirely fictitious creation and that the real author was probably neither a native of St Albans nor an Englishman, but a citizen of the Lower countries. It is likely that the original version was written in Liège about 1357, but this hypothesis, too, is based on rather insecure evidence. More confidently, we can assert that none of the travels recounted by the author need actually have taken place at all, since every geographical, anthropological, botanical or mythological detail could have been gleaned from his library and such well-known sources as Odoric of Pordenone's *Itinerarius* (*c.* 1330), Vincent of Beauvais' *Speculum Naturale et Speculum Historiale* (*c.* 1250), William of Tripoli's *Tractatus de Statu Saracenorum* (*c.* 1270) and a number of others.[11] The amount of written source-material the author used for his own account clearly shows that he did not rely on his own observation, yet neither does it conclusively prove that he himself never set foot on some of the countries he describes. It is therefore impossible to measure the extent to which he can be credited with having created one of the first fictional travellers in Western literature. In any case, the compilation was evidently written for and enjoyed by readers untroubled by theoretical distinctions between fact and fiction, relishing the lively combination of useful information, entertaining phantasy and teasing inventiveness. The air of authenticity created by the first-person narrator obviously contributed to the popularity of his account and satisfied the general interest in miraculous regions, strange creatures and unheard-of social phenomena.

In view of the complicated transmission and affiliation of the manuscripts, it is impossible to be very confident in our judgement of the English translators' abilities or their independence of particular sources. It appears that their familiarity with idiomatic French as well as their literary skills were limited; yet they produced careful prose versions of the most widely read secular text of their time, evidently meant for the increasing number of readers with no or insufficient knowledge of French.

The abridged Bodley version starts with the simple declaration of its aim, to act as a guide for those who want to visit the Holy Land; yet even before we reach the second page, practical considerations and sensible advice recede into the background, and most of the remainder is filled with descriptions of strange countries and the mores of their inhabitants. The fuller Cotton version has a prologue praising Christ's mission on earth and the significance of the Holy Land which the writer claims to have visited himself; this is why he wants to act as a guide to pilgrims and to describe the route he has 'often tymes passed and ryden that way with gode companye of many lordes, God be thonked'.[12]

In both versions, the narrator, who claims to have himself observed and experienced everything he relates, be it ever so improbable and phantastic, appears as an amazingly objective and tolerant witness, posing neither as a boastfully inventive teller of tall stories nor as a satiric Gulliver contrasting strange creatures, their manners and their political or religious convictions with his own country. There is hardly any of the undifferentiated hatred of all heathens to be found in many popular romances. Instead, Mandeville's account is informed by a certain respect for cultural differences and intellectual achievement, and there is a clear sense that the failings of Christianity are largely to blame for the Saracens' occupation of the Holy Land. On this point the narrator is particularly anxious to assert the truth of his own observation. The Bodley version has an interpolation that is particularly interesting, following the Saracens' harsh criticism of the Christians' disobeying the commandments of Christ:

> Trowith this wel, for this haue I bothe herd and sen with mynne eyne and mynne eryn and myne felawys that were with me that weryn of dyuers regionys, for wete ye wel that al be it wondyr to youre heryng, I am not set to lye yow lesyngis. Trowith yif ye welyn. (p. 75.28–32) *tell you lies*

This comes before a passage in which the Sultan speaks to Mandeville in private, enquiring about the state of the Christians and, in his reply, becoming the spokesman of the same harsh criticism regularly found in Christian penitential literature and satire:

> . . . he askede me how that Cristene men ferdyn in oure contres, and I seyde, 'Wel, thour the grace of God.'
> Therto he answerde and seyde, 'Certis, nay, not so. For youre clerkis seruyn not youre God in goode werkis as they shulde, for they shuld yeve lewede men exaumple of good leuynge and they yeve hem examplis of alle wikkednesse. For in festyual dayes, whan the peple shulde gon to cherche for to seruyn God, thanne they gon to the tauerne and ocupien al the day, perschauns and al the nyght aftyr, in dronkenesse and glotenye, as they were bestis out of resoun that wot nat whan they han anow; and aftyr that perchaunce fallynge in fytynge thour dronkenesse with wordys perschaunce tyl euery man sle othir.[13]

The attack on Christian misbehaviour and disregard of their own laws is similar to Langland's account of the seven deadly sins in *Piers Plowman*, Passus V, or the invective by Chaucer's Pardoner against drunkenness, though the effect within this kind of narrative is quite different. The criticism comes from a seemingly disinterested observer, not a cleric, and is part of a travel report designed to instruct, not to preach.

The writer concludes his account with a conventional prayer for his readers, but before that he once more asserts the truth of what he has told:

> Wherfore I prei entierly to alle tho that this bok redyn or writyn that thei redyn no more ne writyn than I haue wretyn, for that I haue wretyn is trewe. (Bodley version, p. 147.8–10)

Mandeville's account moves quickly from one item to the next, with frequent transition from narrative to more descriptive passages and a sense of constant curiosity and unruffled emotion. For the most part, the narrator appears to take every adventure in his stride neither particularly shocked nor frightened by what he sees, but registering every marvel and noting down the strangest customs and beliefs, not to mention the most phantastic natural phenomena and misshapen creatures. Thus, his account is an original combination of guide-book and a collection of tall stories. On the one side, the author gives detailed descriptions of the Holy places and the problems of Christian tourism among the Saracens. These are presented as in no way morally inferior to the pilgrims visiting the sacred localities, who are motivated not only by genuine reverence, but also by sensationalism and, in some cases, even dishonest greed. As an example, we are told that the Sultan had to protect the Holy Sepulcre by a wall because 'some pilgryms that comyn thedyr [*thither*] tokyn [*took*] sum porcioun therof by stalthe [*stealth*] and boryn [*carried*] it away with hem for to kepyn it as for a relyke . . .' (Bodley version, p. 53.6–8). A little earlier we are told that, while the Christian majority in Bethlehem indulge in plenty of wine, the Muslims are forbidden to touch drink. This sanction is illustrated by an anecdote from the life of their prophet, with an ambiguous comment; it allows an interpretation not unconditionally biased in favour of the Christian practice and morals. The narrator also relates that, owing to their previously demonstrated hostility, neither Christians nor Jews are allowed within the immediate vicinity of the temple erected near the Holy Sepulcre; but, as he proudly claims,

> I Iohn Maundeuyle come in there, and elliswhere there me lyked, be vertu of the Soudonis letteris that I hadde; in which letteris he commaunded streytly to alle hese subiectis that they shulde lette me see alle the placis where I come and shewe me as wel the relykys as the place at myn wil, and ledde me from cete to othir yif myster [*need*] were.[14]

He has evidently succeeded in winning the Sultan's personal respect (or so he claims), which again confirms the impression that he has not undertaken this journey in a crusading spirit. On the other hand, this may be a piece of improbable fiction and part of his strategy, designed to give additional authenticity to his account of places nobody else has been able to see for himself.

The question whether his own account is based on personal experience rather than on collecting facts from one or more of the existing accounts, is important not only for reasons of historical biography, but even more for assessing the specific quality of the writer's literary imagination and the precise nature of the fictional *I* he has created. He is clearly anxious for his descriptions to be trusted; they support the biblical histories by frequently referring to localities and the scenes of stories in the Old and New Testaments. This part of the book is evidently designed to appeal to the interests of every church-goer, while the sequel offers more mundane instruction and entertainment.

The narrator's personality is a remarkable literary achievement and contributes significantly to the work's success. Even if every detail of his account were gleaned from earlier travel books and collections of *mirabilia*, the author of the original version has the merit of having shaped his materials, selected from a great mass of available reports and compilations, fictional or otherwise, into a compact and swiftly moving survey of the known world and its amazing phenomena. It is the traveller's lively interest in every new and unexpected social custom, religious belief and freakish whim of nature that drives the narrative forward and keeps up the tension, especially after he has passed the holy places and proceeds to ever stranger and unfamiliar regions. Often, when he finds particularly bewildering habits, he tries to find out their origins: One striking example comes from one of the isles in Prester John's country, where deflowering a virgin is considered to be so dangerous that there is a special group of young men who undertake this risky business for all husbands and are sued as for a criminal offence if the bride is still found a virgin during the second night. The explanation given to Mandeville, not found in any source, is an ancient belief that virgins had poisonous snakes in their bodies which were released by defloration. The passage is a good specimen of Mandeville's narrative style and that of his translators:

> They seyn there and affermyn it for soth that it is a ful perlious thing to takyn a virgyne maydynhed, for they seyn ho so doth, he disposith hym to peril of deth. And yif the husbonde of that woman fynde here a maydyn in the nyght aftyr, so he that shulde an had here maydynhed, be it for dronky*ne*sse or for ony othir cause, dede not the ferste nyght his deuer [*duty*] to the woman, thanne here housbonde shal han his accioun to hym byforn the iuge, as meche as he hadde slayn his fadyr. But at the fyrste nyght that the woman be thus defoiled, they arn so streytly kept aftyr that they dar speke to no man.
>
> I, Ion Maundeuyle, askid hem what was the cause and the skil whi that swich customys weryn vsed ther. And thei seidyn me that in olde tyme some men in that cuntre weryn dede for they refte yynge maydenys of here maydynhed, for they haddyn withinnyn hem, as longe they were virgynys, nederis, and therfor they heldyn that custome in that contre.[15]

It is this curiosity about the astonishing diversity of social customs and the beliefs or superstitions at their roots that seems to me one of the book's most characteristic features and to account for its immense popularity. It informs the indefatigable quest for new wonders and fabulous countries and it satisfies both the natural delight in 'news' of all kind and the belief in the limitless richness of God's creation.

In the end, the reader is assured that the traveller has by no means exhausted this cosmos of possibilities, as he candidly admits: 'There ben manye other dyuerse contrees and manye other merueyles beyonde that I haue not seen, wherfore of hem I can not speke propurly to telle you the manere of hem.'[16] Accordingly, other travellers may still write about their adventures without being accused of boring repetition, 'for men seyn alleweys that newe thinges and newe tydynges ben plesant to here' (p. 228.20–2).

The conclusion of Mandeville's account once more asserts the fiction of a true autobiographical record: After thirty-three years, the knight has returned home, much against his will, because of gout and arthritis, to entertain himself with writing his memoir.[17] It is, if anything, a well-tried literary device, used in picaresque novels as well as in other kinds of autobiographical or confessional writing and it provides a fitting ending to the record of a life spent exploring a world known to the vast majority of its readers (and perhaps even to the author himself) only from hearsay and other written accounts. The different English versions, in prose and verse, point to an unusual diversity of readership and the existence of translators willing to meet the demands of different clients. Their prose is not particularly sophisticated, though hardly less so than that of their sources, but it gives a fair impression of the book's narrative drive and the convincing fiction of genuine observation and enquiring curiosity.

Prose writing of the English mystics

In no other area has Middle English prose developed its own characteristic, original and poetically evocative style as much as in the writings of English mystics: 'On the most demanding of subjects they write in their own tongue at a new level of intensity and complexity in English prose.'[18] The writers usually grouped together as 'mystics' do not form a 'school' and are very different from each other; one may question whether the traditional label gives a just description of their particular significance within the emergence of a devotional lay culture and a vernacular literature of reflexion and pastoral guidance. 'Vernacular theologians' is perhaps a more accurate description.[19] These writers are all basically concerned with the individual soul and its contemplation of the mysteries of God's love, rather than with questions of doctrine, theological controversy or even homiletic practice. They want to make the reader partake in their very personal experience and some of them evidently saw themselves as teachers, yet their emphasis generally is on the inward vision and the condition of the mind required to achieve perfect union with God. The authors often choose an intimate mode of address, as if they were writing to a particular person or group, and in many cases this may well have been the original intention. It is this intensely personal quality that still appeals to the present-day reader more than many other medieval texts.

The earliest of the mystics, Richard Rolle of Hampole (*c.* 1300–49), probably achieved the widest readership. He seems to have left the University of Oxford without a degree and spent most of his later life as a hermit in various places until he retired to Hampole in Yorkshire near a Cistercian convent, where he died.[20] The canon of his works is large; nearly 500 manuscripts contain texts ascribed to him. His writings, the majority of them in Latin, were frequently copied and influenced many other theological thinkers and visionaries. He apparently had his disciples and he entered into controversial debate more readily than later authors, like Julian of Norwich or Margery Kempe, but, like them, he was concerned with lay piety and the inner life of Christians rather than with institutional structures or the church's official teaching. In his writings, he is clearly more interested in the soul's personal relation with God than with ecclesiastical institutions or questions of formal doctrine, though his orthodoxy is never in doubt. Renunciation of the world and contempt of knowledge for its own sake, but most of all the way to individual perfection through participation in God's love, are some of his central themes. After his death, however, his writings were appropriated by laymen, even by Lollards, and he was apparently much read and esteemed as a pastoral guide, but his English works were not among those printed by Caxton or Winkyn de Worde, nor did he achieve the rather more recent popularity of Julian of Norwich or Margery Kempe, far less prominent figures in their own time.

The Cloud of Unknowing *(c. 1390–5)*

The author of this in many ways intriguing work is not known, but he is usually regarded as identical with the person who also wrote *The Book of Privy Councelling*.[21] Like Richard Rolle, and William Langland, for that matter, he writes for educated laymen, not for clerics,[22] and he employs the vernacular, although, even more than these two, he is concerned with its power to convey spiritual truths and guidance. Seventeen manuscripts, from the early fifteenth to the early sixteenth century testify to the book's wide dissemination.[23] It is divided into a Prologue and seventy-five chapters, whose contents are briefly outlined at the beginning. What is particularly impressive about this treatise is the systematic method and the intellectual rigour of definition, even though the author is arguing against formal knowledge and merely rational understanding of God's love. The explanation of his title is a good example; it also shows his critical awareness of the limits of language and of metaphors:

> & wene not, for I clepe [*call*] it a derknes or a cloude, þat it be any cloude congelid of þe hum*o*urs þat fleen [*fly*] in þe ayre, ne ʒit any derknes soche as is in þin house on niʒtes, when þi ca*n*del is oute. For soche a derknes & soche a cloude maist þou ymagin wiþ coriouste of witte [*subtlety of mind*], for to bere before þin iʒen in þe liʒtest day of somer; & also aʒenswarde [*conversely*] in þe derkist of niʒt of wynter þou mayst ymagin a clere schinyng liʒt. Lat be soche falsheed; I mene not þus. For when I sey derknes, I mene a lackyng of knowyng; as alle þat þing þat þou knowest not, or elles þat þou hast forʒetyn, it is derk to þee, for þou seest it not wiþ þi goostly iʒe. & for þis skile it is not clepid a cloude of þe eire [*air*], bot a cloude of vnknowyng, þat is bitwix þee & þi God.[24]

It is a brilliant specimen of expository prose, setting out in simple words the different modes of speaking in similes or images. From the outset, the reader is warned that no effort of the intellect can ever hope to comprehend God, but only total belief in his love. All reasonable creatures, i.e. angels and men, are each in possession of two faculties, the faculty of knowing and the faculty of loving. To the first, God is forever incomprehensible, while by the second, we may obtain spiritual understanding and unending bliss. Step by step the reader is instructed how to rid his or her mind of all false notions, especially intellectual preconceptions that stand in the way of 'þe gracious werk of þis bok' (p. 6) There is no doubt, however, about the exclusive circle eligible for this 'werk'. As the author clearly states in the brief twenty-seventh chapter, it is those who have left the world and have dedicated themselves to a life of contemplation,[25] a distinction quoted, though with different emphasis, in Langland's *Piers Plowman*.

For the *Cloud*-author, the active life, traditionally associated with Martha in the episode from the gospel of St Luke (x, 38–42), is clearly inferior in terms of perfect union with God's love and, though the author explicitly, if grudgingly acknowledges its value for its own sake, he is not really interested in it.[26]

But the reader is also warned against false ideas of contemplation and any pretence of contemplative life. Repeatedly the author returns to the subject of the inadequacy of language to convey spiritual concepts without giving rise to error. An interesting example is his emphatic warning against a literal understanding of 'in' and 'up', or 'nowhere' and 'everywhere', which leads to dangerous error and deceit (chap. 51–3 and 68). The insistence on the spiritual ('goostly') dimension of language, as distinct from its literal meaning, is one of the author's most important contributions to the creation of a vernacular theology. Though he seems much less concerned than Langland with the 'active' life of the Christian, with the needs of a society striving for salvation or the role of the community threatened by corrupt practice and misled by false prophets, he is clearly struggling with some of the same fundamental linguistic problems and just as anxious to reach a lay audience. More directly and informally than the author of *Piers Plowman*, he speaks in a highly individual and intimate voice to a reader in need of direction.

At the outset of *The Cloud of Unknowing*, that reader is asked to take care that no other person should make light of the text by casual or partial perusal, since this might lead him (or her) into error. It seems, though, that the book met some criticism for its alleged obscurity and that the author wrote *The Book of Privy Counselling* to answer such objections. The sequel is much shorter (less than a third) and more closely argued, but, as in *The Cloud of Unknowing*, the author insists on the simplicity of the message and laments the damage done to unspoiled, 'lewed' minds by sophisticated intellectualism of the clergy. The general effect, as the author, with fine homely realism, sees it, is that

þe trewe conceite of þis liȝt werk, þorow þe whiche þe boistousest [*crudest*] mans soule or wommans in þis liif is verely in louely meekenes onyd to [*united with*] God in parfite charite, may no more, ne ȝit so moche, be conceyuid of hem in soþfastnes of spirit, for her blyndnes & here corioustee [*sophistication*], þen may þe kunnyng of þe grettest clerk in scole of a ȝong childe at his A.B.C. (p. 137)

There is a curious contrast between the author's impressive intellectual clarity and his repeated conviction that his message can be grasped by the 'lewed'. No doctrinal subtlety or clerical instruction is needed to enter into union with the love of God. This anti-intellectualism, not unrelated to Langland's distrust of priestly sophistication and dogmatism, lends a colloquial freshness to the author's prose and evidently was in tune with the spiritual climate among a considerable section of the laity, at any rate before a rougher wind of ecclesiastical orthodoxy set in, with the determined persecution of the Lollards and the suppression of many critical or even mildly subversive voices.

Walter Hilton (c. 1340–96), The Scale of Perfection

It has been surmised that the author of *The Cloud of Unknowing* was Walter Hilton, of whose life and writings we know a little more, but there is no real evidence for this, and Hilton's best-known English work, *The Scale of Perfection*, is in important ways different.[27] Like the *Cloud*, Hilton's treatise is addressed to a particular person, in this case an anchoress, but it soon seems to have acquired a much wider readership: *The Scale of Perfection* is extant in forty-one (Book I), and twenty-five (Book II) copies, and it was the first book by one of the Middle English mystics to be printed; Winkyn de Worde's edition of 1494 was produced at the special request of Lady Margaret Beaufort, the mother of King Henry VII, and advertised as a 'hevenly boke more precyous than golde'.[28] Hilton, like the *Cloud*-author, wanted to provide a guide to the perfect life of contemplation for one who has already made her choice: at the end of the concluding chapter (chap. 93) he repeats that his advice does not apply to those who live the active life, but only those who have opted for the contemplative life. His tone is generally more down-to-earth and more toler-ant of alternatives. At least, he states at the outset that according to St Gregory there were two ways of life in Holy Church through which Christians could reach salvation and, though he is only concerned with the contemplative life, he recognises the virtues of the active life (chap. 2), to which he himself belongs. His advice is pastoral and covers not only the stages of contempla-tion (ladder of perfection), but also aids to prayer, remedies against tempta-tion of the devil and, above all, signposts on the way to Jesus and avoidance of sin. There is more of traditional doctrine and practical precept, especially in the first book, than in the *Cloud of Unknowing* and less reflection on the inner life and the power of language to describe it.

The second book introduces itself as as an answer to the request for more instruction, especially as to the image of God in our soul and it proceeds to explain ways of approaching the image and to clear the soul of sinful images. The addressee is assumed to be more conversant with the language of ecclesi-astical teaching, in particular, with the Latin of the Psalms and the New Testament, while the anchoress, for whom Book I was initially written, evidently cannot read the Scripture for herself (chap. 15). The second book, moreover, is concerned with the linguistic means of explaining certain spiritual truths and metaphorical discourse, such as the careful exegesis of 'Jerusalem' as an image for 'sight of pes', signifying 'contemplation in perfit luf of God' or the definition of the terms 'above' and 'within'.[29] This is very similar to some of the *Cloud*-author's explanations, but Hilton's language is less inward and meditative, but rather more practical and homely, even when he is translating common expressions into spiritual ('gostly') meaning:

> For a soule is above al bodily thinge not bi settynge of stede [*its place*], bot bi sotelte [*refinement*] and worthines of kynde [*nature*]. Right so on the selfe wise, God is above al bodily and gostly creatures not bi settynge of stede bot thurgh sotelte and worthines of his unchaungeable blissid kynde. And therfore he that wil wisely seke God and fynden him, he schal not renne out with his thoght as he wolde clymbe aboven the sunne and persen [*pierce*] the firmament, and ymagynen the majeste as it were a light of an hundred sunnes. But, he schal rather drawe downe the sunne and al the firmament, and forgeten it and kesten it bineth him ther he is, and setten al this and al bodily thinge also at noght, and thenke than if he kan gostly [*in spiritual terms*], both of himself and God also. And if he do thus, than seeth the soule above itself and than seeth it heven. (chap. 33, p. 161)

The essence of the mystical experience could hardly be formulated with more sensible clarity and homiletic skill. The goal of true contemplation, as Hilton describes it, is the soul's vision of God in his Trinity and the Blessed Angels. The *Cloud*-author's approach is somewhat different: The 'werk' for which he wants to offer guidance eventually embraces complete mystical union with God. But, though the emphasis may not be quite the same, both writers are united in their insistence on the individual's faculty to obtain salvation and to share in God's love without formal learning or ecclesiastical doctrine. This connects them with the spirit of female piety that found expression in some of the most remarkable and unconventional Middle English Texts, written or dictated by women who certainly did not have the same formal training, let alone contact with any university. Some, like Margaret Kempe, even described themselves as illiterate.[30]

Julian of Norwich (1342–c. 1418) and her Revelations of Divine Love

Julian of Norwich, the most widely read and articulate of the English female mystics, left two accounts of the 'revelations' which appeared to her in May 1373 during a near-fatal illness, as a result of which she spent the rest of her life in meditation on what she saw. We do not know at which point she decided to become an anchoress, but she lived for years as a recluse at an anchorhold attached to St Julian's Church in Norwich.[31] She apparently became quite famous and many visitors, including Margery Kempe, came to her for advice and spiritual guidance.

Julian's *Revelations* have come down in four extant manuscripts. The earlier short version is included in a fifteenth-century anthology of devotional items; the longer version is found in two seventeenth-century manuscripts and an eighteenth-century copy. The longer version, composed by Julian some twenty years after her first visions, expands the account of them by exegesis and meditations on what was revealed to her. Some readers have felt that the author must have acquired some scriptural training during that time, or at least become literate, since, as she claims near the beginning, 'These Revelations were shewed to a simple creature that cowde no letter the yeere of our Lord 1373'.[32] Yet even the early version is nothing like unsophisticated in the way it puts the nature of the 'showings' into words:

> Alle this blyssede techynge of oure Lorde God was schewyd to me in thre partyes, that is be [*by*] bodylye syght, and be worde formede in myne undyrstandynge, and be gastelye [*spiritual*] syght. Botte the gastelye syght I maye nought ne can nought schewe it unto yowe als oponlye and als fullye as I wolde. (chap. 7, p. 189)[33]

Like the author of the *Cloud of Unknowing*, Julian emphatically distinguishes between the kind of experience that can be translated into words and a spiritual ('gastelye') sight which resists cut-and-dried verbalisation. By the first kind of revelation, 'bodylye syght', she evidently means the vivid pictures presented to her mind, even though this was not at first what she desired of God, as she states at the outset:

But in this I desyrede nevere ne bodely syght, ne no manere schewynge of God, botte compassyon, as me thought that a kynde sawlle myght have with oure Lorde Jhesu, that for love wolde become man dedlye [*mortal*]. With hym Y desyrede to suffere, lyeveande in dedlye bodye, as God wolde gyffe me grace.

And in this sodaynlye I sawe the rede blode trekylle downe fro undyr the garlande alle hate [*hot*], freschlye, plentefully, and lyvelye, ryght as me thought that it was in that tyme that the garlonde of thornys was thyrstede [*thrust*] on his blessede heede. (chap. 3, p. 185)

Throughout her account Julian describes such 'bodely syght', chiefly of Christ's Passion, in graphic detail, followed by words coming from Christ, but formed in her soul 'withowten voyce and withowte openynge of lyppes' (chaps 8, p. 191, and 22, p. 209, of the shorter version).[34] Through images and words she reaches an understanding of the full measure of God's love, which she wants to pass on to her readers. The early, shorter version is more spontaneous, intimate and personal in expression; the later redaction not only adds long passages of contemplation and additional comment, but it also introduces many smaller changes, with a consistent tendency to generalisation, and at the same time suppressing a number of individual details, such as the brief passage in which she says that her mother, believing her dead, closed her eyes (chap. 10, p. 194), or her spirited apology for writing as 'woman, leued [*uneducated*], febille, and freylle', a woman who is fulfilling God's will by telling his goodness to readers who will soon forget her once they behold Jesus as the teacher of us all (chap. 6, p. 189). As a woman, Julian is convinced that she cannot possibly claim to be a teacher – 'God forbede that ye schulde saye or take it so that I am a techere, for I meene nought soo, no I mente nevere so'[35] – she feels driven only by a desire to tell of her own experience. The autobiographical, even confessional stance is the main reason for the book's sincere immediacy and lack of any superior condescension. Her revision shows a remarkable growth of confidence and, indeed, ambition, since the long version has turned into a vernacular exposition of the fundamental Christian doctrine, written by a lay woman for lay people like her.

Julian's 'showings' retrace an increasingly close personal relationship between her and her Saviour, whose pastoral affection and comforting guidance establish a tone of loving intimacy characteristic of mystic writing in England and on the continent, but particularly appealing in her own experience of divine love, revealed with unassuming humility and selfless concern for the souls of her fellow-Christians, in a prose of powerful affective intensity as well as conceptual precision. Julian leaves us in no doubt that she is in perfect agreement with what is preached and taught by Holy Church (chap. 16, p. 201), and her language is steeped in scriptural phrases,[36] but her own belief, endorsed by her showings and by the voice of Christ, is almost exclusively fixed on God's love and wrapped in a general movement towards salvation and the certain ultimate defeat of sin. This optimistic attitude, almost diametrically opposed to the aggressive anger of the church's critics such as Langland or the Lollards, culminates in the famous message, several times repeated in the text and reverently quoted by twentieth-century poets: 'Jesus, that in this vision enformid me of all that me nedyth, answerid by this word, and seyd: *Synne is behovabil* [necessary], *but al shal be wel, and al shal be wel, and al manner of thyng shal be wele'* (long version, chap. xxvii, ll. 937–9).[37]

Love is the 'leitmotif' of Julian's discourse about her intimate experience of God and the ultimate ground of all his work. For all its visionary intensity, her language never loses its rational concreteness and an unassuming, homely tone of humane didacticism even when she is dealing with intricate questions of doctrine, especially in the longer version, where she relates that it was only after twenty years that she grasped the mystery of God as Father and as Son. Her method closely follows her own experience, described by her for the benefit of all readers: 'Also in this mervelous example I have techyng with me as it were the begynnyng of an ABC, wherby I may have sum understondyng of our Lordis menyng' (chap. li, ll. 2020–1). The long chapter on God in more than one person can be seen as an example of this progress through revealed images, a struggling after words to make them intelligible and the rephrasing of traditional Christian truths confirmed by personal experience. It is this complete trust in God's love that carries the writer through all tribulations of mortal illness and the Fiend's temptations and confirms her in her knowledge of scriptural wisdom. Only at the end of the longer version has she arrived at what is clearly the heart of her message:

> And fro that time that it was shewid I desired oftentimes to witten what was our Lords mening. And fifteen yer after and more I was answerid in gostly [*spiritual*] understonding, seyand thus: *Woldst thou wetten thi Lords mening in this thing? Wete it wele, love was His mening. Who shewid it the? Love. What shewid He the? Love. Wherefore shewid it He? For love.... thou shalt never knowen ne witten therein other thing without end.* Thus was I lerid that love was our Lords mening. (chap. lxxxvi, ll. 3401–7)

The Book of Margery Kempe

The autobiographical account of the religious experience and unprecedented pilgrimages of Margery Kempe (*c.* 1373–*c.* 1440), an illiterate, yet evidently highly articulate woman, is one of the most remarkable Middle English prose texts and an astonishing document of the 'Age of Chaucer' in a wider sense. The unique manuscript was not publicly known until 1934, though extracts from *The Book of Margery Kempe* were included in a pamphlet printed by William Caxton's successor Winkyn de Worde in 1501.[38] It has quickly become one of the best-known Middle English texts.

The central figure of this unusual autobiography, 'confession' as well as 'revelation', can be called author only in a limited sense, because, by her own report, Margery Kempe could not write, but, feeling herself persuaded by many and at last charged by the Lord himself to leave a record of her life of devotion and communion with Christ, she found the means to do so. At the age of about sixty and some twenty years after her first revelations she met a priest who took down her words. Before that, she had been obeying an inner conviction that she should not write down her revelations too soon. The story of the book's genesis, told in two preambles, is a unique document of divinely inspired authorship, even if some of it may be pious fiction. A first version, made for Margery (who throughout speaks of herself in the third person as 'this creature') by a German clerk, turned out to be unreadable (or illegible) by others, and the priest who eventually agreed to produce a new manuscript experienced opposition by the Fiend before he could proceed with his work. It reads like an edifying miracle, yet at the same time, the circumstantial details produce an effect of reliable authenticity, even modest humour:

> Whan the prest began fyrst to wryten on this booke, his eyn myssyd so that he mygth not se to make hys lettyr, ne mygth not se to mend hys penne. Alle other thyng he mygth se wel anow [*enough*]. He sett a peyr <of> spectacles on hys nose, and than wast wel wers than it was befor. He compleyned to the creatur of hys dysese. Sche seyd hys enmy had envye at hys good dede and wold lett [*stop*] hym yf he mygth, and bad hym do as wel as God wold yeve hym grace and not levyn [*desist*]. Whan he cam agayn to hys booke, he myth [*could*] se as wel, hym thowt [*he believed*], as evyr he dede befor, be day-lyth and be candel-lygth bothe. (ll. 140–9)

At the end of the first part, Margery has to confess that for a time she has spent more hours in her chamber with the writer of her life than in prayer, but the Lord tells her that tears shed by both of them in church would not please him more than the writing, 'for, dowtyr [*daughter*], be this boke many a man schal be turnyd to me and belevyn therin' (chap. 88, ll. 7287–8). The work is offered as witness of the divine grace shown to Margery, not as a historical document or a mere autobiographical record. As the preamble states, the subject of this account was, after many years of an unstable and wilful life, 'parfythly [*perfectly*] drawen and steryd to entren the wey of hy perfeccyon, whech parfyth wey Cryst ower Savyowr in hys propyr persoone examplyd' (ll. 24–6). The priest who wrote down her experience, as she recalled it, was evidently convinced of its truth and value as a model of *Imitatio Christi*.

There is no telling, therefore, to what extent the text reproduces Margery's own words or how far the actual writer felt obliged to introduce some structural order of his own or to shape the events according to his sense of decorum. Most readers, however, have been persuaded by the personal tone and apparently uncensured frankness of the language that Margery is in all essentials recording her experience faithfully and that she was moved by a genuine religious faith; it apparently impressed many who came into contact with her, even though her excesses of crying and weeping whenever she was reminded of Christ's Passion shocked and repelled not a few and she was persistently pursued by venomous slander. It is clear that the sometimes extreme manifestations of her religious fervour were offensive to more conventional contemporaries, arousing suspicions of heresy or at least hypocritical pride. On the other hand, her account reveals an astonishing familiarity with devotional texts and practices as well as a surprisingly retentive memory.

Margery Kempe was probably born around 1373, daughter of a prosperous burgess of King's Lynn (then Bishop's Lynn) in Norfolk, member of Parliament and five times Mayor, besides holder of several other influential civic positions. At 20, she was married and, during the next 20 years, bore her husband 14 children. After the birth of her first child, she experienced a mental breakdown, combined with a religious crisis, frightening apparitions and, at last, a vision of Christ comforting her with the words: 'Dowtyr, why hast thow forsakyn me, and I forsoke neuyr the?'(chap. 1, l. 232). After this, she recovered for a while, but failed to change her sinful ways. She describes herself during this brief period almost like a second Wife of Bath, wearing conspicuously gaudy dress and boasting of her influential kindred. She also tried to make some money of her own by brewing, but, after some initial success, failed disastrously and almost became a moral outcast. By the end of the second chapter, though, she decides to do penance and begins 'to entyr the wey of evyrlestyng lyfe' (chap. 2, ll. 322–3). From then on, her career is a vividly described sequence of visions, intimate conversations with Christ, spiritual resolutions, relapses, temptations and, later in life, a period of some twenty years' pilgrimages to Holy places all over Europe and to the Holy Land. Margery suffers persecution as a heretic; she is arrested several times on her wanderings, questioned by various ecclesiastic authorities and narrowly excapes being burned as a witch or a Lollard.[39]

There is a second part or sequel to the book, written about two years after the first, in which a voyage to Prussia in the company of Margery's daughter-in-law is described. She returns to Lynn, and her account closes with a series of prayers.

Throughout the book, however, as Margery herself admits, there is no strict observance of historical chronology.[40] Not only does her memory work by association rather than according to any premeditated plan; more importantly, her own idea of true relevance differs from that of a reader interested mainly in circumstantial biography. It is the spiritual experience and visionary communion with Christ that is recorded for the reader's contemplation and guidance.

The book is an extraordinary record of an eventful domestic, emotional and religious life and a unique document of personal courage, intellectual independence and spiritual individualism, but one only has to read it alongside a book like *Mandeville's Travels* to see how completely different her interests are and how obsessively she concentrates on her own spiritual life and the reactions provoked by her conspicuous appearance and manner, to the exclusion of everything that contemporary pilgrims found exciting and worth recording on their travels to foreign and exotic regions.[41]

What makes *The Book of Margery Kempe* so different from other mystical writings is the close connection between spiritual or visionary experience and everyday reality. Margery continually has to accommodate her inner life and its often rather troublesome outward manifestations, such as her vow of chastity in marriage and her excessive crying and weeping in public whenever she remembers Christ's Passion, to the demands of daily routine and the very human standards of people around her. She has to negotiate with her husband whom she asks to give up his 'marital rights', until he agrees to a vow of mutual chastity (see chaps 9 and 11); another time she has to face a friar whose sermons she enjoys, but who refuses to let her stay in the same church because of her immoderate, noisy lamentation at Christ's suffering (chap. 61). She is repeatedly accused of being a heretic and a Lollard and almost executed on the spot, but saved either by her own persuasive pleading or by the intervention of impartial outsiders (chap. 13); she even has to appear before the archbishops of York and Canterbury to be examined on her articles of faith (chap. 52), but found unimpeachably orthodox and courageously eloquent in her defence. For an unlearned person who only knows what she has learned from regular church-attendance she is remarkably quick in her answers wherever she is questioned or reproved for her extraordinary behaviour, as in this striking instance, when, attending a church service, she sees an image of the *pietà*:

> And thorw the beholdyng of that pete hir mende was al holy ocupyed in the Passyon of owr Lord Jhesu Crist and in the compassyon of owr Lady, Seynt Mary, be whech sche was compellyd to cryyn ful lowde and wepyn ful sor, as thei sche schulde a deyd. Than cam to hir the ladys preste seying:
> 'Damsel, Ihesu is ded long sithyn.'
> Whan hir crying was cesyd, sche seyd to the preste:
> 'Sir, hys deth is as fresch to me as he had deyd this same day, and so me thynkyth it awt to be to yow and to alle Cristen pepil. We awt evyr to han mende of hys kendnes and evyr thynkyn of the dolful deth that he deyd for us.' (chap. 60, ll. 4958–68)

Throughout her account she shows herself ready to give as good as she gets because she feels sure of acting in accordance with the instructions she receives directly from Christ.[42] Like other mystics, she is thoroughly convinced of being in direct and intimate contact with Jesus whose guidance she accepts even in practical matters, but she is neither a saint heading for martyrdom, nor an anchoress like Julian of Norwich, whom, in a famous chapter, she visits (chap. 18, ll. 1335–81) and who confirms her in her constant obedience to Christ and her disregard of the world's contempt. Margery is not really interested in teaching others and offering a record of her visions and meditations as doctrinal authority, but rather to present her life as an example to others, including unconventional circumstances and more intimate personal details than we normally encounter in mystical writing.

For one thing, Margery refuses to conform to any traditional cliché associated with the social and religious station of women. Unlike the majority of canonised saints, she is a wife and a mother, by medieval consent a genuine obstacle to true sainthood. At a crucial point in Margery's colloquies with Christ, he endorses the accepted gradation of female approaches to perfection – maiden, widow, wife, in descending order – but grants her, though pregnant, an exceptional status because of her exceptional devotion:

> thow the state of maydenhode be mor parfyte and mor holy than the state of wedewhode, and the state of wedewhode mor parfyte than the state [of] wedlake, yet, dowtyr, I lofe the as wel as any mayden in the world. (chap. 21, ll. 1570–4)

Obsession with sexuality as a bar to godliness proves a persistent worry to her and is also one of the clearest expressions of her desperate struggle against social opposition and pressures. Her dilemma as a wife who wants to lead a life of chastity is one of the chief causes of her spiritual crisis and the repeated negotiations with her husband who wants to insist on what society calls 'his rights', are among the most characteristic episodes.[43]

One of the most touching domestic incidents concerns the last illness of her husband, who after falling down the stairs in his home turns into a helpless patient in need of constant nursing. Since the couple, according to their vow of chastity, are living apart, Margery at first has to be sent for, which, naturally, causes some scandal. There is a lively glimpse of oppressive community life, vicious slander and shameless spying:

> And than the pepil seyd, yyf he deyd, hys wyfe was worthy to ben hangyn for hys deth, for-as-meche as sche myth a kept hym and dede not. They dwellyd not togedyr, ne thei lay not togedyr, for (as is wretyn beforn) thei bothyn wyth on assent and wyth fre wil of her eithyr hadden mad avow to levyn chast. And therfor, to enchewyn alle perellys, thei dwellyd and sojowryd in divers placys, wher no suspicyon schulde ben had of her incontinens, for first thei dwellyd togedir aftyr that thei had mad her vow, and than the pepil slawndryd hem and seyd thei usyd her lust and her likyng as thei dedyn beforn her vow-makyng. (chap. 76, ll. 6022–31)

When Margery, in desperation, prays for her husband's life and her delivery from slander, she is told by the Lord to nurse him for the love of Christ, remembering that her husband had once allowed her to live chaste in order to serve the Lord. In return, a miracle of recovery is promised her. Accordingly, the husband lives on for some years to be nursed by her, even to his last days, when he turns completely childish, even as far as all the most primitive bodily functions are concerned:

> And therfor was hir labowr meche the mor in waschyng and wryngyng, and hir costage [*expense*] in fyryng, and lettyd hir ful meche fro hir contemplacyon, that many tymys sche schuld an yrkyd hir labowr, saf sche bethowt hir how sche in hir yong age had ful many delectabyl thowtys, fleschly lustys, and inordinat lovys to hys persone. And therfor sche was glad to be ponischyd wyth the same persone and toke it mech the mor esily, and servyd hym and helpyd hym, as hir thowt, as sche wolde a don Crist himself. (chap. 76, ll. 6072–80)

The episode is evidently told for its exemplary spiritual application; yet at the same time it gives a homely picture of true marital affection and practical charity against a rigorously enforced ideal, however praiseworthy. It is this humane realism, side by side with religious ardour that many readers of *The Book of Margery Kempe* have found especially appealing

Prose narrative: Thomas Malory and *Morte Darthur*

Malory's *Morte Darthur* is the most brilliant achievement of Middle English narrative prose writing and the most influential compilation of Arthurian stories in the language, produced at a time when medieval romance had lost much of its idealistic glamour and was approached with critical eyes and a certain moral scepticism.

Malory's life is not particularly well documented. Even his historical identity is largely a matter of conjecture, though a good many facts that in all probability relate to his person have been brought to light; others are referred to in his *Morte Darthur* and corroborated by historical research.[44] It is very likely that the author came from a Warwickshire family and was born around 1414–18. At the conclusion of his work he describes himself as a knight, who completed the work in the ninth year of the reign of Edward IV, i.e. between March 1469 and March 1470 and who asks all his readers, 'Jentylmen and Jentylwymmen', to pray for him, 'that God sende me good delyveraunce'.[45] Earlier in the book he calls himself 'knyght presoner' (p. 110) and prays for 'good delyveraunce' (p. 226). It seems that he spent several years in prison for various alleged crimes, but also as a victim of the long drawn out feuds between the Lancastrians and the Yorkists. He was first arrested in 1450, accused of various robberies and felonies, but apparently never brought to trial, but kept in several London prisons. It is not clear whether he was a Yorkist or whether he leaned to the other side, but it seems evident that he was deeply involved in the political manoeuvreing and the internecine battles later called the 'Wars of the Roses'. His imprisonments were enforced first by the Lancastrians and later by the Yorkists; between 1450 and 1470 he never seems to have been out of prison for very long, except for the years 1460–8. On the other hand, his confinement, at least during the latter years, must have been liberal enough to allow him access to a rich library of Arthurian material. The text of the *Morte Darthur* suggests that most, if not all, of it was written while the author was behind bars. He was finally released during a brief recovery of the Lancastrian cause in 1470 and died on 14 March 1471, just before another reversal of fortune brought the Yorkist Edward IV back to power.

Malory's work is extant in two versions: for almost four hundred and fifty years the only known text was that printed by William Caxton in 1485; Caxton wrote an interesting preface, discussing the historical truth of the Arthurian stories and their moral value. He also edited Malory's text, with the aim of providing a more coherent structure to the vast, unwieldy material, dividing it into twenty-one books and more than five hundred chapters.[46] In 1934, however, a manuscript of the *Morte Darthur* was discovered in Winchester College which at first seemed much closer to Malory's original composition and to show the extent of Caxton's editorial interference. Though the full details of the text's transmission are by no means entirely clear and the Winchester manuscript also shows a good deal of scribal tampering, it has become the basis of the standard editions.[47] It was produced by two scribes, most probably not before 1470, and, as it has been proved, was for a time in Caxton's London printing shop.[48] Recent studies have suggested that Caxton made use of it; moreover, it can be shown that Vinaver's edition, from which most critics quote, does not reproduce the Winchester text very accurately as far as the division into sections is concerned. Vinaver divides Malory's compilation into eight 'books', treated as more or less completely separate works (hence his title: *The Works of Thomas Malory*), but this is not exactly what the manuscript says, which has only four major sections and a great number of minor divisions, perhaps more representative of scribal conventions than of authorial design.[49] Earlier critics had raised objections to Vinaver's position on literary grounds, and for a time the broader question whether Malory produced a series of different Arthurian stories or a single, coherent narrative was debated with some vigour.[50] More recent changes in critical method and renewed interest in the basics of textual transmission have made this issue appear rather less crucial. Seen in its cultural context Malory's work incorporates a variety of interests and contemporary concerns more relevant to its overall design than formal unity or narrative consistency.[51]

Malory evidently worked with a number of very different sources and his overall plan may have changed more than once in the course of composition if, in fact, he ever had a more specific literary concept than that of producing a comprehensive collection of Arthurian stories, retelling in one volume what he found in various accounts of celebrated heroic deeds and ideals of a bygone age.[52] The book is unique in that it offers the first full-scale biography of King Arthur in English outside the historiographers, from Geoffrey of Monmouth onwards, pieced together mostly from French prose romances and at least two English romances in verse, but united by a new and palpably contemporary vision of the world of chivalry and evidently coloured by experience of fifteenth-century politics and the brutality of warfare, not in the least resembling the heroic idealism of traditional romance. Malory's handling of his sources shows that he deliberately selected and adapted his material so as to form a coherent, if sometimes patchy and uneven narrative.

Some indication of an overall design is suggested by the way Malory used the two major Middle English romances of Arthur's career and death, the *Alliterative Morte Arthure* and the stanzaic *Morte Arthur*, two poems very different in language, poetic style and ethos.[53] The first presents a predominantly tragic view of Arthur's rise and defeat, emphasising his overweening ambition, cruelty and pride, which lead to his ultimate downfall. In the end, the poet 'seems as anti-war as anti-romance'.[54] The stanzaic *Morte Arthur* is as different as can be, recounting an alternative version of Arthur's end, based on the French prose *Mort Artu* where it is closely intertwined with the adulterous love of Lancelot and Queen Guinevere, which plays no part in the alliterative poem. The story is seen in an elegiac and compassionate rather than a heroic and moralistic light; the narrator's sense of pathos and human frailty evidently impressed Malory when he came to this part of his enterprise,[55] possibly more than the great amount of French prose texts on which the larger part of Malory's compilation is based.

The first Book (or section) gives an account of Arthur's origins, his conception, election as King and marriage to Guinevere, the founding of the Round Table and the first adventures of him and his knights. Malory here follows a thirteenth-century French prose romance, *La Suite du Merlin*, and it appears from the 'explicit' that there was originally no settled plan to go any further. His personal situation may have had something to do with it:

AND THIS BOOKE ENDYTH WHEREAS SIR LAUNCELOT AND SIR TRYSTRAMS COM TO
COURTE. WHO THAT WOLL MAKE ONY MORE LETTE HYM SEKE OTHER BOOKIS OF
KYNGE ARTHURE OR OF SIR LAUNCELOT OR SIR TRYSTRAMS; FOR THIS WAS DRAWYN
BY A KNYGHT PRESONER, SIR THOMAS MALLEORRÉ, THAT GOD SENDE HYM GOOD
RECOVER. AMEN.[56]

It is at this point that Malory takes up the story from the alliterative *Morte
Arthure*, as if he had just discovered a new text to provide him with one more
instalment. There is no question of a simple translation: Malory's version is
only half as long as the poem; he is evidently anxious to speed up the action
and to skip over passages that serve to heighten the epic sweep of the old poet,
holding up the swift passage from one hostile encounter and warlike triumph
(or defeat) to the next.[57] The author clearly realised that a prose narrative
demands a different style from that of the heroic alliterative long line. At the
same time he seems to have come to a decision about the larger potential of
his project and the possibility of many further episodes and chivalric adventures,
involving several others of Arthur's most famous knights. This is clearly shown
by the way he parts company with his model at the point where Arthur's trium-
phant career turns into tragedy and the final battle sequence begins. Immediately
before this turning point Malory follows the alliterative poem fairly closely, even
to the point of incorporating some of its lines in his prose account:

> . . .
> Wē will by the Cross-days   encrǫch thēse landes   *Rogation days, invade*
> And at the Christenmass day   bē crowned there-after,
> Regne in my rēaltees   and hǫld my Round Tāble,
> With the rentes of Rōme,   as mē best līkes;
> Sēnn graithe over the grẹte sẹ   with good men of armes   *Then proceed*
> Tō revenge the Renk   That on the Rood dīed!'   *Man, Cross*
> (ll. 3212–17)

Malory's 'translation' reads like this:

> . . . and comly be Crystmas to be crowned, hereafter to reigne in my asstate and to
> kepe my Rounde Table with the rentys of Rome to rule as me lykys; and than, as I
> am avysed, to gete me over the salte se with good men of armys to deme for his deth
> that for us all on the roode dyed'. (p. 145)

From here, the two accounts proceed along diametrically different lines: the
alliterative poem describes the sudden reversal of Arthur's fortunes, Mordred's
treachery and the final battle, with the King's death at Glastonbury in more
than a thousand lines (ll. 3218–4346). Malory, in contrast, evidently realised
that many more texts existed, describing further adventures of Arthur and the
knights of the Round Table, and he therefore replaced the whole passage by a
new, very brief conclusion to this episode, leaving himself free to add any
number of further continuations.

Malory's Arthur, crowned emperor by the Pope, is asked by a council of
knights and lords to let them all return home 'to sporte us with oure wyffis'.

214

His ready consent, with homely wisdom and a proverb, seems like an explicit comment on the heroic Arthur of the alliterative poem: ' "Ye say well," seyde the kynge, "for inowghe is as good as a feste, for to attemte God overmuche I holde hit not wysedom. And therefore make you all redy and turne we into Ingelonde." ' (p. 146) Queen Guinevere and many other noble wives give a joyful welcome to the King and his victorious followers. The 'explicit' promises more of their adventures to come:

> HERE ENDYTH THE TALE OF THE NOBLE KYNGE ARTHURE THAT WAS EMPEROURE HYMSELF THOROW THE DYGNYTÈ OF HIS HONDYS.
> AND HERE FOLOWYTH AFFTIR MANY NOBLE TALYS OF SIR LAUNCELOT DE LAKE. (p. 146)

The proud Arthur, destroying himself by overweening pride, is not for Malory, who turns to different traditions for his own portrait.

Four groups of episodes based on French prose romances follow, each mainly centred around one or a group of Arthur's knight's (Lancelot, Gareth, Tristram, Galahad) until the most successful part of Malory's work is reached, his version of the final phase and the mutual extinction of the Arthurian court and the Round Table. For this section, Malory used the French *Mort Artu* as well as the English stanzaic *Morte Arthure*, but, by tightening the narrative structure, focusing on the characters' conflicting loyalties and, above all, by his deliberately distancing, yet highly suggestive prose style he provided a new sense of inevitable catastrophe and moral impasse that made his version the most impressive and influential of Arthurian narratives in English.[58] It can also be seen as a decisive breakthrough of prose as a medium of telling stories, no less successful and popular than verse. England's first printer, William Caxton, evidently sensed this, when, along with French prose romances, he chose Malory's *Morte Darthur* as one of the first major ventures of his new press.

Malory's fictional portrait of Arthurian chivalry is a curious blend of literary tradition, newly revived ideals and contemporary experience.[59] Though it employs many of the trappings of romance as well as its transcendental aspirations, it is firmly rooted in human laws of behaviour and the moral standards of a particular Christian society, eventually disrupted and broken by its own failings. This is best seen in the last two books, the finest part of Malory's compilation and his most original achievement.[60] The tragedy of Arthur's Round Table and a whole world of values and ideals is not the result of one single 'tragic flaw', though some of the explanations offered by the protagonists seem to suggest simple answers, in particular Guinevere's haunting speech when, in the presence of her ladies, she bids Lancelot goodbye, urging him never to see her again:

> 'Thorow thys same man and me hath all thys warre be wrought, and the deth of the moste nobelest knyghtes of the worlde; for thorow oure love that we have loved togydir ys my moste noble lorde slayne . . . for thorow the and me ys the f[lou]re of kyngis and [knyghtes] destroyed. (720, 15–17, 29–30)

This may be true as far as the plot and an ultimate moral assessment are concerned, but the text suggests a number of other causes, and the reader's sympathy is painfully divided.[61] Throughout the text, there is no comfortable allotting of guilt and responsibility or a sense of strict moral enquiry, but a fatal clash of loyalties and a feeling of inexorable doom. The narrator does not attempt to explore his characters' inner lives or their psychological conflicts; he simply registers the human drama taking its course. Where agents of the disaster are blamed, the blame is given to the personal enemies of Guinevere and Lancelot, not to the adulterous lovers, though it is they who in the end confess themselves the causes of the entire tragedy. The king himself, as the narrator explains, would much rather wink at his queen's illicit affair with his best knight than be forced into action by a public scandal and risk the outward harmony of the Round Table.[62] In a most revealing passage, added by Malory to his sources, Arthur declares that the glory of his Round Table is nearer to his heart than the love of his queen:

> . . . And therefore,' seyde the kynge, 'wyte you well, my harte was never so hevy as hit is now. And much more I am soryar for my good knyghtes losse than for the losse of my fayre quene; for quenys I myght have inow, but such a felyship of good knyghtes shall never be togydirs in no company. And now I dare sey,' seyde kynge Arthur, 'there was neuer Crystyn kynge that ever hylde such a felyshyp togydyrs. And alas, that ever sir Launcelot and I shulde be at debate!' (685, 28–35)

For Arthur, the fellowship of his knights of the Round Table is the centre of his world; its very existence guarantees the uniqueness of his universe and its ethical foundations. By the standards of this society, it is broken up not so much through Lancelot's adulterous relationship with the King's wife, but through the envy and hate of the knights who make it public, thus producing a situation where Lancelot has to defend the honour of the Queen, and the King has to make war against his best knight in order to escape public humiliation. It is a society where loss of face and open shame are crucial, not private guilt or individual conscience.[63]

At the same time, the action of the last two books, in particular Lancelot's relationships with women, introduce personal conflicts and confrontations that involve more private aspects of character and a new sense of interiority.[64] Conventional episodes of battle, tournament and knightly adventure give place to more intimate scenes of individual emotions, suspicion, jealousy, vindictive anger and amorous obsession. In this respect Malory's final books come closer to our idea of the novel than any previous Middle English narrative and, though for the most part he merely appears to re-tell stories found in earlier volumes, his own treatment adds a new dimension of psychological insight and complex personalities. At the same time, he deliberately gives a different slant to some of the crucial episodes, in particular the love of Lancelot and Guinevere, the ultimate cause of all the tragedy. As Malory tells it, it is not so much a story of an erotic passion, such as that of Chaucer's Troilus, but an example of true loyalty and faith. Chivalric love here is an ideal bond rather than a sensual experience and, though it is, in the end, condemned as sinful it yet brings out the best knightly qualities in the lover. Unlike the French authors, Malory's narrator is more interested in the noble aspects of the mutual attraction and in the sad difference between his own age and the glorious times of Arthur, as he explains in a particularly characteristic passage:

> For, as the Freynshhe booke seyth, the quene and sir Launcelot were togydirs. And whether they were abed other at other maner of disportis, me lyste nat thereof make no mencion, for love that tyme was nat as love ys nowadayes. (676, 1–4)

The short paragraph is also a specimen of Malory's individual prose style. He is not a sophisticated stylist, nor does he try to impress by ornate phrases, vivid images or showy rhetoric. His range of registers is comparatively narrow, but it would be misleading to call his prose artless, unambitious and unconsciously successful.[65] Conscious or not, it has a simple directness, a haunting intensity of pathos and an unobtrusive precision. For all its lack of tonal variety it can be most expressive when it comes to changes of mood or temper, especially in dialogue where Malory frequently achieves a sense of genuine exchange between personalities quite different from verse narrative.

One of the most touching episodes is the death of the Fair Maid of Astolat after Lancelot has refused her love. When her dead body arrives at Arthur's court and her story is revealed, there is a tense scene, related by Malory with characteristic restraint, yet hinting at the psychological drama under the polite surface, as the queen, in the presence of her husband and his knights, reproaches her lover for not showing the maid more kindness:

> 'Sir,' seyde the quene, 'ye myght have shewed hir som bownté and jantilnes whych myght have preserved hir lyff.'
> 'Madame,' seyde sir Launcelot, 'she wolde none other wayes be answerde but that she wolde be my wyff othir ellis my paramour, and of thes two I wolde not graunte her. But I proffird her, for her good love that she shewed me, a thousand pound yerely to her and to her ayres, and to wedde ony maner of knyght that she coude fynde beste to love in her harte. For, madame,' seyde sir Launcelot, 'I love nat to be constrayned to love, for love muste only aryse of the harte selff, and nat by none constraynte.'
> 'That ys trouth, sir, 'seyde the kynge, 'and with many knyghtes love ys fre in hymselffe, and never woll be bonde; for where he ys bonden he lowsith hymselff.' (641, 29–41)

There is no open criticism of Lancelot's behaviour, except from the queen, who is herself guilty of adulterous love.[66] Her remark and Lancelot's reply suggest to the reader an unspoken exchange between the two lovers, while the king seems blissfully unaware of what is really going on. Scenes like this show Malory's narrative prose at its most expressive: without rhetorical flourish and conspicuous verbal artistry, yet eloquent in its evocation of complex emotion and unarticulated mental processes. It is he, more than any other English author, who has made the stories of Arthur and the Knights of the Round Table so fascinating to many later writers and thus become an essential part of the British cultural inheritance.[67]

Notes

1. For a useful survey and guide, see *Middle English Prose: A Critical Guide to Major Authors and Genres*, ed. A. S. G. Edwards (New Brunswick, 1984). Cf. also *The Medieval Translator. The Theory and Practice of Translation in the Middle Ages*, ed. Roger Ellis (Cambridge, 1989) for an introduction into some problems and practices of medieval translation.

2. For the text of the preface see 'Trevisa's Original Prefaces on Translation: A Critical Edition', ed. Ronald Waldron in *Medieval English Studies Presented to George Kane*, ed. E. D. Kennedy, R. Waldron and J. S. Wittig (Woodbridge, 1988), pp. 285–99. Extracts are given in several anthologies, e.g. *Chaucer to Spenser: An Anthology*, ed. Derek. Pearsall (Oxford, 1999), pp. 230–1, or *A Book of Middle English*, ed. J. A. Burrow and Thorlac Turville-Petre, second edition (Oxford, 1996), pp. 215–22. On Trevisa see the useful account, with full bibliography, by David C. Fowler, *John Trevisa* (Aldershot, Hants., 1993), re-issued as part of *English Writers of the Late Middle Ages*, ed. M. C. Seymour, Authors of the Middle Ages, I, 1–4 (Aldershot, Hants., 1994), pp. 65–126; cf. also John Taylor, *The Universal Chronicle of Ranulf Higden* (Oxford, 1966); on Trevisa see pp. 134–40.

3. Extracts in Pearsall's anthology, pp. 232–3. See Anne Hudson, *Lollards and their Books* (London, 1985) and *The Premature Reformation: Wycliffite Texts and Lollard History* (Oxford, 1988), and the older, still useful study by Margaret Deanesly, *The Lollard Bible and Other Medieval Versions* (Cambridge, 1920). A good up-to-date survey is Steven Justice, 'Lollardy', in *The Cambridge History of Medieval English Literature*, ed. David Wallace (Cambridge, 1999), pp. 662–89.

4. Indeed, some Middle English prose texts have become surprisingly popular with non-academic readers, especially in modern English translations. As Nicholas Watson states: 'Unlike most writers, Julian, the *cloud-author* and Kempe are more widely read outside universities than they are inside', in 'Middle English Mystics', *The Cambridge History of Medieval English Literature*, p. 543.

5. A full account of Middle English prose writing in its historical context is to be found in *The Cambridge History of Medieval English Literature*.

6. Cf. the account of its transmission and the bibliography in the latest edition, *The English Text of the Ancrene Riwle. The 'Vernon' Text*, ed. Arne Zettersten and Bernhard Diensberg, *EETS*, 310 (2000), Introduction, pp. ix–xxii.

7. This series of letters, from members of a prosperous Norfolk family, written between 1425 and *c.* 1500 is a particularly interesting document of the business dealings and family politics and personal life in a particular social context. See *The Paston Letters*, ed. N. Davis, 2 vols (Oxford, 1971); Davis has also edited *Selections* (Oxford, 1958) and *Selections in Modern Spelling* (Oxford, 1963).

8. The 'Insular Version' is, according to M. C. Seymour, a French recension, made in England before 1375, of the original French text. See the list of manuscripts in Appendix B, 'The Scribal Tradition of *Mandeville's Travels* in England', in *The Metrical Version of Mandeville's Travels*, ed. M. C. Seymour, *EETS*, 269 (1973), pp. 193–7. The texts of the metrical version and of the Latin Harley version (Appendix A) are quoted from this edition. A fuller list of manuscripts, including the 'Continental Tradition' (97 manuscripts), the 'Insular Tradition' (81 manuscripts) and the 'Liège Tradition' (85 manuscripts, some of them in French, Latin, German, Danish and Czech), and of editions is to be found in M. C. Seymour, *Sir John Mandeville* (Aldershot, Hants, 1993), re-issued as part of *English Writers of the Late Middle Ages*, ed. M. C. Seymour, Authors of the Middle Ages, I, 1–4 (Aldershot, Hants., 1994), pp. 1–64. The list also mentions a number of fragments and lost manuscripts not included in the count. A particularly interesting case is British Library MS. Additional 24189 which contains 28 illustrations of

the first five chapters, based on a Latin or Czech text written in Bohemia. For a facsimile of the pictures with commentary see *The Travels of John Mandeville. A Manuscript in the British Library. Introduction and Commentaries on the Plates by Josef Krása* (George Braziller, Inc., New York, 1983). The volume is another interesting document of the work's vast popularity all over Europe.

9. *The Bodley Version of Mandeville's Travels*, ed. M. C. Seymour, EETS, 253 (1963), p. 3.

10. The Latin text on which this version is probably based has 'plures desiderant audire de terra sancta, id est de terra promissionis' (pp. 2.5–6).

11. See Seymour's notes in *The Bodley Version of Mandeville's Travels*, p. 149 and *passim*. A fuller version made around 1400, conflated from several earlier texts and preserved in British Library MS. Cotton Titus C. xvi, is one of the only two extant unabridged English texts of *Mandeville's Travels*. The 'standard' edition of this version is *Mandeville's Travels*, ed. M. C. Seymour (Oxford, 1967).

12. Seymour's edition, p. 3. The author also asserts that he has translated the book out of Latin into French and then again from French into English, 'that euery man of my nacoun may vnderstonde it' (p. 4). He asks his readers to confirm the truth of what he relates and to correct any errors or omissions. 'For thinges passed out of longe tyme from a mannes mynde or from his syght turnen sone into forgetynge, because that mynde of man ne may not ben comprehended ne withholden for the freeltee of mankynde' (p. 4). The modest apology is interesting in view of the often incredible facts and events to follow.

13. Bodley version, pp. 77.7–18; the Cotton text is very similar at this point, p. 100.

14. Bodley version, p. 57.14–19; see Cotton version, p. 60.

15. Bodley, p. 109.17–32; see Cotton version, pp. 206–7.

16. Cotton version, p. 228; the abridged Bodley version only repeats the conventional formula that it would take too long to describe all the wonders he saw on his journey (Bodley, p. 145.25–8), though the author may have mistranslated the Latin 'Multe quidem et alie sunt patrie, aliaque plura mirabilia que non vidi in partibus illis' [*There are yet many and different regions and more different wonders in those parts which I have not seen*] (p. 144.25–6).

17. 'And now I am comen hom mawgree myself to reste for gowtes artetykes that me distreynen, that diffynen the ende of my labour ayenst my wille, God knoweth. And thus takynge solace in my wreched reste recordynge the tyme passed I haue fulfilled theise thinges and putte hem wryten in this boke, as it wolde come into my mynde, the yeer of grace a m.ccc and lvi in the xxxiiii yeer that I departede from oure contrees' (Cotton version, p. 229.20–7).

18. See *English Mystics of the Middle Ages*, ed. Barry Windeatt (Cambridge, 1994), for a convenient anthology of texts, newly edited, with introduction and bibliography; the quotation is on p. 1.

19. See Nicholas Watson, 'The Middle English Mystics' in *The Cambridge History of Medieval English Literature*, pp. 539–65. Watson, in spite of the title of his chapter, considers the whole concept of 'Middle English mystics' anachronistic and a creation of early twentieth-century English catholicism, whose priorities were devotional rather than historical (pp. 543–4). He prefers the term 'vernacular theologians' for these writers, since 'Rolle, the *Cloud*-author and the rest are involved in the same socio-political discussion as Chaucer, Langland and the Lollards' (p. 544). On some general background see the important chapter by Vincent Gillespie, 'Vernacular Books of Religion' in *Book Production and Publishing in Britain 1375–1475*, ed. Jeremy Griffiths and Derek Pearsall, Cambridge Studies in Publishing and Printing History (Cambridge, 1989), 317–44.

20. See Nicholas Watson, *Richard Rolle and the Invention of Authority,* Cambridge Studies in Medieval Literature, 13 (Cambridge, 1991), for a general evaluation, especially the chapter ' "Mixed life": the English Works' pp. 222–56. See also Hope Emily Allen, *Writings Ascribed to Richard Rolle, Hermit of Hampole, and Materials for his Biography*, Modern Language Association Monographs, series 3 (New York, 1927). For his English writings see *English Writings of Richard Rolle*, ed. H. E. Allen (Oxford, 1931) and *Richard Rolle: Prose and Verse from MS. Longleat 29 and related manuscripts*, ed. S. J. Ogilvie-Thomson, EETS, 293 (1988). For some excerpts from his writings, including two of his hymns, see Windeatt, *English Mystics of the Middle Ages*, pp. 15–66.

21. *The Cloud of Unknowing* and *The Book of Privy Counselling*, ed. Phyllis Hodgson, EETS, 218 (1944); extracts in *English Mystics of the Middle Ages*, ed. Windeatt, pp. 67–77 and 78–105 (*Book of Privy Counselling*), and in *Chaucer to Spenser*, ed. Pearsall, pp. 292–6. Translation by Clifton Wolters (Harmondsworth, 1961). See also *Deonise Hid Diuinite and Other Treatises on Contemplative Prayer Related to* The Cloud of Unknowing, ed. Phyllis Hodgson, EETS, 231 (1955), for some anonymous texts closely related to *The Cloud of Unknowing*, if not by the same author.

22. In fact, he addresses himself to a disciple, a twenty-four year old (chap. 4), but he also envisages other readers, though only such as are prepared to peruse the book in its entirety, not cursorily or in selected passages; see Prologue.

23. Hodgson's edition is based on British Library MS Harley 674, a careful early fifteenth-century manuscript. There are also two Latin translations, independent of each other, another indication of the text's popularity; see Hodgson, pp. xxv–vii.

24. *The Cloud of Unknowing* and *The Book of Privy Counselling*, ed. Phyllis Hodgson, chap. 4, p. 23.

25. 'ʒif þou aske me who schuld worche, þus, I answere þee: alle þat han forsaken þe worild in a trewe wille, & þer-to þat ʒeuen hem not to actyue liif, bot to þat liif þat is clepid contemplatyue liif' (p. 63).

26. See chapters 17–21, where the story of Christ's visit to Mary and Martha is treated at some length, but chiefly to defend the contemplatives against the complaints of the Marthas of this world. Christ's reply to Martha is thus rephrased: 'Actyues, actyues! Make ʒow as besi as ʒe kan . . . & medel ʒow not of contemplatyues' (chap. 21, p. 55).

27. Walter Hilton, *The Scale of Perfection*, ed. Evelyn Underhill (London, 1923), slightly modernised; extracts from both books in *English Mystics of the Middle Ages*, ed. Windeatt, pp. 149–72, and from several other writings, pp. 108–48 and 173–80; see also Walter Hilton, *The Ladder of Perfection. A New Translation by Leo Sherley-Price* (Harmondsworth, 1957). Cf. also Joseph E. Milosh, *The Scale of Perfection and the English Mystical Tradition* (Madison, 1966). Hilton studied in Cambridge; he possibly lived some time as a hermit and later became canon of the Augustinian priory of Thurgarton near Southwell, where he died in 1394. He wrote in Latin as well as in English.

28. See Windeatt, p. 149.

29. See book II, chaps 21 and 33, in Windeatt, pp. 157–63.

30. See the important arcticle by Felicity Riddy, ' "Women talking about the things of God": a late medieval subculture', in *Women and Literature in Britain 1150–1500*, ed. Carol Meale, Cambridge Studies in Medieval Literature, 17 (Cambridge, 2nd ed., 1996), pp. 104–27.

31. See *The Shewings of Julian of Norwich*, ed. Georgia Ronan Crampton (Kalamazoo, Michigan, 1994), with good introduction and notes; *A Book of Showings to the Anchoress Julian of Norwich*, ed. Edmund Colledge and James Walsh, 2 vols (Toronto, 1978), with useful introduction, and Julian of Norwich, *A Revelation of Love*, ed. Marion Glasscoe (Exeter, 1976, rev. 1986), also *Julian of Norwich's Revelations of Divine Love (The Shorter Version) ed. from B.L. Add. MS 37790*, ed. Frances Beer, Middle English Texts, 8 (Heidelberg, 1978) and *English Mystics of the Middle Ages*, ed. Windeatt,

pp. 181–213 (complete shorter version) and pp. 214–26 (extracts from longer version); extracts in *Chaucer to Spenser*, ed. Pearsall, pp. 297–303 (he prefers the longer version as 'more gracefully written and more famous', p. 297); Julian of Norwich, *Revelations of Divine Love*, translated into modern English and with an introduction by Clifton Wolters (Harmondsworth, 1966). See also the important study by Nicholas Watson, 'The Composition of Julian of Norwich's *Revelation of Love*', *Speculum*, 68 (1993), 637–83, and Watson, 'Middle English Mystics', *The Cambridge History of Medieval English Literature*, pp. 557–60.

32. Chap. 2 of the longer version. Quotations of this versions are from the edition by Crampton, accessible also through http://www.lib.rochester.edu/camelot/teams/julian2.htm The shorter version is quoted from Windeatt's anthology.

33. Cf. longer version, chap. ix, ll. 340–3.

34. See the longer version, chaps xiii, ll. 500–1 and xlviii, ll. 2829–30.

35. Chap. 6, p. 189. The longer version has no such disclaimer at this point; instead, the author is anxious to insist on the perfect orthodoxy of all her visions: 'But in al thing I leve as Holy Church levith, preachith, and teachith. For the feith of Holy Church, the which I had afornhand understonden and, as I hope, by the grace of God wilfully kept in use and custome, stode continualy in my sight, willing and meneing never to receive onything that might be contrary therunto' (chap. ix, ll. 335–8). It seems that the older Julian, known and sought after as spiritual authority, could no longer pretend not to be a teacher; on the other hand, she possibly had to guard against objections to her kind of revelation or even a suspicion of heresy, as Margery Kempe had to.

36. See J. A. W. Bennett, *Middle English Literature*. Edited and completed by Douglas Gray, The Oxford History of English Literature, I.2 (Oxford, 1986), p. 334; the whole chapter on mystical writing and on Julian of Norwich in particular is worth reading.

37. See also ll. 956–9: '*It is sothe that synne is cause of al this peyne, but al shal be wele, and al shal be wele, and all manner thing shal be wele.* These words were seyd full tenderly, shewyng no manner of blame to me ne to non that shall be safe.' The first version is much less emphatic at this point (chap. 13, pp. 198–9). Cf. the use of the quotation in T. S. Eliot's *Four Quartets* ('Little Gidding') and in Iris Murdoch's novel *The Bell* (London, 1958), chap. 12.

38. See *The Book of Margery Kempe*, ed. Barry Windeatt, Longman Annotated Texts (Harlow, 2000), critical edition, with rich annotation and bibliography. Quotations are from this edition; see also *The Book of Margery Kempe*, ed. Sanford Brown Meech and Hope Emily Allen, *EETS*, 212 (1940, repr. 1961); there is a good modern translation by Barry Windeatt, *The Book of Margery Kempe*, Penguin Classics (Harmondsworth, 1985, repr. with revised bibliography, 1994), with a helpful introduction.

39. For the chronology of her life, as far as it can be gathered from her text and the writing of the manuscript see Windeatt's edition, pp. vii-viii and 2–9. Windeatt offers some interesting speculation on the identity of the priest and his part in the book's composition.

40. See preamble, ll. 134–7: 'Thys boke is not wretyn in ordyr, every thyng after other as it wer don, but lych as the mater cam to the creatur in mend whan it schuld be wretyn, for it was so long er it was wretyn that sche had forgetyn the tyme and the ordyr whan thyngys befellyn.'

41. See Windeatt, pp. 22–7, on Margery's individual style and its independence of traditional genres.

42. Christ himself tells her that 'I schal yeve the grace inow to answer every clerke in the love of God' (517–8).

43. See especially chapter 11 and Windeatt's introduction to his edition, pp. 9–18: 'Backgrounds and foremothers', for some women saints, whose life may have been a model for Margery.

44. See P. J. C. Field, *The Life and Times of Sir Thomas Malory*, Arthurian Studies, 29 (Cambridge, 1993), for a very thorough account of the known and the conjectured facts about Malory. The best introduction to Malory's work and to Malory studies is *A Companion to Malory*, ed. Elizabeth Archibald and A. S. G. Edwards, Arthurian Studies, 37 (Cambridge, 1996). P. J. C. Field's contribution to this volume, 'The Malory Life-Records', pp. 115–30, gives a concise summary of the documentary evidence and his views on Malory's career.

45. *Malory: Works*, ed. Eugène Vinaver (Oxford, 1954, rev. ed. 1971), p. 726. Quotations are from this edition.

46. Caxton's preface, slightly abridged, is most easily accessible in *Chaucer to Spenser,* ed. Pearsall, pp. 465–6. The volume also contains most of the last book, with a helpful headnote and brief bibliography. For a complete facsimile of Caxton's volume (863 printed pages) see *Sir Thomas Malory: Le Morte Arthur. Printed by William Caxton, 1485*. Introduction by Paul Needham (London, 1976).

47. The most convenient complete edition is *Malory: Works*, ed. Vinaver, in one volume; the best critical edition, with commentary: *The Works of Sir Thomas Malory*, ed. Eugène Vinaver, rev. P. J. C. Field, 3rd edn, 3 vols (Oxford, 1990). For a complete facsimile of the Winchester manuscript (British Library MS Add. 59678) see *The Winchester Malory. A Facsimile*, Introduction by N. R. Ker, *EETS, Supplementary Series*, 4 (1976), and for a well documented analysis of the editorial history, Carol M .Meale, ' "The Hoole Book": Editing and the Creation of Meaning in Malory's Text', in *A Companion to Malory*, pp. 3–17. The superior textual authority of the Winchester manuscript is even more seriously questioned in P. J. C. Field, *Malory: Text and Sources*, Arthurian Studies, 40 (Cambridge, 1998); see especially 'The Earliest Texts of Malory', pp. 1–13, and 'The Choice of Texts for Malory's *Morte Darthur*', pp. 14–26.

48. See Lotte Hellinga, 'The Malory Manuscript and Caxton', in *Aspects of Malory*, ed. Toshiyuki Takamiya and Derek Brewer, rev. ed. (Cambridge, 1986), 127–41.

49. See Meale's description of the manuscript and Caxton's possible use of it in: ' "The Hoole Book": Editing and the Creation of Meaning in Malory's Text', in *A Companion to Malory*, pp. 8–17, and the studies referred to by her.

50. See the important article by Derek Brewer, ' "the hoole book" ', *Essays on Malory*, ed. J. A. W. Bennett (Oxford, 1963), pp. 41–63, and the collection *Malory's Originality: A Critical Study of Le Morte Darthur*, ed. R. M. Lumiansky (Baltimore, 1964).

51. See Felicity Riddy, *Sir Thomas Malory* (Leiden, 1987), for a convincing attempt to place Malory within his cultural environment. An excellent new discussion is the same author's, 'Contextualizing *Le Morte Darthur*: Empire and Civil War', in *A Companion to Malory*, pp. 55–73.

52. He himself calls his compilation 'the hoole book of kyng Arthur and of his noble knyghtes of the Rounde Table' (726, 10–11). For a good and up-to-date account of Malory's sources see Terence McCarthy, 'Malory and his Sources' in *A Companion to Malory*, pp. 75–95, and Field, *Malory: Text and Sources*.

53. The most accessible edition of both Middle English poems is *King Arthur's Death. The Middle English Stanzaic Morte Arthur and Alliterative Morte Arthure*, ed. Larry Benson, Exeter Medieval Texts and Studies (Exeter, 1986; first published Indianapolis, 1974). See also the chapter on 'The matter of Britain' in W. R. J. Barron, *English Medieval Romance*, Longman Literature in English Series (London, 1987), pp.132–76, with useful bibliography. Barron also treats Malory's *Morte Darthur* in this connection (pp. 147–53); it seems appropriate to include the work here as well, as a particularly important document of Middle English prose writing.

54. Barron, *English Medieval Romance*, p. 142. For a collection of different approaches to the poem see *The Alliterative Morte Arthure. A Reassessment of the Poem*, ed. Karl Heinz Göller, Arthurian Studies, 2 (Cambridge, 1981), with a good summary of research, pp. 7–14.

55. See Dieter Mehl, *The Middle English Romances of the Thirteenth and Fourteenth Centuries* (London, 1969), pp. 186–93, and Barron, pp. 142–7.

56. Vinaver's edition, p. 110. In his note, the editor suggests that Malory may have failed to obtain further material, and he rightly concludes that 'The phrase can legitimately be taken to refer, not to a possible completion of an unfinished work, but to further works on similar themes' (p. 739).

57. See Vinaver's commentary, pp. 739–41, and, for a more detailed analysis, his three-volume edition, pp. 1366 ff.

58. For a useful account of Malory's prose see P. J. C. Field, *Romance and Chronicle: A Study of Malory's Prose Style* (London, 1971); for two particularly stimulating and original studies of Malory's style and vision see also Mark Lambert, *Malory: Style and Vision in* Le Morte Darthur, Yale Studies in English, 186 (New Haven, 1975), and Jill Mann, *The Narrative of Distance, The Distance of Narrative in Malory's* Morte Darthur, The William Matthews Lectures 1991 (London, 1991).

59. See Richard Barber, 'Malory's *Le Morte Darthur* and Court Culture under Edward IV', *Arthurian Literature*, 12, ed. James P. Carley and Felicity Riddy (Cambridge, 1993), pp. 133–56, and Richard Barber, 'Chivalry and the *Morte Darthur*' in *A Companion to Malory*, pp. 19–35. For a perceptive and useful study see also Christoph Houswitschka, *Politik und Liebe in der Literatur des englischen Spätmittelalters am Beispiel von Thomas Malory*, Sprache und Literatur: Regensburger Arbeiten zur Anglistik und Amerikanistik, 36 (Frankfurt am Main, 1991).

60. I have not seen a better account of this last section than that of Mark Lambert in *Malory: Style and Vision in* Le Morte Darthur, 'The Last Tales', pp. 124–221. My own reading of Malory is greatly indebted to his. For a useful survey see C. David Benson, 'The Ending of the *Morte Darthur*', in *A Companion to Malory*, pp. 221–38.

61. 'In these last books of *Le Morte Darthur* causation is multiple and complex . . . Gawain, Lancelot and Guinevere each take absolute responsibility for the disaster because each could have prevented it, not because each entirely caused it', Lambert, *Malory: Style and Vision in* Le Morte Darthur, p. 160.

62. 'For, as the Freynshe booke seyth, the kynge was full lothe that such a noyse shulde be upon sir Launcelot and his quene; for the kynge had a demyng of hit, but he wold nat here thereoff, for sir Launcelot had done so much for hym and for the quene so many tymes that wyte you well the kynge loved hym passyngly well' (674, 37–41).

63. Cf. Lambert: 'It is Malory himself, not just his characters, for whom honor and shame are more real than innocence and guilt', *Malory: Style and Vision in* Le Morte Darthur, p. 179; he concludes, 'the lovers are not felt to be guilty of betrayal but to be risking shame and disaster', p. 199.

64. See Elizabeth Edwards, 'The Place of Women in the *Morte Darthur*', in *A Companion to Malory*, pp. 37–54, especially pp. 51–4.

65. See the very good account of Malory's prose style by Jeremy Smith, 'Language and Style in Malory', in *A Companion to Malory*, pp. 97–113, and Field, *Romance and Chronicle: A Study of Malory's Prose Style*.

66. Malory's sources give a different account; Lancelot is blamed by the maid's letter as well as by Arthur; cf. McCarthy, 'Malory and his Sources', p. 87.

67. See A. S. G. Edwards, 'The Reception of Malory's *Morte Darthur*' in *A Companion to Malory*, pp. 241–52, for an informative survey, with useful bibliographical notes.

Conclusion

There is no simple way of defining the end of the 'Age of Chaucer'. Certainly, after Lydgate, Hoccleve and the Middle Scots poets, especially Henryson's *Testament of Cresseid*, and Douglas's translation of Virgil, with its attack on Chaucer, active engagement with Chaucer's poetic heritage and that of his contemporaries appears to have calmed down and given way to other literary occupations. Malory, in particular, seems to be completely untouched by Chaucer's art, and his fascination with the Arthurian world is a far cry from 'th' olde dayes of the Kyng Arthour, / Of which that Britons speken greet honour'.[1] Yet it would be wrong to underestimate the impact of Chaucer on the authors of the sixteenth century. The printed collections of Caxton and his successors secured the presence and availability of some of the more important texts. Chaucer's works alone were published in a number of influential editions.[2] For a long time, however, the canon was not absolutely fixed, and a surprising amount of non-Chaucerian material came to be included, in particular Henryson's *Testament of Cresseid* and several poems by Lydgate.[3] But hardly any writer after 1500 can reasonably be called a 'Chaucerian'. Poetic models and influences rapidly changed under the influence of humanism and the Italian Renaissance, and the major Tudor poets generally looked elsewhere for genuine inspiration, for new material and a fresh poetic grammar. In addition, major changes in English pronunciation, vocabulary and prosody made the language of Chaucer and his period increasingly appear quaint against the fashions of court and city. Nevertheless, the old poets were by no means as thoroughly ignored as twentieth-century criticism, with its anachronistic compartmentalisation, frequently suggests. Shakespeare's reading of Chaucer, not very often paid very close attention to, is astonishingly extensive, though the poet is mentioned by name only once in the possibly non-Shakespearean Prologue to *The Two Noble Kinsmen*, an effective dramatisation of the 'Knight's Tale'. The passage deserves quoting because, apart from obvious salesmanship, it shows the prestige and market-value yet attached to the poet:

> We pray our play may be so, for I am sure
> It has a noble breeder and a pure,
> A learned, and a poet never went
> More famous yet 'twixt Po and silver Trent.
> Chaucer, of all admired, the story gives;
> There, constant to eternity, it lives.[4]

Whoever wrote the prologue, the whole of the play itself confirms Shakespeare's familiarity with Chaucer, begun at least twenty years earlier, with *The Rape of*

Lucrece, A Midsummer Night's Dream, Romeo and Juliet, and most evident in *Troilus and Cressida*.[5] Shakespeare's rewriting of Chaucer's tragic poem shows him treating the source with the respectful independence that is characteristic of him whether he dramatises Roman history, Italian novellas or popular myth. There is no evidence that he recognised and appreciated all the qualities we associate with Chaucer's poetry or his personal tone; the distance in time between the two poets seems vast, and Chaucer seems to have receded into the past where he has joined the great classic poets.

More immediate and openly acknowledged at first sight is Chaucer's impact on another great Elizabethan poet, Edmund Spenser (*c.* 1552–99), whose first important series of poems, *The Shepheardes Calender*, published anonymously in 1579 and reprinted four times within twenty years, attempts to revive the pastoral tradition of Theocritus and Virgil, inspired also by Continental models, like the French poet Jean Marot and the Italian Baptista Mantuanus, whose Eclogues were first published in 1498. It is a far cry from Chaucer's relaxed and utterly unpedantic reading of Ovid or Virgil, yet Spenser makes a point of referring to Chaucer as the great master, who appears as under the name of Roman poet Tityrus, the God of Shepherds, who, as Spenser says in the December Eclogue, taught him to sing and whose language he makes an effort to adopt.[6] The mysterious E. K., who added his pseudo-learned commentary to the first edition of the *Calender*, begins his commendatory letter with a tribute to 'the olde famous Poete Chaucer: whom for his excellencie and wonderfull skil in making, his scholler Lidgate, a worthy scholler of so excellent a maister, calleth the Loadestarre of our Language: and whom our Colin clout [the poet Spenser] in his Æglogue calleth Tityrus the God of shepheards, comparing hym to the worthiness of the Roman Tityrus Virgile.'[7] Chaucer is already quoted with the reverence accorded to a classical author, respected as much for his reputation as for genuine closeness. It is clear that we are at a definite remove from the 'Age of Chaucer', whose language and poetic style are for Spenser almost as distant as his foreign models and for his commentator as much in need of 'glossing' as the allusions to classical Goddesses and nymphs.[8]

Notes

1. *The Canterbury Tales*, III, 857–8.

2. See Pynson's edition of 1526, in three parts, and the editions of William Thynne (1532, 1542), John Stow (1561) and Thomas Speght (1598). See also the important study by Alice S. Miskimin, *The Renaissance Chaucer* (New Haven, CT, 1975), and the interesting collection of essays, *Rewriting Chaucer. Culture, Authority, and the Idea of the Authentic Text, 1400–1602*, ed. Thomas A. Prendergast and Barbara Kline (Columbus, Ohio, 1999).

3. See the particularly useful bibliography by Russell A. Peck, *Chaucer's* Romaunt of the Rose *and* Boece, Treatise on the Astrolabe, Equatorie of the Planetis, *Lost Works, and Chaucerian Apocrypha. An Annotated Bibliography 1900 to 1985* (Toronto, 1988).

4. John Fletcher and William Shakespeare, *The Two Noble Kinsmen*, ed. Lois Potter, The Arden Shakespeare, Third series (Walton-on-Thames, 1997), Prologue, ll. 9–14.

5. On Shakespeare's reading of Chaucer see in particular the excellent discussion by E. Talbot Donaldson, *The Swan at the Well: Shakespeare Reading Chaucer* (New Haven, 1985) and, more from the Shakespearean angle, Ann Thompson, *Shakespeare's Chaucer: A Study in Literary Origins* (Liverpool, 1978). Cf. also my 'Chaucerian Comedy and Shakespearean Tragedy', *Jahrbuch der Deutschen Shakespeare-Gesellschaft West*, 1984, 111–27.

6. 'For he of *Tityrus* his songs did lere', *The Poetical Works of Edmund Spenser*, ed. J. C. Smith and E. D. Selincourt (Oxford, 1912, many times reprinted), *The Shepheardes Calender*, December, l. 4.

7. *The Poetical Works of Edmund Spenser*, p. 416. Glossing 'Tityrus' in the February eclogue, E. K. writes: 'I suppose he meane Chaucer, whose prayse for pleasant tales cannot dye, so long as the memorie of hys name shall liue, and the name of Poetrie shal endure' (p. 426).

8. Cf. also C. S. Lewis's verdict on Spenser's indebtedness to Chaucer: 'Chaucer and pseudo-Chaucer were less important to him than he himself liked to believe.' *English Literature in the Sixteenth Century Excluding Drama*, The Oxford History of English Literature (Oxford, 1954; repr. 1990 as *Poetry and Prose in the Sixteenth Century*), p. 356.

Chronology

DATE	ENGLISH LITERATURE	POLITICAL AND CULTURAL EVENTS
1327–77		Reign of Edward III
1337–1453		Hundred Years' War
c. 1338		Giovanni Boccaccio (1313–75), *Il Filostrato*; *Decameron* (1348–51)
1341		Francesco Petrarca (1304–74) crowned poet laureate in Rome; *Canzoniere* (from 1348)
1346		Battle of Crécy: English victory
1348 ff., 1361		Black Death in England
1356		Battle of Poitiers: English victory
1360		Treaty of Brétigny: temporary peace with France
1360		Jean de Mandeville, *Voyage d'Otre Mer*; one of the earliest versions of *Mandeville's Travels*
1330–84		John Wyclif: Latin writings, condemned by Pope Gregory XI (1377) and by University of Oxford (1381)
c. 1330–1408	John Gower *Mirrour de l'Omme* (c. 1374–9) *Vox Clamantis* (c. 1385) *Confessio Amantis* (c. 1386–90), rev. 1393	
c. 1342–1400	Geoffrey Chaucer *The Book of the Duchess* (c. 1368–9) *The House of Fame* (c. 1380) *The Parliament of Fowls* (c. 1382) *Troilus and Criseyde*, perhaps simultaneously with translation of Boece, *Consolatio Philosophiae* (c. 1381–6) *The Legend of Good Women* c. 1386–7; Prologue revised 1394–5 *The Canterbury Tales* (c. 1387–1400)	
1350–5	*Winner and Waster* (alliterative debate poem)	
1350–70	*The Prick of Conscience*	
c. 1342–c. 1415	Julian of Norwich *Revelations of Divine Love* (c. 1373, early version; after 1393, later version)	

1351		Statute of Labourers: attempt to fix wages and prices after Black Death
c. 1362–1390	William Langland, *Piers Plowman* Z-Text, A-text, B-text, C-text	
1374		Death of Francesco Petrarca
1375		Death of Giovanni Boccaccio
1377–99		Reign of King Richard II
1399–1413		Reign of King Henry IV
1378–1417		'Great Schism': two rival Popes in Rome and Avignon
1381		Peasants' Revolt in England
1380–92	English translation of 'Wycliffite Bible'	
c. 1381	*The Cloud of Unknowing*	
c. 1395	Walter Hilton (*c.* 1340–96), *The Scale of Perfection*	
1387	John Trevisa's (1326–1412) translation of Ranulf Higden's *Polychronicon*	
c. 1390	*Parlement of the Thre Ages* (alliterative debate)	
c. 1390–1400	MS British Library Cotton Nero A.x. *Pearl, Patience, Cleanness, Sir Gawain and the Green Knight*	
c. 1390	Vernon Manuscript (Bodley Eng. poet.a.1.): Large collection of mainly religious and devotional verse and prose	
c. 1368–*c.* 1426	Thomas Hoccleve *The Regement of Princes* (*c.* 1411–12) *Complaint, Dialogue with a Friend* (*c.* 1421–2)	
c. 1370–1449	John Lydgate *Troy Book* (*c.* 1412–20) *The Siege of Thebes* (*c.* 1421–2) *The Pilgrimage of the Life of Man* (*c.* 1426–8) *The Fall of Princes* (*c.* 1431–8)	
c. 1373–*c.* 1439	Margery Kempe *The Book of Margery Kempe* (*c.* 1436–8)	
1401		Statute *De Heretico Comburendo*: suppression of Lollards; first Lollards burned
1407–9		*Constitutions* of Thomas Arundel, Archbishop of Canterbury 1399–1414: licensing of vernacular preaching required and English translation of Scripture forbidden

228

1413–22		Reign of Henry V
1414		Lollard revolt of Sir John Oldcastle (Lord Cobham); Oldcastle executed (1417)
1415		Battle of Agincourt, English victory
1420		Treaty of Troyes: Henry V acknowledged heir to French crown
1430–1		Joan of Arc captured and burned at Rouen
c. 1416–71	Sir Thomas Malory	
1422–71		Reign of Henry VI
c. 1424	James I (1394–1437), *The Kingis Quair*	
c. 1448	Richard Holland, *The Buke of the Houlat*	
1450s		Latin Bible printed by Johannes Gutenberg in Mainz
1453		End of Hundred Years War; all French possessions lost, except Calais
1453		Constantinople taken by the Turks
c. 1422–*c.* 1492	William Caxton, first English printer First edition of Chaucer's *Canterbury Tales* (1478) First edition of Gower's *Confessio Amantis* (1483) First edition of Malory's *Morte Darthur* (1485)	
1455–85		The Wars of the Roses between the Houses of York (white rose) and Lancaster (red rose); first battle of St Albans
1460		Battle of Northampton: Henry VI captured by the Yorkists
1461		Battle of Towton: Edward IV acclaimed king
1471		Henry VI restored to the throne; battle of Barnet: Henry VI deposed and murdered
1471–83		Reign of Edward IV
1483–5		Reign of Richard III
1485		Battle of Bosworth: Richard III killed; accession of Henry VII, first Tudor King
1485–1509		Reign of King Henry VII
1495	Winkyn de Worde's editions of Chaucer's *Canterbury Tales* and Malory's *Morte Darthur*	
1488–1513		James IV King of Scotland
1513		Battle of Flodden: devastating victory of the English over the Scots
c. 1425–*c.* 1505	Robert Henryson, *Morall Fabillis, Testament of Cresseid*	

c. 1456–*c.* 1513	William Dunbar
	The Golden Targe, Twa Mariit
	Wemen (*c.* 1508)
c. 1475–1522	Gavin Douglas
	The Palice of Honour (*c.* 1508)
	Translation of Virgil's *Aeneid*
	(*c.* 1510)

Bibliography

Bibliographies

Brown, Carleton and Robbins, Rossell Hope, *The Index of Middle English Verse* (New York, 1943); Supplement by R. H. Robbins and J. L. Cutler (Lexington, KY, 1965). (Full list of extant Middle English verse, arranged alphabetically by first lines.)

Watson, George, *New Cambridge Bibliography of English Literature*, vol. I (600–1600) (Cambridge, 1974). (Comprehensive bibliography, including literary, historical and cultural material.)

Wells, John Edwin, *A Manual of the Writings in Middle English 1050–1400* (New Haven, 1916, with 9 Supplements to 1941). (Completely revised, from 1967 under title *A Manual of the Writings in Middle English Literature 1050–1500*, first under the editorship of Burke Severs, then Albert E. Hartung. An indispensable bibliographical handbook, with brief introductions to texts, criticism and full bibliographies.)

Annual bibliographies

Annual Bibliography of English Language and Literature, ed. for the Modern Humanities Research Association (Cambridge, 1921–). (Includes reviews and individual contributions in collections, Festschriften, etc.)

International Bibliography of Books and Articles on the Modern Languages and Literatures, ed. for the Modern Language Association of America (New Yorks, 1956–). (Comprehensive listing, with little annotation; current volumes accessible through the Internet.)

The Year's Work in English Studies, ed. for the English Association (London, 1921–). (Critical summary with some evaluation.)

See also the annual bibliographies in *Studies in the Age of Chaucer* (1979–) and *Yearbook of Langland Studies* (1987–), also accessible through the Internet (see the New Chaucer Society Web page: http://ncs.rutgers.edu).

Electronic resources

Much bibliographical and other information, including texts, articles and additional sources, can be accessed through the Internet. Some useful sites only can be listed here, as a first introduction to a rapidly increasing and constantly changing virtual library. A useful site, with links to a great deal of texts and secondary material is: http://www.luminarium.org/lumina.htm

Corpus of Middle English Verse and Prose http://www.hti.umich.edu/c/cme/ (Large corpus of Middle English texts in mostly reliable editions.)

Electronic Text Centre: The Middle English Collection http://etext.lib.virginia.edu/mideng.browse.html (Large corpus of Middle English texts in reliable editions, with links to many other texts and library resources.)

TEAMS Texts http://www.lib.rochester.edu/camelot/teamstmsmenu.htm (Large range of recently edited student editions, with introductions and notes.)

Labyrinth: Resources for Medieval Studies http://www.georgetown.edu/labyrinth/ (Good range of texts and plenty of secondary material, with links to modern studies and other national cultures.)

Anthologies

Burrow, J. A. (ed.), *English Verse 1300–1500* (London, 1977).

Burrow, J. A. and Turville-Petre, Thorlac (eds), *A Book of Middle English*, 2nd edn (1996). (Briefer excerpts, with good, mainly linguistic commentary.)

Pearsall, Derek (ed.), *Chaucer to Spenser. An Anthology* (Oxford, 1999). (A most useful and comprehensive collection of texts, with good annotation, lexical, textual and factual.)

General studies of the period

Anderson, Bonnie S. and Judith P. Zinsser, *A History of their Own. Women in Europe from Prehistory to the Present*, vols I–II (Harmondsworth, 1990).

Blake, N. F. (ed.), *The Cambridge History of the English Language*, vol. II: *1066–1476* (Cambridge, 1992). (An authoritative account of the linguistic developments during the Middle English period. Of particular interest: N. F. Blake, 'The Literary Language', pp. 500–41.)

Blamires, Alcuin (ed.), *Woman Defamed and Woman Defended. An Anthology of Medieval Texts* (Oxford, 1992). (A wide-ranging collection of texts on an old theme.)

Deanesly, Margaret, *The Lollard Bible and Other Medieval Versions* (Cambridge, 1920, repr. 1966).

Duffy, Eamon, *The Stripping of the Altars: Traditional Religion in England, 1400–1580* (New Haven, 1992). (A challenging study of orthodoxy, popular religion and unrest in late medieval England.)

Green, Richard Firth, *Poets and Princepleasers: Literature and the English Court in the Late Middle Ages* (Toronto, 1980). (An important account of the relationship between literature and court at the time of Chaucer and later.)

Harvey, Barbara, *Living and Dying in England: The Monastic Experience* (Oxford, 1993).

Horrox, Rosemary (ed.), *Fifteenth-Century Attitudes: Perceptions of society in late medieval England* (Cambridge, 1994). (Ten essays by different authors on various aspects of English culture and society.)

Hudson, Anne, *Lollards and Their Books* (London, 1985).

Hudson, Anne, *The Premature Reformation: Wycliffite Texts and Lollard History* (Oxford, 1988). (Seminal Study of an important area of Middle English literature.)

Keen, M. H., *England in the Later Middle Ages* (London, 1973).

Knowles, David, *The Religious Orders in England*, 3 vols (Cambridge, 1948–59). (An important handbook.)

Kratzmann, Gregory, *Anglo-Scottish Literary Relations 1430–1550* (Cambridge, 1980).

McFarlane, K. B., *Lancastrian Kings and Lollard Knights* (Oxford, 1972).

McKisack, May, *The Fourteenth Century, 1307–1399* (Oxford, 1959).

Myers, A. R., *England in the Late Middle Ages, 1307–1536*, Pelican History of England, vol. IV, rev. edn (Harmondsworth, 1961). (Useful survey of political and social history, including chapters on literature and art.)

Pantin, W. A., *The English Church in the Fourteenth Century* (Cambridge, 1955, repr. Toronto, 1980).

Pearsall, Derek and Salter, Elizabeth, *Landscapes and Seasons of the Medieval World* (London, 1973). (A splendidly illustrated discussion, ranging from classical traditions to Gavin Douglas.)

Scattergood, V. J. and Sherborne, J. W. (eds), *English Court Culture in the Later Middle Ages* (London, 1983). (An important collection of essays.)

Smalley, Beryl, *The Study of the Bible in the Middle Ages*, 3rd rev. edn (Oxford, 1963).

Stevens, John, *Words and Music in the Middle Ages: Song, Narrative, Dance and Drama, 1050–1350*, Cambridge Studies in Music (Cambridge, 1986).

Stevens, John, *Music and Poetry in the Early Tudor Court* (London, 1961; rev. edn Cambridge, 1979). (A particularly valuable and influential study.)

Medieval literature and literary theory

Boitani, Piero and Torti, Anna (eds), *Poetics: Theory and Practice in Medieval English Literature. The J. A. W. Bennett Memorial Lectures.* Seventh Series. Perugia, 1990 (Cambridge, 1991).

Carruthers, Mary J., *The Book of Memory: A Study of Memory in Medieval Culture*, Cambridge Studies in Medieval Literature, 10 (Cambridge, 1990). (A fascinating account of medieval attitudes towards memory, texts and transmission.)

Copeland, Rita, *Rhetoric, Hermeneutics, and Translation in the Middle Ages: Academic Traditions and Vernacular Texts* (Cambridge, 1991).

Ellis, Roger (ed.), *The Medieval Translator: The Theory and Practice of Translation in the Middle Ages* (Cambridge, 1989). (An interesting collection of essays by different authors.)

Gradon, Pamela, *Form and Style in Early English Literature* (London, 1971). (An important study of general concepts of Middle English literature, such as allegory, structures and realism.)

Griffiths, Jeremy and Pearsall, Derek (eds), *Book Production and Publishing in Britain 1375–1475* (Cambridge, 1989). (An important collection of essays by different authors on an often neglected subject.)

Lewis, C. S. *The Discarded Image. An Introduction to Medieval and Renaissance Literature* (Cambridge, 1964). (An excellent survey of basic texts and contexts.)

Machan, Tim William, *Textual Criticism and Middle English Texts* (Charlottesville, 1994). (An original and stimulating discussion of editorial problems, with particular application to Middle English texts.)

Minnis, A. J. and Brewer, Charlotte (eds), *Crux and Controversy in Middle English Textual Criticism* (Cambridge, 1992). (A useful collection of essays by various authors on editorial problems of Middle English Literature.)

Minnis, A. J. and Scott, A. B. (eds), *Medieval Literary Theory and Criticism c. 1100– c. 1375: The Commentary Tradition* (Oxford, 1988). (A valuable anthology of writings on literary theory in the Middle Ages, with extensive introductions.)

Patterson, Lee, *Negotiating the Past: The Historical Understanding of Medieval Literature* (Madison, 1987). (An important and stimulating series of chapters on literary theory and individual texts.)

English literary history

Aers, David, *Community, Gender, and Individual Identity: English Writing 1360–1430* (London, 1988). (Takes a new look at late Middle English literature in the light of recent developments in social, economic and cultural history.)

Aers, David (ed.), *Culture and History 1350–1600: Essays on English Communities, Identities, and Writing* (New York, 1992). (A very useful collection of essays on the wider contexts of literary history.)

Bennett, J. A. W., ed. and completed by Douglas Gray, *Middle English Literature, The Oxford History of English Literature*, vol. I, part II (Oxford, 1986). (A very useful account of Middle English writing from *The Owl and the Nightingale* to Langland, but excluding Chaucer, who is treated in an earlier volume of the series.)

Benson, C. David, *The History of Troy in Middle English Literature: Guido delle Colonne's Historia Destructionis Troiae in Medieval England* (Woodbridge, 1980).

Boitani, Piero, *English Medieval Narrative in the 13th and 14th Centuries* (Cambridge, 1982). (A valuable survey of Middle English narrative verse, culminating in Chaucer who occupies more than half of the book.)

Bolton, W. F., *The Middle Ages*, Sphere History of Literature in the English Language, vol. I, rev. edn (London, 1986). (Various good essays on different genres and authors.)

Burrow, John A., *Medieval Writers and Their Work. Middle English Literature and its Background 1100–1500* (Oxford, 1982). (A very helpful introduction, particularly to 'some of the chief differences which confront the reader of modern literature'.)

Burrow, John A., *Essays on Medieval Literature* (Oxford, 1984). (Stimulating essays on various Middle English authors and poems, most of them previously published.)

Burrow, John A., *Ricardian Poetry. Chaucer, Gower, Langland and the* Gawain *Poet* (London, 1971). (A challenging study of four authors and some common characteristics of their work.)

Finke, Laurie A., *Women's Writing in English: Medieval England* (London, 1999). (General account of the role of women in medieval English literature, society and some important women writers, e.g. Julian of Norwich, Margery Kempe and the Paston women.)

Ford, Boris (ed.), *Medieval Literature: Chaucer and the Alliterative Tradition*, The New Pelican Guide to English Literature, vol. I, part I (Harmondsworth, 1982). (Essays by different authors on Middle English literature, its background and individual works.)

Guddat-Figge, Gisela, *Catalogue of Manuscripts Containing Middle English Romances*, Texte und Untersuchungen zur Englischen Philologie (München, 1976). (A very useful description of manuscripts, most of which contain other material beside romances.)

Jack, R. D. S. (ed.), *The History of Scottish Literature*, vol. I: *Origins to 1660* (Medieval and Renaissance) (Aberdeen, 1988).

Legge, M. Dominica, *Anglo-Norman Literature and its Background* (Oxford, 1963). (A very useful account of an often neglected area.)

Lewis, C. S., *The Allegory of Love. A Study in Medieval Tradition* (Oxford, 1936; many times reprinted). (A true 'classic'. One of the most learned as well as elegant and stimulating accounts of a central theme in medieval literature, with chapters on the *Roman de la Rose*, Chaucer, Gower, Lydgate and others.)

Loomis, Roger Sherman, *Arthurian Literature in the Middle Ages* (Oxford, 1959). (A collaborative history by different authors.)

Meale, Carol M. (ed.), *Women and Literature in Britain, c. 1150–1500*, 2nd edn, Cambridge Studies in Medieval Literature, 17 (Cambridge, 1996). (An excellent collection of original essays by different scholars.)

Medcalf, Stephen (ed.), *The Later Middle Ages*, The Context of English Literature (London, 1981). (An interesting general account of the period, especially the cultural context.)

Oakden, J. P., *Alliterative Poetry in Middle English*, 2 vols (Manchester, 1930, 1935). (Ground-breaking study of Middle English alliterative poetry, more technical than critical.)

Owst, G. R., *Literature and Pulpit in Medieval England: A Neglected Chapter in the History of English Letters and of the English People*, 2nd edn (Oxford, 1961). (A seminal study of the debt of Middle English literature to the art of preaching and religious instruction.)

Pearsall, Derek, *Old English and Middle English Poetry*, The Routledge History of English Poetry (London, 1977). (A particularly stimulating account, taking special note of the historical context and of manuscript transmission.)

Reed, Thomas L., *Middle English Debate Poetry and the Aesthetics of Irresolution* (Columbia, 1990).

Salter, Elizabeth, *Fourteenth-Century English Poetry: Contexts and Readings*, ed. Derek Pearsall and Nicolette Zeeman (Oxford, 1983). (An original survey of fourteenth-century English writing.)

Salter, Elizabeth, *English and International: Studies in the Literature, Art and Patronage of Medieval England*, ed. Derek Pearsall and Nicolette Zeeman (Cambridge, 1988). (A collection of important essays, most of them previously published.)

Spearing, A. C., *Medieval Dream-Poetry* (Cambridge, 1976). (A helpful survey of an important subject.)

Spencer, H. Leith, *English Preaching in the Late Middle Ages* (Oxford, 1993).

Taylor, John, *English Historical Literature in the Fourteenth Century* (Oxford, 1987).

Turville-Petre, Thorlac, *The Alliterative Revival* (Cambridge, 1977).

Wallace, David (ed.), *The Cambridge History of Medieval English Literature* (Cambridge, 1999). (An authoritative and modern collaborative account of the period 1066–1547, not confined to the best-known and often studied authors and texts, but surveying the full historical and literary context.)

Wenzel, Siegfried, *Preachers, Poets and the Early English Lyric* (Princeton, 1986).

CHAUCER, Geoffrey (1340–1400)

Bibliography
Griffith, Dudley David, *Bibliography of Chaucer 1908–1953* (Seattle, 1955). (Attempts a complete listing of publications on Chaucer, without annotation; continued by Crawford, William E., *Bibliography of Chaucer 1954–63* [Seattle, 1967], Baird, Lorrayne Y., *A Bibliography of Chaucer 1964–1973* [Boston, MA, 1977], and Baird-Lange, Lorrayne Y. and Schnuttgen, Hildegard, *A Bibliography of Chaucer 1974–1985* [Hamden, CT, 1988]). See also the annual bibliographies in *Studies in the Age of Chaucer* (1979–), also accessible through the Internet (see the New Chaucer Society Web page: http://ncs.rutgers.edu).

Texts
Benson, Larry D. (ed.), *The Riverside Chaucer* (Boston, 1987). (Completely rev. from F. N. Robinson's edn (2nd edn, Boston, 1957). (Most frequently used and quoted edition of Chaucer's works, with generous commentary.)

Donaldson, E. Talbot (ed.), *Chaucer's Poetry: An Anthology for the Modern Reader*, 2nd edn (New York, 1975). (Omits the prose tales, but provides admirable commentary.)

Manly, John M. and Rickert, Edith (eds), *The Text of the Canterbury Tales*, 8 vols (Chicago, 1940). (A thorough account of all manuscripts, recording all variants; useful for reference.)

Ruggiers, Paul, G. (ed.), *A Variorum Edition of the Works of Geoffrey Chaucer* (Norman, Okla., 1983-). (A multi-volume edition in progress; an excellent example of a volume that provides a judicious conspectus of textual and critical issues is Derek Pearsall's edition of *The Nun's Priest's Tale* [Norman, OK, 1984].)

Windeatt, Barry, A. (ed.), Geoffrey Chaucer, *Troilus and Criseyde: A new edition of 'The Book of Troilus'* (London, 1984). (An invaluable edition of the poem, with excellent commentary and Boccaccio's *Il Filostrato* as parallel text where possible.)

Studies
Blake, Norman, E., *The Textual Tradition of the Canterbury Tales* (London, 1985). (A detailed and controversial account of the manuscript tradition and theories of the text's genesis.)

Boitani, Piero, *Chaucer and the Imaginary World of Fame* (Cambridge, 1984). (A wide-ranging study of the *House of Fame* and its background.)

Boitani, Piero (ed.), *Chaucer and the Italian Trecento* (Cambridge, 1983). (An invaluable collection of essays on Chaucer and Anglo-Italian literary relations in the fourteenth century.)

Boitani, Piero and Mann, Jill (eds), *The Cambridge Chaucer Companion* (Cambridge, 1986). (A useful collection of essays on important aspects of Chaucer's art.)

Brewer, Derek, *Chaucer: The Poet as Storyteller* (London, 1984). (A stimulating survey, one of a number of particularly useful books Brewer has written on various aspects of Chaucer.)

Brewer, Derek (ed.), *Chaucer and Chaucerians: Critical Studies in Middle English Literature* (London, 1966). (A valuable collection of essays by different authors on various aspects of Chaucer, including his immediate successors.)

Brewer, Derek (ed.), *Chaucer: The Critical Heritage*, 2 vols (London, 1978). (An indispensable collection of early responses to Chaucer.)

Brewer, Derek (ed.), *Writers and Their Background: Geoffrey Chaucer* (London, 1974). (A useful collection of essays by different authors on various aspects of Chaucer's art, his reading and the culture of his age.)

Bryan, W. F. and Dempster, Germaine (eds), *Sources and Analogues of Chaucer's Canterbury Tales* (1941; New York, 1958). (An indispensable collection of source texts.)

Burnley, David, *A Guide to Chaucer's Language* (London, 1983). (An excellent discussion of important issues connected with Chaucer's language and style.)

Cooper, Helen, *The Canterbury Tales*. Oxford Guides to Chaucer (Oxford, 1989). (Most useful and discriminating survey of problems, criticism and research.)

Crow, Martin M. and Olson, Clair C. (eds), *Chaucer Life-records* (Oxford, 1966). (Indispensable collection of records relating to Chaucer's life and political career.)

Donaldson, E. Talbot, *Speaking of Chaucer* (London, 1970). (Particularly stimulating and sometimes provocative collection of essays by Donaldson, most of them previously published.)

Donaldson, E. Talbot, *The Swan at the Well: Shakespeare Reading Chaucer* (New Haven, 1985). (A spirited study of Shakespeare's debt to Chaucer.)

Eckhardt, Caroline D., *Chaucer's General Prologue to the* Canterbury Tales*: An Annotated Bibliography 1900 to 1982*, The Chaucer Bibliographies (Toronto, 1990). (A comprehensive international bibliography, with reliable summaries; other volumes have already appeared or are in preparation.)

Kean, P. M., *Chaucer and the Making of English Poetry*, 2 vols (London, 1972). (A sensitive and wide-ranging survey.)

Lawton, David, *Chaucer's Narrators*, Chaucer Studies, 13 (Cambridge, 1985). (Excellent, stimulating discussion of an often debated problem.)

Mandel, Jerome, *Building the Fragments of the Canterbury Tales* (Cranbury, NJ, 1992).

Mann, Jill, *Chaucer and Medieval Estates Satire: The literature of social classes and the General Prologue to the* Canterbury Tales (Cambridge, 1973). Ground-breaking study of a much-discussed text.

Mann, Jill, *Geoffrey Chaucer*. Feminist Readings (Hemel Hempstead, 1991). (An assessment of Chaucer's portrayal of women.)

Mehl, Dieter, *Geoffrey Chaucer: an introduction to his narrative poetry* (Cambridge, 1986).

Minnis, A. J., *Chaucer and Pagan Antiquity*, Chaucer Studies, 8 (Cambridge, 1982). (A fine study of Chaucer's reading of classical literature and legend.)

Minnis, A. J., with Scattergood, V. J. and Smith, J. J., *The Shorter Poems*. Oxford Guides to Chaucer (Oxford, 1995). (The best survey of recent and established scholarship and criticism on the shorter poems.)

Muscatine, Charles, *Chaucer and the French Tradition* (Berkeley and Los Angeles, 1957). (One of the most influencial books on Chaucer's method and style.)

Nolan, Barbara, *Chaucer and the Tradition of the 'Roman Antique'* (Cambridge, 1992).

Patterson, Lee, *Chaucer and the Subject of History* (London, 1991).

Pearsall, Derek, *The Life of Geoffrey Chaucer. A Critical Biography* (Oxford, 1992). (By far the best critical biography of the poet.)

Pearsall, Derek, *The Canterbury Tales* (London, 1985). (One of the most helpful general treatments of the *Canterbury Tales*.)

Percival, Florence, *Chaucer's Legendary Good Women* (Cambridge, 1998). (A wide-ranging and sensible study of the *Legend of Good Women*.)

Prendergast, Thomas A. and Kline, Barbara (eds), *Rewriting Chaucer: Culture, Authority and the Idea of the Authentic Text 1400–1602* (Columbus, OH, 1999). (Collection of essays by various authors on the early transmission and adaptation of Chaucer's text.)

Robertson, D. W., *A Preface to Chaucer: Studies in Medieval Perspectives* (Princeton, 1962). (One of the most controversial and influential books on Chaucer's poetry and that of his time.)

Rowland, Beryl (ed.), *Companion to Chaucer Studies*, rev. edn (New York, Oxford, 1979). (Very useful collection of 22 articles by various authors, surveying the scholarship of important aspects of Chaucer's poetry.)

Spurgeon, Caroline F. E., *Five Hundred Years of Chaucer Criticism and Allusion, 1357–1900* (Cambridge, 1925). (A very useful collection of early references to Chaucer.)

Strohm, Paul, *Social Chaucer* (Cambridge, MA, 1989). (Important study of Chaucer's social position and audience and its implications for his poetry.)

Wallace, David, *Chaucerian Polity: Absolutist Lineages and Associational Forms in England and Italy* (Stanford, 1997). (Unconventional and thought-provoking look at Chaucer's poetics within a European context, particularly his association with the Italian Renaissance.)

Wimsatt, James I., *Chaucer and His French Contemporaries: Natural Music in the Fourteenth Century* (Toronto, 1991). (Comprehensive study of Chaucer's French contemporaries and their influence on his poetry.)

Windeatt, Barry A., *Troilus and Criseyde*, Oxford Guides to Chaucer (Oxford, 1992). (Thorough and judicious guide to the poem and most of its problems.)

GOWER, John (*c.* 1330–1408)

Texts

Macaulay, G, C. (ed.), *The English Works of John Gower*. Edited from the Manuscripts, with Introduction, Notes and Glossary, 2 vols, EETS, ES, 81, 82 (1900–1). (Still the standard edition.)

Bennett, J. A. W. (ed.), *Selections from John Gower*, Clarendon Medieval and Tudor Series (Oxford, 1968). (Useful selection, with good commentary.)

Studies

Echard, Siân and Fanger, Claire, *The Latin Verses in the* Confessio Amantis. *An Annotated Translation* (East Lansing, 1991). (Very useful collection, with a substantial preface by A. G. Rigg.)

Fisher, John H., *John Gower. Moral Philosopher and Friend of Chaucer* (New York, 1964). (Magisterial and indispensable study of the poet, in particular the historical context and literary relationships.)

Gallacher, Patrick J., *Love, the Word, and Mercury. A Reading of John Gower's* Confessio Amantis (Albuquerque, 1975). (Interesting study of the role of speech and word in the poem.)

Minnis, A. J. (ed.), *Gower's* Confessio Amantis. *Responses and Reassessments* (Cambridge, 1983). (Stimulating collection of new essays on various aspects of Gower's great English poem, attempting to dispell conventional prejudices and 'allow Gower the courage of all his convictions'.)

Nicholson, Peter, *An Annotated Index to the Commentary on Gower's* Confessio Amantis, Medieval and Renaissance Texts and Studies, 62 (Binghamton, NY, 1989). (Most useful line-by-line commentary, listing significant references to every passage from over 350 editions, books and articles.)

Nicholson, Peter (ed.), *Gower's* Confessio Amantis. *A Critical Anthology* (Cambridge, 1991). (Useful anthology of critical essays and chapters from books published between 1908 and 1982.)

Schmitz, Götz, the middel weie. *Stil und Aufbauformen in John Gowers 'Confessio Amantis'*, Studien zur englischen Literatur, 11 (Bonn, 1974). (Style and structure in the *Confessio*.)

Yeager, R. F., *John Gower's Poetic: The Search for a New Arion* (Cambridge, 1990). (Important and wide-ranging study of Gower's language, style and poetic techniques.)

LANGLAND, William

Texts

Schmidt, A. V. C. (ed.), William Langland, *The Vision of Piers Plowman. A Critical Edition of the B-Text Based on Trinity College, Cambridge, MS B.15.17*, 2nd edn (London, 1995). (The most useful and affordable student edition.)

Pearsall, Derek (ed.), *Piers Plowman by William Langland. An Edition of the C-Text* (London, 1978). (The best and most helpfully annotated edition of the C-Text.)

Schmidt, A. V. C. (ed.), William Langland, *Piers Plowman. A Parallel-Text Edition of the A, B, C and Z Versions*, vol. I: Text (London, 1995). (Very useful parallel edition of the four texts, though yet with no commentary.)

Kane, George (ed.), *Piers Plowman: The A Version* (London, 1960; 2nd edn, 1988).

Kane, George and Donaldson, E. T. (eds), *Piers Plowman: The B Version* (London, 1975; 2nd edn, 1988).

Russell, George and Kane, George (eds), *Piers Plowman: The C Version* (London, 1997). (The three volumes of the Kane edition are a monument of textual scholarship, with thorough examination of all the manuscripts; the editorial principles have been much debated.)

Rigg, A. G. and Brewer, Charlotte (eds.), *Piers Plowman: The Z-Version* (Toronto, 1983).

William Langland, *Piers the Plowman, Translated into modern English with an introduction*, by J. F. Goodridge, Penguin Classics (Harmondsworth, 1959; often reprinted). (Good modern translation, with useful commentary.)

William Langland, *Piers Plowman. A New Translation of the B-Text*, by A. V. C. Schmidt, The World's Classics (Oxford, 1992). (Very readable and thoughtful translation, with helpful introduction and commentary.)

Studies

Alford, John A. (ed.), *A Companion to* Piers Plowman (Berkeley, Los Angeles, London, 1988). (An excellent collection of essays, bringing together the essential information on most major aspects of Langland's poem.)

Baldwin, Anna P., *The Theme of Government in Piers Plowman*, Piers Plowman Studies, 1 (Cambridge, 1981).

Bloomfield, Morton W., *'Piers Plowman' as a Fourteenth-Century Apocalypse* (New Brunswick, 1961). (A seminal study of Langland and the apocalyptic tradition.)

Brewer, Charlotte, *Editing* Piers Plowman. *The evolution of the text.* Cambridge Studies in Medieval Literature, 28 (Cambridge, 1996). (Fascinating account of the editions and the editors of this puzzling text and its complex transmission.)

Du Boulay, F. R. H., *The England of* Piers Plowman: *William Langland and His Vision of the Fourteenth Century* (Cambridge, 1991).

Burrow, John A., *Langland's Fictions* (Oxford, 1993). (Particularly sensitive account of the poet's extraordinary 'fictive imagination'.)

Coleman, Janet, *Piers Plowman and the* Moderni (Rome, 1981). (An interesting account of some of the philosophical contexts of Langland's work.)

Donaldson, E. T., *'Piers Plowman': The C-Text and its Poet* (New Haven, 1949). (One of the best general accounts of the C-Text.)

Godden, Malcolm, *The Making of Piers Plowman* (London, 1990). (A sensible introduction to the poem, its structure and its most distinctive themes.)

Goldsmith, Margaret E., *The Figure of Piers Plowman: The Image on the Coin*, Piers Plowman Studies, 2 (Cambridge, 1981.)

Hussey, S. S. (ed.), *'Piers Plowman': Critical Approaches* (London, 1969). (A useful collection of previously unpublished essays.)

Kane, George, *Piers Plowman: The Evidence of Authorship* (London, 1965). (A cogent and convincingly argued presentation of the evidence for Langland's authorship of all three versions of *Piers Plowman*. A kind of preliminary statement to the groundbreaking Athlone edition [ed. George Kane].)

Middleton, Anne, 'Piers Plowman', in *A Manual of the Writings in Middle English 1050–1500*, ed. J. Burke Severs and Albert E. Hartung, vol. VII (New Haven, 1986), pp. 2211–34 and 2417–43. (A particularly helpful and discriminating account of Langland scholarship.)

Pearsall, Derek, *An Annotated Critical Bibliography of Langland* (Ann Arbor, 1990). (An indispensable guide to research, critically annotated and judiciously selective.)

Simpson, James, *Piers Plowman. An Introduction to the B-Text* (London, 1990). (A stimulating introduction to the poem within the context of the literary and cultural history of the later English Middle Ages.)

Vasta, Edward (ed.), *Interpretations of Piers Plowman* (Notre Dame, 1968). (A good collection of 'classic' critical accounts.)

THE *GAWAIN*-POET

Texts
Andrews, Malcolm and Waldron, Ronald (eds), *The Poems of the Pearl Manuscript* (London, 1978, rev. edn, Exeter, 1987). (Reliable edition of the four poems.)

Gollancz, Sir Israel (ed.), *Pearl, Cleanness, Patience and Sir Gawain, facsimile of British Museum MS Cotton Nero A. x.*, EETS, 162 (1923, repr. 1971).

Tolkien, J. R. R. and Gordon, E. V. (eds), *Sir Gawain and the Green Knight*, rev. Norman Davis (Oxford, 1967). (The 'classic' edition of this poem, with good notes and commentary.)

Studies
Andrew, Malcolm, *The Gawain-Poet: An Annotated Bibliography, 1839–1977* (New York, 1979.)

Blanch, Robert J., *Sir Gawain and the Green Knight: A Reference Guide* (Troy, New York, 1983). (A full annotated bibliography up to 1978.)

Brewer, Derek and Gibson, Jonathan (eds), *A Companion to the Gawain-Poet*. Arthurian Studies, 38 (Cambridge, 1997). (A particularly valuable collection of new essays on many central aspects of this author.)

Burrow, John A., *A Reading of* Sir Gawain and the Green Knight (London, 1965). (Still one of the most sensible and helpful introductions to the poem.)

Davenport, W. A., *The Art of the Gawain-Poet* (London, 1978).

Lecklider, Jane K., Cleanness: *Structure and Meaning* (Cambridge, 1997). (A thorough and helpful investigation into the liturgical and exegetical traditions behind the poet's use of biblical passages and their manuscript dissemination.)

Putter, Ad, *An Introduction to the* Gawain-Poet (Harlow, 1996). (A stimulating, fresh introduction to the poems of the *Gawain*-manuscript and their background.)

Spearing, A. C., *The Gawain-Poet. A Critical Study* (Cambridge, 1970). (A sensible reading of the four poems ascribed to the *Gawain*-Poet.)

LYDGATE, John (*c.* 1370–1450)

Texts

Bergen, H. (ed.), *Lydgate's Troy Book, EETS, ES*, 97 (1906), 103 (1906), 106 (1910), 126 (1935, for 1920).

Bergen, H. (ed.), *Lydgate's Fall of Princes, EETS, ES*, 121–4 (1918–19).

Erdmann, Axel (ed.), *Lydgate's Siege of Thebes, EETS, ES*, 108 (1911) and (ed. A. Erdmann and E. Ekwall) 125 (1930).

Furnivall, F. J. (ed.), *The Pilgrimage of the Life of Man*, translated by John Lydgate, *EETS, ES*, 77 (1899), 83 (1901), (Introduction, notes, glossary by K. B. Locock) 92 (1904); repr. as one volume 1973.

MacCracken, H. N. (ed.), John Lydgate, *The Minor Poems*, Part I, *EETS, ES*, 107 (1911).

Norton-Smith, John (ed.), John Lydgate, *Poems*, Clarendon Medieval and Tudor Series (Oxford, 1966). (Useful selection, with good commentary.)

Studies

Pearsall, Derek, *John Lydgate*, Medieval Authors (London, 1970). (Fullest and most stimulating account of the poet, his work and his environment.)

Schirmer, Walter F., *John Lydgate. A Study in the Culture of the XVth Century*, trans. Ann E. Keep (London, 1961; first published in German 1952). (A sensible and detailed study.)

HOCCLEVE, Thomas (*c.* 1368–*c.* 1437)

Texts

Blyth, Charles R. (ed.), Thomas Hoccleve, *The Regiment of Princes*, Middle English Texts (Kalamazoo, Michigan, 1999). (A useful edition, 'designed for classroom use'.)

Burrow, J. A. (ed.), *Thomas Hoccleve's Complaint and Dialogue, EETS*, 313 (1999). (Text re-edited and fully annotated; with good up-to-date bibliography.)

Furnivall, Frederick, J. (ed.), *Hoccleve's Works*, I: *The Minor Poems, EETS, ES*, 61 (1892), rev. by J. Mitchell and A. I. Doyle, reissued in one volume with part II (1970).

240

Furnivall, Frederick, J. (ed.), *Hoccleve's Works*, III: *The Regement of Princes, EETS, ES,* 72 (1897).

Seymour, M. C. (ed.), *Selections from Hoccleve* (Oxford, 1981). (Useful and well annotated selection.)

Studies

Burrow, J. A., *Thomas Hoccleve* (Aldershot, Hants., 1994), reissued as *English Writers of the Late Middle Ages*, ed. M. C. Seymour, Authors of the Middle Ages, I, 1–4 (Aldershot, Hants., 1994), pp. 185–248). (Brief, stimulating introduction, with valuable bibliography.)

Mitchell, Jerome, *Thomas Hoccleve. A Study in Early Fifteenth-Century Poetic* (Urbana, 1968).

THE MIDDLE ENGLISH LYRIC

Texts

Arn, M.-J., *Fortunes Stabilness: Charles of Orleans's English Book of Love*, Medieval and Renaissance Texts and Studies (Binghamton, 1994).

Brook, G. L. (ed.), *The Harley Lyrics. The Middle English Lyrics of MS Harley 2253* (Manchester, 1948).

Brown, Carleton (ed.), *English Lyrics of the XIIIth Century* (Oxford, 1932).

Brown, Carleton (ed.), *Religious Lyrics of the XIVth Century.* 2nd edn, rev. by G. V. Smithers (Oxford, 1957).

Brown, Carleton (ed.), *Religious Lyrics of the XVth Century* (Oxford, 1939).

Davies, R. T. (ed.), *Medieval English Lyrics. A Critical Anthology* (London, 1963). (A fine anthology, with useful introduction and commentary.)

Greene, Richard Leighton (ed.), *Early English Carols* (Oxford, 1935).

Greene, Richard Leighton (ed.), *A Selection of English Carols*, Clarendon Medieval and Tudor Series (Oxford, 1962). (Selection from Greene's earlier collection, with a very useful introduction and commentary.)

Robbins, Rossell Hope (ed.), *Secular Lyrics of the XIVth and XVth Centuries*, 2nd edn (Oxford, 1955).

Robbins, Rossell Hope (ed.), *Historical Poems of the XIVth and XVth Centuries* (New York, 1959). (A particularly useful anthology.)

Steele, R. and Day, M. (ed.), *Charles of Orleans: The English Poems, EETS,* 215, 220 (1941, 1946; reprinted 1970).

Studies

Gray, Douglas, *Themes and Images in the Medieval English Religious Lyric* (London, 1972). (Sensible and useful account of the various forms of Middle English religious lyrics and their development.)

Woolf, Rosemary, *The English Religious Lyric in the Middle Ages* (Oxford, 1968). (Full and sensitive discussion of many aspects.)

MIDDLE SCOTS LITERATURE

Texts

Bawcutt, Priscilla and Riddy, Felicity (eds), *Longer Scottish Poems,* vol. I: 1375–1650 (Edinburgh, 1987). (Excellent anthology of many otherwise hardly accessible texts, with useful commentary.)

Bawcutt, Priscilla (ed.), *The Poems of William Dunbar*, 2 vols, published by the Association for Scottish Literary Studies, 27–8 (Glasgow, 1998).

Coldwell, David F. C. (ed.), *Vergil's Aeneid Translated into Scottish Verse by Gavin Douglas*, Scottish Text Society, 4 vols (Edinburgh, 1957–64).

Fox, Denton (ed.), *The Poems of Robert Henryson* (Oxford, 1981).

Gopen, George D. (ed.) *The Moral Fables of Aesop* by Robert Henryson: *An Edition of the Middle Scots Text, with a Facing Prose Translation, Introduction, and Notes* (Notre Dame, IN, 1987).

Kindrick, Robert L. (ed.), *The Poems of Robert Henryson*, Middle English Texts (Kalamazoo, Michigan, 1997). (Students' Edition.)

Kinghorn, A. M. (ed.), *The Middle Scots Poets*, York Medieval Texts (London, 1970). (Very useful anthology with notes.)

Kinsley, James (ed.), *The Poems of William Dunbar* (Oxford, 1979).

Norton Smith, John (ed.), James I of Scotland, *The Kingis Quair*, Clarendon Medieval and Tudor Series (Oxford, 1971).

Small, John (ed.), *The Poetical Works of Gavin Douglas*, 4 vols (Edinburgh, 1874).

Tasioulas, J. A. (ed.), *The Makars: The Poems of Henryson, Dunbar and Douglas*, Canongate Classics, 88 (Edinburgh, 1999). (A useful collection, with introduction and notes for the non-specialist.)

Studies

Bawcutt, Priscilla, *Dunbar the Makar* (Oxford, 1992). (Excellent general account of Dunbar's life and writings.)

Bawcutt, Priscilla, *Gavin Douglas: A Critical Study* (Edinburgh, 1976). (Perceptive account of Douglas's career and writings, in particular his translation of the Aeneid.)

Gray, Douglas, *Robert Henryson*, Medieval and Renaissance Authors (Leiden, 1979). (Useful study of the poet and his literary achievement.)

Ridley, Florence H., 'Middle Scots Writers', in *A Manual of the Writings in Middle English 1050–1500*, iv, ed. Albert E. Hartung (New Haven, 1973), pp. 961–1060, 1123–284. (Thorough account of scholarship on the chief Middle Scots writers.)

MIDDLE ENGLISH PROSE

Studies

Edwards, A. S. G. (ed.), *Middle English Prose: A Critical Guide to Major Authors and Genres* (New Brunswick, 1984). (An indispensable guide.)

Fowler, David C., *John Trevisa* (Aldershot, Hants.,1993), re-issued as part of *English Writers of the Late Middle Ages*, ed. M. C. Seymour, Authors of the Middle Ages, I, 1–4 (Aldershot, Hants., 1994), pp. 65–126.

Mandeville's Travels

Texts

Seymour, M. C. (ed.), *Mandeville's Travels* (Oxford, 1967). (Standard edition of one of the best and fullest texts, BL MS Cotton Titus C.xvi.)

Seymour, M. C. (ed.), *The Bodley Version of Mandeville's Travels, EETS*, 253 (1963). (Critical edition of a shorter version in Bodley MS e Musaeo 116.)

Seymour, M. C. (ed.), *The Metrical Version of Mandeville's Travels*, EETS, 269 (1973). (Critical edition of the metrical version preserved in the Coventry Corporation Record Office.)

Studies

Higgins, Iain Macleod, *Writing East: The 'Travels of Sir John Mandeville'* (Philadelphia, 1997).

Seymour, M. C., *Sir John Mandeville* (Aldershot, Hants, 1993), reissued as part of. *English Writers of the Late Middle Ages*, ed. M. C. Seymour, Authors of the Middle Ages, I, 1–4 (Aldershot, Hants., 1994), pp. 1–64. (Brief, useful introduction, with valuable bibliography of manuscripts, prints and secondary material.)

The Middle English Mystics

Texts

Windeatt, Barry (ed.), *English Mystics of the Middle Ages* (Cambridge, 1994). (A valuable collection of texts, newly edited from the manuscripts, with useful commentary and bibliography.)

Hodgson, Phyllis (ed.), *The Cloud of Unknowing* and *The Book of Privy Counselling*, EETS, 218 (1948).

Hodgson, Phyllis (ed.), Deonise Hid Diuinite *and Other Treatises on Contemplative Prayer Related to* The Cloud of Unknowing, EETS, 231 (1955)

Wolters, Clifton (trans.), *The Cloud of Unknowing* (Harmondsworth, 1961). (A translation into modern English.)

Walter Hilton, *The Scale of Perfection*, ed. Evelyn Underhill (London, 1923).

Sherley-Price, Leo (trans.), *The Ladder of Perfection* (Harmondsworth, 1957).

Julian of Norwich, *Julian of Norwich's Revelations of Divine Love. (The Shorter Version)*, ed. Frances Beer, Middle English Texts, 8 (Heidelberg, 1978). (Good critical edition, with useful commentary an annotation).

Julian of Norwich, *A Book of Showings to the Anchoress Julian of Norwich*, ed. E. Colledge and J. Walsh, 2 vols (Toronto, 1978). (Critical edition of the Paris manuscript, with useful introduction.)

Julian of Norwich, *The Shewings of Julian of Norwich*, ed. Georgia Ronan Crampton (Kalamazoo, Michigan, 1994). (Annotated edition of the longer version, from MS Sloane 2499, with useful introduction and notes.)

Julian of Norwich, *A Revelation of Love*, ed. Marion Glasscoe, Exeter Medieval Texts (Exeter, 1976, rev. edn, 1986). (Annotated edition of the longer version, from MS Sloane 2499.)

Julian of Norwich, *Julian of Norwich: Revelations of Divine Love and The Motherhood of God*, ed. Frances Beer (Woodbridge, 1999). (A translation of the short version, including some chapters from the longer version on the Motherhood of God, with an introduction on Julian within the context of the mystical tradition and an Intepretative Essay.)

Julian of Norwich, *Revelations of Divine Love*, translated into modern English and with an introduction by Clifton Wolters (Harmondsworth, 1966).

Studies

Abbott, Christopher, *Julian of Norwich: Autobiography and Theology* (Woodbridge, 1999). (An exploration of Julian as a lay person writing from her own experience and the character of her theology.)

Baker, Denise Nowakowski, *Julian of Norwich's Showings: From Vision to Book* (Princeton, NJ, 1994). (On the intellectual background and the transformation of the short text into the longer version.)

Glasscoe, Marion, *English Medieval Mystics: Games of Faith* (London, 1993).

Glasscoe, Marion (ed.), *The Medieval Mystical Tradition in England*. 5 vols (Exeter, 1980, 1982; Cambridge, 1984, 1987, 1992). (Collections mostly of conference papers on various *Lollard* topics in connection with English mystical writing.)

Knowles, David, *The English Mystical Tradition* (London, 1961).

Milosh, Joseph E., *The Scale of Perfection and the English Mystical Tradition* (Madison, 1966).

Riehle, Wolfgang, *The Middle English Mystics* (London, 1981). (A study of Middle English mystical writing, with particular emphasis on style and the use of metaphor.)

The Book of Margery Kempe

Texts
Meech, Sanford Brown and Allen, Hope Emily (eds), *The Book of Margery Kempe*, EETS, 212 (1940). (Critical edition with commentary and glossary.)

Windeatt, Barry (ed.), *The Book of Margery Kempe*, Longman Annotated Texts (Harlow, 2000). (Critical edition, with generous annotation and full bibliography.)

Windeatt, Barry (trans.), *The Book of Margery Kempe* (Harmondsworth, 1985, with revised bibliography, 1994). (A helpful modern version, with good introduction.)

Studies
Staley, L., *Margery Kempe's Dissenting Fictions* (Philadelphia, 1994).

Tanner, N. P., *The Church in Late Medieval Norwich, 1370–1532* (Toronto, 1984). (Close study of a particular regional religious climate.)

Sir Thomas Malory (c. 1416–71)

Texts
Malory, Sir Thomas, *The Works of Sir Thomas Malory*, ed. Eugène Vinaver, 3rd edn, rev. P. J. C. Field, 3 vols (Oxford, 1990). (Critical edition, based on the Winchester manuscript.)

Malory, Sir Thomas, *Works*, ed. Eugène Vinaver, 2nd edn (Oxford, 1971). (Good one-volume edition of the Winchester text.)

Malory, Sir Thomas, *Le Morte D'arthur*, ed. Janet Cowen, with introduction by John Lawlor, 2 vols (Harmondsworth, 1969). (Complete text, based on Caxton's edition of 1485.)

Studies
Archibald, Elizabeth and Edwards, A. S. G. (eds), *A Companion to Malory*, Arthurian Studies, 37 (Cambridge, 1996). (A helpful collection of essays by various authors on many aspects of Malory's art and its critical reception.)

Benson, Larry D., *Malory's Morte Darthur* (Cambridge, MA, and London, 1976).

Field, P. J. C., *The Life and Times of Sir Thomas Malory*, Arthurian Studies, 29 (Cambridge, 1993). (A thorough study of the extant documents and inferences about Malory's life and environment.)

Field, P. J. C., *Romance and Chronicle: A Study of Malory's Prose Style* (London, 1971). (A valuable investigation into Malory's style.)

Lambert, Mark, *Malory: Style and Vision in* Le Morte Darthur, Yale Studies in English, 186 (New Haven, 1975). (A stimulating and original study of Malory's style and vision.)

Mann, Jill, *The Narrative of Distance, The Distance of Narrative in Malory's* Morte Darthur, The William Matthews Lectures 1991 (London, 1991). (A detailed examination of Malory's narrative method.)

Takamiya, Toshiyuki and Brewer, Derek, eds, *Aspects of Malory* (Cambridge, 1981, rev. 1986). (An important collection of essays, with a bibliography by T. Takamiya, pp. 179–93.)

Index

Note: *Bracketed page-numbers refer to bibliographical entries in the notes*

Adams, Robert (105)
Aers, David (105)
Aesop 176–7, 178
Alein de Lille (Alanus ab Insulis) 17, 56
  De Planctu Naturae 88, 176, 184
Alford, John A. (105)
Allegory *87–102*
Allen, Hope Emily (220), (221)
Alliterative Morte Arthur, see Morte Arthur,
Ancrene Riwle 195, (218)
Andrew, Malcolm (124), 125, 126
Anglo-Norman 1, (6)
Animal Fable 46–7, 51, *170–81*, 191
Anne Boleyn 164
Archibald, Elizabeth (222)
Arn, M.-J. (170)
Arthour and Merlin 2, (6)
Arthur, King of Britain 68, *212–17*, 222–7
Arundel, Archbishop 194–5
Ascenius 187
Augustine, Church-Father 35–6
Austen, Jane
  Mansfield Park 25, 56
  Northanger Abbey 74, (79)

Baldwin, Anna (105)
Barber, Richard (223)
Barker-Benfield, B. C. (6), (191)
Barney, Stephen A.
Barron, W. R. J. (125), 213, 222, (223)
Bartholomaeus Anglicus
  De Proprietatibus Rerum 128, 176, 194
Bawcutt, Priscilla (190), (192), 193
Beer, Frances (220)
Bennett, J. A. W. (77), (170), (221), (222)
Benson, C. David (59), (104), 136, 152–3, (223)
Benson, Larry D. (6), (55), (125), (192), (222)
Bergen, H. (152), 153
Bible 46
  Book of Daniel 65, 70
  1 Corinthians 107
  Jonah 109–16, 124

Psalms 97, 107
Revelation 106
St John 165, (172)
St Luke 113, 202, 220
St Matthew 94, 101–2, 107, 110–11, 113, 124
Blake, Norman (57), (58)
Blamires, Alcuin (57), (192)
Blanch, Robert J. (125)
Blanchfield, Lynne (104)
Bloomfield, Morton W. (78)
Boccaccio, Giovanni 10–11, 17
  Decameron 37, 39–40, 43, 50, 57, 59
  De Casibus Virorum Illustrium 53, *141*
  Filocolo
  Il Filostrato 23–32, 136
  De Mulieribus Claris 34
  Teseida 32, 41
Boece (Boethius) 46, 53, 154, 174, 182
  Consolatio Philosophiae 3, 8, 12–13, 28, 30 65, 88, 116
Boffey, Julia (6), (190), (191)
Boitani, Piero (6), (55), (56), (57), (191)
Book of Margery Kempe 6, 201, 202, 205, *207–11*, 221
Book of Privy Counselling 202
Brewer, Charlotte (7), (104), 105
Brewer, Derek S. (55), 108, (124), (190), (222)
Broich, Ulrich (77)
Brook, G. L. 158, (170), 171
Brown, Carleton (170), 171
Bryan, W. F. (54), (57), (78)
Bullough, Geoffrey (54), (79)
Bunyan, John
  Pilgrim's Progress 87, 98
Burke, John J., Jr. (57)
Burrow, John (56), (78), 84, 106, 107, 108, (124), 125, 155, 191, (218)

Calin, William (58)
Campbell, Lily B. (154)
Carley, James P. (223)
carol *161–4*, (170)
Catherine of Arragon, English Queen 163

Caxton, William 8, 22, 187, 201, 207, 212, 215, 222, 224
Charles, Duke of Orleans 160, (170)
Chaucer, Geoffrey 1–6, *8–59*, 60, 62, 64, 70, 77, 80, 97, 108, 119, 127, 128, 129–32, 133, 139, 146, 150, 151, 154, 155, 174–5, 176, 180, 184, 185, 188, 219, 224–5, 226
   Book of the Duchess 14–16, 30, 78, 125, 128, 129, 149
   'Canon Yeoman's Tale' 42
   Canterbury Tales 5, 32, *36–54*, 62, 72, 133, 139–40, 169, 176
   'Clerk's Prologue' 164
   'Clerk's Tale' 43, 50, 52, 53
   'Cook's Tale' 41, 43, 49, 50
   'Friar's Tale' 43–4
   'Franklin's Tale' 47–8, 49
   'General Prologue' 37–8, 54
   House of Fame 9, 16, *19–22*, 23, 27, 34, 35, 138, 190
   'Knight's Tale' 40, 49, 58, 133, 140, 174, 224
   Legend of Good Women 11–12, 31, *32–6*, 38–9, 51, 133, 142–3, 188, 190, 191
   'Man of Law's Prologue and Tale' 45–6, 52, 71–2
   'Man of Law's Epilogue' 105
   'Merchant's Tale' 47, 50–1, 138, 152, 171, 185
   'Miller's Prologue' 37, 47
   'Miller's Tale' 36, 40, 41, 43, 44, 49
   'Monk's Prologue and Tale' 32, 42, 53, 142
   'Nun's Priest's Tale' 36, 46–7, 51, 115, 176
   Parliament of Fowls 16–19, 176
   'Pardoner's Prologue' 90, 198
   'Parson's Prologue' 54
   'Parson's Tale' 36, 40, 53, 65
   'Physicians Tale' 52–3
   'Prioress' Tale' 51–2
   'Reeve's Tale' 40, 43, 44, 49–50
   'Retraction' 13, 47, 54, 64, 76, 158
   'Second Nun's Tale' 51
   'Squier's Tale' 49
   'Summoner's Tale' 43, 191
   'Tale of Melibee' 36, 38, 44–5, 53
   'Tale of Sir Thopas' 42, 44, 45, 49
   'To Rosemounde' *158–9*
   'Troilus and Criseyde' 3, 13, 18, *22–32*, 33, 53, 60, 78, 128, 133, 136, 138, 139, 149, 153, 155, 174, 181–3, 185, 191–2, 216, 224

'Wife of Bath's Prologue' 41–2, 148, 185
'Wife of Bath's Tale' 68, 224
Childs, Wendy (6)
Christine de Pisan (55)
   Epistre au Dieu d'Amours 155
Clemen, Wolfgang 2, (55)
Cloud of Unknowing 2, 202–3, 204, 205
Col, Pierre 12
Coldwell, David F. C. 199
Coleman, Janet (106)
Colledge, Edmund (220)
Cooper, Helen (57), 140, 153
Courtly Love 18, 25–7, 123, 129–32, 133, 159
Crampton, Georgia Ronan (220), (221)
Crane, Susan (6)
Crow, Martin M. (55)
Cutler, John L. (171)

Damico, Helen (153)
Dante Alighieri 10–11, 34, 44, 154
   Divina Commedia 21, 53, 104
Davenport, W. A. (124–5)
David, Alfred (170)
Davis, Norman (124), (170), (218)
Davies, R. T. (170), 171
Day, Mabel (170)
Deanesley, Margaret (218)
Dearmer, Percy (171)
Deguileville, Guilaume, *Pélerinage de la Vie Humaine* 140
Delany, Sheila (56)
Delveccio, Doreen (78)
Dempster, Germaine (54), (57), (78)
Deschamps, Eustache (55)
Destruction of Troy (allterative)
Dickens, Charles, *The Mystery of Edwin Drood* 36
Dickins, Bruce (192)
Diensberg, Bernhard (218)
Diller, Hans Jürgen (77)
Donaldson, E. Talbot (56), (58), (104), (226)
Douglas, Gavin 173, *186–90*
   Enead 186–90, 224
   Palace of Honour 190
dream vision 116–19, 123, 189, 190
Dronke, Peter (107)
Dryden, John 41, 58
Du Boulay, F. R. H. (105)
Duggan, Hoyt N. (7), (105)
Dunbar, William 173, *183–6*
   Goldyn Targe 184–5, 190
   Tretis of Two Married Women 185–6

Echard, Siân (77)
Edward II, King of England 172
Edward III, King of England 10
Edward IV, King of England 212
Edwards, A: S. G. (6), (124), (190), (191), (218), 222, (223)
Edwards, Elizabeth (223)
Ekwall, A. (153)
Eliot, T. S.
    Four Quartets 221
Ellis, Roger (218)
English language 1, 4, 63, 135, 152, 194
Erdmann, Axel (153)
Esch, Arno (78)

fabliau 37, 49–51
Fanger, Claire (77)
Farnham, Willard (154)
Field, P. J. C. 222, (223)
fin amour see Courtly love
Fisher, John H. 70, 77
Fletcher, John 41, (225)
Foakes, R. A. 8, (54)
Forester, Richard 60
Fowler, David C. (105), 218
Fox, Denton (6), 181, 183, (190), 191
Fox, J. (170)
Frank, Robert Worth (57)
French language 1, 135, 152, 160, 194, 195, 196, 197, 219
friars 164, 168–9, 180
Froissart, Jean (55)
Furnivall, Frederick J. (58), 141, 153, (155)

Gawain-Poet 3, *108–126*
    Cleanness 113–16, 123
    Patience 109, *110–13*, 114, 116, 119, 123
    Pearl 104, 109, *116–19*, 123
    Purity, see Cleanness
    Sir Gawain and the Green Knight 3, 109, *119–23*, 125–6, 161
Gest Hystoriale of the Destruction of Troy 3, 152–3
Gibson, Jonathan 124
Gillespie, Vincent (219)
Glasscoe, Marion (220)
Godden, Malcolm (105), 106
Godfrey of Viterbo
    Pantheon 69, 79
Göller, Karl Heinz (222)
Goldsmith, Margaret E. (106)
Gollancz, Sir Israel (155)
Goodridge, J. F. (104)

Gopen, George D. (191)
Gordon, E. V. (124)
Goundolf, Anne 60
Gower, John 2, 3–4, 6, *60–79*, 127, 143, 146, 150, 158, 172, 174, 185
    Confessio Amantis 4, 45, 60, 61 *62–77*
    Mirrour de l'omme (Speculum hominis) 61
    Vox Clamantis 61
Gray, Douglas 164, 171, 172, 191, 221
Greene, Richard Leighton 161–2, (170), (172)
Griffiths, Jeremy (7), (219)
Gualterus Anglicus 177
Guddat-Figge, Gisela (7)
Guido delle Colonne
    Historia Destructionis Troiae 128, 135, 136, 137–8, 152–3
Guillaume de Lorris *see Roman de la Rose*

Hammond, Antony (78)
Hammond, Eleanor P. (154)
Hanna, Ralph III (106), 192
Havely, N. R. (56)
Hellinga, Lotte (222)
Henry IV, King of England 10, 60, 62, 128
Henry V, King of England 128, 135, 139, 141, 168
Henry VI, King of England 128, 141, 144, 145, 150, 168
Henry VIII, King of England 164, 186
Henryson, Robert 173, *176–83*
    Moral Fables 176–81, 189
    Orpheus and Euridice 183
    Testament of Cresseid 3, *181–3*, 191–2, 224
Herman, John P. (57)
Heyworth, P. L. (107)
Hibbard, Laura *see* Loomis
Higden, Ranulf
    Polychronicon 194
Hilton, Walter 2, 220
    The Scale of Perfection 203–5
Historia Apolonii Tyrii
Hoccleve, Thomas (55), *146–51*, 172, 224
    Complaint 147, (155)
    Dialogue 147
    'La Male Regle de T. Hoccleve' 147
    Letter of Cupid to Lovers 148, 155
    Regement of Princes 146, *149–51*, 155
    Series 147–9
Hodgson, Phyllis (220)
Holland, Richard
    Buke of the Howlat 175–6

Homer 23
  Iliad 58
Hopkins, Andrea (125)
Horace 128
Houswitschka, Christoph (223)
Howard, Donald (58)
Hudson, Anne (218)
Humphrey, Duke of Gloucester 4, 7, 141, 142, 143, 144, 145, 146
Hussey, S. S. (106)

Isidore of Seville, *Etymologiae* 99–100
Italy 1
Ives, Carolyn (190)

James the First, King of Scotland
  Kingis Quair 173–5
James II, King of Scotland
James IV, King of Scotland 173, 186
Jean de Meun 55
  see also *Roman de la Rose*
Jenkins, Priscilla 106
Joan of Beaufort 174
Joan, Countess of Westmoreland
John of Gaunt, Duke of Lancaster 14
Julian of Norwich 201, 202, *205–7*, 210, (220–1)
Justice, Steven (218)

Kane, George 81, (104), 105, 106
Kean, Patricia M. (56), (59)
Keen, M. H. (7)
Kempe, Margery see *Book of Margery Kempe*
Kennedy, E. D. (218)
Ker, N. R. (222)
Kerby-Fulton, Kathryn 82, 105
King Horn 158
Kinghorn, A. M. (190)
Kinsley, James (192)
Kirkpatrick, Robin (56), (58)
Kiser, Lisa J. (56)
Kline, Barbara 190, (225)
Knott, T. A. (105)
Kolve, V. A. (57)
Krása, Josef (219)

Lambert, Mark 223
Langland, William 81–3, 85, 95, 108, 202, 203, 206, 219
  Piers Plowman 2, 3, 5, 62, *80–107*, 111, 163, 169, 198, 202
Language, see English, French, Latin language

Latin language 1, 77, 78, 91, 135, 152, 164–6, 187–8, 193, 195, 196, 201, 219
Laud Troy Book 152–3
Laurence de Premierfait 142
Lawrence, D. H.
  Lady Chatterley's Lover 81
Lawton, David (55)
Lecklider, Jane K. 113, (124)
Lewis, C. S. (78), 152, 226
Legge, M. Dominica (6)
Le Morte Arthur (stanzaic) 213, 215
Le Suite de Merlin (French) 213
Livy (Livius) 35, 52
Locock, K. B.
Lollards 82–3, 142, 145–6, 154, 155–6, 168–9, 201, 203, 206, 209, 210, 219
Loomis, Laura Hibbard (7), (58)
Lumiansky, R. M. (222)
Lydgate, John 4, 6, 8, *127–46*, 159, 172, 174, 178, 224
  Complaint of a Loveres Lyfe 128–32
  'Defence of Holy Church' 145
  Fall of Princes 135, *141–4*
  Mumming at Windsor 145
  Pilgrimage of the Life of Man 140–1
  Siege of Thebes 135, *139–40*
  Temple of Glass 133–5
  Troy Book 128, *135–9*, 141
  lyrics *157–72*

Macaulay, G. C. (7), 61, (77)
MacCracken, H. N. 144, (1515), 154
Machan, Tim William (7), (105)
Machaut, Guillaume de 55, 160
Mackenzie, W. Mackay (192)
Macrae-Gibson, O. D. (6)
Macrobius 46
Malory, Sir Thomas 6, *211–17*, 222–3
  Morte Darthur 211–17, 222–3
Mandel, Jerome (57)
Mandeville's Travels 195–201, 209
Mann, Jill (56), 105, 106, (223)
Mantuanus, Baptista 225
Manuscripts 4–5, 80–2, 157–8, 160, 164
  Aberystwyth: National Library of Wales, MS Peniarth 392D (Hengwrt) 47, 58
  Auchinleck, *see* Edinburgh
  London:
  British Library, Additional 24189: 218–19
  British Library, Additional 37790: 220
  British Library, Additional 59678 (Winchester MS) 222

British Library, Cotton Nero A.x: 108, 109, (124)
British Library, Cotton Titus C.xvi: 219
British Library, Harley 674: 220
British Library, Harley 978: 157
British Library, Harley 2253: 157-8, 167, 168
British Library, Harley 4866: 155
British Library, Sloane 2593: 171
Cambridge:
University L. Ee. 1.12: 165
University L. Ff .5.48: 172
Durham:
University L. Cosin V.iii.9: (155)
Edinburgh:
National Library of Scotland, Advocates 1.1.6 (Bannatyne) 184, 191
National Library of Scotland, Advocates 19.2.1 (Auchinleck) 2
National Library of Scotland, Advocates 19.3.1: 165, (172)
National Library of Scotland, provisional shelf-mark: Acc. 4233 (Asloan) 191
Ellesmere, *see* San Marino
Lincoln Cathedral 132: 161
Manchester: Rylands L., Lat. MS 395: 172
Oxford:
Bodleian L. Arch. Selden. B.24: 6
Bodleian L. Douce 322: 164
Bodleian L. e. Musaeo 116: 197, 219
Bodleian L. Rawlinson D.913: 170
Bodleian L. Rawlinson Poet 163: 158
Bodleian L. Selden Supra 53: (155)
Bailliol College 354: 163
San Marino: Huntington (Ellesmere) 47, 58
Mapheus Vegius 187
Margaret Beaufort 204
Margaret Tudor 186
Marot, Jean 225
Marotti, Arthur (170)
Marriage of Sir Gawain 68
Martianus Capella, *De Nuptiis . . .* 133
McCarthy, Terence (222), (223)
Meale, Carol M. 57, (220), (222)
Medcalf, Stephen (7), (155)
Meech, Sanford Brown (221)
Mehl, Dieter (55), (56), 57, (78), (106), (125), (191), (223), (226)
Middle Scots *173-93*
Middleton, Anne (59)
Milosh, Joseph E. (220)

Minnis, Alistair J. (7), 55, (57), (78), (79), (170)
Minot, Laurence 168
Mirror for Magistrates 141, (154)
Miskimin, Alice S. (225)
Mitchell, Jerome 154
Morte Arthure (alliterative) 3, 213, *214-15*
Mort Artu (French) 213, 215
Murdoch, Iris
  The Bell 221
Muscatine, C.
Mystics *201-11, 219-20*

Needham, Paul (222)
Nicholson, Peter (78), (79)
Nolan, Barbara
Norton-Smith, John 151, 154, 191

Oakden, J. P. (124)
Odoric of Pordenone, *Itinerarius* 197
Ogilvie-Thomson, S. J. (229)
Oldcastle, Sir John 155-6, 169, 172
Olson, Clair C. (55)
Ovid 13, 128, 190, 225
  Fasti 65
  Heroides 20, 35, 36
  Metamorphoses 16, 34, 67, 70-1, 78
Owen, Charles A. (57)
Owst, G. R. 106

Pace, George B. (218)
Parkinson, David (190)
Paston Letters 195, 218
Patterson, Lee (55), (59)
Paulus Diaconus
  Gesta Langobardorum 69
Pearsall, Derek (6), (7), 9, 40, 51, 54, (55), 58, 70, (78), 88, 93, (104), 105, 106,107, 127, 134, 140, 143, 150, 151, 152, 153, (170), (171), 191, 192, 193, (218), (219), (221), (222)
Peasants' Revolt 61, 83
Peck, Russell A. (225)
Percival, Florence (56)
Petrarca, Francesco (Petrarch) 10-11, 43, 154, 172
  Canzoniere 25
Phaedrus 177
Pope, Alexander, *The Rape of the Lock* 46
Potter, Lois (58), (225)
Prendergast, Thomas A. (190), (225)
Prudentius, *Psychomachia* 90
Putter, Ad 124
Pynson, Thomas 225

Querelle de la Rose 11
Quinn, William A. (56)

Reichl, Karl (56)
Renaud de Louens 44
Richard II, King of England 4, 10, 60, 62, 172
Riddy, Felicity (220), 222, (223)
Ridley, Florence H. 182, (192)
Rigg, A. G. (70), (104)
Robbins, Rossell Hope (154), 160, 161–2, 164, 167, 168, (170), 171, 172
Robertson, D. W. (55)
Robertson, Elizabeth (59)
Robins, William (79)
Robinson, Peter (58)
Rolle, Richard 2, 201–2, (220)
Roman de la Rose 3, 8, 11–12, 17, 18, 19, 32, 51, 52, 53, 59, 65, 66, 78, 83, 84, 87, 88, 95, 115, 116, 128, 129, 132, 133, 140, 152, 184–5, 190
Roman de Renart 176
Roman de Thebes 140
Romance 45, 49, 67–9, 71–2, 74–5, 93, 99, 101–2, 119, 198, 211, 213–15, 222–3
Rowland, Beryl (55), (192)
Rowe, Donald W. (56)
Russell, George (104)

Saints' Legend 45
Salter, Elizabeth (6), (171), (192)
Scattergood, V. J. (6)
Schick, J. (152)
Schirmer, Walter (151), 152
Schmidt, A. V. C. (104), (105), 107
Schmitz, Götz (77), 192
'Scottish Chaucerians' 173, 190
Selincourt, E. D. (226)
Seymour, M. C. 154, 218, 219
Shakespeare, William 8, 151, 192
    A Midsummer Night's Dream 225
    Pericles, Prince of Tyre 72, (78), 79
    Rape of Lucrece 224–5
    Romeo and Juliet 225
    Troilus and Cressida 138, 225
    Two Noble Kinsmen 41, 224
Shaw, Martin (171)
Sherley-Price, Leo (220)
Sherborne, J. W. (6)
Simpson, James 98, 105, 106, 107
Skeat, W. W. 80–1, (105)
Small, John (193)
Smith, J. C. (226)
Smith, Jeremy (223)

Smithers, G. V. (170)
Spearing, A. C. (124), (125)
Speght, Thomas 191, (225)
Spenser, Edmund 225, 226
Shepheardes Calender 225, 226
Spurgeon, Caroline (54)
St Paul 46–7
Statius 23
Steele, R. (170)
Stemmler, Theo (77)
Stevens, John (171), (172)
Stone, W. G. (58), (153)
Stow, John 225
Stratmann, Gerd (77)
Strohm, Paul (151), 154
Surrey, Henry Howard, Earl of 186
Suso, Heinrich
    Horologium Sapientiae 148
Swanton, Michael (170)

Takamiya, Toshiyuki (222)
Tale of Beryn 58, 153
Taylor, John (218)
Tasioulas, J. A. (191)
Theocritus 225
Thompson, Ann (226)
Thynne, Francis 191–2
Thynne, William 181, (191), (225)
Tolkien, J. R. R. (124)
Torti, Anna (191)
Trevisa, John 194, (218)
Trivet, Nicholas 72
Turville-Petre, Thorlac (218)

Underhill, Evelyn (220)

Vinaver, Eugène 212–13, 222, 223
Vincent of Beauvais, *Speculum Naturale et Speculum Historiale* 197
Virgil 23, 44, 128, 225
    Aeneid 19–20, 35, 58, 112, 124, 186, 193

Waldron, Ronald (124), (218)
Wallace, David 5, (6), (55), (78), 105, (151)
Walsh, James (220)
Watson, Nicholas (6), 218, 219, (220), (221)
Weddynge of Sir Gawen 68
Wenzel, Siegfried (77)
Wetherbee, Winthrop (78), 79
Wickham, Glynne (154)
William of Tripoli, *Tractatus de Statu Saracenorum* 197

Williams, Ralph Vaughan (171)
Windeatt, Barry (56), 219, 220, 221
Wimsatt, James I. (55), (170)
Wittig, H. S. (218)
Wolters, Clifton (220), (221)
Woolf, Rosemary (106)

Wyclif, John 83, 194
Wynkyn de Worde 201, 207

Yeager, R. F. 77, (79)

Zeeman, Nicolette (7), (171)
Zettersen, Arne (218)